Theorizing Culture

An interdisciplinary critique
after postmodernism

Edited by

Barbara Adam
University of Wales, Cardiff

Stuart Allan
University of Glamorgan

UCL
PRESS

First published in 1995 by UCL Press

UCL Press Limited
University College London
Gower Street
London WC1E 6BT

The name of University College London (UCL) is a registered
trade mark used by UCL Press with the consent of the owner.

British Library Cataloguing-in-Publication Data
A CIP catalogue record for this book is available from the British Library.

ISBNs:
1-85728-328-7 HB
1-85728-329-5 PB

Typeset in Baskerville.
Printed and bound by
Biddles Ltd, Guildford and King's Lynn, England.

Contents

CONTENTS

Acknowledgements

We would both like to express our gratitude to the School of Social and Administrative Studies, UWCC, for its financial support with respect to the preparation of the manuscript in its final version. We would further like to thank Simon Hopper for standardizing the chapters into the required computer format, and Anne Mable for her careful copy-editing of the text.

Finally, we also take pleasure in acknowledging the enthusiastic support of Justin Vaughan, Senior Editor at UCL Press.

Barbara Adam and Stuart Allan
Wales, 1995

Contributors

Barbara Adam teaches social theory and women's studies at the University of Wales, Cardiff. She has written numerous papers and two books (*Time and social theory* and *Timewatch. The social analysis of time*) on social time, is the founder editor of *Time and Society* and currently an ESRC Fellow under the Global Environmental Change programme.

Stuart Allan lectures on media and cultural studies at the University of Glamorgan. He has published in the areas of media sociology, critical discourse analysis and the cultural dynamics of nuclearism. In 1993 he joined the journal *Time and Society* as Assistant Editor. He is currently engaged in research on the Welsh news media.

Karen Atkinson is a lecturer in language studies at the University of Glamorgan. Prior to 1992, she taught sociolinguistics at Roehampton Institute in London. She has published on intergenerational communication, on the "co-operativity" of all-female discourse, and on official discourses of public health. Currently she is working on a book about language, women and old age.

Paul Atkinson is Professor of Sociology at the University of Wales, Cardiff. He has published extensively on medicine, education, and qualitative research methods. His recent books include *Fighting familiarity* (with Sara Delamont), published by Hampton Press, *Medical work and medical talk* and *Varieties of qualitative data analysis* (with Amanda Coffey), both published by Sage, and *Microcomputing and qualitative data analysis* (with Anna Weaver), published by Avebury.

Taieb Belghazi is a lecturer in English at the Faculty of Letters in Rabat, Morocco. He completed his Ph.D. at the Centre for Critical and Cultural Theory in Cardiff, Wales, on *Time and postmodernism*. He has written and translated a number of articles on literary criticism, and is currently working on a book dealing with the issues of national culture, postcolonialism and postmodernism in the Moroccan context, entitled *Postnationalism?*

Fred Botting lectures on theory and Romantic literature at Lancaster University. He completed his doctoral work at the University of Wales, Cardiff. He has published articles on theory, Romanticism and postmodernism, and, in 1991, a book *Making monstrous: Frankenstein, criticism, theory* (Manchester University Press). An introduction to Gothic writing, *Gothic*, is forthcoming from Routledge.

Cynthia Carter is a lecturer in mass communications with the Centre for Journalism Studies, University of Wales, Cardiff. Research interests and publications primarily focus on analyses of familial ideology in the media, discourses of violence against women in the British press, and the media's construction of "global" and "local" forms of identity.

Amanda Coffey is a lecturer in sociology in the School of Social and Administrative Studies, University of Wales, Cardiff. She has published on gender and education, and on the sociology of professional accountancy training. Her current research interests include initial teacher training, and women and citizenship. Her publications include *Varieties of qualitative data analysis* (with Paul Atkinson).

Brian Doyle has taught, researched and published in communication, cultural and media studies since 1981. He is Field Leader for Society and Culture in the School of Humanities and Social Sciences at the University of Glamorgan.

Andrew Edgar is a lecturer in philosophy at the University of Wales, Cardiff. He is the author of articles in the areas of moral and political philosophy and critical theory. He is currently acting director of the Centre for Applied Ethics at Cardiff.

Simon Hopper is completing postgraduate work at the University of Wales, Cardiff, on the conceptions of rationality in Max Weber and the Frankfurt School. He currently teaches part-time at the University of Glamorgan. His main research interests are in the fields of social theory, the history of ideas, and the sociology of knowledge.

Samantha Humphreys is currently undertaking postgraduate research, and teaching media and cultural studies part-time at the University of Glamorgan.

CONTRIBUTORS

Glenn Jordan teaches cultural and media studies at the University of Glamorgan. He previously taught at the University of Illinois. He has published on cultural theory, racism and Black intellectual history. He is the co-author (with Chris Weedon) of *Cultural politics: class, gender, race and the postmodern world* (Basil Blackwell 1995).

Hughie Mackay is Staff Tutor at the Open University in Wales, working on a course on media, culture and identities. He is also a principal lecturer at the University of Glamorgan. He researches and teaches in sociological and cultural studies perspectives on technology. Current research includes prototyping in system design, the social construction of the object-orientated paradigm in computing, and the Welsh news media.

Rob Middlehurst is a senior lecturer in language studies/creative writing and Course Leader for the Communication Studies Award at the University of Glamorgan. Research interests include issues of communication and persuasion, and the interrelationship between writing, culture and society. He has recently been involved in research on public health discourse for Health Promotion Wales.

Jane Moore is a lecturer in the Centre for Critical and Cultural Theory at the University of Wales, Cardiff. She is co-editor of *The feminist reader: essays in gender and the politics of literary criticism* (1989), and has written essays on Mary Wollstonecraft and critical theory.

Christopher Norris is Professor of the history of ideas at the University of Wales, Cardiff. His recent books include *What's wrong with postmodernism? Critical theory and the ends of philosophy* (1990), *Spinoza and the origins of modern critical theory* (1991), *Uncritical theory: postmodernism, intellectuals and the Gulf War* (1992), *The truth about postmodernism* (1993), and *Truth and the ethics of criticism* (1994).

Timothy Robins teaches media and cultural studies at the University of Glamorgan. He is also conducting postgraduate research at the Department of Cultural Studies, University of Birmingham.

Peter Sedgwick is a lecturer in philosophy at the University of Wales, Cardiff. He is the author of a number of articles on the relationship between postmodernism and analytic philosophy. He is the editor of *A Nietzsche reader* (Basil Blackwell 1995).

Chris Weedon teaches critical theory, cultural studies and women's studies at the University of Wales, Cardiff. Her books include *Feminist practice and poststructuralist theory* (1987). She is the co-author (with Glenn Jordan) of *Cultural politics: class, gender, race and the postmodern world* (Basil Blackwell 1995).

Brian Winston is Director of the Centre for Journalism Studies and Professor of Mass Communications at the University of Wales, Cardiff. His books include *Misunderstanding media* (Routledge & Kegan Paul 1986) and *Claiming the real: the documentary film revisited* (BFI 1995).

Theorizing culture: an introduction

Barbara Adam and Stuart Allan

The principal aim of *Theorizing culture: an interdisciplinary critique after post-modernism* is to engage a series of theorists and researchers, positioned across the breadth of the social sciences and humanities, in the task of theorizing culture. Depending on who is doing the talking, of course, "culture" may be made to signify any number of different material processes. Accordingly, this collection of essays has been organized to provide the reader with an extensive range of interdisciplinary modes of critique. The individual contributors are located in a variety of academic disciplines, including critical theory, English and literary studies, language studies, sociology, philosophy, media and cultural studies, and thus each of them prioritizes a distinct conceptual and methodological agenda. All of the writers nevertheless share a commitment to securing a fresh approach to theorizing cultural forms, practices and identities, a project to be achieved by looking beyond the limitations engendered by that troublesome word "postmodernism".

Are we currently witnessing the "twilight" of postmodern cultural theory?[1] In our view, the answer is a cautiously hopeful "yes". Still, it is our contention that in this "era of Posts", terms such as "postmodernism", "postcolonialism", "postfeminism" and even "post-History" are increasingly commanding much of the conceptual terrain for cultural research. It appears to be the case that a more familiar vocabulary of analytical categories, such as "representation", "ideology", "experience" and "reality", is in the process of being slowly displaced into the academic dustbin. This when the word "culture", in contrast, seems to be appearing everywhere, its meaning stretched to the point that attempts to specify the non-cultural run into severe difficulties. The degree to which the postmodernists have recast the terms of academic debate is apparent, for a startling implication of this general tendency to embrace "culture" is the all too frequent conceptual dis-articulation of questions concerning how cultural power is woven into the very texture of everyday life.

It is our opinion that critical approaches to theorizing culture, that is, attempts to explicitly foreground the complex economic, political and ideological materiality of cultural processes in time and space, need to intervene across the contested terrain marked by the term "postmodernism". To ignore these at times perplexing, often acrimonious debates about whether or not we are living in a "postmodern age" is to ignore, simultaneously, how their particular terms of reference are quietly redrawing the parameters of "what counts" as cultural theory. Theories of culture, we would suggest, cannot be separated from cultural critique, that is, from the need to engage with specific cultural problematics in a way that underscores their relevance to the contradictory reproduction of social divisions and hierarchies across the social field. The particular reasons why it is the case that "postmodern" modes of thought have come to enjoy such recognition (if not ready acceptance) in cultural theory thus need to be directly addressed in a manner that is reflexive about their perceived advantages as well as their disadvantages.

For some cultural theorists, the "postmodern turn" is regarded as a necessary one due to the conceptual unravelling of the organizing tenets of modernism. Many of them seek to demonstrate how, in their view, postmodern cultural theory succeeds in calling into question the modernist belief – or, more to the point, the hope – that there is some "innocent" knowledge to be "discovered" that forms the bedrock upon which we may build our "impartial" theories, our science and politics, and our morals and values. This type of cultural theory, its advocates insist, shows us that what is collectively defined as "knowledge" is always culturally specific, always articulated from a particular viewpoint and interest position consistent with certain social rules and conventions. Postmodern cultural theory thus challenges modernist assumptions about the "universality" of "reason", even the premiss that there exists an "external reality" to be "detected" through "scientific" modes of investigation. It queries a "rationality" that allows all humans to agree on what is "real" and "right", "just" and "humane". It stresses, instead, that there is a contingency, temporality and situational logic for any definition of "the world out there". As such, this type of cultural theory destabilizes our multidisciplinary reliance on a realm amenable to the practices of "objective", "detached" and "neutral" research enquiry, thereby calling into perpetual dispute our "facts" about the social world and the "disinterested" language of representation available to "reflect" them.

Postmodern cultural theory, in controverting the validity of this "metaphysics of presence", that is, the assumption that something real exists "in the world out there" independent of the observer, constitutes an attack on narrative knowledge. In its place, this theoretical project looks to affirm the contextual and constitutive nature of culture, arguing that we are inextricably implicated in our subject matter; as Ermarth (1992: 23) writes, "each day, in countless and intensely realised details, we reinvent Paris, Detroit, and Gaza". Familiar distinctions between "form" and "content", or between "subject" and "object", are to be dismissed with a sweep of the hand, a strategy that applies irrespective of whether we are dealing with aesthetic, historical, political or scientific representations of "reality". In this way, postmodern cultural theory unsettles any faith in Reality as an absolute, one that exists beyond the limits of interpretation and interest. It insists that temporal and spatial relations not only condition our descriptions of the social world, but actually construct the contending validity-claims that make up that social world in the first place. Once the "master" or "metanarratives" of science are demonstrated to be as perspectival as they are provisional, then Reality is quickly pluralized into a series of different definitions about the social world which happen to be "in play" at a given time and place. It then follows that we may similarly dismiss any belief in the universal axioms of Truth; instead, we may advance a formulation of "truth" as being just another contradictory effect of what is a multiplicity of heterogeneous discourses.

Adherents to postmodern cultural theory maintain that only once we have rejected the absolutes and universals that otherwise underpin our "will to knowledge" will we be able to recognize the theorist's constitutive involvement in the subject matter of his or her own theoretical practice. They suggest that as soon as we acknowledge this crucial presupposition, we will begin to appreciate the potential this approach to theory possesses for leading us to a deeply moral stance. Confronted with the partial, necessarily conditional nature of "reality" and "truth", we are forced to address, in turn, a range of ethical choices engendered by our theorizing. The situated, constitutive self can no longer hide behind the imperialism of unifying conceptual schemes embodied in "master" narratives; rather, each one of us has to engage with the fluid ambiguities and uncertainties of tentative, "local" stories or accounts. Significantly, however, we would suggest that it is precisely at this point that it becomes clear how little of this radical potential is currently being realized in the name of postmodern cultural theory. This is to say that, despite its theoretical potential for active engagement, commitment and "life politics" (Giddens 1991), this type of theory recurrently prioritizes cultural plurality and invention for their own sake. The rich diversity of cultural forms, practices and identities is being celebrated at the expense of a critical analysis of their implication in the daily renewal of the pernicious logics of class, sexism, racism, homophobia, ageism and nationalism, amongst others, that are all too indicative of "postmodern" societies.

Quite rightly, therefore, we find widespread concern over postmodernism that extends well beyond the charge that it is a politically conservative form of theorizing, one that has only academic ivory towers as its terms of reference. Critics point to a perception that there is an increasing number of cultural theorists (only some of whom are explicitly marching under the banner of postmodernism) who appear content to simply describe the "pleasures" of various "textual surfaces", or relations of "parody" and "pastiche", when researching a particular cultural problematic. These theorists are then condemned for depriving cultural theory of a basis from which to adjudicate between truth-claims and, as a result, a "foundation" upon which to anchor active political empowerment for social change. Similarly, the argument is made that it does not follow from this conceptual shift to embrace "cultural difference" that an interventionist politic may be dismissed as being constitutive of an outdated "metanarrative", of being "essentialist" in its strategic commitment to disrupting the organization of cultural hegemony across the social field. Postmodernism, many of its critics contend, fosters political indecision to the point that its often well-intentioned adherents risk becoming lost in the nihilism of "relativism".

Accordingly, the contributors to *Theorizing culture* seek to leave behind the oppositional logics of modernism that continue to map, to a considerable degree, the theoretical landscape according to choices of position between "foundationalism" and "relativism", or between single epistemologies and plural ontologies. We need, instead, to affirm the contextual complexity of cultural life in the late-twentieth century so as to centre, for purposes of critique, relations of power as being both repressive and productive in their regulation of bodies, institutions and communities. As the editors of this volume, we have encouraged our contributors to displace the "view from no-where" indicative of much postmodern cultural theorizing in order to allow for the position of "now-here": inescapably local, partial and fragmentary, and yet contextual, interconnected and globalizing. In our view, we as researchers cannot simply appropriate the particular "advantages" of postmodern cultural theory and then selectively ignore or displace those aspects that complicate matters. Rather, we need to reflexively examine how we are temporally and spatially situated within the institutional dynamics of theoretical production so that we may then, in turn, proceed to challenge their attendant "micropolitics".

The stakes for a critical approach to cultural theory have never been higher. While, in our view, it is appropriate to acknowledge that the self-legitimating modernist narrative of human progress has lost its conceptual authority, clearly it is not possible to endorse what can all too easily become a postmodernist "shrug of indifference" to the heterogeneous matrices of social conflicts pervading society. This collection of essays thus seeks to assess the current state of research in cultural theory in the light of the competing truth-claims of postmodernist discourses while, at the same time, explicitly acknowledging the material contingencies of theoretical work in an interdisciplinary context. This is to underscore, from the outset, that the political, economic and ideological materiality of culture shapes the (often unspoken) rules by which the very normalcy of everyday life is defined, policed and resisted. Without the "neutral ground" of modernism beneath our feet, we face profound moral and ethical choices, that is, we encounter culturally specific questions regarding how best to contribute to the public re-articulation of a democratic politic.

Notes

1. In using the phrase "postmodern cultural theory", it is not our intention to suggest that it constitutes a singular, totalized object. Rather, it is employed here as a form of analytical shorthand to stand in for what is a vast array of contending approaches that rely upon some configuration of "postmodernism" in their engagement with a particular cultural problematic. We wish to acknowledge from the outset of this book, therefore, that precisely what is meant by "postmodernism" will vary from one contributor's chapter to the next.

References

Ermarth, E. D. 1992. *Sequel to history: postmodernism and the crisis of representational time.* Princeton, New Jersey: Princeton University Press.
Giddens, A. 1991. *Modernity and self-identity.* Cambridge: Polity.

PART I
Truth, reality and cultural critique

Introduction to Part I

The contributors to this first section of the book approach the problematic of cultural critique in the context of postmodernist debates about "truth" and "reality". The emphases of their discussions range from the use of rhetorical devices in the construction of narratives to the practice of reflexivity in academic culture, from inscriptions of the body in fiction and notions of "the Real" in Lacanian psychoanalysis to poetry as source of the critical Utopian moment, from representations of AIDS in public health documents to the "will to facticity" inflected in news discourse. Despite these diverse interests and perspectives, the chapters nevertheless cohere around a shared concern with the capacity of contemporary cultural theory for retaining a critical edge, for prioritizing the dynamic politics of truth-claims about reality and the necessity for engaging with matters of ethics.

Christopher Norris, in the opening chapter entitled "Culture, criticism and communal values: on the ethics of enquiry", sets the scene for several of the key debates taking place across the pages of this book. At issue is the need to critique certain relativist trends in recent cultural theory within the specific context of postmodernism, particularly what he calls "the fashionable rhetoric of 'otherness' – of alterity, radical difference, heterogeneity and so forth – that has gone along with this relativizing drift across various disciplines of thought". Norris makes the case (via a reading of Derrida on Levinas) that such notions are both philosophically untenable and a source of much confusion in present-day thinking about questions of ethics and politics. Postmodernist thinkers like Lyotard have worsened matters, in his view, through their skewed understanding of history, their rejection of a typecast "Enlightenment" metanarrative, their misreading of precursors such as Kant and their failure to perceive the disabling consequences of a relativism pushed to this dogmatic extreme.

In the next chapter, "Realism and its discontents: on the crisis of cultural representation in ethnographic texts", Paul Atkinson and Amanda Coffey proceed to elaborate upon several of these issues through an examination of the ethnography of culture and the culture of ethnography. They begin by pointing out that a number of theoretical developments – including postmodernism, feminist research and the "rediscovery" of rhetoric – are being blamed by some researchers for plunging ethnography into an exigent "crisis of representation". It is Atkinson and Coffey's contention, however, that this perception of a "crisis" has been an unnecessarily exaggerated response. Accordingly, they suggest that a renewed interest in the rhetoric of inquiry offers a series of positive opportunities for the contemporary ethnographer who is attempting to look beyond the epistemological and theoretical upheavals characteristically associated with postmodernism.

This concern with questions of rhetoric and the construction of ethnographic narratives is followed by "Reflexivity in academic culture", Simon Hopper's discussion of the reflexive turn in theory. He identifies the need for a reflexivity that turns on the self without ending up in the futile reflexive regress associated by some critics with postmodernism. He argues that critical accounts of academic culture should move beyond the rather abstract discussions of the writer–text–reader relationship so as to explore the wider cultural contexts of knowledge. In his view, we need to take account of the issues surrounding the production, reception and reproduction of academic culture, issues that tend to be displaced by an exclusively textual approach. By placing the emphasis on reflexivity, Hopper contends, we stand to gain a potentially powerful, collective project that poses a political challenge to the *taken-for-granted* framework of the human sciences.

In "Theorizing the body's fictions", Jane Moore takes a feminist literary perspective on the issues of truth, cultural representation and political practice. She examines the contemporary feminist debate on essentialism that has arisen in the context of, and partly to counter, a postmodern scepticism towards truth. Specifically, Moore is concerned with the implications for feminist theory of the return of the body as the referent of sexual difference. Without minimizing the importance of the materiality of the body for identity and action, she problematizes the contention that the anatomical body yields the truth or reality of sexual difference. In order to articulate and theorize these issues, she engages with Jeanette Winterson's short novel, *Written on the body*. By focusing on what literature has to say about the reality of the body, and what postmodern theory has to say about literature, Moore explores the conditions of contemporary meanings of the sexed body.

From an engagement with cultural constructions of the body we move to a psychoanalytic encounter with the radical potential of the subconscious. In "Culture, subjectivity and the real; or, psychoanalysis reading postmodernity",

Fred Botting argues that, in these "postmodern times", reality is not what it used to be. This chapter, in seeking to address the issue of who claims the right to define reality, centres on the problem of subjectivity. Specifically, Botting argues that Lacanian psychoanalysis provides a framework for examining postmodern culture and its effects on identity and psychic wellbeing. He proceeds, in turn, to identify cultural responses to postmodernity in terms of particular states of mourning and psychosis, thereby raising intriguing questions about the necessary function and possibility of a unifying, regulating cultural principle. Indeed, it is the desire for this "paternal metaphor", Botting suggests, that escapes both the metanarratives of Enlightenment thought and the radical relativist position typically associated with postmodernism.

Andrew Edgar and Peter Sedgwick, in their chapter entitled "Adorno, Oakeshott and the voice of poetry", are concerned with postmodernist criticism of Enlightenment thought and, in particular, with the "manifestation of reason" in a culture dominated by science. The authors focus on the work of the neo-Hegelian philosophers Adorno and Oakeshott in order to demonstrate that it is possible to take a sceptical approach to reason without, at the same time, collapsing into an uncritical celebration of pluralism and diversity. Oakeshott's concept of a "voice of poetry", they suggest, opens up the possibility of articulating a critical Utopian moment in all social relations. Edgar and Sedgwick then proceed to demonstrate how Adorno's account of "tradition" focuses this mode of argument in an analysis of past and present mundane social practice, one that is antithetical to both Enlightenment science and postmodernism.

"Representing AIDS: the textual politics of health discourse" is the title of Karen Atkinson and Rob Middlehurst's contribution to this section's discussion. This chapter highlights the degree to which postmodern cultural theory has neglected linguistic specificity in its accounts of discourse. Having first foregrounded a series of issues regarding how discourses may be theorized as being indicative of the wider organization of power relations within society, this chapter proceeds to consider recent work specifically dealing with language, AIDS and cultural activism. Atkinson and Middlehurst then seek to explore, by integrating critical and literary theory with a form of close textual analysis, how the politicization of HIV and AIDS is discursively constituted through health promotion materials. Their analysis of both "mainstream" and "alternative" documents explicates several points of ideological contestation in the conceptualization and framing of HIV and AIDS issues, thereby underscoring how the very materiality of the cultural meanings in play is itself a "linguistic battlefield".

Finally, this section of the book ends with Stuart Allan's chapter "News, truth and postmodernity: unravelling the will to facticity", in which he seeks to extend a number of the themes raised above in the context of researching news discourse. It is his contention that some researchers of news media culture, anxious to retain notions of "objectivity" and "bias", are relying upon certain modernist notions of "reality" to support their claims that are untenable. Specifically, where these researchers implicitly assume that journalists possess the capacity to symbolically translate "the world out there" (the world beyond our immediate experience) in an "impartial" manner, the ensuing critique of "news bias" is frequently restricted to considering the degree to which this "reality" has been distorted in the resultant news narrative. Consequently, Allan suggests that we need to render analytically visible the very invisibility of the truth-claims embedded in these "factual" accounts of reality by unravelling what he terms "the will to facticity" as it is implicated in the news text's regulation of truth.

CHAPTER 1

Culture, criticism and communal values: on the ethics of enquiry

Christopher Norris

Introduction

"What is truth?" asked Pontius Pilate, jesting – or so the tale goes – and did not stay for an answer. If the question comes up at all nowadays in the context of cultural theory then it is likely to receive little more by way of serious or reasoned response. For many – poststructuralists in particular – the very mention of "truth" is enough to evoke first a sceptical, then a mildly pitying, and then – if one persists in raising the matter – a downright contemptuous response. After all, don't we *know* (after Saussure) that language is a system of relationships and differences "without positive terms"; that the link between signifier and signified is strictly "arbitrary"; that signs are caught up in an endless process of intertextual differing–deferral; and therefore (QED) that notions like reference, reality and truth simply drop out of the picture, mere remnants of an old "metaphysical" (or logocentric) prejudice that has now been deconstructed once and for all (Saussure 1974). And if this is not enough to convince the stubborn party then they had best be advised – on no lesser an authority than Foucault – that such talk is *always and everywhere* a product of power/knowledge interests, an effect of that domineering drive within discourse whose operations are masked behind a specious rhetoric of reason, enlightenment and truth (see Foucault 1977, 1980). At this point – if not before – the arguments tend to run out.

I trust I am not alone in thinking this to be a lamentable state of affairs. For there is something to worry about when a movement of thought gets so far out of touch with the standards and values – not to mention the common decencies – of open argumentative debate. All the more so when its followers make a habit of denouncing those bad old dogmatic ("Enlightenment") notions of truth, reason, critique, etc., while effectively placing their own ideas beyond reach of criticism or counter-argument. Of course this might be seen as just another version of the self-refuting paradox built into all relativist doctrines.

5

That is to say, if such arguments are valid then there must be at least *one* truth-claim exempted from the general (relativist) rule, i.e. the claim that "all truths are relative", or again, that all arguments in the end come down to a matter of consensus belief. In the case of poststructuralism the truths that enjoy this privileged status are those having to do with language (or "discourse") as the ultimate horizon of intelligibility. Thus one simply has to accept – on pain of exclusion from the right-thinking fold – that language is a network of differential signs, that these signs refer to nothing outside or beyond their own structural economy, that "reality" is a construct out of this or that language-game, discourse, signifying practice, or whatever. If it is asked what reason the poststructuralists can offer for advancing these (surely) less than self-evident claims, then the answer is most often: thus spake Saussure. And it is always the same few talismanic passages that are cited by way of scriptural warrant. Chief among them are Saussure's now famous remarks on the "arbitrary" nature of the sign, on the absence of so-called "positive" terms, and on the fact that different languages have a different range of semantic, conceptual or categorical distinctions.

What these theorists tend to ignore – and for obvious reasons – is the following series of awkward points about Saussure's much-vaunted "revolution" in linguistics. First: his project was a relatively specialized affair, designed to counterbalance the prevalent stress on historical (diachronic) aspects of language, and adopted for the mainly heuristic purpose of excluding those other dimensions (e.g. reference) that could not be theorized in structural-synchronic terms. Saussure is clear enough – though in passages that scarcely rate a mention on the standard (poststructuralist) account – that these concerns were set aside for the sake of achieving an adequate degree of conceptual rigour from his own methodological standpoint, and not because he thought them otiose, wrongheaded or simply beside the point. A more attentive perusal will discover nothing in the *Cours de linguistique générale* that can possibly be read as lending support to such a wholesale dismissive attitude. Nor, for that matter, would the case be much strengthened had Saussure indeed made the kinds of exorbitant claim that are nowadays attributed to him. For there is something decidedly suspect – a throwback to the pre-Enlightenment age of faith – in the notion that arguments can be made good simply by appealing to the wisdom enshrined in some canonical text. This is perhaps the most retrograde aspect of much that currently passes for "advanced" theoretical thinking in the human and social sciences. Hence the second main objection to poststructuralism's use of Saussure: that it treats his text with the same kind of piecemeal but dogmatic fixation on a few sacred points that has characterized the wranglings of theological discourse down through the ages. That is to say, it exploits the *Cours* as a convenient sounding-board for its own doctrinal preconceptions, and thus ignores Saussure's claim to have brought about a specific theoretical advance in certain well-defined areas of structural–linguistic enquiry. (For further arguments to this effect see Anderson 1983, Tallis 1988, Eagleton 1991, Cunningham 1993.)

This claim was not lost upon an earlier generation of theorists, those (like Althusser, Macherey and Goldmann) who understood more of the intellectual background – especially in philosophy of science – that went along with the promotion of Saussurean linguistics as a pilot discipline for other fields of research (see especially Althusser 1990; also Gutting 1989 and Norris 1991). But such is the turnover rate in present-day intellectual fashion that these are considered mere name-antiquities, honoured (if at all) with nostalgic fondness for that age of high theoreticist illusion. What price theoretical rigour, consistency, truth-conditions and so forth when it is known for a fact – or with presumptive warrant from Saussure – that all such ideas are "constructed in language", have meaning only by virtue of their role within some localized interpretive community, or exist solely as figments of an epistemic will-to-power vested in the discourse of logocentric reason? No matter that Saussure, on all the evidence to hand, would have regarded this doctrine as utterly foreign to the nature and ambitions of his own undertaking. No matter that the claims of structural linguistics – and its relevance to other fields of thought – were staked upon a strong version of the argument from conditions of possibility, that is, the *a priori* criteria that a theory must satisfy in order to count as a valid contribution to knowledge. As I say, these aspects of Saussure's work were precisely what appealed to thinkers in other fields – anthropology, poetics, political theory – who welcomed the prospect of a radical break (an epistemological *coupure*) with prevailing explanatory norms. Structural linguistics could thus be seen as converging with that movement in philosophy of science, represented most notably by Bachelard and Canguilhem, which likewise sought to define the conditions under which a discipline could properly assert some claim to theoretical validity. But this is now treated as a bygone episode in the history of thought, a distant prelude to the dawning awareness that science – like philosophy – is just one "discourse" among others, a language-game with its own favoured idioms and metaphors, but without any privilege in point of epistemological rigour or truth.

Relative truths

If Bachelard is remembered nowadays it is chiefly for works like *The psychoanalysis of fire*, his essays in reflection on those modes of metaphoric or creative reverie that stand, so to speak, at the opposite pole from the scientific language of concept and logical inference (Bachelard 1964; also 1969, 1971). What is thereby forgotten – one might say repressed – is the fact that these writings were themselves a part of his epistemological project, his attempt to distinguish more clearly between the two realms of thought. It is a plain misreading of Bachelard's work to extract from it the modish (quasi-Derridean) doctrine that "all truth-claims are fictions", "all concepts just sublimated metaphors" or "'science' merely the name we attach to some currently prestigious language-game". On the contrary: Bachelard's aim was to prevent such promiscuous levelling of the difference – the more than contingent, linguistic or localized (culture-specific) difference – between scientific epistemologies on the one hand and poetic–metaphorical "reverie" on the other (Bachelard 1968, 1984; see also Lecourt 1975, Tiles 1984, Gutting 1989). This placed him squarely at odds with the current poststructuralist wisdom, as well as with the neo-pragmatist idea – advanced by Richard Rorty and Stanley Fish, among others – that truth can be defined, for all practical purposes, as what is "good in the way of belief", and hence as what happens to fit in with some going range of metaphors, language-games or "final vocabularies" (Rorty 1982, Fish 1989).

That Saussure should now be routinely co-opted by adepts of this ultra-relativist view is, to say the least, something of an irony, given his methodo-logical concerns and his desire to set linguistics on the path towards a genuine (structural–synchronic) science of language. Such was indeed the main source of its appeal for that earlier generation of theorists who saw in it – as likewise in Bachelard's work – a means of articulating the difference between meta-phor and concept, ideology and science, natural (everyday) language on the one hand and theoretical discourse on the other. But in both cases, Saussure and Bachelard, these claims were lost from view with the postmodern turn towards an out-and-out conventionalist theory of science, knowledge and rep-resentation that treated such ideas as merely a species of "metalinguistic" delu-sion. Thus Bachelard was read – or standardly invoked – as arguing that all scientific concepts could in the end be traced back to their subliminal source in some privileged metaphor, model or intralinguistic paradigm. And Saussure's theoretical commitments counted for nothing in comparison with the prospects that were opened up by treating all theories (his own presumably among them) as "constructed in" or "relative to" some localized signifying practice. For it could then be maintained – without fear of contradiction on reasoned philosophical grounds – that literary critics were among the van-guard party in a coming "revolution" of the instituted order of discourse, an event whose signs they were able to read though their knowledge that "reality" was merely the figment of a naturalized (though in fact merely "arbitrary") relation between signifier and signified. Richard Harland has coined the useful term "superstructuralism" to describe this curious conjuncture of a *soi-disant* "radical" semioclastic zeal to subvert the very groundwork of bourgeois representation with a thoroughly idealist reversal of priorities between material (or socio-economic) base and cultural (linguistic or literary) super-structure (Harland 1987; see also Mowitt 1993). Its emergence can be traced with some precision in the passage from a work of high structuralist rigour like Barthes' *Mythologies* (1957/1972), where the Saussurean model is systemati-cally deployed in uncovering the sources of mystification, to the same writer's more ebulliently "textualist" *S/Z* (1970) where the very idea of such a (quasi-)"scientific" approach is denounced as just one more ruse in the service of existing power/knowledge relations. Henceforth – according to Barthes – any talk of "reality" or "truth" can be seen for what it is, a mere product of the drive to place limits on the otherwise open-ended play of codes, languages, sig-nifying practices, etc.

Nor are such notions by any means confined to the wilder fringes of post-modern intellectual fashion. They find support in a whole range of kindred ideas advanced by neo-pragmatist adepts like Rorty and Fish; by followers of Wittgenstein, mainly in the social sciences, much given to talk of "language-games" and "forms of life" (see for instance Winch 1958, Phillips 1977, Bloor 1983); by holists and anti-foundationalists of various colour; by proponents of the so-called "strong programme" in sociology of knowledge (Bloor 1976, Barnes 1982, 1985, Fuller 1988, Woolgar 1988); by Foucauldians ever ready to diagnose symptoms of the ubiquitous epistemic will-to-power; and by sceptical debunkers of science (Paul Feyerabend chief among them) who espouse an an-archist "theory" of knowledge that rejects all criteria of truth, method, logic, consistency and proof (Feyerabend 1975, 1978, 1992). On this latter view – enthusiastically adopted by postmodern cultural theorists – philosophy of sci-ence has no unique or well-defined object-domain, and certainly no special claim in matters of epistemological warrant. It can best be treated as a hybrid genre that draws freely on the insights of discourse-theory, sociology, cultural history, narrative poetics, psychoanalysis and any other discipline with some-thing to offer by way of interpretive guidance. For if science itself is just one more voice in what Rorty (following Oakeshott) calls the "cultural conversa-tion of mankind", then clearly we can have no reason – aside from professional or guild interests – for regarding philosophy of science as in any way a special or privileged discipline.

It is worth pursuing the implications of this argument since they are taken on board – whether wittingly or not – by a good many people in the humanis-tic disciplines who equate "science" with the grim paternal law of reason, authority and truth. Thus the great virtue of Feyerabend's writings is that they push all the way with this ultra-relativist case, and hence provide a useful litmus-test for thinkers in other disciplines tempted by the doctrine's heady appeal but not (perhaps) altogether clear what its claims amount to. For one thing it means renouncing any distinction between the "context of discovery" for scientific work (i.e. the various social, cultural or psycho-biographical factors typically adduced by historians of science) and the "context of justification". This latter is the sphere wherein – according to the standard view – such factors should be deemed strictly irrelevant, since the work in question must stand or fall on its merits as properly assessed through procedures of experimental testing, theoretical consistency, inference to the best explanation, etc. (The argument receives its classical account in Reichenbach 1938.) But, as Feyerabend sees it, this distinction is just one of the ways in which "science" – or the discourse of technocratic reason – has managed to impose its dominant values upon a culture increasingly subject to forms of destructive means-end rationality. Only by curbing these false epistemic pretensions can we hope to resist its further encroachment into the human and social lifeworld.

Hence Feyerabend's various case studies are designed to knock away those delusory props of objectivity, truth, method, disinterested (value-free) enquiry and so forth, and thus to restore a sense of the radical contingency – along with the various motivating interests – that are always at work when scientists engage in some particular research project. The best-known example of this deflationary approach is Feyerabend's treatment of the issue between Galileo and Cardinal Bellarmine, standardly viewed as a textbook case of early modern science (equated with reason, autonomy and freedom of intellectual conscience) in conflict with the entrenched forces of religious bigotry and dogma. On the contrary, he argues: it was Galileo who fudged the observational data to fit in with his theory, and who moreover ignored the church's very reasonable position, i.e. that the scientist had a prior obligation to respect the interests of social stability and communal peace (Feyerabend 1975). After all, if there is no truth in such matters – if the debate comes down to just a play-off between competing (geocentric and heliocentric) metaphors – then the issue is not closed on strictly scientific grounds and it remains possible to present Galileo as a narrow-minded zealot of the new science and Bellarmine as taking a larger, wiser and more principled view of the question. Such is the virtue, as Feyerabend sees it, of collapsing that old and pernicious distinction between the "context of discovery" and the "context of justification". It allows us to reopen issues of ethical and socio-political responsibility that philosophy of science has mostly ignored on account of its adherence to a dogmatic (self-serving) image of scientific method and truth. This was the view that Feyerabend maintained when, in a subsequent open letter, he advised the latterday church authorities that they should hold out against the pressure to retract in the case of Bellarmine v. Galileo, and not show themselves over-impressed by the weight of scientific "evidence" (Feyerabend 1992). Such consistency is perhaps unexpected in one who is otherwise more than happy to junk every last precept of logical thought, from the protocols of inductive inference and experimental proof to the law of non-contradiction. But of course Feyerabend can turn straight round and reply that he doesn't care at all for such boring old forms of *tu quoque* rejoinder – the stock-in-trade of philosophi-cal discourse from Socrates down – since an anarchist is free to make up new rules as the game goes along.

Still, one may suspect that there is something very wrong not only with Feyerabend's arguments but also with an intellectual culture that accords them such high visibility and status. One reason for this, as I have suggested already, is the spirit of *ressentiment* among cultural theorists and literary intellectuals who know their own disciplines to possess nothing like an adequately reasoned or principled basis, and who thus seize upon any opportunity to cast "science" in the same indigent role. Another, more respectable motive is the widespread awareness that some applications of science have indeed given rise to a whole range of social and ethical problems, not to mention those looming ecological crises that threaten catastrophe on a global scale. In this context it is hardly surprising that Feyerabend's message should have gained credence among people – including large sections of the Left–liberal or radical intelligentsia – well-disposed towards any such creed that purports to demolish the truth-claims of scientific method. What remains less than clear is how those threats can be averted, or those problems solved, if not through the better, more en-lightened practice of a science that respects both its own disciplinary impera-tives and the interests and values of society at large. (See for instance – from a range of very different philosophic and ethico-political perspectives – Passmore 1979, Laudan 1984, Maxwell 1984, Fox Keller 1985, Bhaskar 1986, Harding 1986, Harré 1986, Fuller 1989, Trigg 1980, Sorrell 1994.)

The same problem arises with those blanket postmodernist assaults on the philosophic discourse of modernity that treat all truth-claims as manifestations of the epistemic will-to-power, and that thus end up by denying the very possi-bility of reasoned or principled critique. Foucault offers perhaps the most strik-ing case of this confusion between normative and normalizing discourse, that is to say, between truth as arrived at by respecting the standards of probative, veridical or good-faith enquiry and truth as laid down by some coercive tribu-nal with powers to enforce its authority. (For some pointed criticisms see Barrett 1992, McNay 1992; also Norris 1993.) Hence also the perverse mis-reading of intellectual history that equates the Enlightenment – most fissile and heterodox of movements – with the voice of some capitalized monologic truth bent upon suppressing all differences of view.

Enlightenment and its others

No doubt this goes a long way towards explaining the current high stock of anticognitivist doctrines – postmodernism, neo-pragmatism and kindred trends – that would seek to level science to the status of merely one language-

11

game (or culture-specific "form of life") among others. For we shall then do justice – so the argument runs – to that whole range of social interests and values that have suffered the violence of an instrumental reason whose hallmark is the brutal exploitation of nature and humanity alike. In this respect postmodernism picks up the line of argument first developed with a certain gloomy relish by Adorno & Horkheimer in their book *Dialectic of enlightenment* (1972). And it is open to much the same criticisms, among them – as Habermas has justly remarked – the fact that it adopts a reductive, monolithic or undifferentiated concept of "reason", one that ignores the various roles or functions that have separated out within the "public sphere" of concerned participant debate (Habermas 1987). Thus it fails to acknowledge the crucial distinction between reason as a form of narrowly instrumental (means-end) rationality and reason as the exercise of critical or reflective intelligence brought to bear upon precisely such real or potential abuses. In Adorno's case this failure gave rise to what Habermas terms a "performative contradiction", that is, a mode of utterance that continues to rely upon forms of rational argument (analysis, diagnosis, critique, negative dialectic) while expressly denouncing "reason" and all its works. Indeed, one can think of no other theorist whose writing exhibits this strange inconsistency – this tension between overt or programmatic statement and actual procedures of thought – to the degree that is manifest everywhere in Adorno's work. What it shows to often startling effect, given Adorno's otherwise highly rigorous standards of reflexive autocritique, is the way that a naïve (quasi-positivist) conception of "science" and its associated truth-claims can produce a whole series of aporetic blind-spots resulting from the tendency to equate reason with the technocratic will-to-power.

Hence, also, as I have argued elsewhere, the curious disjunction in Foucault's work between his passionate (intensely ethical) commitment to exposing those sources of oppression and his resolute refusal – on Nietzschean grounds – to acknowledge any truth-claims, principles or values that could equip that project with a normative basis (Norris 1993). This confusion is typical of the current crusade against "Enlightenment" precepts of whatever kind, equated as they are – through a partial and distorted reading of intellectual history – with the ascendance of reason in a narrowly positivist (scientistic) mode and the drive to subordinate other spheres of value to the imperatives of brute technological "progress". The result, most often, is a twofold deficit: a lack of any adequate criteria for distinguishing on the one hand truth from falsehood, and on the other hand just (progressive or equitable) from unjust (retrograde or exploitative) modes of ethical conduct, social practice, civil and political institutions, etc. What is crucial here is the perceived role of science – or of cognitive and epistemic truth-claims – *vis-à-vis* the ethico-political sphere where such claims may be subject to further debate from the standpoint of agents with a shared human interest in promoting the common good. For there is an evident link between the hostility towards science in many quarters of "advanced" cultural debate and those other forms of extreme epistemological scepticism that have gained wide currency in various disciplines.

Among them one might instance the call – by Richard Rorty (1980) and others – for a turn towards narrative or hermeneutic models as a substitute for the old, constructive or problem-solving paradigm of philosophical enquiry; the idea of "thick description" (as opposed, say, to structural analysis) advanced by Clifford Geertz and his numerous disciples in the field of comparative ethnography (Geertz 1983); the constant citation of Wittgenstein on "language-games" or cultural "forms of life" by social theorists and communitarian moral philosophers anxious to avoid any taint of "Enlightenment" (i.e. universalist) thinking (Winch 1958, Bloor 1983); the appeal to holistic doctrines of meaning and truth among philosophers likewise sensitive to the charge of "foundationalism" in whatever residual guise (for a critical survey see Fodor & Lepore 1991); and of course – a point on which all these doctrines converge – the deflationary view of science that treats it as just one cultural activity among others, enjoying no privileged epistemic status and best understood through the means afforded by sociology of knowledge, historical and contextual studies, or the above-listed range of interpretive options. What unites these ideas – across otherwise large differences of view – is the desire to cut loose from any lingering attachment to truth-claims, grounds, validity-conditions or other such tokens of a misplaced regard for "science" as the paradigm of disciplined thought. And this desire is expressed – as in Lyotard's work – through a marked devaluation of the cognitive (or epistemic) phrase-regime, equated with the will to subsume all discourse under a single self-legitimizing rule, that whereby intuitive or sensuous presentations are "brought under" adequate concepts, or phrases subjected to the governing tribunal of judgment on evidential grounds. Hence Lyotard's triple postmodernist injunction: to "wage war on totality", to "save the honour of the name" and to maximize the range of discursive differentials, that is to say, the open-ended variety of language-games, speech-act genres or "first-order natural pragmatic narratives" (Lyotard 1987). Only thus can we avoid what he (like Foucault) regards as the "blackmail" of Enlightenment reason.

Terry Eagleton has remarked on the curious way that Lyotard's undoubted erudition goes along with a propensity to reinvent the wheel when making such heavy weather of long-familiar problems like the fact/value distinction (Eagleton 1989). Thus he might have saved himself a deal of perplexity – though also, in the process, missed some fine chances for high postmodernist mystification – by attending to Hume's thoughts on the topic rather than pursuing the Kantian (or quasi-Kantian) sublime into regions of radical "heterogeneity". But we should also recall, in this connection, that it was Kant – much maligned or strategically misread by advocates of the postmodern turn

– who raised these issues to their highest point of articulate philosophical grasp. Indeed, his main purpose in the three *Critiques* was to demarcate the various (distinct but interrelated) orders of knowledge and judgment whose co-operative working was the precondition of human intellectual, moral and socio-political advancement (Kant 1933, 1952, 1956). Thus philosophy fell into all kinds of error, Kant argued, if it confused the order of determinate (theoretical or scientific) concepts with that of reflective or speculative ideas; or the phenomenal realm of science, causality and law-governed explanation with the noumenal realm of practical reason (ethics); or again, if it sought to bring "ideas of reason" (regulative ideas like peace, progress, democracy and the *sensus communis* of an enlightened public sphere) under the rules of evidence and conceptual adequacy entailed by judgments in the cognitive mode. Philosophical endeavours were worse than useless if they offered no guard against the manifold illusions that flowed from these elementary category-mistakes. For the way would then be open to both those forms of corrosive scepticism – epistemological and ethical – which Kant considered such a scandal to philosophy, and whose effects as he encountered them in the writings of Hume had famously aroused him from out of his "dogmatic slumbers". That is to say, they produced on the one hand a doubt as to the truth-claims (or the powers of theoretical understanding) evinced in various branches of the natural sciences, and on the other – conversely – an illegitimate extension of just those claims into the realm of ethics or practical reason, a realm wherein the ideas of freewill and autonomy must at all costs be saved from the threatening encroachment of determinist or causal-explanatory models.

Such was Kant's argument in the section of his first *Critique* devoted to the "paralogisms of pure reason". These were the aporias that typically came about through seeking some determinate (empirical or cognitive) content for ideas – including those of freedom, responsibility, the good of democratic institutions, etc. – that properly belonged to the exercise of thought in its speculative mode, and that could not be confirmed – or disconfirmed – by reference to the epistemic rule requiring that intuitions be brought under adequate concepts. So it was vital – Kant thought – to maintain these distinctions in the face of any argument (like Hegel's after him) that viewed them as historically contingent or relative to this or that cultural time and place. For otherwise ethics would reduce to just a branch of anthropology or applied psychology; practical reason (in the Kantian sense) to merely – as Foucault and other latterday sceptics would have it – a species of epiphenomenal illusion; and morality itself to just a cynical variant on the determinist maxim *tout comprendre, c'est tout pardonner*.

In short, there are some large questions bound up with Kant's much-criticized "doctrine" of the faculties. Moreover, they are questions that continue to preoccupy philosophers even where the idiom has shifted towards a more linguistic or scaled-down "descriptive" register. Among them are those current double-aspect arguments that recommend that we treat human actions, motives and interests as "falling under" both a causal-determinist description and an alternative (but not incompatible) view that takes account of the reasons that agents offer by way of argued or principled justification (see for instance Davidson 1980). At any rate it seems fair to suggest that Foucault and his poststructuralist disciples have been somewhat premature in proclaiming the demise of that transient "discourse" of Enlightenment reason wherein (supposedly) "man" first appeared as a specular figment of his own imaginary, a chimerical hybrid creature, or – Kant according to Foucault – a strange kind of "empirico-transcendental doublet" (Foucault 1970). Indeed, as I have argued more fully elsewhere, one can go a long way towards explaining the normative confusions in Foucault's work by examining the sequence of distorted visions and revisions that marked his various engagements with Kant (Norris 1993). And the same applies to many in the current postmodernist (or counter-Enlightenment) camp whose adversarial gestures are often nothing more than an unwitting repetition of themes first explored by Kant in the "Paralogisms of Pure Reason".

Lyotard presents a rather different case since he knows very well what is at stake in these arguments. Thus for instance he deploys the paralogisms, with pointed intent, as a lever for unsettling the entire conceptual edifice wherein they should figure (on the standard account) as a kind of cautionary outwork, a propaedeutic means for warding off forms of "transcendental" illusion (Lyotard 1987). In fact it might appear that Lyotard displays an exemplary fidelity to Kant, as for instance by evoking the Kantian sublime – that figure of the radical "incommensurability" between phrase-regimes – as a salutary check upon the cognitive drive to suppress or obliterate the speech-act "differend", and hence to adjudicate in matters beyond its own (strictly limited) domain. But this is to ignore the very partial – if you prefer, "strong revisionist" – character of Lyotard's reading of Kant. More specifically: his reading is "postmodern" in the sense that it promotes (or exploits) just those elements in Kant's thinking – among them the sublime *qua* emblem of absolute heterogeneity – that facilitate the passage from modernity to counter-modernity, or from an ethos of enlightened mutual understanding to an ethos of the differend premised on the idea of strictly non-negotiable "phrases in dispute". It thus falls in very readily with the current high vogue among cultural and literary theorists for talk of "otherness", "difference", "radical alterity" and the like.

Such talk derives partly from poststructuralist sources, no doubt through some vague analogy with Saussure's theory of language as a differential system of contrasts and relationships "without positive terms". But it has also gained credence – in writers influenced by the work of Emmanuel Levinas – from the notion of ethics as involving a primordial encounter with the absolute "other", an encounter that constitutes the ethical relation as such, and that should therefore take precedence over all other (e.g. historical, social or cognitively oriented) modes of human concern (Levinas 1969, 1981). In particular it calls for a radical break with what Levinas views as the dominant tradition of Western (post-Hellenic) thought, that which locates epistemology – or the subject-centred quest for knowledge and truth – at the heart of philosophical endeavour. For the effect of such thinking has been either to marginalize ethical questions or to treat them (like philosophers from Plato to Descartes, Kant and Husserl) as somehow dependent upon our first getting clear about issues of truth, knowledge or adequate conceptual representation.

Levinas follows Heidegger – up to a point – in recounting the history of "Western metaphysics" as the history of an error, a deep-laid oblivion, or a swerving away from the demand placed upon it by an ethic of radical otherness. Nevertheless he reads Heidegger (as Heidegger himself read Nietzsche) as occupying the role of "last metaphysician", one who strove to overturn or transvalue that history while remaining captive to some of its predominant motifs (see especially Heidegger 1979). For on this account Heidegger failed to think through his "destruction" of onto-theological concepts and categories to the point where they might have opened on to that moment of the ethical encounter with otherness *before* "philosophy" as such, and before even the obscure intimations of a long-lost primordial Being that Heidegger sought to reveal (Heidegger 1962, 1993). Fundamental ontology was in this sense not so much a break with the prevailing (epistemological) tradition as an attempt to transform and revitalize its innermost resources by returning to a common point of origin. And since that origin, according to Levinas, *already* marked the site of a covering-over – a forgetfulness of ethics *qua* "radical alterity" in the quest for Being as the self-same ground of authentic agency and thought – it should therefore be seen as yet another variant of the will-to-truth within Western metaphysics that evades or defers the unthinkable challenge of an absolute, unmediated otherness.

Far be it from me to defend Heidegger against Levinas's strictures. One is inclined to welcome any criticism that might just be of use in weaning disciples off his potent brand of fake etymopoeic profundity, his drastic misreading of philosophers like Kant and Husserl, and his (to say the least) dubious conviction that the truth of Being was exclusively vouchsafed to thinkers at home in those languages – Greek and German – that between them monopolized the wisdom of the ages (for more detailed argument, see Norris 1990). From here it was no great distance to Heidegger's espousal of Nazi ideology during the 1930s and his subsequent (post-war) continuing belief in the "inner truth and greatness" of the National Socialist movement (Bourdieu 1991, Rockmore 1992, Ott 1993, Wolin 1993). Nor should we forget – in the present context –

that this high-handed talk of "Western metaphysics" as some kind of immemo-
rial lapse from grace went along with an equally blanket and reductive charac-
terization of "science", one that maintained little sense of the distinction
between science and technology, and that treated them both as disastrous
emanations of the old epistemic ("metaphysical") will to truth (Heidegger
1977). Hence, ironically, the marked resemblance between Heidegger's thinking on this topic and the theses propounded in *Dialectic of enlightenment* (Adorno
& Horkheimer 1972) and later works by Adorno (1973a,b). It is a case –
crudely put – of anti-scientism making strange bedfellows, aligning Adorno
(foremost among critics of the Heideggerian "jargon of authenticity") with
exactly that counter-Enlightenment ethos whose errors and dangers he diagnosed elsewhere with such pinpoint accuracy. Nothing could more clearly
illustrate Habermas's point about the normative confusions that always result
from this failure to distinguish the modalities of "reason" in its various
(instrumental, theoretical, ethico-political and critical-emancipatory) spheres
(Habermas 1987). And if any further evidence were needed then one might
adduce Heidegger's notorious pronouncement to the effect that there was no
real difference – no difference pertinent to "thinking" at this elevated level –
between mechanized agriculture, production-line techniques and the mass-
manufacture of corpses in the Nazi gas-ovens (see Schirmacher 1989; also
Zimmerman 1991).

Of course this statement exhibits a degree of crassness and moral stupidity
that far surpasses the milder forms of value-relativism endorsed by postmodernists like Lyotard. But it may nonetheless stand as a cautionary index, a
pointer to what looms at the end of the road that these thinkers are currently
travelling. For in their case also it is taken as read – with frequent (overt or
implicit) reference to Heidegger – that "reason" equates *tout court* with the
monologic discourse of instrumental (means-end) rationality, and hence that
there can be no moral distinctions worth making between its various malign
manifestations. The same tendency is visible in certain forms of "depth-
ecological" approach to issues of environmental concern, arguments that likewise draw inspiration from Heidegger, and whose upshot – very often – is to
implicate not only "science" or "reason" but the entire realm of human
activities and purposes in a so-far unexpiated history of crimes against the
natural and animal world. One can see why such thinking has been dubbed
"neofascist" by critics who fear – not without reason – that it will get environ-
mentalism a bad name (see the arguments assembled in Zimmerman 1993).
For it brings out most vividly the dangers courted by a reactive (counter-
Enlightenment) outlook that reduces humanity to its lowest common denomi-
nator, that is to say, its (no doubt well-attested) drive to recruit or exploit every
kind of natural and human resource in the service of brute, unthinking
technological "progress". At the very least this betrays a refusal to acknowl-

edge those other, more progressive or enlightened uses of reason that have produced – what would otherwise be wholly unaccountable – the revulsion against just such humanly degrading forms of the destructive will-to-power over nature. At worst it produces a contempt for humanity (taken as somehow the logical consequence of a concern for other animals or for the natural environment) much akin to Heidegger's anti-humanist stance, his attitude of "open reverence" before nature that none the less enabled him – "consistently" enough – to offer that truly appalling pronouncement with regard to technology and the gas-chambers. For at a certain point the assault upon "science", narrowly conceived, leans over into a wholesale assault upon reason, likewise reduced (together with the human beings who now become merely its unwitting executants) to the same dead level of a technocratic drive divorced from all forms of reflective, ethical or emancipatory interest.

Science, criticism and ethics

This is why current attitudes to science can often serve as a litmus-test – so to speak – of attitudes adopted in the wider (ethical and socio-political) sphere. Heidegger provides the most striking instance, despite his efforts to disguise (or to dignify) a downright contempt for science through obscurantist talk about the "question of technology" as somehow predestined – inescapably bequeathed – by the entire prehistory of "Western metaphysics" to date. Nevertheless, as I suggested above, it is far from clear that Levinas provides a much better alternative when he urges a return to the "primordial" locus of ethics, construed as the encounter with an absolute Other which, more radically even than Heidegger's discourse on Being, exceeds all the limiting concepts and categories of that same (onto-theological) tradition. Jacques Derrida raises some pertinent questions with regard to this strictly exorbitant claim in his early essay "Violence and metaphysics" (Derrida 1978). "The other, as other, is not only an alter ego", Levinas writes. In the moment of ethical encounter, quite simply, ". . . it is what I myself am not" (quoted in Derrida 1978: 125). Of course there are contexts – familiar contexts, those of "decency" and "everyday life" – which dispose us to adopt the belief that "the other is known through sympathy, as an other like myself, as alter ego" (quoted in Derrida 1978: 125). But Levinas rejects such reassuring habits of thought with all the rigour, all the force of uncompromising principle that Kierkegaard once brought against the ethical claims of Hegelian *Sittlichkeit*. Or rather: where Hegel had himself objected to the "formalist" character of Kantian ethics, that is, Kant's conceiving of moral law in rigorous abstraction from the manifold contexts of human social and historical experience, Levinas will criticize both Kant and Hegel – along with the entire tradition of thought on such topics from Plato to Husserl – for their failure to acknowledge the ethical instance as that which cannot be reduced to the terms of this familiar (intra-philosophical) debate.

Hence the title of Levinas's best-known work, *Totality and infinity* (Levinas 1969). Philosophers have quelled the voice of the Other – the infinitely Other – through their totalizing will to negate or transcend such signs of absolute difference. In so doing they have reduced ethical questions to the level of a common intelligibility, a sphere of supposedly shared values and knowledge-constitutive interests where difference is admitted only (as with Hegel) on condition that it ultimately yield to some higher act of reflective or synthesizing consciousness. Indeed, one misrepresents Levinas by invoking that time-honoured metaphor of *voice* as the internalized demand that conscience makes upon the otherwise unregenerate promptings of instinct, self-interest or desire. For he, no less than Derrida, mistrusts the appeal to such an inward tribunal whose dictates are identified with practical reason in its legislative role as arbiter of universal right. It is therefore not the voice but the *face* of the other that bears this mute yet eloquent witness to the claims upon us of one whose alterity refuses even our best-willed efforts to negotiate the distance between self and Other. Such would be the opening, in Derrida's words,

> of a question, in the inversion of transcendental symmetry, put to philosophy as logos, finitude, history, violence: an interpellation of the Greek by the non-Greek at the heart of a silence, an ultralogical affect of speech, a question that can be stated only by being forgotten in the language of the Greeks; and a question that can be stated, as forgotten, only in the language of the Greeks. (Derrida 1978: 133)

So these are the stark alternatives, as Levinas presents them. (That Derrida takes a somewhat different view, thus removing this passage from the ambit of straightforward approving paraphrase, should be evident already from the pointed apposition of those two last clauses.) Only by confronting the challenge to think *outside and beyond* all its inherited conceptual resources will philosophy avoid that "egological" gesture of containment – that move to comprehend and thus assimilate the absolute other – which has hitherto exerted an implacable hold upon the discourse of reason and truth. "All the classical concepts interrogated by Levinas are thus dragged toward the *agora*, summoned to justify themselves in an ethico-political language that they have not always sought – or believed that they sought – to speak, summoned to transpose themselves into this language by confessing their violent aims" (Derrida 1978: 97). At very least there is room for doubt as to the close affinity (even, as some recent commentators have argued, the relationship of mutual dependence) between his own and Levinas's projects.

19

Simon Critchley goes yet further in his detailed exegetical account of the two thinkers (Critchley 1992). If there is – as Derrida has often maintained – an ethical moment proper to deconstruction, then it can only emerge (Critchley argues) through a reading that would find its way through and beyond the aporias of deconstructive thought, and acknowledge the absolute priority of ethics as that which alone gives both projects their ultimate meaning and purpose. On this account deconstruction is a kind of staging-post or half-way house between "totality" and "infinity", epistemology and ethics, or the sovereign *logos* of Western (Hellenic) tradition and its other as figured in the texts and the customs of a different – primarily Judaic – ethical culture. But we need only look again at the above-cited passage from Derrida ("All the classical concepts . . . ") to perceive certain problems that arise with this markedly partisan Levinasian reading of "Violence and metaphysics". After all, it is made clear that the "violence" in question is not *exclusively* that which pertains to those "classical concepts" in their drive to monopolize the discourse of truth and reason. There is also the violence with which, in Derrida's words, they are "dragged toward the *agora*", summarily called upon to "justify themselves", and to do so (moreover) in a language – an "ethico-political" language such as Levinas brings to bear – that they themselves "have not always sought – or believed that they sought". And so it comes about that the classical concepts are transposed out of their original element – that of the Hellenic or "ontotheological" tradition – and obliged to confess their "violent aims" before an ethical tribunal whose precepts and values are of a wholly different order. It seems, to say the least, a rather violent proceeding, and one in which the confession is extracted not only under duress but in a court where the judge, jury and prosecuting counsel appear to speak very much with a single voice.

One could speculate at length on what Lyotard might have to say concerning this flagrant suppression of the narrative *differend*, this casting of reason (or its "classical concepts") in the role of a solitary defendant whose every attempt at self-justification will surely be struck down as irrelevant by the rules of the court. But it is not much use invoking Lyotard here since he, like Levinas, will admit of no ethical claim save that which elevates alterity – or the difference-principle – to the status of sole and absolute criterion in matters of dispute between rival parties (Lyotard 1987). And this is why, *pace* Critchley, one has to read an essay such as "Violence and metaphysics" not as a kind of deconstructive prelude to the wisdom enshrined in Levinas's thought, but – on the contrary – as a *critique* of Levinasian ethics, one that refuses to locate all violence on the side of those much-maligned "classical concepts". For here as with Lyotard there is a danger that genuine (substantive or principled) distinctions between truth and falsehood or right and wrong will be pushed out of sight through the promotion of "difference" to a point where it exerts plenipotentiary powers. Such would be the point at which truth-claims, arguments, concepts and reasons are ruled *de jure* inadmissible simply on account of their presuming to state some determinate fact of the matter, to refute some other (false or ungrounded) item of evidential witness, to criticize the logic, consistency or truth of those arguments brought against them, or to claim due warrant and justification – on principled grounds – for the plea thus submitted on their own behalf. This is why Lyotard ends up by denying that one could ever properly refute a right-wing revisionist "historian" of the Holocaust like Faurisson (Lyotard 1987). It would be wrong no matter how groundless his factual claims, how absurd his display of pseudo-scholarship, or how repugnant his ethico-political stance. For to do so – to invoke such self-assured standards of serious, responsible scholarly enquiry – would infringe upon his right to reject those standards and pursue some entirely different project with its own *sui generis* criteria.

It might seem tactless or worse to compare Levinas's profound meditations on the Holocaust and its significance for our thinking about ethics, philosophy and history with Lyotard's self-inflicted dilemma in the face of a malignant ideologue like Faurisson. But the comparison is justified in this respect at least: that an ethics of absolute "difference", "alterity" or "otherness" is one that on principle denies itself recourse to a *sensus communis* of shared human values and truth-seeking interests, a realm wherein the rival parties to any such dispute might hope to find some common ground of mutual intelligibility. Thus Levinas and Lyotard both take their stand on the existence of strictly non-negotiable disputes that admit of no possible mediating instance – no appeal to agreed-upon criteria of reason or justice – that could offer some equitable means of resolving the issue. And in both cases this ethic goes along with a marked devaluation of all modes of knowledge – epistemic, cognitive, scientific, theoretical, epistemo-critical and so forth – that might otherwise assume a more prominent role (as they have for philosophers from Kant to Husserl) in a project seeking to dispel the various sources of ignorance, prejudice and error. All of which points towards philosophy of science as the arena wherein these issues are currently raised with the greatest urgency and force. Thus defenders of a critical-realist ontology – notably Roy Bhaskar – have an interest not only in rendering intelligible the ideas of scientific knowledge, truth and progress, but also in preserving that ethical or socio-political dimension where science can be seen as furthering the ends of emancipatory critique (see Bhaskar 1986, 1989 and 1993).

In this they join hands – across the widening gulf of more recent Francophile thought – with those philosophers, Bachelard and Canguilhem among them, who acknowledged the conventional, the metaphorical and error-prone character of much scientific thought, but who none the less maintained that science advanced precisely through the criticism – the more adequate conceptualization – of its own formative past (see Bachelard 1968, 1984; also

21

Lecourt 1975, Tiles 1984, Gutting 1989). "Formative", that is, in the sense of providing an explanatory (socio-historical) context for the study of those vari-ous conceptual revolutions or paradigm shifts that had marked the more significant stages of its progress to date. In other words, it was possible to defend the distinction between science and erroneous (i.e. proto- or pseudo-) science while taking full account of those multiform changes in the very conception of scientific truth – of theory, methodology, validity-conditions, experimental protocols and so forth – that properly engaged the interest of cultural historians and sociologists of knowledge. Again it is a matter – a fairly elementary matter one would think – of respecting the difference between "context of discovery" and "context of justification". For otherwise philosophy of science could offer no credible or coherent explanation of what Peter Munz, in his aptly titled book on the topic, refers to as "our knowledge of the growth of knowledge" (Muntz 1985; also Laudan 1979, Rescher 1979, Smith 1981).

These distinctions have been pretty much ignored – or rejected out of hand – by the present-day company of postmodern sceptics, Wittgensteinians, neo-pragmatists and revisionist historians of science. What they all have in common is a strong desire to discredit any idea of truth as something more than localized (or contingently warranted) belief, joined with a tendency – pushed to its absurdist limit in Feyerabend's writing – to collapse issues of validity or justification into questions for the biographer, the psychoanalyst or the sociologist of knowledge. A major point of entry for these and kindred doctrines has been through the various successive waves of French cultural fashion, in particular (as I have argued) that version of the Saussure-inspired "linguistic turn" which construes all truth-claims – along with their attendant "sub-jectpositions" – as relative to (or "constructed in") this or that language, discourse, Lyotardian "phrase-genre", etc. Undoubtedly much of this thinking has its source, at whatever distorting remove, in Bachelard's seminal reflections on the role of metaphor, figural language or analogical representation in the prehistory of the natural sciences. But it was not until structuralism ceded to poststructuralism as the last word in "radical" theory – emblematically, with the late-70s switch of allegiance from Althusser to Foucault – that it also gave up on any version of Bachelard's quest for well-defined "epistemological breaks", and hence accomplished the passage to a species of wholesale cultural-linguistic relativism. And this in turn opened the way for that post-modern *doxa* that views both the natural and the human "sciences" as so many language-games recurrently prone to delusions of epistemological grandeur.

Worst of all, so it is argued, is the form that such delusions take when they set up to legislate in realms beyond their own, strictly limited (epistemic or cognitive) domain, and thus give rise to Habermasian talk of the "unfinished project of modernity". For this project contravenes the difference-principle (or Lyotard's incommensurability-thesis) on two main counts. First, it assumes that there is no sharp divide – no radical disjunction of realms – between knowledge-constitutive (or epistemic) interests and an ethical will to ameliorate the human condition by attaining a better, more enlightened understanding of what constitutes progress in the sphere of intersubjective conduct and relations. (This is also why Kant, in his Preface to the first *Critique*, confutes his present-day anti-foundationalist critics by insisting that a shared commitment to such values is the precondition for *every* branch of intellectual endeavour, including the natural sciences and works of theoretical enquiry.) Secondly, it sees no reason in principle to suppose that human beings (or cultures) may be so far divided one from another – or committed to such diverse, incommensurable "forms of life" – as to rule out any prospect of achieving consensus except through coercive (and thus *a fortiori* non-consensual) means. On the contrary: there is evidence and reason to believe that ethical advances most often come about – quite simply, that we treat each other better – through the kind of principled yet tolerant allowance that results from an enhanced understanding of the interests that unite "us" and "them" across otherwise considerable differences of ethos and culture. For it is a minimal requirement of any such advance that we should recognize *both* the fact of this alterity *and* the fact that we become thus aware of it – or willing to acknowledge its claims upon us – only by virtue of our human capacity to respect others by (so far as possible) placing ourselves in their position. And this requires in turn that our sense of their "otherness" should *not* reach the point (the potentially violent or paranoid point) where difference is raised into some kind of shibboleth or ethical absolute. For we should then lack even the most rudimentary resources for understanding what they say, respecting what they mean, or treating them as human in any (to us) intelligible sense of that term. (For further argument to this effect, see Norris 1994.)

That the above set of claims will strike many readers as hopelessly *dépassé* – just a throwback to quaint old "Enlightenment" ways of thought – offers as reliable an index as any of what Lyotard means by his talk of our current "postmodern condition" (Lyotard 1983). Still one may take leave to doubt that this condition should be seen as a wished-for deliverance from the ideas and values thus cheerfully consigned to the scrap-heap of intellectual history. Indeed, there is a strong case for viewing it as a thoroughly regressive and mystified conception, one which – if followed through consistently – would sever all ties of mutual understanding and obligation between persons, between cultures and (not least) between ethics and other dimensions of human enquiry. We can best see this counter-argument at work in the pages of "Violence and metaphysics" that Derrida devotes to Husserl, more specifically, to questioning Levinas's charge that the entire project of transcendental phenomenology is merely a last and desperate attempt to reassert the privilege standardly attached to the self-knowing, self-acting, self-grounding subject of

23

epistemological tradition. Thus, according to Levinas, "by making the other, notably in the *Cartesian meditations*, the ego's phenomenon, constituted by analogical appresentation on the basis of belonging to the ego's own sphere, Husserl allegedly missed the absolute alterity of the other, reducing it to the same" (quoted in Derrida 1978: 123). And again: "to make the other an alter ego . . . is to neutralize its absolute alterity" (quoted in Derrida 1978: 123). But then the question arises: on what possible (alternative) basis can we recognize the Other as another *person*, that is to say, as not belonging to our field of phenomenal perception in just the same way as inanimate objects of experience like rocks and stones, or (arguably) trees, or (yet more arguably) animal creatures of various non-human species?

Of course there is room for much debate – for instance, among "deep" ecologists – as to whether such distinctions are ethically desirable, or where (if at all) the line should be drawn between phenomenal and creaturely modes of being. Nor should we assume that "depth" in these matters necessarily equates with a humane or civilized ethic, a point sometimes made by those critics of deep ecology who note its very marked Heideggerian strain of contempt for all merely human (or humanist) values (see Zimmerman 1993). But Derrida's argument begins farther back, at the stage – with Husserl – where thought first encounters this need to distinguish the demands made upon us by the various modes of phenomenal "appresentation". At any rate I would venture the following claims, all of which receive ample warrant from the text. First: it is indeed a *critique* of Levinasian ethics, and not – as might be gathered from some recent commentators – just a skirmishing prelude to Derrida's acknowledgement of the deeper kinship between their two projects. Secondly: that critique goes by way of an argument very much in the Kantian (and, self-evidently, the Husserlian) mode; that is to say, a negative transcendental argument that points out the conditions of *im*possibility that render Levinas's statements strictly untenable. Thirdly: what is at issue here is not only the relation between self and other but also, more specifically, the extent to which our very conception of "the Other" – and our sense of obligation in face of such demands – arises from a *prior and essential* capacity to achieve self-knowledge through reflection on our own experience as real-world, situated moral agents. From which it follows (fourthly) that there *is not and cannot be* an ethics of radical "alterity", one that would respect the Levinasian injunction to renounce all thinking that involves recourse to the intersubjective, to the *sensus communis* of shared human interests, or to the sphere of an "egological" (yet none the less ethical) reflection on the self and its relationship to the other. To the "other", that is, as an alter ego whom we are able to recognize – across and despite all differences of language, culture, gender, formative tradition and so forth – as *like us* in certain crucial (distinctively human) respects and radically *unlike* the objects that otherwise constitute our field of experience.

Again one is aware of likely objections from the depth-ecological quarter. What entitles us, these thinkers might ask, to claim (with Husserl, as Derrida reads him) that we possess phenomenological warrant for reserving "ethics" to the privileged sphere of human interpersonal relations, and thereby excluding the concern with nature – in all its rich and threatened variety – from the ambit of properly ethical concern? I should note that Derrida has returned to this question in a recent essay on Heidegger where it is raised with precisely such objections in mind (Derrida 1987). Moreover, a prominent theme in that essay is the ease with which depth-ontological talk of the Heideggerian variety gives rise on the one hand to a strain of anti-humanist (or post-metaphysical) thinking with – to say the least – dubious ethical and political consequences, and on the other to a certain residual anthropomorphism that dogmatically excludes animal life from the realm of authentic *Dasein*.

These misgivings have indeed become steadily more apparent in the course of Derrida's various engagements with Heidegger over the past three decades. They are first signalled in his essay "The ends of man" (1968), albeit in the somewhat muted form that has often witnessed Derrida's desire – a generous and properly ethical desire – to do justice to thinkers whose work has greatly influenced his own, but with whom he is none the less obliged to take issue on principled philosophic grounds (for English translation, see Derrida 1982a). In his latest texts that critical distance has increased to the point where Derrida's commentaries on Heidegger are more in the nature of symptomatic or diagnostic readings (Derrida 1989). And this despite what many hostile critics have seen – not without some justification – as an over-generosity on Derrida's part, a redemptive strategy that deploys all manner of subtle hermeneutical techniques in order to save Heidegger from his own worst devices. All the same it should be clear to any unprejudiced reader that Derrida has always criticized that strain of anti-humanist thinking, very largely inspired by Heidegger, whose numerous variations on the "end of" theme – the end of man, the end of philosophy, the end of metaphysics – have exerted such a potent and continuing influence on the currency of "advanced" theoretical debate.

One result of such thinking is to remove ethics – or whatever survives of that "discourse" – to a level of depth-ontological concern where it no longer makes sense in humanly intelligible terms, or as having do with such discredited notions as agency, will, practical reason or political responsibility. And this in turn goes along with the severance of truth – likewise pushed back to a primordial dimension "beyond" or "before" all its merely metaphysical determinations down through the history of Western thought – from any possible reckoning in terms of scientific, epistemological or knowledge-constitutive interests. For there is, as I have argued, a close relation between these two aspects of Heidegger's thought. The reduction of "science" to technology, and of "reason" to the realm of merely instrumental (means-end) rationality, is that which on the one hand enables Heidegger to issue his famous pronouncement "science does not think", and on the other opens the way to his proclaimed wholesale "destruction" of the Western (post-Hellenic) metaphysical and humanist tradition of thought. It might seem perverse, given their much-publicized differences of late, to suggest even a minimal alignment between Derrida's and Habermas's readings of Heidegger (see for instance Habermas 1987). But on this much at least they are agreed: that there exist real dangers, of philosophical confusion and worse, in any thinking that so resolutely seeks to break with all the concepts and categories, the values and enabling assumptions, of that same "metaphysical" tradition. More specifically: it risks engendering what Derrida reveals – through a textual exegesis much closer than anything that Habermas sees fit to provide – as the depth-ontological indifference towards questions (of knowledge and ethical comportment alike) that Heidegger treats as belonging to the epoch of a "human, all-too-human" error.

To offer an adequately detailed reading of these texts would further complicate an already complex argument. But my summary account may help to define what is at stake when Derrida effectively turns back the charge that Levinas brings against Husserl, that is, his claim that the project of transcendental phenomenology is just another variant of the logocentric drive to contain or suppress all signs of an alterity beyond its conceptual grasp. Thus, according to Levinas,

> . . . concepts suppose an anticipation, a horizon within which alterity is amortized as soon as it is announced precisely because it has let itself be foreseen. The infinitely-other cannot be bound by a concept, cannot be thought on the basis of a horizon; for a horizon is always a horizon of the same, the elementary unity within which eruptions and surprises are always welcomed by understanding and recognized. (Derrida 1978: 95)

In which case Husserl's project would indeed stand condemned – along with that entire prehistory of thought that it claims to pass in critical review – as nothing more than a massively elaborated stratagem for avoiding the ethical question. All the more so in that Husserl sees the "crisis" of the European sciences (both the natural and the human sciences, philosophy pre-eminent among them) as resulting from the rift between a mindless positivism devoid of reflective or critical content and a reactive tendency that responds to this impoverished condition by swinging straight across to the opposite (relativist) extreme (Husserl 1978). Such, according to Husserl, was the widespread tendency that manifested itself in such emergent disciplines as sociology of knowledge, comparative ethnography and those contextualist approaches to the history of science or philosophy that relativized truth to some particular (e.g. linguistic or cultural) locale. Behind them loomed the ultimate threat of a Nietzschean "transvaluation of values" that would seek to undermine every last standard of truth, reason and critique. Any hope of reversing this widespread drift must rest (he argued) upon philosophy's willingness to question its own most foundational or axiomatic beliefs, but to do so in a rigorous and principled way that answered the sceptic point-for-point on grounds of the sceptic's choosing. Only thus could the sciences, natural and human, be saved from their otherwise inevitable lapse into forms of irrationalist (or nihilist) abandon that Husserl – writing in the period before World War Two – saw as inextricably bound up with the drift towards global catastrophe.

It is a similar diagnosis that Habermas offers in his early book *Knowledge and human interests* (Habermas 1971). His project – like Husserl's – has a twofold purpose: to think its way back through those errors and distortions that had overtaken the philosophic discourse of modernity, and then (as it were, on the positive side) to redeem the emancipatory values still latent within that discourse. Thus it is not so much "science" (in the blanket Heideggerian pejorative sense) that has brought this situation about, but rather a narrowly positivist conception of science that equates with the brute technological will-to-power, and that hence creates a radical disjunction of realms between "knowledge" and "human interests". But from Levinas's viewpoint – as expressed in his early book on Husserl – this can only constitute yet another episode in that misbegotten history of thought whose governing principle is the exclusion of ethics from its field of primordial concern. "More than any other philosophy, *phenomenology*, in the wake of Plato, was to be struck with light. Unable to reduce the last naïveté, the naïveté of the glance, it predetermined Being as object" (Derrida 1978: 95). For if ethics is *by very definition* that which "philosophy" has kept off bounds – so that even when purportedly raising such questions it has redefined them on its own (intra-philosophical) terms – then of course ethics can find no place within a project that avowedly seeks to vindicate the truth-claims of philosophy through a yet more rigorous critical review of its grounding suppositions and values. Husserl would then stand as the latest, most resourceful and hard-pressed defender of a tradition of thought whose contemporary "crisis" was not so much a threat from outside that tradition – from the forces of militant unreason – as a deep-laid liability nurtured within it from the time of its Greek origins. Such would at least be Levinas's case: that Husserl bears witness to this ancient complicity by denominating *science* as the privileged sphere wherein thought both confronts that epochal "crisis" and is destined – if at all – to transcend or resolve it.

Beyond relativism

I trust that it will now be clear why I have devoted such a lengthy excursus to this three-way encounter on the question of ethics and epistemology between Husserl, Levinas and Derrida. What is at issue for each of them is the relation between "crisis" and "criticism", that is to say, the extent to which philosophy (and the human sciences in general) may still exercise a rightful claim to represent the interests of enlightened understanding through a critical reflection on its own past history. For Levinas, this question merely serves to obscure the violence implicit in all such attempts to subjugate ethics to epistemology, or to "represent" the other on terms laid down by a discourse of self-legitimizing reason and truth. For Derrida, conversely, Levinas has misread Husserl – submitted his texts to the hermeneutic "violence" of a partial and appropriative reading – through this fixed preconception that concern for the other excludes all concern with those questions (critical, epistemological, etc.) whose province is that of the first-person subject in its various modes of reflective self-knowledge or "egological" enquiry. Thus (in Derrida's words) "if the other was not recognized as ego, its entire alterity would collapse". Or again: "if the other were not recognized as a transcendental alter *ego*, it would be entirely in the world and not, as ego, the origin of the world" (Derrida 1978: 125).

Such is the argument in its technical ("conditions of possibility") form, as derived from Kant and re-stated in terms of a directly Husserlian provenance. But we should not be misled into thinking such arguments utterly remote from the context of everyday human social and moral concern. What emerges from Husserl's complex, often tortuous, investigations is also (in a very precise sense of that phrase) what we *know from experience*: that we can best understand other people by observing their behaviour, interpreting their motives, consulting their interests and so forth, on the basis of a knowledge that comes of our sharing the same lifeworld. For this is nothing less than a precondition for treating them as human beings, that is to say, as physically-embodied creatures who exist "in the world" and are subject (like us) to the conditions of phenomenal experience, but also as beings who can think, reason, will and judge under just those conditions, and who thus exercise a claim – again like us – to ethical autonomy and selfhood. It is in virtue of respecting both of these requirements that Husserl, in Derrida's estimate, cannot be held guilty of the charge brought against him by Levinas.

Again I would make the point that this argument has a bearing on issues beyond the sphere of Husserlian exegesis, transcendental phenomenology, or even of "ethics" as a specialized discourse whose terms no doubt derive from an expert tradition of intra-philosophical debate. But that "beyond" is not the realm of an absolute alterity that would repudiate all commerce with the interests of philosophic reason. No more is it alien to those values of "decency" and "everyday life" that (according to Levinas) incorrectly lead us to believe "that the other is known through sympathy, as an other like myself, as an alter ego". Rather, it is a question of philosophy's seeking to articulate the conditions of possibility wherein such "decent", "everyday" values receive something more by way of reasoned and principled justification. At both levels – insofar as they can be thus crudely distinguished – our relation to the "other" must involve our *knowledge* of that other (i.e. as given under the aspect of phenomenal "appresentation"), and also our awareness of what Derrida calls its "originary non-phenomenality". Only thus can we balance the respect due them as co-participants in the ethical sphere with a shared understanding of the various constraints – bodily, physical, circumstantial, etc. – that in practice operate to narrow the range of free-willed (autonomous) agency and choice.

No doubt such talk will strike many readers as a throwback to Kant's unworkable dualism, his idea of "man" (or the subject of philosophy from Kant to Husserl) as a kind of "transcendental-empirical doublet", a creature somehow (impossibly) straddling the noumenal realm of practical reason and the realm of phenomenal appearances. On this view there is simply no point in pursuing issues that have long since lost any relevance or urgency that they once seemed to possess. But it is far from clear that the problem has been resolved – or shown up as a pseudo-problem – by treating it (along with Foucault) as merely the figment of some bygone discursive formation, or recommending (with the Wittgensteinians, postmodernists and liberal-communitarians) that we adopt a more minimalist or socially contextualized notion of the self. Thereby one might hope to coax philosophy down from its high metaphysical delusions and so – in the words of Stanley Cavell – "lead us back, via the community, home" (Cavell 1969: 43). Still there is a sense in which this reassuring counsel amounts to no more than a shuffling evasion of the deeper (jointly epistemological and ethical) issue. For such an argument is utterly bankrupt of resources when it comes to explaining how knowledge could ever advance beyond the stage of uncritical consensus belief, or again, how the dictates of moral conscience may sometimes require that one think, judge or act in a manner sharply at odds with the currency of in-place societal norms.

These cases may be rare but they are hardly unthinkable, as witness the various fictive instances that have always been a focus of the novelist's concern, from Huck Finn saying he'd rather go to Hell than turn in the runaway slave to the crises of conscience and commitment explored by existentialist writers such as Sartre and Camus. They have also figured prominently in the work of ethical philosophers who either look to fiction as a source of illustrative material or who raise similar issues by setting out to construct their own preferred range of imaginary test-case scenarios. (For examples of these two approaches see Nussbaum 1990 and Parfit 1984.) But of course these fictive analogies can only make sense – only strike us, that is to say, as possessing a certain exemplary force – against a background knowledge of those real-world conditions under which moral agents may sometimes be called upon to repudiate the mores or the cultural values of their own time and place. Such would be the case of those who lost their lives in resisting the Nazi rise to power, in refusing various forms of unjust or repressive doctrinal imposition, or in the struggle waged against the apartheid regime in South Africa. For one can scarcely begin to make sense of these examples – to do them justice in descriptive or evaluative terms – if one adopts a version of the postmodern-pragmatist or the liberal-communitarian line that treats ethical questions as always relative to some localized "language-game" or cultural "form of life". (See O'Neill 1989 for a pointed critique of these trends in present-day ethical theory.)

But this does not mean – as Lyotard suggests in *Just gaming* – that such judgments are wholly unaccountable, that they issue from the prompting of some "other" voice within us whose summons (like that of the Kantian sublime) defies all attempts at reasoned or principled justification (Lyotard & Thébaud 1985). Nor does it require, in Levinasian terms, that this voice be taken as the call of an absolute or infinite alterity, one that would exceed even Lyotard's residual sense of the subject for whom – or in whom – the sublime registers its power to subvert all the ground-rules of reasoning judgment. For despite this difference between them as to the source or locus of that "otherness", still it is the case that both Lyotard and Levinas go far towards rendering ethics an ultimate mystery, a realm wherein thinking must proceed always "without criteria", since otherwise it will always end up by committing some infraction of the ethical differend. I have already offered reasons – with reference to Derrida's critique of Levinas – for holding this to be a strictly unintelligible argument, one that would destroy any possibility of mutual understanding between self and other, and that would thus translate (ironically enough, given Levinas's overt claims) into a species of transcendental solipsism. But the objection is more than technical, as can readily be seen if one asks what might follow from this thinking of ethics as a call from the beyond of an infinite alterity that adjures us to relinquish all the presuppositions of "decent", "everyday" human understanding.

This risk can only be increased, moreover, when the absolute in question is insistently equated with a certain, quite specific religious or cultural tradition. In Levinas's case this tradition is that of a privileged Judaic openness to the thinking of absolute alterity, as against the opposing (Helleno-Christian) drive to annex or to "amortize" infinite difference in the name of a reason supposedly bound to a logic of identity or the "self-same" in thought. Derrida's critique of Levinas is in large part a negative-transcendental ("conditions of impossibility") argument to the effect that there is simply no thinking of ethics

– no conceiving the other as another *person* – unless on the basis of an intersubjectivity that reckons with precisely those aspects of experience, cognitive interests among them, which Levinas so zealously seeks to exclude. There are similar arguments to be found at many points in Derrida's work, notably in his essay "The supplement of copula", where the issue is again that of "Greek" metaphysics and whether we could ever intelligibly claim to think our way somehow "outside" or "beyond" the domain of its (supposedly) culture-specific concepts and categories (Derrida 1982b).

That no such thinking is possible – that we cannot even raise these questions except in terms that will always already have been provided by that same tradition – is one part of Derrida's answer, arrived at (again) through the strictest, most rigorous form of transcendental deduction. But this should not (I repeat) be taken to indicate that his essay deals only with questions of a specialized philosophical import. For he also makes the point, here as in "Violence and metaphysics", that *as a matter of necessity* there are terms for mutual understanding that transcend (in both the technical and the broader sense of that word) the manifold differences that no doubt exist between languages, cultures, communal life-forms, etc. And this may remind us – if we still need reminding after recent events in the former Yugoslavia, eastern Europe, Palestine and elsewhere – of the dangers that arise when the difference-principle (or the notion of radical alterity) is promoted to a high point of doctrine. For it can all too easily undergo the change from an attitude of good-willed tolerant respect for the diversity of human values and beliefs to a paranoid outlook that defines the other as indeed an alien being, one who – at the limit – ceases to embody any claim to shared humanity or personhood.

It is worth pausing over this figure of "embodiment" since it serves to focus all the issues that arise in Derrida's reading of Levinas and Husserl. Also, it helps to situate those issues in the wider context that I have tried to keep in view throughout this chapter, namely the relation between science (or knowledge in its cognitive, epistemic or phenomenal modes) and the realm of human ethical concern. The following passage from "Violence and metaphysics" is perhaps most crucial in this regard, so I shall cite it at length.

> Bodies, transcendent and natural things, are others in general for my consciousness. They are outside, and their transcendence is the sign of an already irreducible alterity. Levinas does not think so; Husserl does, and thinks that "other" already means something when things are in question. Which is to take seriously the reality of the outside world. Another sign of this alterity in general, which things share here with others, is that something within them too is always hidden, and is indicated only by anticipation, analogy, and appresentation . . . But in the case of the other as transcendent thing, the principled possibility of an

31

originary and original presentation of the hidden visage is always
open, in principle and a priori. This possibility is absolutely rejected in
the case of Others. The alterity of the transcendent thing, although
already irreducible, is such only by means of the indefinite incompleteness of my original perceptions. Thus it is incomparable to the alterity
of Others, which is also irreducible, and adds to the dimension of
incompleteness (the body of the Other in space, the history of our relations, etc.) a more profound dimension of nonoriginality – the impossibility of going around to see things from the other side. But without
the first alterity, the alterity of bodies (and the Other is also a body,
from the beginning), the second alterity could never emerge. (Derrida
1978: 124)

No doubt there are many and varied ways of unpacking this densely argued
passage. Its immediate context is of course the issue between Levinas and
Husserl as regards the project of transcendental phenomenology and its (real
or supposed) reduction of ethics – of our comportment *vis-à-vis* the Other – to
the sphere of self-locked "egological" concern. Derrida not only repudiates
this charge (so to speak) on Husserl's behalf, but shows how we could never
encounter that Other *as another person* except on the basis of a knowledge that
comes of our existing in a shared phenomenological lifeworld. For it is precisely by virtue of this common horizon – this putting oneself in the Other's
place within a shared set of spatio-temporal co-ordinates – that we encounter
the distinctive mode of "transcendence" that opens the ethical dimension.
That is to say, it is the condition of possibility for our understanding first that
there exist objects in the world that are not just pieces of our own mental fur-
niture; and then for our grasping those crucial respects in which the Other (i.e.
the other person) is not merely a phenomenal other, or an item in the field of
our perceptual experience, but a being whose "alterity" demands recognition
in a manner quite distinct from that which pertains to the givenness of objects
or inanimate bodies.

In short, Levinas misreads Husserl – does his thinking an injustice, a manifest, even "violent" injustice – while also propounding an ethics of absolute
(infinite) difference or alterity that quite simply cannot be construed in
humanly intelligible terms. And this has to do with his resolute refusal (like
Kierkegaard's (1941) before him) to admit the continuity that exists between
the realms of understanding, of reflective self-knowledge, and of other-regarding principles. For to deny this continuity is also to reject the most basic of
enabling conditions for ethical thought in general, that is to say, the knowledge
that other beings exist, that they are subject (like us) to all the pressures and
constraints of a physically embodied existence, and that we cannot – to repeat
– *do them justice* as moral agents without interpreting their words and actions in

the light of this shared knowledge. The argument is capable of adequate re-statement in a range of philosophical vocabularies outside the somewhat specialized Husserlian idiom. Thus it is often implicit (as I noted above) in dis-cussions of the freewill/determinism issue that treat human acts as construable under two alternative (but not incompatible) descriptions, on the one hand that of *reasons* that the agent concerned might accept as an adequately justified account of her motives, interests or principles in thus acting, and on the other that of *causes* that may yet appear, to an external observer, as possessing some explanatory force (see for instance Nagel 1986). Then again, it clearly relates to the Kantian distinction between noumenal and phenomenal realms, with the difference that here – for Derrida as indeed for Husserl – there can be no access to the former (that is, to the "suprasensible" realm of ethics or practical reason) except by way of an ethics that also encompasses our creaturely exist-ence as sentient beings.

Conclusion

It will now perhaps be clear why I have conducted this discussion along two tracks of argument, the one having to do with postmodernist ideas about difference, otherness, radical incommensurability and so forth, and the other with present-day forms of ontological or epistemic relativism as manifest espe-cially in philosophy of science. Where these ideas converge is on the thesis – common to Levinas and Lyotard – which holds that the interests of justice can only be served by raising alterity to a high point of principle, by maximizing the range of discursive or narrative differentials, and by seeking to dislodge the cognitive phrase-regime (or the subject-centred epistemology of knowledge and truth) from its position of unwarranted pre-eminence.

One could instance many other tributary sources, among them the Witt-gensteinian appeal to "language-games" (or cultural "forms of life"), each pos-sessed of its own internal criteria, its own *sui generis* dimension of sense-making values and norms (Wittgenstein 1953). For on this account it follows that any criticism of such language-games is always and necessarily beside the point – or sure to involve some form of injustice – since it will *de facto* issue from a dif-ferent (external) standpoint that fails to respect those immanent criteria, and that thus cannot possibly achieve understanding on terms acceptable to the speakers – or the "native informants" – concerned. (For the best-known state-ment of this view, see Winch 1958.) And it is then a short step to those varieties of extreme relativist thinking as applied to the history and philosophy of science that likewise see nothing but arrogance or ethnocentric prejudice in the notion of scientific truth as in any way distinct from – or capable of rising above – its own localized contexts of discovery. Here also it is taken for granted that truth-claims, criteria, validity-conditions and so forth are intrinsically as many and various as the language games, life-forms, conceptual paradigms or research programmes that make up this or that (no matter how highly specialized) interpretive community.

Least of all should science or its allied (cognitive) language-game be allowed to stray over into the ethical domain where no such ground-rules properly apply. For this would constitute a particularly grievous infraction of the speech-act *differend*, a failure to reckon with the fact/value antinomy, or – in Levinas's terms – just one more instance of that drive to assimilate ethics (or the demand laid upon us by the call of an infinite otherness) to the sphere of "self-same" epistemological thought. More than that, it would amount – so these arguments suggest – to a species of wholesale determinism that ignores the difference between reasons and causes, between persons or agents and objects or events in the world, or again, between the realm of freely willed (other-regarding) ethical choice and those phenomena that the natural sciences seek to explain as falling under the laws of causal necessity. It is this latter objection that I think goes furthest towards accounting for the currently widespread hostility to science, and also for the high prestige of those doctrines – hermeneutic, sociological, postmodern, poststructuralist, neo-pragmatist, communitarian and so forth – that relativize scientific truth-claims to some local or culture-specific context of belief.

But there is (as I have suggested) reason to think that this hostility results from a number of deep-laid errors or misapprehensions. In part these have to do with science and its characteristic methods, procedures, disciplinary constraints, etc., matters that tend to be treated – if at all – with the kind of blanket and ill-informed criticism that comes of mistaking one particular (obsolete) paradigm of scientific truth, that of a crude and unreflective positivism, for the enterprise of "science" as a whole. Much the same applies to the two closely related issues of freewill/determinism and the fact/value dichotomy. For here also one gets a very different picture if one turns aside from the fashion-prone discourse of cultural theory and looks instead to those other, more thoughtful approaches that acknowledge the extent of causal (that is to say, material or socio-economic) determinants in human thought and action with a view to making ethical allowance – as well as social and political provision – for the practical limits that are often imposed upon our powers of autonomous choice. Moreover this suggests what is wrong with any thinking, like Lyotard's, that erects Hume's fork – the supposed disjunction between fact and value, or the cognitive and evaluative phrase-genres – into a wholesale incommensurability-principle that equates justice with a point-blank refusal to offer reasons, arguments or justifying grounds for this or that ethical commitment. It is, to say the least, a curious feature of such thinking that it treats Hume's dilemma as a startling new discovery while taking no account of recent work (in ethics and philosophy of mind and action) that points a way beyond this false antinomy by stressing the close relationship between value-judgments, reasons and knowledge-constitutive interests. One consequence of this – as likewise of the arguments propounded by Ted Honderich and other defenders of a qualified determinist outlook – is to help us think more constructively about science and its claims upon the shape and limits of our freedom (Honderich 1987). For there can then be no possible reason (aside from mere ignorance or prejudice) for denying that science may produce the kinds of knowledge that contribute to a better, more humane understanding of ethical and socio-political issues.

There is also room for doubt as to the liberating or emancipatory potential of those various ultra-relativist approaches – from the "strong programme" in sociology of knowledge to the manifold forms of the linguistic or hermeneutic "turn" – that are seen as offering a wished-for deliverance from the iron laws of scientific determinism. Thus it is worth pointing out that there is nothing so dogmatic – so tightly sealed off from any prospect of challenge on argued, reasoned or principled grounds – than a relativist orthodoxy that would view all truth-talk as merely a product of this or that language-game, discourse, paradigm, "interpretive community" or whatever. For if this were the case, as Hilary Putnam has remarked, then we would always willy-nilly be in the position of understanding other people, other cultures and other communities by our own interpretive lights, that is to say, according to the values or beliefs that happened to prevail within our society (Putnam 1983). Thus relativism is both conceptually incoherent – for reasons that have long been familiar to philosophers – and apt to produce some unfortunate consequences by way of its covert (or, in Rorty's case, its disarmingly open and genial) ethnocentrism (see Rorty 1991). My point here, as also in the long excursus via Derrida and Levinas, is that high-toned talk of "alterity" and "otherness" is not much use when it comes to deciding how best to treat others – how to make allowance for their interests, motives, pressures of circumstance, complexities of moral choice, etc. – on the only basis we have for such decisions, that of our shared humanity. For if we start out from the opposite conviction, i.e. that other people may (for all we know) have interests and values utterly incommensurable with our own, then it follows first that we couldn't make sense of any particular (context-specific) difference of views, and secondly that we would have no choice but to interpret them on our cultural terms.

This is why relativism so easily slips across from an attitude of tolerant pluralist regard for the variety of human cultures to a blank incapacity for the kind of thinking that would sometimes encounter a genuine challenge to its own habits of belief. And this applies just as much in the ethical domain as to issues raised by epistemology or philosophy of science. In each case the relativist is at a loss to explain how we could ever make significant *discoveries*, either in the natural and human sciences (through achieving a better, more adequate order of explanatory or conceptual grasp), or again – the equivalent in ethical terms – through the encounter with differing value-systems or principles of judgment. For it is a precondition of our making such discoveries, as Donald Davidson and others have argued, that the differences in question should always show up against a background horizon of beliefs held in common and – beyond that – a working assumption (Davidson's "principle of charity") that most of those beliefs hold true across and despite any localized problems of communicative grasp. In short, "whether we like it or not, if we want to understand others, we must count them right on most matters" (Davidson 1984: 197). And again: "the methodological problem of interpretation is to see how, given the sentences a man [*sic*] accepts as true under given conditions, to work out what his beliefs are and what his words mean" (Davidson 1984: 162).

From which it follows in turn that "a theory is better the more of its own resources it reads into the language for which it is a theory" (Davidson 1984: 229). "Better", that is, in the following three senses. Such a theory would (1) help to explain what actually goes on in the process of interpreting other people's meanings, intentions and beliefs; (2) provide a strong counter-argument to the relativist case; and (3) open up the further possibility – as argued above – that we might find reason to examine and revise some of our own more parochial beliefs insofar as they prove inadequate when measured against those other (different but by no means unintelligible) ways of thought. For the attitude of counting others (like ourselves) necessarily "right on most matters" is also what allows us sometimes to see where things have gone wrong, whether in our own or in their understanding, or indeed in the process of translation between such differing views. If it is ruled out pretty much *de rigueur* by the dominant trends in present-day cultural, social and literary theory, then – one is tempted to conclude – so much the worse for that theory.

References

Adorno, T. W. 1973a. *Negative dialectics*, tr. E. B. Ashton. London: Routledge & Kegan Paul.

Adorno, T. W. 1973b. *The jargon of authenticity*, tr. K. Tarnowski and F. Will. London: Routledge & Kegan Paul.

Adorno, T. W. & M. Horkheimer 1972. *Dialectic of enlightenment* tr. J. Cumming. New York: Seabury Press.

Althusser, L. 1990. *"Philosophy and the spontaneous philosophy of the scientists" and other essays*, G. P. Elliott (ed.). London: Verso.

Anderson, P. 1983. *In the tracks of historical materialism*. London: Verso.

Bachelard, G. 1964. *The psychoanalysis of fire*, tr. A. C. M. Ross. London: Routledge & Kegan Paul.

Bachelard, G. 1968. *The philosophy of no: a philosophy of the new scientific mind.* New York: Orion Press.

Bachelard, G. 1969. *The poetics of space,* tr. M. Jolas. Boston: Beacon Press.

Bachelard, G. 1971. *The poetics of reverie,* tr. D. Russell. Boston: Beacon Press.

Bachelard, G. 1984. *The new scientific spirit.* Boston: Beacon Press.

Barnes, B. 1982. *T.S. Kuhn and social science.* Oxford: Basil Blackwell.

Barnes, B. 1985. *About science.* Oxford: Basil Blackwell.

Barrett, M. 1992. *The politics of truth: from Marx to Foucault.* Cambridge: Polity.

Barthes, R. 1957/1972. *Mythologies: a selection,* tr. A. Lavers. London: Jonathan Cape.

Barthes, R. 1970. *S/Z,* tr. R. Miller. London: Jonathan Cape.

Bhaskar, R. 1986. *Scientific realism and human emancipation.* London: Verso.

Bhaskar, R. 1989. *Reclaiming reality.* London: Verso.

Bhaskar, R. 1993. *Dialectic: the pulse of freedom.* London: Verso.

Bloor, D. 1976. *Knowledge and social imagery.* London: Routledge & Kegan Paul.

Bloor, D. 1983. *Wittgenstein: a social theory of knowledge.* New York: Columbia University Press.

Bourdieu, P. 1991. *The political ontology of Martin Heidegger.* tr. P. Collier. Cambridge: Polity.

Cavell, S. 1969. *Must we mean what we say?* Oxford: Oxford University Press.

Critchley, S. 1992. *The ethics of deconstruction: Derrida and Levinas.* Oxford: Basil Blackwell.

Cunningham, V. 1993. *In the reading gaol.* Oxford: Basil Blackwell.

Davidson, D. 1980. *Essays on actions and events.* Oxford: Clarendon Press.

Davidson, D. 1984. *Inquiries into truth and interpretation.* London: Oxford University Press.

Derrida, J. 1978. Violence and metaphysics: an essay on the thoughts of Emmanuel Levinas. In *Writing and difference,* tr. A. Bass, 79–153. London: Routledge & Kegan Paul.

Derrida, J. 1982a. The ends of man. In *Margins of philosophy,* tr. A. Bass, 109–36. Chicago: University of Chicago Press.

Derrida, J. 1982b. The supplement of copula. In *Margins of philosophy,* tr. A. Bass, 175–205. Chicago: University of Chicago Press.

Derrida, J. 1987. Geschlecht II: Heidegger's hand. In *Deconstruction and philosophy: the texts of Jacques Derrida,* J. Sallis (ed.), 161–96. Chicago: University of Chicago Press.

Derrida, J. 1989. *Of spirit: Heidegger and the question,* tr. G. Bennington and R. Bowlby. Chicago: University of Chicago Press.

Eagleton, T. 1989. *The ideology of the aesthetic.* Oxford: Basil Blackwell.

Eagleton, T. 1991. *Ideology: an introduction.* London: Verso.

Feyerabend, P. 1975. *Against method.* London: New Left Books.

Feyerabend, P. 1978. *Science in a free society.* London: New Left Books.

Feyerabend, P. 1992. *Farewell to reason.* London: Verso.

Fish, S. 1989. *Doing what comes naturally: change, rhetoric, and the practice of theory in literary and legal studies.* Oxford: Oxford University Press.

Fodor, J. & E. Lepore 1991. *Holism: a shopper's guide.* Oxford: Basil Blackwell.

Foucault, M. 1970. *The order of things: an archaeology of the human sciences.* London: Tavistock.

Foucault, M. 1977. *Language, counter-memory, practice*, D. F. Bouchard & S. Simon (eds). Oxford: Basil Blackwell.

Foucault, M. 1980. *Power/knowledge: selected interviews and other writings*, C. Gordon (ed.). Hemel Hempstead, England: Harvester Wheatsheaf.

Fox Keller, E. 1985. *Reflections on gender and science*. New Haven, Connecticut: Yale University Press.

Fuller, S. 1988. *Social epistemology*. Bloomington, Indiana: Indiana University Press.

Fuller, S. 1989. *Philosophy of science and its discontents*. Boulder, Colorado: Westview Press.

Geertz, C. 1983. *Local knowledge: further essays on interpretive anthropology*. New York: Basic Books.

Gutting, G. 1989. *Michel Foucault's archaeology of scientific knowledge*. Cambridge: Cambridge University Press.

Habermas, J. 1971. *Knowledge and human interests*, tr. J. Shapiro. London: Heinemann.

Habermas, J. 1987. *The philosophical discourse of modernity: twelve lectures*, tr. F. W. Lawrence. Cambridge: Polity.

Harding, S. 1986. *The science question in feminism*. Ithaca, New York: Cornell University Press.

Harland, R. 1987. *Superstructuralism*. London: Routledge.

Harré, R. 1986. *Varieties of realism: a rationale for the social sciences*. Oxford: Basil Blackwell.

Heidegger, M. 1962. *Being and time*, tr. J. MacQuarrie and E. Robinson. New York: Harper & Row.

Heidegger, M. 1977. *The question concerning technology*, tr. W. Lovitt. New York: Harper & Row.

Heidegger, M. 1979. *Nietzsche*, vol. I: *The will to power*, tr. D. F. Krell. New York: Harper & Row.

Heidegger, M. 1993. *Selected writings*, D. F. Krell (ed.), 2nd enlarged edn. London: Routledge.

Honderich, T. 1987. *A theory of determinism*, vol. I: *Mind and brain*; vol. II: *Consequences of determinism*. Oxford: Oxford University Press.

Husserl, E. 1978. *The crisis of European sciences and transcendental phenomenology*, tr. D. Carr. Evanston, Illinois: Northwestern University Press.

Kant, I. 1933. *Critique of pure reason*, tr. N. Kemp Smith. London: Macmillan.

Kant, I. 1952. *Critique of judgement*, tr. J. C. Meredith. Oxford: Clarendon Press.

Kant, I. 1956. *Critique of practical reason*, tr. L. W. Beck. New York: Bobbs-Merrill.

Kierkegaard, S. 1941. *Fear and trembling*, tr. W. Lowrie. Princeton, New Jersey: Princeton University Press.

Laudan, L. 1979. *Progress and its problems*. Berkeley: University of California Press.

Laudan, L. 1984. *Science and values*. Berkeley: University of California Press.

Lecourt, D. 1975. *Marxism and epistemology: Bachelard, Canguilhem and Foucault*. London: New Left Books.

Levinas, E. 1969. *Totality and infinity*, tr. A. Lingis. Pittsburgh: Duquesne University Press.

Levinas, E. 1981. *Otherwise than being, or beyond essence*, tr. A. Lingis. The Hague: Martinus Nijhoff.

Lyotard, J-F. 1983. *The postmodern condition: a report on knowledge*, tr. G. Bennington and B. Massumi. Manchester: Manchester University Press.

Lyotard, J-F. 1987. *The differend: phrases in dispute*, tr. G. van den Abbeele. Manchester: Manchester University Press.

Lyotard, J-F. & J-L. Thébaud 1985. *Just gaming*. Manchester: Manchester University Press.

Maxwell, N. 1984. *From knowledge to wisdom*. Oxford: Basil Blackwell.

McNay, L. 1992. *Foucault and feminism*. Cambridge: Polity.

Mowitt, J. 1993. *Text: on the genealogy of an antidisciplinary object*. Durham, North Carolina: Duke University Press.

Muntz, P. 1985. *Our knowledge of the growth of knowledge*. London: Routledge & Kegan Paul.

Nagel, T. 1986. *The view from nowhere*. Oxford: Oxford University Press.

Norris, C. 1990. *What's wrong with postmodernism?* Hemel Hempstead, England: Harvester Wheatsheaf.

Norris, C. 1991. *Spinoza and the origins of modern critical theory*. Oxford: Basil Blackwell.

Norris, C. 1993. *The truth about postmodernism*. Oxford: Basil Blackwell.

Norris, C. 1994. *Truth and the ethics of criticism*. Manchester: Manchester University Press.

Nussbaum, M. C. 1990. *Love's knowledge: essays on philosophy and literature*. Oxford: Oxford University Press.

O'Neill, O. 1989. *Constructions of reason: explorations of Kant's practical philosophy*. Cambridge: Cambridge University Press.

Ott, H. 1993. *Heidegger: a political life*, tr. A. Blunden. London: HarperCollins.

Parfit, D. 1984. *Reasons and persons*. Oxford: Oxford University Press.

Passmore, J. 1979. *Science and its critics*. London: Duckworth.

Phillips, D. L. 1977. *Wittgenstein and scientific knowledge: a sociological perspective*. London: Macmillan.

Putnam, H. 1983. *Realism and reason*. Cambridge: Cambridge University Press.

Reichenbach, H. 1938. *Experience and prediction*. Chicago: University of Chicago Press.

Rescher, N. 1979. *Scientific progress*. Oxford: Basil Blackwell.

Rockmore, T. 1992. *On Heidegger's Nazism and philosophy*. Hemel Hempstead, England: Harvester Wheatsheaf.

Rorty, R. 1980. *Philosophy and the mirror of nature*. Oxford: Basil Blackwell.

Rorty, R. 1982. *Consequences of pragmatism*. Hemel Hempstead, England: Harvester Wheatsheaf.

Rorty, R. 1991. On ethnocentrism: a reply to Clifford Geertz. In *Objectivity, relativism, and truth*, 203–10. Cambridge: Cambridge University Press.

Saussure, F. de 1974. *Course in general linguistics*, tr. W. Baskin. London: Fontana.

Schirmacher, W. 1989. *Technik und Gelassenheit*. Freiburg: Karl Alber.

Smith, P. J. 1981. *Realism and the progress of science*. Cambridge: Cambridge University Press.

Sorrell, T. 1994. *Scientism: philosophy and the infatuation with science*. London: Routledge.

Tallis, R. 1988. *Not Saussure*. London: Macmillan.

Tiles, M. 1984. *Bachelard: science and objectivity*. Cambridge: Cambridge University Press.

Trigg, R. 1980. *Reality at risk: a defence of realism in philosophy and the sciences.* Hemel Hempstead, England: Harvester Wheatsheaf.

Winch, P. 1958. *The idea of a social science and its relation to philosophy.* London: Routledge & Kegan Paul.

Wittgenstein, L. 1953. *Philosophical investigations,* tr. G. E. M. Anscombe. Oxford: Basil Blackwell.

Wolin, R. (ed.) 1993. *The Heidegger controversy: a critical reader.* Cambridge, Mass.: MIT Press.

Woolgar, S. (ed.) 1988. *Knowledge and reflexivity: new frontiers in the sociology of knowledge.* London: Sage.

Zimmerman, M. E. 1991. *Heidegger's confrontation with modernity: technology, politics, art.* Bloomington, Indiana: Indiana University Press.

Zimmerman, M.E. 1993. Rethinking the Heidegger–deep ecology relationship. *Environmental Ethics* **5**, 195–224.

CHAPTER 2

Realism and its discontents: on the crisis of cultural representation in ethnographic texts

Paul Atkinson and Amanda Coffey

Introduction

The first time the observer's glass was filled he emptied it. Then he noticed that the others after taking a swig from theirs, handed it on. Perhaps on the same analogy, when one man's nice-looking wife came in half way through, another man, friend of the first, gave her a good kiss. It was all free and easy and went with a terrific swing, but order was kept and there were certain rules, like keeping silence during the solos. Mostly the women asked the men to dance. Everyone danced, old, middle-aged and young.

The striking feature of the dancing was the rolling tempo, less nerve-taut than American swing and hot rhythm, somewhat less martial than the tune Noel Gay wrote for the *Lambeth walk* . . . This tempo the pianists and dancers managed to introduce into waltzes and fox-trots, but it was most obvious when they danced their "own" dances, with improvised steps. The dancers faced each other, by two and two, or by three and three, with linked arms. They did jigging steps with their feet, plus some high kicking, then the two lines crossed over, turned and reformed. As they crossed, they walked in the half-lilting, half-swaggering way that Lupino Lane used in his *Lambeth walk*. For the men it is a swagger, arms out from the sides, like a boxer playing for position; for the women it is more of a lilt, with hips swaying. The two get mixed, though, when the men dress as women and behave like them – which is part of the tradition. Also men dance with men and women with women quite freely (Harrison & Madge 1939/1986: 146–7).

With a co-researcher we are at the stand and I stare, boldly but with propriety: never meeting another's eye for more than a passing split second, not fixing my gaze anywhere and certainly not anywhere in particular. There I am, not alone, looking but not obviously staring; also eating and drinking as I do so; it is lunchtime; other women together in booths, one clutch of boys similarly; at the back of the pub various people sat at separate tables but conducting, with silences, a joint conversation. In come two men, unshaven, dischevelled [*sic*], suspect wet stains down trouser fronts, a smell noticeable even from some yards distant. One stands immediately in front of me, stares fixedly at me and says something routinely obscene whilst jiggling his hand in a suspiciously commodious trouser pocket. "Piss off" I say (appropriately, I think) and remove us to the back of the pub. We sit at a table for two. My colleague eating and quite unaware of the spectacle, misses the return of the wino who stands before us, rolled up newspaper end-up over his crotch and with one encircling hand masturbating it with accompanying groans punctuated by more obscene remarks. Civil inattention rules among my fellow-diners.

I dither: what to do? I contemplate my dinner, the other diners, my eating unawares colleague, and ponder previous experiences when bar staff had found such things quite in order. I march past the symbolically masturbating wino to the bar, tell a barwoman who leaves me while she tells the manager. I tell the tale to him in my smoothest non-Rochdalean voice, ask him if he'd be so good as to do something about "it", leaving "it" an empty category. The man is ejected along with his equally dampish colleague. My colleague is interested, but as she says, what can you expect when the Sally Army hostel is right by the back door to the bar. We finish our meal, me in a fume about the wino in particular, the sexual political strangeness of men in general. Thirty seconds later the wino leers from out of a doorway and says his routine obscenity. A neap tide of fury drowns me, but as usual I dam it up. (Poland & Stanley 1988: 83–4)

These two observations of everyday life are separated by 50 years. The actual settings have probably changed much less in that period than the ways in which they are inscribed in the respective texts. The first is derived from the Mass Observation project; the second is by a feminist sociologist. Something has clearly changed in the way that social observers describe social settings and social actors, and how they write about their own work as observers. It is not simply a difference between the apparent enjoyment of the first observer, and the disgust and fury of the second (although that has something to do with it). Rather, the differences reflect quite important shifts in the written discourse of social scientists. The first displays a remarkable degree of self-assurance, even insouciance. The observer/author displays remarkably little doubt or hesitancy. The description reflects an author who experiences and writes about the social scene from a position that seems to be unproblematic and taken-for-granted. Although the narrator is present in the text, swigging from his glass, there is a clear separation between the observer and the observed. The latter are regarded with an assured and slightly quizzical gaze. The actors are objects of a detached curiosity. The observer seems to take for granted an implicit superiority. There is an air of "knowing" about the written text. It is unproblematic and uncritical. The descriptions and comparisons seem naïve in their self-confidence. The second extract has a very different air. The observer–narrator is directly engaged in the activities she describes, and writes herself "into" the text itself. The self of the ethnographer is treated as being of equal interest to the actions of the observed. In both extracts gender-relevant action is described. What is noticeable, however, is how very differently "gendered" the two accounts are. The first describes social actors in terms of men and women *per se*. It also describes cross-dressing and gendered action in unreflective, matter-of-fact ways. The second, by contrast, is gendered not only in terms of content but also in terms of the construction of the text itself. The observer as well as the observed have gendered selves that form part of the research experience and the textual output (for a similar comparison, see Hey 1986).

This difference in how ethnographic texts can represent social phenomena – and some of the changes that have intervened between the two texts – form the point of departure for this chapter. How can two accounts of broadly similar kinds of social scene, derived from observational research, be so very different? Perhaps more pointedly, why are the texts constructed in such different ways, and what are the consequences for the representation of social "reality"? Taking our examples as a point of departure, then, we examine some contemporary debates about the ethnographic representation of culture; we thus reflect on the culture of ethnography.

Debates about the representation of cultural phenomena have nowhere been more vigorous – and occasionally acrimonious – than in the field of ethnographic writing. Originating in North American cultural anthropology and thence spreading more widely, debates over the production of ethnographic texts have concentrated on the *textual construction of reality* (Atkinson 1990). It is significant that such debates have emerged most starkly within the discipline of anthropology. Historically, anthropology, especially in the United Kingdom, has been marked by a certain degree of methodological and epistemological self-confidence. Whatever the theoretical disputes that characterized anthropology for many years, they were conducted against a stable background of paradigmatic assumptions. In other words, there was a bedrock of implicit certainty and faith in the fundamental subject matter of anthropology itself. Central to those taken-for-granted foundations was the conduct and writing of ethnography. Similarly, the performance of the fieldwork itself was treated as equally unproblematic. This does not mean that anthropologists did not encounter or report practical problems of operating "in the field". Rather, the fundamental conceptualization of anthropological endeavour itself remained largely unchallenged. The period between the early fieldwork of culture-heroes such as Malinowski (e.g. 1922) or Radcliffe-Brown (e.g. 1922) and the recent past was marked by a very stable academic culture (Stocking 1983, Clifford 1986). The conduct of ethnographic fieldwork remained central to the academic work and identity of the social anthropologist. The period spent in the field was virtually a *sine qua non* of membership in a tightly bounded discipline. The force of anthropological fieldwork as a *rite de passage* must be recognized. Equally it should be recognized that the anthropological initiate's passage depends not solely on his or her experience of the field. Of course it is imperative that the novice should go there and be there: first-hand experience of the field is a necessary condition for incorporation into the anthropological community. The anthropologist's membership of the discipline also depends on turning the fieldwork into textual representations. In itself fieldwork is not enough. One must also produce the ethnography (that is, the ethnographic monograph). Traditionally, the professional and academic status passage has been completed and confirmed by the construction of a major text. The anthropological monograph, therefore, is the culmination of the ethnography and the legitimating mark of the anthropologist. The relationships between fieldwork, text production and the discipline of anthropology, have then developed over time. The anthropologist was identified with his or her people, who in turn were identified with and in the ethnography. The ethnographic monograph thus became the embodiment of the discipline itself and the identity of its practitioners. Within the classical period of British and American anthropology the ethnographic monograph enshrined a series of standardized representations of societies and (by implication) of their authors (Boon 1982). There are, of course, other modes of ethnographic representation, including film. They are equally conventional and artful as any written text (cf. Crawford & Turton 1992, Loizos 1993).

Given the importance of the ethnography as textual product it is little wonder that radical assaults on its status should strike at the roots of the discipline. Thus in recent years, anthropology – once so stable – has experienced a *crisis of representation*. The textual foundations have been shaken and, along with them, the intellectual faith that has informed their production and reception. The status of ethnographic texts has also come under scrutiny from within sociology (Atkinson 1990, 1992, Hammersley 1992). In many ways this has proved a less critical issue for this discipline than for anthropology, not least because ethnographic methods and monographs are much less central to sociology as a whole. Important though qualitative research is in many fields of empirical sociology, it does not underpin the entire academic enterprise as it

does for anthropology. The critiques of ethnography in sociology have sometimes followed directions similar to those in anthropology.

The early years of ethnographic sociology at the University of Chicago, for
instance, were founded upon modes of realist writing. There were – as we discuss later – clear affinities between the work of the Chicago sociologists and
the literary styles of novelists working in Chicago at the same period (in the
1920s). There were links between the literary and academic circles, and they
shared cultural perspectives. Both groups were intellectuals grappling with the
rapidly changing material and social fabric of the metropolis around them. For
many years, those realist styles of textual representation were taken for granted
among sociologists. In the recent past, however, sociologists have, like anthropologists, turned a more critical gaze towards their own representations of culture, and their cultures of representation.

To some extent, however, the sociological critique has different origins from
that of the anthropologists. Sociologists have followed arguments more overtly
derived from within sociology itself. The influence of symbolic interactionism
on the development of ethnography – most notable in urban and organizational settings – has, for instance, led directly to an evaluation of the *language*
of ethnographic work (Richardson 1990a, 1994, Hastrup 1992). Likewise,
the development of an extensive research methods literature (notable for its
absence in anthropology until very recently) led sociologists to address the craft
skills involved in writing ethnographic texts. More recently still, sociologists
have turned their attention to critical issues in reading and evaluating ethnographic texts and their arguments (Hammersley 1991, 1993, Atkinson 1992).

Ethnography, then, across the disciplines of sociology and anthropology has
been the subject of recent problematizing and questioning. In particular the
texts that are written and read as an outcome of ethnographic fieldwork are no
longer (if they ever were) left to stand alone as unproblematic. Rather the
textual practices of ethnographers are in themselves open to scrutiny. In this
chapter we aim to explore some of the trends, developments and intellectual
challenges that have contributed to this so-called crisis in the production (and
reception) of ethnographic texts. We consider what the consequences are both
for the nature of ethnographic texts and for the status of the ethnographic
method. Several of the positions and critiques we discuss have been associated
with the general thrust of postmodernism. Postmodernism has certainly contributed to reappraisals of cultural representation, in the human sciences and
beyond. To that extent, the relevance of postmodernism must be acknowledged. On the other hand, we shall also suggest that recent developments in
the culture of ethnography are not dependent on postmodernism *per se*. Many
current tendencies can be understood as *developments* of anthropological and
sociological perspectives, rather than radical departures from them.

The "rediscovery of rhetoric" and the questioning of privilege

The radical reassessment of the very foundations of anthropological and socio-logical knowing has been paralleled by wider developments in the human disciplines. In many quarters a wide, if diffuse, intellectual movement may be identified under the rubric of the "rhetoric of inquiry". This tendency draws on various philosophical and critical sources. It has addressed the structure and content of, amongst others, history, economics, psychology and sociology. It has also been directed towards the physical and biological sciences (Gilbert 1977, Law & Williams 1982). In part, this movement reflects the "rediscovery of rhetoric". Rhetoric is no longer consigned to the margins of legitimate scholarship; it has more recently been recognized as central to scholarly work and production. The classical theory and practice of rhetoric was concerned with argumentation and persuasion. The separation of rhetoric and science in Enlightenment thought implied a radical distinction between two contrasted sets of commitments. On the one side stand together science, reason, logic, method and evidence. On the other side are ranged rhetoric, persuasion, opinion and ornamentation. The aspirations of modern scholarship were firmly rooted in such dualities. The separation of rhetoric from logic in the creation of modern disciplinary knowledge parallels a number of other, equally fundamental, separations and dichotomies. It established the possi-bility of an observer armed with a neutral language of observation (since untouched with rhetoric) and thus allowed for the elementary distinction between that observer and the observed. The rediscovery of rhetoric creates the possibility of removing such distinctions: of removing the distance between the subjects and objects of inquiry, and questioning the taken-for-granted canons of science and reason. Arguments that scientific accounts and texts have rhetorical qualities and are *produced* challenge long-held distinctions between scientific fact and textual production: between the reality of the natural–scientific world and narrative accounts of the social world. (For other accounts of representation of the natural and social, see Bazerman 1988, Lynch & Woolgar 1990, Myers 1990, Lutz & Collins 1993.)

Such a weakening of cultural boundaries is also advocated from a more overtly ideological perspective. In particular, the distinction between the observer and the observed has been scrutinized and questioned by critics of the ethnographic tradition. They draw on criticisms of ethnography's com-plicity with the intellectual and material projects of a Western imperialism. Perhaps the best known of such critiques remains that of Edward Said (1978) and his sustained commentary on the *orientalism* of Western observation. Dealing specifically with the Near and Middle East, Said traces the historical processes whereby that Orient (or Levant) was appropriated by the gaze of

46

European observers. Napoleon's encyclopaedic survey of Egypt is at once a type-case and a microcosm for such a historical process. In its course, the oriental became one version of the other: that is, the subjugated and muted object of a dominating discourse. An orientalizing perspective thus established a fundamental difference between a Western observer and an Eastern other. The oriental could thus be invested with a range of essential qualities that could be contrasted with those of the inherently superior West. In enumerating and classifying the exotic characteristics of the oriental, then, the privileged observer establishes a position of authority, which is inscribed in the text of exploration, description and classification (Marcus 1992). A virtually identical set of issues can be described for the encounters of the Old World with the New in the conquest and appropriation of the Americas. From the earliest accounts of the Spanish conquests through to the accounts of nineteenth-century explorers and ethnologists, the continent has been populated by others and appropriated through the accompanying representations. The texts of exploration and exploitation repeatedly inscribe the metropolitan perspective (Todorov 1984, Pratt 1992).

The rediscovery of rhetoric at the textual level *and* the parallel questioning of the orientation of Western observation are trends that have questioned the privileged position of the observer (and in turn the position of ethnographer as writer). In turn the textual products of observation and work across a spectrum of disciplines have been topics of increasing scrutiny.

Feminism and ethnography

The privileged position of the observer–author may also be – and has been – identified as a gendered one. The argument is not about the over- or under-representation of men and women as ethnographic authors: many of the classic ethnographies have in fact been written by women. Rather, it is about the relationships between ethnography, gender and feminism at more fundamental levels. The issues include feminist perspectives on research and interpretation.

By and large, the original authors of the critiques of anthropological ethnography paid rather little attention to feminist theory *per se*. Their interests were congruent, however, and drew on some common roots. Feminists have grappled with qualitative methods and the ethnographic experience in general (Olesen 1994), and with textual forms of cultural representation in particular. Clough (1992), for instance, articulates a feminist view, drawing on psychoanalytic perspectives. She argues that from a feminist standpoint one can see the standard realist accounts of ethnography as incorporating unconscious fantasies and desires concerning race, gender or class. Realism, she argues, suppresses those unconscious processes under the guise of factual discourse. Wolf (1992) also addresses the feminist perspective on ethnography and representation. She suggests that reflexive, self-critical attitudes are particularly characteristic of feminist thought. Feminism in general encourages an examination of power and powerlessness, the mutual obligations of researcher and researched. She implies that feminist scholars were exploring these issues independently of their becoming fashionable topics among male anthropologists. As Wolf also suggests, the heightened sensibilities of feminist scholars have led directly towards problems of representation. In a similar vein Mascia-Lees et al. (1989) draw attention to a concern among feminist anthropologists for modes of understanding (including writing) that do not reduce women to the position of voiceless *objects*, but treat them as subjects in their own right, entitled to their own voices. This echoes the very foundations of the feminist research process – the concern with voice and authority, accounts and experience (Smith 1989, Olesen 1994). This feminist strain of ethnographic critique is reminiscent of the distinction, first elaborated by Shirley and Edwin Ardener (e.g. Ardener 1975), between dominant and muted groups. This view proposes that there are fractions of the population whose culture, or world view, is dominant (e.g. men, upper classes, dominant ethnic groups). There are others, the dominated (e.g. women, lower classes, suppressed minorities) who are *muted* in that they are deprived of their own culturally legitimated means of expression. Muted groups are seen – and must often see themselves – through the categories of the dominant. They are visible and audible only through the eyes or voices of the dominating groups. As a consequence, they cease to be the subjects of their own experiences and actions; they are reduced to being the objects of other subjects. They are subjugated in that sense. It is argued, therefore, by feminists and other critics of classic ethnographic discourse that the "others" of such inquiry and such description are rendered mute. Indeed, when the objects of ethnography are already dominated (as are women, for instance), the ethnographic gaze may be in danger of performing a kind of double subjugation (Trinh 1989).

The argument of "domination" as part of the ethnographic endeavour is only one possible reading of such work, however. In many contexts – most strongly, perhaps, among sociologists working in their own society – there has been a quite overt intention to use ethnography to recuperate the experiences of otherwise invisible and un-voiced groups. Sociological ethnography frequently favours the underdog, giving voice to underprivileged and powerless groups (Nader 1974, Bell 1978, Richardson 1990b). From within the so-called second Chicago School of urban ethnographers, Howard Becker (1967) advocated the methodological advantages of a form of partisanship. When he asked "Whose side are we on?", he pointed out that it is incumbent of the ethnographer *not* to take on trust the world views of the powerful or the dominant. It is imperative to take seriously and to give voice to the underdogs. This reversal of the normal hierarchy of credibility and legitimacy is not simply a vulgar exercise of intellectual rebelliousness on the part of the social scientists. One does so not merely as a gesture of defiance. On the contrary, it is a necessary prerequisite to an adequate understanding and representation of otherwise muted categories and cultures. Indeed, it is noteworthy that the history of ethnography in Western societies has been consistently characterized by studies of the marginal, the stigmatized, the dispossessed. In Britain and the United States equally, the roots of urban ethnography are to be found in studies of the urban poor, the slums of the great cities, ethnic minorities and their distinctive urban areas.

This rather different reading of ethnographic work, however, does not altogether let the production of ethnographic texts off the hook. It may be argued that such ethnographies of Western urban settings partake equally of the "orientalizing tendencies" identified among anthropologists studying exotic cultures. And there is some truth in that. There may have been in some quarters a condescending view of the more exotic characteristics of slums and their denizens. The "nuts and sluts" tradition evident in studies of deviance is occasionally coloured by an orientalizing attitude towards the colourful and the bizarre. There is, perhaps, the desire *épater les bourgeois* by confronting the culturally mainstream reader with stark contrasts of mores and material circumstances. Nevertheless, those tendencies must be set against much more enduring and pervasive commitments on the part of sociological ethnographers. For in various ways, ethnographers have been convinced of the necessity to reverse the normally taken-for-granted hierarchies of credibility. Ethnographers seek to give the marginalized or the deviant a social presence. They are represented as social actors endowed with the capacity for rational social action. Their culture is treated seriously and with respect: the goal of cultural relativism is a methodological imperative for ethnographic researchers. In other words then, it is misleading to equate all (or indeed, any) ethnography with the worst excesses of an orientalizing gaze. There is a world of difference, in terms of intentions and outcomes, between the ethnographic enterprise on the one hand and the exploitative scrutiny of dominating and appropriating discourses on the other. The problem of representation in ethnographic texts is not, moreover, primarily moral in origin. It is not necessary to adopt a radically critical or polemical perspective in order to recognize that ethnographic writing is not straightforward. The major issue is how to use the variety of available textual formats and devices to reconstruct social worlds, *and* to explore how those texts are then received by both the cultural disciplines and the social worlds we seek to capture.

Language and genre in ethnographic writing

The use of textual conventions to produce written texts can be identified as a further point of discontent within the ethnographical endeavour. We must recognize – as in other contexts of social-scientific discourse – that there is no neutral medium of representation available for the ethnographer. We use the resources of natural language available to all. We use the conventions of written language too in making and reading academic texts – such as ethnographic monographs or journal papers. The formats that academics use are *conventional*. In other words, there is no "natural" way of describing and writing about social scenes, actors and actions. Even though we are so used to some ways of writing that we treat them uncritically, as natural, that should not blind us to the fact that – far from being natural in any sense – they are conventional resources. The authors of academic texts draw on a repertoire of conventional devices in order to construct their authoritative texts. Equally, the readers of those self-same texts draw on the same stock of literary conventions in order to make sense of them. We do not need to assert that the meaning of a text is totally determined by the use or interpretation of particular devices or conventions in order to recognize that there are socially shared conventions of reading and writing that exert a major influence on the production and reception of academic texts. We have become accustomed to particular kinds of texts that have been adopted to embody the results of ethnographic work. Or, to put it in more formally literary terms, there have developed particular *genres* of ethnographic writing (Atkinson 1992). These have close affinities with other kinds of non-fiction writing. There are also links with genres of fictional writing as well. In general, those genres reflect our conventional assumptions about realism and authenticity in written accounts.

The affinity between fictional writing and ethnographic writing has been identified by Krieger (1984) who likens the production of an ethnographic text to the creation of a novel. In such cases the author is responsible for creating and peopling a social world and has the task of telling a plausible (and interesting, believable) story. Storytelling has been explored and used as a way of producing accounts, narratives and other texts of ethnography (Denzin 1994); indeed Wolcott (1994) suggests that organizing and presenting qualitative studies (including ethnography) as a mystery novel enables a popular genre to be brought to bear. The "I just couldn't put it down" praise of an ethnographic text is praise indeed and something most of us writing ethnography would seek to achieve.

The historical and stylistic continuities between ethnography and fiction can be traced to the early years of ethnographic sociology at the University of Chicago. It is well known that some of the earliest studies in urban sociology that we would today characterize as ethnographic were undertaken at the

University of Chicago in the first decades of this century. The urban sociologists and the novelists of Chicago focused on common subject matter, and on similar stylistic approaches. Some of those commonalities have been explored by Cappetti (1993). Sociologists and novelists occupied not just the same city, but a shared intellectual and social milieu. By and large both groups were "new" intellectuals, conscious of their distance from the old established academic and cultural centres of the East Coast. Sociologists and novelists alike found inspiration in European authors such as Balzac or Zola. They were members of the same social circles. The affinities between urban sociology and realist fiction were multiple and reciprocal. Cappetti documents in some detail how novelists and sociologists wrote their representations of the city, and the common ground between them, focusing on three novelists: James Farrell, Nelson Algren and Richard Wright. Farrell is a particularly apt choice, insofar as he studied sociology at Chicago, and so is a microcosm of the mutual influences of fiction and sociology. James Farrell's subject matter – as in his famous *Studs Lonigan* trilogy – directly echoed that of the Chicago sociologists. The work of Thrasher on the gang paralleled Farrell's account of the young Lonigan and his contemporaries (although, as Cappetti indicates, the social backgrounds of Studs Lonigan and Thrasher's gang-members were far from identical). As Cappetti (1993: 143) herself notes:

> Following Robert Park's invitation, Farrell quite literally subjected a white middle-class neighbourhood to the estranged gaze of ethnography, a discipline born among foreign cultures and subsequently brought home to observe the urban poor. Studs' life comes to stand for a society and a time – the United States during the 1920s – becoming a narrative metaphor for the destruction of youth and the future that came to fruition during the Depression. Farrell used urban sociology and ethnography in the spirit of the radical social questioning that . . . inspired such different movements as surrealism, the Chicago school of urban sociology, the WPA arts projects of the 1930s, and the Frankfurt School.

Despite the potential influence of other literary styles, the "realist" approach has been dominant in the development of ethnographic writing. Van Maanen (1988) indeed has identified literary realism as the dominant mode of representation. As Van Maanen characterizes it, the realist mode implies an impersonal, all-but-invisible narrator. It is presented from the point of view of one impartial author whose point of view is the dominant, even the sole, one. It is a genre of authoritative reportage. As a style, as a collection of literary devices, such realist writing is a massively familiar one for the construction of factual, authoritative accounts. There is, therefore, the danger of taking it for granted, and hence of treating it as a natural way of representing the social. Despite this tendency towards a realist approach, it remains by no means clear that literary realism is the only – or even the best – way to produce accounts of varied social worlds. Indeed, as Atkinson (1983) noted, there is something of a paradox in the use of what one might call a "straightforward" realism for ethnographic purposes. There is a tension between the conventions of realism and the assumption of most ethnographic work. For most ethnographers – whether sociology or anthropology be their primary discipline – recognize the complexity of social life and its collective representations. Equally, they recognize the fundamentally constitutive nature of language. That is, language use creates and constructs social reality. Interpretative anthropologists, for instance, are committed to the ideals of *thick description*, while symbolic interactionists equally endorse an interpretative sociology that places language at the heart of an essentially constructivist view of reality and representation. And yet conventional realism is founded on a very different treatment of language. Such realism has historically encouraged little or no explicit concern for the language of representation itself. Realism treats language as a taken-for-granted resource. The realism of conventional writing, Atkinson argued, may therefore result in "thin" description. Such arguments – that narratives and descriptions from a single, implicit point of view may not do justice to the complexity of cultural forms – have given rise to various alternative approaches.

Experiments and alternatives

Partly for reasons we have discussed already, there have been various attempts at more "experimental" forms of writing. Rather than the tidy certainties of realist writing, various commentators have called for texts that are more "open", more "messy" or more fragmented. In transgressing the normal conventions of realist texts, such alternative forms of ethnographic writing would simultaneously do two things. First, they would challenge and highlight the very conventionality of much ethnographic writing itself. Secondly, they would allow for a creative exploration of more complex modes of representation. Further, therefore, while the conventionality of all modes of representation is recognized, there is more than a hint in such arguments that complex texts may be more faithful to the complexities and contours of social life.

Experimental writings, or as Richardson (1994) prefers, "experimental representations", have come largely in the wake of feminist explorations of writing practices (see above) and postmodernist perspectives on language, method and genre. The postmodern concern with deconstruction and with doubt about conventional discourses and genres has added the move towards more imaginative and experimental types of writing practice in all of the authorial disciplines (see Clifford & Marcus 1986, Geertz 1988, Morris 1988, Denzin 1991, Lather 1991). Equally, experimental textual forms can be seen as an extension of symbolic interactionism, the theoretical and methodological foundation of sociological ethnography. Experimental writing can here be viewed as a continuation of the ethnographer as a reflexive practitioner. The new genres and textual forms that have come with experimentation are varied and involve a blurring of textual conventions and boundaries. A common thread however is *the violation of prescribed conventions*, and the transgression of the boundaries of (social science) writing genres (Richardson 1994).

One such variety of "experimental" writing has involved a so-called "dialogic" approach. This stands in contrast to the "monologic" mode associated with conventionally realist accounts. In the latter, it is argued, there is but the one dominant perspective. The text is written from the single point of view. The authorial voice of the narrator-ethnographer (for all its impersonal self-effacement) implicitly claims a singular authority. The text embodies a single "voice". The dialogic text, on the other hand, is intended to include a multiplicity of voices and perspectives (Dwyer 1977, 1979). Dialogic perspectives derive, in part at least, from various readings of the work of Bakhtin (see Holquist 1990, Allan 1994). It follows that the experimental text may have a more fragmented surface. The conventional ethnography has relied upon varieties of narrative presentation. Again, those narratives – small narratives of everyday life, or grander narratives of institutions – have normally been constructed from a single authorial perspective. More experimental forms of ethnography may in effect disrupt such narrative presentations. The dramatic unities of time and space may be disrupted, while persons and events are represented (or reconstructed) through diverse and fragmentary texts.

The normal conventions of realist representation may then be replaced or supplemented by more imaginative and mixed literary styles or genres. In turn these different styles may give a less authoritative and "realer" picture of the social worlds that are being described. Some ethnographic authors have therefore tried, self-consciously, to use alternative forms of writing. They have included the use of dramatic conventions, with social action reconstructed in the form of a play or script (e.g. Ellis & Bochner 1992). The use of overtly "fictional" styles of writing may be essayed, such as a so-called "stream of consciousness" fictional style. Even more overtly "different" is the use of poetry. At least one author has reconstructed part of her sociological work in the form of a poem – taking the actual words of an informant and arranging them into the form of verse: Richardson (1992) told Louisa May's story of her life through poetic verse which reflects both Richardson's "poetic self" and Louisa May's life story (cf. Denzin 1994). Such experimental work attains an authenticity of a different order from the realism of conventional ethnography: it captures the *ethnopoetics* of an informant's life-history and accentuates their qualities. (By ethnopoetics we mean the everyday forms of rhetoric and spoken perform-ance of social actors.) Equally extreme, perhaps, is the use of what is being called "ethnographic fiction". That is, the contrived fictionalizing of social action and social actors – sometimes in order to convey what are regarded as authentic accounts of sensitive settings and issues. In the construction of eth-nographic fiction, the wheel of interactions between literary and scholarly work comes full circle.

The more general affinities between experiential ethnographic writing and the postmodernist rubric are clear here. Postmodernism, in recognizing and celebrating the diversity of styles and representations, encourages a variety of genres and their promiscuous mixing in the form of pastiche. It questions the monovocal expression of truth or authenticity in favour of a polyvocal celebra-tion of diversity. It transgresses the smooth surface of narrative logic, and endorses a multi-faceted fragmentation. There is, therefore, much in the postmodernist movement to commend various radical re-evaluations of ethnographic writing. On the other hand, it is not necessary to appeal to post-modernism *per se*. It is arguable that the possibilities for textual experimen-tation are contained within the modernist movement in literature. Modern literature provides us with a multiplicity of textual formats and devices for the construction of written representations. Modernist fiction found many ways, for instance, of representing the mingling of external events and inner dia-logue; of reconstructing the minutiae of extraordinarily detailed description; of linking factual reportage with the fantastic. By adopting some of these "new" conventions and by experimenting in similar ways, ethnographic texts can also be viewed as undergoing a modernist movement.

Conclusion

Contemporary debates and developments concerning ethnographic writing in anthropology and sociology have considerable relevance beyond those specific domains of social science. The issues – as we have tried to illustrate – reflect yet broader currents in contemporary thought: feminism and the rhetorical turn among them. At the same time, these developments contribute to the treatment of representation as problematic. They thus are drawn into that loose assemblage of ideas known as postmodernism. We conclude, however, by noting that it is not necessary to endorse the most extreme postmodernist pos-ture as a consequence.

The critiques of ethnographic representation may lead some commentators towards a radically "textual" view of the matter. It may be concluded, to put it at its simplest, that there is nothing beyond the ethnographic text, and that the ethnography has no referential value in the attempt to construct accounts of particular social worlds. Such a view proposes a fundamental assault on the authority of the anthropologist or sociologist as author, and on the claims of the ethnographic text for authoritative, factual status.

In our view such radical textualism is not called for, and is not a necessary consequence of contemporary reflection. It is right to question a vulgar realism that pays no heed to the nature of its own language and its own textual conventions. It is right to acknowledge that there is nothing natural about the textual conventions of realism as a style of composition. It is equally right to recognize that ethnographies are, in that sense, *composed*. There can be no quarrel with attempts to identify the textual formats and the literary or rhetorical devices that are normally deployed by ethnographers. Nonetheless, we believe that such a recognition constitutes an extension of the ethnographic imagination rather than a radical threat to it.

Ethnographers have for many years recognized that their research is possible by virtue of our basic, socially shared competencies. In order to participate in and understand the social world around us, we use the research methods of everyday life. We draw on the resources of everyday language and of interaction ritual in order to become social inquirers. We routinely recognize the essential reflexivity of such exercises: that is, the degree to which the observer is implicated in the observed. Indeed, we start to dissolve that dualism. In the same fashion, we are free to acknowledge our reliance on the conventional resources of written language in making (and reading) our ethnographies. We understand the reflexivity of our textual practices just as thoroughly as we do the reflexivity of our data collection and analysis. A rejection of vulgar positivism need not lead to the abandonment of every semblance of method, nor of all claims to authoritative discourse. Equally, a rejection of vulgar realist assumptions about writing do not automatically lead to the nihilism of a purely "textualist" approach. We need rather to examine and to use the conventions of written representation – in all their variety – in order to construct scholarly works that do justice to the complexities of social life and to the subtleties of ethnographic inquiry.

References

Allan, S. 1994. "When discourse is torn from reality": Bakhtin and the principle of chronotopicity. *Time and Society* **3**, 193–218.

Ardener, S. (ed.) 1975. *Perceiving women.* London: Malaby.

Atkinson, P. 1990. *The ethnographic imagination: textual constructions of reality.* London: Routledge.

Atkinson, P. 1992. *Understanding ethnographic texts.* Los Angeles: Sage.

Atkinson, P. A. 1983. Writing ethnography. In *Kultur und Institution*, H. J. Helle (ed.),

103. Berlin: Duncker & Humblot.

Bazerman, C. 1988. *Shaping written knowledge: the genre and activity of the experimental article in science.* Madison: University of Wisconsin Press.

Becker, H. S. 1967. Whose side are we on? *Social Problems* **14**, 239–47.

Bell, C. 1978. Studying the locally powerful. In *Inside the whale*, C. Bell & S. Engel (eds), 14–40. Oxford: Pergamon.

Boon, J. A. 1982. *Other tribes, other scribes.* Cambridge: Cambridge University Press.

Cappetti, C. 1993. *Writing Chicago: modernism, ethnography, and the novel.* New York: Columbia University Press.

Clifford, J. 1986. Introduction: partial truths. In *Writing culture: the poetics and politics of ethnography*, J. Clifford & G. E. Marcus (eds), 1–26. Berkeley: University of California Press.

Clifford, J. & G. E. Marcus (eds) 1986. *Writing culture: the poetics and politics of ethnography.* Berkeley: University of California Press.

Clough P. 1992. *The end(s) of ethnography.* Los Angeles: Sage.

Crawford, P. I. & D. Turton (eds) 1992. *Film as ethnography.* Manchester: Manchester University Press.

Denzin, N. 1991. *Images of postmodern society.* Los Angeles: Sage.

Denzin, N. 1994. The art and politics of interpretation. In *Handbook of qualitative research*, N. K. Denzin & Y. S. Lincoln (eds), 500–15. Los Angeles: Sage.

Dwyer, K. 1977. On the dialogic of fieldwork. *Dialectical Anthropology* **2**, 143–51.

Dwyer, K. 1979. The dialogic of ethnology. *Dialectical Anthropology* **4**, 205–24.

Ellis, C. & A. P. Bochner 1992. Telling and performing personal stories: the constraints of choice in abortion. In *Investigating subjectivity: research on lived experience*, C. Ellis & M. G. Flaherty (eds), 79–101. Los Angeles: Sage.

Geertz, C. 1988. *Works and lives: the anthropologist as author.* New York: Basic Books.

Gilbert, G. N. 1977. Referencing as persuasion. *Social Studies of Science* **7**, 113–22.

Hammersley, M. 1991. *Reading ethnographic research: a critical guide.* Harlow, England: Longman.

Hammersley, M. 1992. *What's wrong with ethnography?* London: Routledge.

Hammersley, M. 1993. The rhetorical turn in ethnography. *Social Science Information* **32**, 23–37.

Harrison, T. & C. Madge 1986 (first published 1939). *Britain by mass observation.* London: Century Hutchinson.

Hastrup, K. 1992. Writing ethnography: state of the art. In *Anthropology and autobiography*, J. Okely & H. Callaway (eds), 116–33. London: Routledge.

Hey, V. 1986. *Patriarchy and pub culture.* London: Tavistock.

Holquist, M. 1990. *Dialogism: Bakhtin and his world.* London: Routledge.

Krieger, S. 1984. Fiction and social science. In *Studies in Symbolic Interaction*, vol. V, N. Denzin (ed.), 269–86. Greenwich, Connecticut: JAI Press.

Lather, P. 1991. *Getting smart: feminist research and pedagogy with/in the postmodern.* London: Routledge.

Law, J. & R. J. Williams 1982. Putting the facts together: a study of scientific persuasion. *Social Studies of Science* **12**, 535–58.

Loizos, P. 1993. *Innovation in ethnographic film: from innocence to self-consciousness.* Manchester: Manchester University Press.

Lutz, C. A. & J. L. Collins 1993. *Reading National Geographic.* Chicago: University of Chicago Press.

Lynch, M. & S. Woolgar (eds) 1990. *Representation in scientific practice*. Cambridge, Mass.: MIT Press.

Malinowski, B. 1922. *Argonauts of the Western Pacific*. London: Routledge & Kegan Paul.

Marcus, J. 1992. *A world of difference: Islam and gender hierarchy in Turkey*. London: Zed.

Mascia-Lees, F. E., P. Sharpe, C. B. Cohen 1989. The postmodernist turn in anthropology: cautions from a feminist perspective. *Signs* **15**, 7–33.

Morris, N. 1988. *The pirate's fiancee: feminism, reading and postmodernism*. New York: Verso.

Myers, G. 1990. *Writing biology: texts in the social construction of scientific knowledge*. Madison: University of Wisconsin Press.

Nader, L. 1974. Up the anthropologist: perspectives gained from studying up. In *Reinventing anthropology*, D. Hymes (ed.), 284–311. New York: Vintage Books.

Olesen, V. 1994. Feminisms and models of qualitative research. In *Handbook of qualitative research*, N. K. Denzin & Y. S. Lincoln (eds), 158–74. Los Angeles: Sage.

Poland, F. & L. Stanley 1988. *Feminist ethnography in Rochdale*. Manchester: University of Manchester Studies in Sexual Politics.

Pratt, M. L. 1992. *Imperial eyes: travel writing and transculturation*. London: Routledge.

Radcliffe-Brown, A. R. 1922. *The Anadaman Islanders*. Cambridge: Cambridge University Press.

Richardson, L. 1990a. Narrative and sociology. *Journal of Contemporary Ethnography* **19**, 116–35.

Richardson, L. 1990b. *Writing strategies: reaching diverse audiences*. Los Angeles: Sage.

Richardson, L. 1992. The consequences of poetic representation: writing the other, rewriting the self. In *Investigating subjectivity: research on lived experience*, C. Ellis & M. G. Flaherty (eds), 125–37. Los Angeles: Sage.

Richardson, L. 1994. Writing: a method of inquiry. In *Handbook of qualitative research*, N. K. Denzin & Y. S. Lincoln (eds), 516–29. Los Angeles: Sage.

Said, E. 1978. *Orientalism*. New York: Pantheon.

Smith, D. E. 1989. Sociological theory: methods of writing patriarchy. In *Feminism and sociological theory*, R. A. Wallace (ed.), 34–64. Los Angeles: Sage.

Stocking, G. W. 1983. *Observers observed: essays on ethnographic fieldwork*. Madison: University of Wisconsin Press.

Todorov, T. 1984. *The conquest of America: the question of the other*. New York: Harper & Row.

Trinh, Minh-ha T. 1989. *Woman, native*. Bloomington, Indiana: Indiana University Press.

Van Maanen, J. 1988. *Tales of the field: on writing ethnography*. Chicago: University of Chicago Press.

Wolcott, H. F. 1994. *Transforming qualitative data: description, analysis and interpretation*. Los Angeles: Sage.

Wolf, M. 1992. *A thrice told tale: feminism, postmodernism and ethnographic responsibility*. Palo Alto, California: Stanford University Press.

CHAPTER 3

Reflexivity in academic culture

Simon Hopper

Introduction

Although considerable scholarly attention has been paid to cultural practices within the natural sciences, there has been a comparative neglect of social science and the humanities (Becher 1989). This is beginning to change as the issue of "reflexivity" becomes a major, even fashionable, topic throughout these latter areas (for shorthand I shall refer to the social sciences and the humanities together as the human sciences), forming part of a wider concern with postmodernist questions of representation and objectivity. At present, however, the dominant approach to reflexivity in the human sciences has been to highlight and examine the rhetorical and/or textual construction of academic discourse through the use of "new literary forms" and self-questioning texts. This chapter argues that taken on its own this approach is inadequate to the goal of a reflexive academic culture, and I hope to show both why this is the case and also what other directions analyses of reflexivity can take in the future.

In the first part of the chapter, I outline what I mean by academic culture and why reflexivity is an important issue in the human sciences. In the second part, I critically examine the textual approach to reflexivity in a single field, the social studies of science, focusing in particular on the assumption that reflexivity is a property and possibility only at the level of the individual academic text. There I will argue that this assumption ignores the wider cultural and social processes outside of the text that shape the constitution of academic culture. In the final section, I outline an alternative approach to reflexivity that incorporates reflexive textual analysis into a wider collective project, one that aims to make the human sciences more consciously aware of the diverse aspects that make up academic culture.

Academic culture, postmodernism and the problem of reflexivity

The phrase "academic culture" is used here to refer to the interests, resources, constraints and processes that constitute the academy as a form of life. By "academy" I mean the institutions and people committed to tertiary education and research. Academic culture is thus the sum total of the social, economic, political and symbolic practices that are associated with these twin goals of teaching students and the pursuit of knowledge. It stretches from the external funding of, and attitude towards the academy, through to the formal and informal arrangements of universities and colleges, the attributes of academics and academic discourse, and to the content of academic knowledge itself, both pedagogical and scholarly. Traditionally, reflection upon academic culture from within has been from one of two perspectives: either that of higher education policy concerned with funding, qualifications and the relationship between academia and the wider society; or a discussion as to the nature and status of academic knowledge conducted in terms of methodology and epistemological validity. In the past, despite the attempts of a few schools of thought to connect and extend these two levels of analysis (such as the sociology of knowledge), academic culture has appeared to be blissfully unaware of its own social construction. Of course, this lack of awareness is only displayed at the formal level of scholarly knowledge. At the informal level, there exists a fully developed "folk knowledge" about the pragmatic workings of academia, a point that is acknowledged below. This unfortunate situation is changing, however, as academics in a number of disciplines have sought to foreground the problematic of reflexivity. Academics are increasingly using the tools and resources of their own disciplines to analyze and reflect upon their own disciplines. It is to the rise of this reflexivity that I now turn.

It is now becoming increasingly common to attach the historically specific label of "modernist" to the notion that the human sciences provide (or can provide) objective, empirically verified and essentially true knowledge about human culture and society. The modernist view of knowledge production (and the knowledge that it produced) had previously formed part of the political order, both legitimating and being legitimated by the power of the modern nation state in the West (Bauman 1987, 1992, Bourdieu 1991). In the postmodern world, where the market and globalization are increasingly dominant, the modernist self-image of academic knowledge is no longer seen as acceptable. Instead, the human scientist is limited to "interpreting" rather than "legislating" over what is truth, beauty or the good life (Bauman 1987). This shift from absolute to relative claims of truth and rightness can be seen, for example, in Foucault's (1980: 126–133) championing of the locally and specifically situated intellectual against the universal intellectual of the modernist era exemplified by Sartre.

Although both the portrayal of postmodernism as a "fundamental break" with modernism and modernity and its basis in empirical social change have been challenged (Giddens 1990 and Featherstone 1988, respectively), the concept is useful insofar as it suggests why academics throughout the human sciences have begun to explicitly question their own taken-for-granted assumptions. If Bauman (1987) is correct, then the declining power of the state has led to academic prescriptions increasingly being seen – by those both inside and outside academia – as mere interpretations that are open to challenge and criticism. Fundamental assumptions of academic knowledge, such as objectivity, value-neutrality, rationality, logic, the distinction between subject (the academic) and object (society and culture), assumptions that can be traced back to Descartes, have been challenged from within the human sciences. These wide-ranging and disparate critiques form what is labelled "postmodernism", although an exact definition of this term has been notoriously difficult to sustain. Postmodernism has encouraged the human scientist to look critically at his or her situation and the practices of representation, objectification and prescription that form it. Many disciplines are still trying to come to terms with such uncertainty and ambiguity, yet it appears that the move towards greater self-analysis and critique is a major trend within current academic culture. Such a move of "turning-back-upon-oneself" constitutes the problem of reflexivity as it is discussed here.

To avoid confusion, the use of "reflexivity" in this chapter is to be distinguished from two other uses of the term. In ethnomethodology, the term often refers to the hermeneutical problem of making sense of accounts, what Ashmore calls the "constitutive circularity of accounts" (Ashmore 1989: 32), by which he means that in order to make sense of an account one needs to know what it refers to, but to know what is referred to one must already have made sense of the account. The second use of "reflexivity" has been in social theory, where it is employed to describe the self-monitoring features of (post)-modern societies (Giddens 1991, Beck 1992, Beck et al. 1994, Lash & Urry 1994). My conception of reflexivity does share some features with the latter use, with the exception that it is used in this chapter at the level of the academy rather than at either the societal or global levels.

Reflexivity in the social studies of science

Rather than attempt to survey and discuss reflexivity across the human sciences, it would make more sense in this context to focus upon a particular field, in this case contemporary social studies of science (hereafter SSS).

60

Although I am using the social studies of science as my example, another field in which issues of reflexivity and representation have become prominent is ethnography (for an account of how such issues have been treated in ethnography see the chapter by Paul Atkinson and Amanda Coffey in this volume). Within SSS attempts at conceptualizing and resolving the problem have concentrated upon issues of textual authority and rhetoric, employing "new literary forms" (Woolgar 1988) to destabilize and question the representational functions of social scientific discourse. My position is that this approach is too narrow to form the basis of reflexivity, reducing as it does academic knowledge and culture to its textual manifestations. To support this claim I intend to show some internal difficulties with the textual approach, and then proceed to argue that we should see reflexivity as an intersubjective, social and political project to be carried on at both the personal/textual level and at an institutional/collective level.

Reflexivity has been an issue in sociology since Gouldner (1971) and an explicit issue in SSS since at least Gruenberg's influential discussion (1978). Gruenberg notes that reflexivity "is an aspect of all social science, since any statement which holds that humans necessarily act or believe in particular ways under particular circumstances refers as much to the social scientist as to anyone else" (Gruenberg 1978: 322). This level of self-reference is not necessarily a vicious one as the social scientist is not usually in the situation that his or her statements describe or explain. In SSS, however, general statements made about its object, scientific knowledge, necessarily refer to SSS itself to the extent that social science follows or claims to follow scientific methodology. More generally, SSS is referring to itself when it makes claims about all forms of knowledge: true or false; scientific or non-scientific. Thus the social studies of science are inherently open to claims about the inevitability of reflexivity, that its theories and methods can, and should, be applied to itself.

Within SSS reflexivity has shifted from being merely a potential issue to an openly pursued and debated problem. This is due to its appeal as a critical weapon to both those outside and inside the field. Reflexivity has been used by external critics, such as Trigg (1978) and Laudan (1981), in what is termed the *tu-quoque* argument: "This position (theory, argument) is incoherent (illegitimate, mistaken) because when reflexively applied to itself the result is an absurdity: self-contradiction (-refutation, -destruction, -undermining)" (Ashmore 1989: 86). Reflexivity has also been used in a similar way as a weapon by those within the field to attack rivals: X claims that Y ignores the consequences of Y's research (theories, explanations) for their own position (research, theories, explanations) (Woolgar 1981, Mulkay 1984, Ashmore 1989). More recently, however, the perceived negative value of reflexivity has been challenged by a number of figures within SSS, arguing that "the apprehension of reflexivity as a *problem* for social science is an unnecessary and overly restrictive interpretation" (Woolgar & Ashmore 1988: 2; their emphasis). Instead they see it as a fruitful and progressive line of inquiry.

The routes that the advocates of reflexivity have generally taken to solve or celebrate reflexivity have been overwhelmingly literary. This is because of a "linguistic turn" in the field, part of a wider trend within the human sciences of analyzing disciplinary objects (society, history, law) with literary modes of analysis. In SSS the shift has been towards a focus on scientific discourses and how scientists represent reality and their own representations of reality (Potter 1988, Woolgar 1988, Woolgar & Ashmore 1988). This focus was later extended to SSS itself, with Woolgar arguing that "we need to explore forms of literary expression whereby the monster [reflexivity] can be simultaneously kept at bay and allowed a position at the heart of our enterprise" (Woolgar 1982, quoted in Woolgar & Ashmore 1988: 4).

Writers adopting the textual approach, such as Malcolm Ashmore, Michael Mulkay and Steve Woolgar, employ a number of textual devices to draw attention to the constructed and rhetorical nature of their own texts. Such devices include the intervention of a second authorial voice (Pinch & Pinch 1988, Woolgar & Ashmore 1988, Wynne 1988, Woolgar 1989), a play-like dialogue (Mulkay 1984, Ashmore et al. 1989), a lecture or speech (Mulkay 1985, Ashmore 1989), a newspaper article (Ashmore et al. 1989) and even a self-referential encyclopaedia (Ashmore 1989). All of these devices are attempts to bring to the awareness of the reader the point "that conventional textual forms depend upon a conception of the author as a passive, neutral agent of representation" (Woolgar 1989: 141), or alternatively, "that interpretation goes on all the time, that the idea of one reading – a singular correspondence between text and meaning – is illusory" (Woolgar & Ashmore 1988: 4). A taste of the resulting style can be seen in the following passage of Woolgar's:

> For example the hidden hand of the author (observer) – the agent for presenting this argument – could be revealed just at the point when readers least expect it.
> – Is this where I come in?
> – If you must.
> – I don't much like your tone. I thought we had agreed that my entrance was to be the major highlight of the whole argument, that the appearance of a *different* voice would be the best way of making the point.
> – Which point?
> – That it is not possible to effectively demonstrate the importance of the role of the agent of representation using the standard univocal textual form.

– Yes, I agreed it would be better to try to *demonstrate* the point rather than to just keep on stating it. (Woolgar 1989: 140)

Although the textual approach to reflexivity can be both entertaining and thought-provoking one can question the use of such an approach in a number of ways. The constant pointing by "reflexive" texts to their own constructed nature does tend to undermine their readability and persuasive power. Indeed the deliberate attempt is often made to undermine their own textual authority until they reach the contradictory position of privileging the non-privileged nature of their text, e.g. Ashmore (1989), Woolgar (1989). As Ashmore (1989) points out, however, the paradoxical nature of a position is not enough, by itself, to eliminate that position. Paradoxes remain paradoxes despite being labelled as such, and indeed the partial intent of Ashmore (1989) is to explore and revel in the paradoxes that reflexivity throws up, instead of thinking that we can or should resolve them.

The key problem with the textual approach is that it treats reflexivity as a desirable possibility at the level of the individual text, and as a feature to be found in an author's representational practices. What these assumptions ignore are, first, the impossibility of a fully reflexive text, and secondly, that even if this were possible it would not be necessarily desirable to think of reflexivity in this way. A fully reflexive text cannot exist because of the dependence of texts on what Goffman (1974) calls a "frame". A frame is a set of assumptions and conventions that organize or guide the interpretation of an action or statement, such as the seriousness in which it is to be taken or the presumed relationship the action has to reality. The frame is a resource, indeed an indispensable resource, for the making and understanding of an action or statement. In *Frame analysis*, Goffman (1974) analyzes the ways in which frames can become broken, that is, when the frame is transformed from a resource to a topic as in the way Pirandello's plays take as their topic the conventions of the theatrical frame thereby highlighting the question of reflexivity.

Within SSS, the writer may be able to break the frame that he or she is in, such as the empiricist monologue, by pointing to and analyzing the frame, or through the introduction of a second authorial voice or reference to the monologic conventions. The crucial point, however, is that the writer can never write outside of frames; he or she can twist and turn the focal point of the text, yet can never escape the necessity of having to speak in a frame, a frame that invariably remains outside of the author's control. Goffman, commenting on French film maker Godard's device of making the process of cinematography visible in his films, sees this attempt to escape the frame as displaying bad faith (although this does not stop Goffman from displaying it himself in the introduction to *Frame analysis*):

This evidence of bad faith holds not merely for Godard and not merely for tricky filmmakers but for anyone in any frame who tries to convey something about the character of the frame he [*sic*] is employing; the posture he thereby assumes inevitably denies awareness of the frame in which *that* posture is struck. (And this holds as well for one whose intent is to direct attention to this effect.) The actor describing himself acting necessarily engages in an act he cannot include in the description; he can appear to succeed in the try but cannot then describe the trying; he can try to describe trying to describe himself describing, but then there is another try that characterises him and escapes his description. (Goffman 1974: 404, note 45, his emphasis)

SSS texts employing new literary forms can be seen as being the textual equivalent of Godard's films, with a constant layering and re-layering of comments and meta-comments, each deconstructing the previous comment's assumptions. Yet at each point there are aspects of framing that elude the writer's control: in pointing to some previously unexamined presuppositions, the writer makes further assumptions from which to examine others. Thus any piece of writing, whether conventional or attempting to be reflexive, contains a necessary element of blindness in order to say something. It has to chart a course between total reflexivity, reflecting on the reflection, and the dogmatic assertion of statements. This is what Ashmore calls the Scylla and Charybdis of reflexivity: "the Rock of Principled Purity, with its constraints leading inexorably to Silence and the Sea of Complacent Practice, which constantly threatens to lull us back into Science" (Ashmore 1989: 193).

We therefore need to modify our notion as to what constitutes reflexivity, abandoning the conception of reflexivity as a goal realizable only within an individual text. Reflexivity as total-reflection is not only impossible (leading to a solipsistic navel-gazing silence), but also not necessarily desirable. Indeed if the aim of reflexivity is to open up a dialogue about academic practice then why does this have to be conceived of as being constituted solely of self-analysis of textual forms through ever more radical textual forms? As Pinch & Pinch (1988) point out, even in multivocal texts the author retains control over the voices and hence the dialogue remains within relatively narrow limits. There is nothing self-evident about reflexivity that limits us to being reflexive about our own texts within those texts. Such an attempt, I hope to have shown above, is bound to fail because it always retains unexamined assumptions and principles in order to actually say something. What I want to do now is suggest where, outside and beyond the dead-end of textualism, we may locate more fruitful lines of reflexive inquiry.

Reflexivity as a collective project

The alternative approach that I want to propose is that we see reflexivity not only as a project for individual authors to carry out in their own texts, but as a collective process within the academic culture of the human sciences. That is to say, I want to argue for a widening out of the dialogue to involve the whole range and complexity of a field or discipline. This wider process of reflexivity would involve, in turn, the analysis of more than just the textual manifestations of academic knowledge and culture. Reflexivity would refer not to an individual author in an individual text but instead to a dialogue between academics (as well as academics and non-academics) and to the wide variety of processes beyond epistemology that shape the construction of academic knowledge. This dialogue would not be a radical break, since academics have always held an acute awareness of the economics, politics and customs of academia. Such practical reasoning has, however, been hidden and subdued in formal academic discourse itself. This is not only because of the dominance of the empiricist monologue, but also because academic culture itself has not been deemed an object worthy of the attention of research by either academics or those who fund them. This chapter is intended to challenge that assumption and to argue instead that we should make academic culture a topic of study in its own right. The textual account of reflexivity also pursues this goal, but it does so without providing a comprehensive account of academic culture and thus narrows reflexivity to representations of representations.

If we look at what the textual approach ignores we can see that there are at least three areas that cannot be reduced to merely textual manifestations: conditions of production, reception and reproduction. By ignoring the material conditions of knowledge production, this approach is unable, for instance, to answer the following questions Delamont asks of sociology of science: "Why are there so few women working in the sociology of science; such a small proportion of publications in the field by women; so few women on the editorial boards of the journals?" (Delamont 1989: 209). These are questions about the role of gender in the production of SSS, a role that cannot be explored merely through the more thorough textual analysis of SSS (although this would play a part). Instead one would have to look at the relative opportunities for men and women in the human sciences and the processes whereby differences in publications, promotions and memberships of fields are produced.

The textual approach also ignores the differences that occur in the reception of academic knowledge by readers. It adopts an attitude similar to that of the psychoanalytic perspective within cultural studies, in that it has "been content to deduce audience responses from the structure of the text" (Morley 1992: 59). This assumption that texts determine interpretations ignores Latour's point that "readers seem to be much more devious, harder to take in, much cleverer in deconstruction, much faster in fiction-making than is assumed by those writers who, with some arrogance, believe that others believe" (Latour 1988: 168). In addition to this, it ignores the fact that a single text can be interpreted in a number of ways, depending upon the identity and context of interpreters, or their position either inside or outside the hierarchies of academia. There has been little attempt to study the audience of academia in the same way the audiences of popular culture have been researched. We need to be aware, then, of how the knowledge of the human sciences is received and used by readers, be they academics in the same field, other academics, students or those outside of the university.

The textual approach also ignores the reproduction of knowledge. By "reproduction" I mean the analysis of the ways in which the human sciences maintain themselves as ongoing forms of life, that is, how they maintain a sense of relative continuity. This can include the ways in which the human sciences distinguish and maintain themselves as separate disciplines through the construction of traditions, the socialization of academics and the justificatory practices the disciplines utilize to acquire and retain funding. Such an analysis would also ask how the current structures of power and status in the human sciences are formed and reproduced. The textual approach to reflexivity has done little to illuminate this aspect of the human sciences and is content to focus upon abstract issues of representation. An important exception is the analysis of the rhetorical strategies in which texts locate themselves in relation to an important or well-known tradition and attempt to build upon it, this chapter being an example of such a strategy.

These three dimensions of academic knowledge and culture are largely ignored by the textual approach to reflexivity, discussed only where they manifest themselves textually, and even then usually sidelined in favour of the more epistemological problems of representation. I would argue, in contrast, that if we reconceptualize reflexivity as a collective process rather than as an issue for individual authors, then such questions of production, reception and reproduction should become the focal point of inquiry. Such a conception of reflexivity is an inherently political one, asking, as it does, about the role and maintenance of power relations both within academic culture and between the academy and society. Needless to say, then, the questions it raises about such issues are perhaps questions that some in and outside of the human sciences might not want to be asked.

This conception of reflexivity is radically different from previously proposed forms of self-analysis within the human sciences. As Woolgar rightly points out, however:

> As soon as practitioners start talking programmatics (that is, as soon as
> they start talking about how research ought to be done, rather than

just doing it), they often forget the most cherished tenets of their own practice . . . As soon as the discussion moves to a consideration of "the state of the field", its "prospects for future development", "possible new directions", an assessment of "what has been achieved", and so on, all commitment to relativism is dropped. (Woolgar 1992: 332)

Therefore, unlike Woolgar, I believe that taking relativism and reflexivity seriously involves more than just playing with textual forms. Once one has realized that reflexivity is a desirable feature of academic culture, a realization that can itself perhaps be traced to marginal locations within the disciplines, then the quest for ever more radical and challenging literary forms will not suffice. What is required, instead, is greater attention being paid within the human sciences to their own cultural practices as they inform the social institutions of academia, such as the university and the academic career, and their role in the production, reception and reproduction of knowledge.

Conclusion

This chapter began with an outline of the development of the textual approach to reflexivity. It then argued that such an approach was trapped in the assumption that reflexivity had to occur within a single text and, moreover, that the only way to challenge this is to undermine the pertinent representational and rhetorical practices. This is an impossible task, and in any case, ignores or displaces important dimensions of academic knowledge and culture, namely their production, reception and reproduction. If practitioners of the human sciences are to explore these dimensions in addition to the role of rhetoric in academic discourse, then the issue of reflexivity must be widened out to become a collective process within academia. In this way, supposedly natural hierarchies and customs will be confronted. This form of questioning means that reflexivity will pose a political challenge to human scientists. If we are honest with ourselves, however, we may see that such an analysis will not destroy the human sciences, but rather enrich our own understanding and practice of the human sciences as a form of life, its academic culture.

References

Ashmore, M. 1989. *The reflexive thesis: wrighting sociology of scientific knowledge.* Chicago: University of Chicago Press.
Ashmore, M., M. Mulkay, T. Pinch 1989. *Health and efficiency: a sociology of health economics.* Milton Keynes, England: Open University Press.

Bauman, Z. 1987. *Legislators and interpreters: on modernity, post-modernity and intellectuals.* Cambridge: Polity.

Bauman, Z. 1992. *Intimations of postmodernity.* London: Routledge.

Becher, T. 1989. *Academic tribes and territories: intellectual inquiry and the culture of disciplines.* Milton Keynes, England: SHRE/Open University Press.

Beck, U. 1992. *Risk society: towards a new modernity.* London: Sage.

Beck, U., A. Giddens, S. Lash 1994. *Reflexive modernization.* Cambridge: Polity.

Bourdieu, P. 1991. Universal corporatism: the role of intellectuals in the modern world. *Poetics Today* **12**, 655–69.

Delamont, S. 1989. *Knowledgeable women: structuralism and the reproduction of elites.* London: Routledge.

Featherstone, M. 1988. In pursuit of the postmodern. *Theory, Culture and Society* **5**, 195–215.

Foucault, M. 1980. *Power/knowledge: selected interviews and other writings 1972–1977.* Hemel Hempstead, England: Harvester Wheatsheaf.

Giddens, A. 1990. *The consequences of modernity.* Cambridge: Polity.

Giddens, A. 1991. *Modernity and self-identity.* Cambridge: Polity.

Goffman, E. 1974. *Frame analysis: an essay on the organisation of experience.* London: Penguin.

Gouldner, A. W. 1971. *The coming crisis of Western sociology.* London: Heinemann.

Gruenberg, B. 1978. The problem of reflexivity in the sociology of science. *Philosophy of the Social Sciences* **8**, 321–43.

Lash, S. & J. Urry 1994. *Economies of signs and space.* London: Sage.

Latour, B. 1988. The politics of explanation: an alternative. In *Knowledge and reflexivity: new frontiers in the sociology of knowledge*, S. Woolgar (ed.), 155–76. London: Sage.

Laudan, L. 1981. The pseudo-science of science? *Philosophy of the Social Sciences* **11**, 173–98.

Morley, D. 1992. *Television, audiences and cultural studies.* London: Routledge.

Mulkay, M. 1984. The scientist talks back: a one-act play with a moral, about replication in science and reflexivity in sociology. *Social Studies of Science* **14**, 265–82.

Mulkay, M. 1985. *The word and the world: explorations in the form of sociological analysis.* London: Allen & Unwin.

Pinch, T. & T. Pinch 1988. Reservations about reflexivity and new literary forms or why let the devil have all the good tunes? In *Knowledge and reflexivity: new frontiers in the sociology of knowledge*, S. Woolgar (ed.), 178–97. London: Sage.

Potter, J. 1988. What is reflexive about discourse analysis? In *Knowledge and reflexivity: new frontiers in the sociology of knowledge*, S. Woolgar (ed.), 37–52. London: Sage.

Trigg, R. 1978. The sociology of knowledge. *Philosophy of the Social Sciences* **8**, 289–98.

Woolgar, S. 1981. Interests and explanation in the social study of science. *Social Studies of Science* **11**, 365–94.

Woolgar, S. 1982. Laboratory studies: a comment on the state of the art. *Social Studies of Science* **12**, 481–98.

Woolgar, S. (ed.) 1988. *Knowledge and reflexivity: new frontiers in the sociology of knowledge.* London: Sage.

Woolgar, S. 1988. *Science: the very idea.* London: Ellis Horwood/Tavistock.

Woolgar, S. 1989. The ideology of representation and the role of the agent. In *Dismantling truth: reality in the postmodern world*, H. Lawson & L. Appignanesi (eds), 131–44. London: Wiedenfeld & Nicolson.

Woolgar, S. 1992. Some remarks about positionism: a reply to Collins and Yearley. In *Science as practice and culture*, A. Pickering (ed.), 327–42. Chicago: University of Chicago Press.

Woolgar, S. & M. Ashmore 1988. The next step: an introduction to the reflexive project. In *Knowledge and reflexivity: new frontiers in the sociology of knowledge*, S. Woolgar (ed.), 1–11. London: Sage.

Wynne, A. 1988. Accounting for accounts of the diagnosis of multiple sclerosis. In *Knowledge and reflexivity: new frontiers in the sociology of knowledge*, S. Woolgar (ed.), 101–22. London: Sage.

CHAPTER 4
Theorizing the body's fictions

Jane Moore

One is not born a woman; one becomes one. (Simone de Beauvoir 1949)

One is both born and constructed as a woman. (Rosi Braidotti 1989)

The sexed body: a question of essence?

The question of the body, a perennial topic of feminist theory and philosophy in general, is permanently in dispute. Is sexual difference rooted in the biological body, thereby making sexual identity synonymous with anatomy, or is anatomy simply the representation, the ultimate figure, of culturally constructed meanings of man and woman? Is it possible, even, to polarize the debate in this way? The absence of a consensus has kept alive the fascination with these questions about the body. In a postmodern present, however, they have taken on a new significance for feminist theory. Postmodernism's loss of faith in the metanarratives of truth and progress, together with its distrust of metaphysical absolutes, has involved a new generation of poststructuralist feminist theorists in an obligatory return to the question of sexual essence.

The work of Rosi Braidotti (1989, 1991) is representative of an increasing suspicion among feminist theorists towards the way in which predominantly male theorists of the postmodern have inscribed a notion of the "feminine" as a metaphor for the crisis of traditional master narratives in a way that, according to Braidotti, does not bear directly on the historical experience of women or on their anatomical difference. Concerned that the material reality of women's lived experiences is in danger of being erased, she calls on feminists to rethink the politics of sexual difference with the stress falling on the essential difference of women from men.

Forty years on from de Beauvoir's radical refusal of any notion of a fixed female nature or essence, Braidotti urges feminists to be suspicious of the theory that everything is culturally constructed. Sexual identity, she claims, is at least as much a fact of nature as it is a cultural fiction. Her argument takes issue with the work of feminist poststructuralist theorists, who, following on from de Beauvoir, stressed the reactionary implications for feminist politics of theories of biological determinism that rest on the realist assumption that representations of the body are purely secondary to its material reality. The problem with a belief in simple referentiality, as Jane Gallop argued, is that

> it cannot recognize that the reality to which it appeals is a traditional ideological construction, whether one terms it phallomorphic, or metaphysical, or bourgeois, or something else. The politics of experience is inevitably a conservative politics, for it cannot help but conserve traditional ideological constructs which are not recognized as such but are taken for the "real". (Gallop 1988: 99)

Poststructuralism's proposition that meanings are constructed in language and that they are cultural and ideological, not natural or neutral, provided feminists with the theoretical tools to challenge patriarchal accounts of the world that justified woman's inferior social and economic status by appealing to a pre-cultural and unequal sexual difference.

While Braidotti acknowledges that it is necessary for a feminist theory of change to work with poststructuralist accounts of subjectivity that would release the meaning of woman from the closure of biological determinism, she is somewhat more concerned that the development of poststructuralist theory (by mainly French and predominantly male philosophers) has emphasized the textual construction of meanings to the point of losing sight of the material or bodily reality of sexual difference. In an essay entitled "The politics of ontological difference", Braidotti (1989) proposes that the crisis of knowledge that defines a postmodern condition is specifically a crisis of the "masculine" values of reason and truth. Traditionally, Western philosophy has constructed its truth-seeking project around the ideal image of "the man of reason" (Braidotti 1989: 89). In the postmodern condition, however, "woman" and "feminine" have come to function primarily as privileged metaphors for the crisis of rational and masculine values, for non-truth. But they have done so, and this is the root of Braidotti's objection, in a way that "is not directly related to either the discursivity or the historical presence of real-life women" (Braidotti 1989: 89).

Alice Jardine, in her book *Gynesis* (1985), which is largely in sympathy with Braidotti's distrust of the implications for feminism of the postmodern crisis of the metaphysical categories, Man, Meaning, Truth, The Subject, describes the process of the metaphorization of woman to which Braidotti refers as one

that has involved, above all, a reincorporation and reconceptualization of that which has been the master narrative's own "non-
knowledge", what has eluded them, what has engulfed them. This
other-than-themselves is almost always a "space" of some kind (over
which the narrative has lost control), and this space has been coded as
feminine, as *woman*. (Jardine 1985: 25)

Jardine glimpses a future for feminism in the possibility that these spaces,
which although "coded as *feminine*" do not designate a person or a thing but
are to be thought of as a mode of textual resistance to "Reason", could nonetheless become the site of a new feminist aesthetic that would begin to free
women, and men, from "Man's Truth" (Jardine 1985: 61). Yet she also shares
Braidotti's suspicion that the process of "the putting into discourse of
'woman'" (Jardine 1985: 25) is not bringing men's domination of philosophy to
an end, but is, instead, allowing them to construct new theories of meaning
over woman's dead body.

Expanding this criticism, Braidotti argues that "far from being a reactive
movement of critical opposition, the feminism of sexual difference is also the
active gesture of affirmation of women's ontological desire" (Braidotti 1989:
90). The feminist project, as Braidotti defines it, is definitively bound up with
the establishment of women's sexual and bodily difference and the will "to
change the concrete social conditions of sex-relations and of gender stratifica-
tion" (Braidotti 1989: 97). On this understanding of feminism, it follows that a
feminist criticism that does not directly relate to the reality of the female body
cannot be properly said to be a feminist politics at all. And it is on this basis
that Braidotti calls on feminist critics to refuse postmodernism's disembodiment of sexual difference and to recognize instead the essential, metaphysical,
difference of woman's sexual being. Her defence of essentialism rests on the
following premisses:

> First, that in order to make sexual difference operative as a political
> option, feminist theoreticians should re-connect the feminine to the
> bodily sexed reality of the female, refusing the separation of the
> empirical from the symbolic, or of the material from the discursive, or
> of sex from gender. Secondly, that this project is important as both the
> epistemological basis for feminist theory and the grounds of political
> legitimation for feminists in the social, economic, political, and theo-
> retical context of the postmodern and the post-industrial condition.
> Thirdly, that in thinking about sexual difference one is led, by the very
> structure of the problem, to the metaphysical question of essence.
> (Braidotti 1989: 93)

Describing the question of essence as an ontological one, ontology "being the branch of metaphysics that deals with the structure of that which essentially *is*, or that which is implied in the very definition of an entity" (Braidotti 1989: 93), she argues that rather than reproducing the "facile anti-intellectualism of those who see metaphysics as 'woolly thinking'" or those who would "reduce it to an ideologically incorrect option", feminists should instead "take seriously the critique of discourse about essences as the historical task of modernity" (Braidotti 1989: 93).

My aim in this essay is indeed to take seriously Braidotti's injunction to reconsider the discourse about essences and to do so within the specific theoretical framework of postmodernism. However, although I share Braidotti's belief that the language of essentialism cannot be easily ignored when one is thinking about the question of sexual difference, I do not believe that the future of feminism depends on a reaffirmation of the bodily roots of that difference. Nor do I believe that feminism is finally incompatible with postmodernism's interrogation of metaphysical absolutes. In the process of outlining what I find problematic about Braidotti's defence of essentialism, I propose to turn to both Sigmund Freud's and Jean-François Lyotard's analyses of the problem of gaining a knowledge of the body in itself, in its essence, and also to Jeanette Winterson's fictional exploration of the same problem in her short novel, significantly entitled *Written on the body* (1992).

The certainty of sexual difference

Braidotti is right, in my view, to highlight the metaphysical status of sexual difference in Western culture. Human bodies *are* sexed. This much would appear obvious. As Sigmund Freud pointed out, in the ordinary course of things we are given to making a spontaneous distinction between the sexes and the habit of doing so does not usually cause us any problems: "When you meet a human being, the first distinction you make is 'male or female?' and you are accustomed to make the distinction with unhesitating certainty" (Freud 1991: 146). The immediate certainty of difference, Freud implies, is proof enough of its existence. It goes without saying that one is male or female. It is simply like that: it is a metaphysical fact. Similarly, Braidotti claims in defence of her essential womanliness "it is a fact, it is like *that*: 'I' am sexed. 'I' have been a woman – socially and anatomically – for as long as 'I' have existed, that is to say, in the limited scale of my temporality, forever" (Braidotti 1989: 101).

Still, as Freud also recognized, however strong our feeling is that we are essentially male or female, the appeal to metaphysics is unable in and of itself, in its essence, to contribute to our understanding of the formation of masculine and feminine identities. Moreover, the appeal to anatomical science only adds to the confusion. "Anatomical science", Freud tells us, shares our certainty about sexual difference "at one point and not much further. The male sexual product, the spermatozoon, and its vehicle are male; the ovum and the organism that harbours it are female" (Freud 1991: 146). But after this it is impossible to establish fixed differences between the sexes. Even the sexual organs themselves are not sufficient evidence of the existence of two distinct and, in consequence, incommensurably different sexes; for, according to Freud, science has identified

> the fact that portions of the male sexual apparatus also appear in women's bodies, though in an atrophied state, and vice versa in the alternative case. It regards their occurrence as indications of *bisexuality*, as though an individual is not a man or a woman but always both – merely a certain amount more the one than the other. (Freud 1991: 147)

On the basis of science's affirmation of bisexuality, Freud concludes that "what constitutes masculinity or femininity is an *unknown characteristic* which anatomy cannot lay hold of" (Freud 1991: 147; my emphasis).

Braidotti would agree with Freud that the appeal to anatomical science is unable in and of itself to lay hold of the meanings of masculinity and femininity that circulate in society. She acknowledges the need for a theory that would highlight the construction of sexual identities in language and culture and thus explain how meanings of masculinity and femininity can change between cultures and across history. In this respect she argues that it would be disastrous for feminism to forgo theories of representation in favour of an exclusive return to essentialism. "Being-a-woman", Braidotti asserts, is not entirely a biological condition, it is also a cultural and linguistic one:

> My "being-a-woman", just like my "being-in-language" and "being-mortal" is one of the constitutive elements of my subjectivity. Sexual difference is ontological, not accidental, peripheral, or contingent upon socio-economic conditions; that one be socially constructed as a female is an evidence, that the recognition of the fact may take place in language is clear, but that the process of construction of femininity *fastens and builds upon anatomical realities is equally true.* (Braidotti 1989: 101; my emphasis)

And yet, as the above quotation demonstrates, while Braidotti is certain that femininity is as much a product of culture as it is of nature, she is still more certain that the signifier is unable to say everything about the anatomical reality of a body whose existence precedes the process of the construction of femininity. While it would be a nonsense to contradict Braidotti on this point – at birth infants are (usually) visibly and physically sexed male or female – the problem remains, which is also Freud's problem, that if what constitutes sexual identity is an "unknown characteristic which anatomy cannot lay hold of", to what degree is it possible to speak with any certainty of the existence of sexual essences?

One answer to the question would be, we do have the notion of a sexual essence and that's all there is to it. This is in many senses the answer that Braidotti gives. A striking feature of her essay is its unwillingness to define sexual essence except as something that is essentially undefinable, something that both precedes and exceeds the communicative function of language. In terms of sexual essence, all that language can do is *evoke* the idea of the existence of something that resists full or adequate representation. Braidotti writes, for example, that "something in the fact of "being-a-woman" is in excess of the feminist identity" (Braidotti 1989: 95). To ask what this excess is that cannot be contained within the political language of feminism would prohibit any answer on the essay's own terms other than a metaphysical one. The essay suggests no possible answer to the question apart from one that would reinvoke sexual essence as a mysterious and metaphysical force that resists analysis.

It is possible, however, to question the implications for feminism and for postmodernism, of such an answer. To begin with, there is the obvious risk that a definition of "woman" that stresses her essential and in consequence incommensurable difference from man produces a separatist feminist politics that confines women within a social and sexual sphere that is totally alien to men. It is therefore difficult to understand how Braidotti's appeal to metaphysics can produce the feminist politics of change that she calls for. To speak of an essential or metaphysical sexual difference is not to describe that difference and it is certainly not to resolve it; it is a way of retaining its elusiveness, of affirming its transcendental and incontestable truth. On the other hand, it is also necessary to acknowledge Braidotti's argument that in the context of postmodernism's disembodiment of sexual difference feminism must emphasize the essential nature of the sexual difference in order to begin the "positive project of turning difference into a strength, of affirming its positivity" (Braidotti 1989: 101). Not to do this, Braidotti insists, would equally carry the danger of leaving unchanged the actual social and historical existence of real women's lives.

Is there, then, no way out of this impasse? Is feminism necessarily obliged to run the risk of metaphysical closure in the name of political change? And must it also corral into fixed categories the sexual undecidability that is the consequence of both Freud's thesis of bisexuality and of postmodernism's interrogation of metaphysical absolutes? To put the question differently, is it possible to retain the excitement and debate that comes from not knowing the full measure of the sexual difference without thereby sacrificing the feminist project to change the concrete social conditions of sex relations? Finally, is postmodernism incompatible with feminism?

All of these questions return once again to the problem of metaphysics, and by extension, to postmodernism. The question of metaphysics, I now want to suggest, provides the framework for much of the philosophical and aesthetic theories of meaning that, in their common suspicion of truth, essence and substance, are called postmodern. Jacques Derrida and Jean-François Lyotard, to name but two of the most influential philosophers of the late (postmodern) twentieth century, share in common, whatever else differentiates their work, the aim of interrogating and complexifying metaphysics.[1] Certainly they are highly suspicious, even contemptuous, of metaphysical categories; for Lyotard, metaphysics does amount to a form of "woolly-thinking",[2] but the process by which he arrives at this conclusion is analytical not simply judgemental, and it is to his analysis of the metaphysics of sexual difference that I now want to turn.

The uncertainty of sexual difference

In an essay entitled "Can thought go on without a body?", Jean-François Lyotard (1991a) offers an alternative approach to theorizing the metaphysics of sexual difference. For Lyotard, no less than Braidotti, the defining feature of an ontological notion of sexual essence is precisely its unrepresentability in language. But while this recognition leads Braidotti to confirm the ontological and metaphysical roots of sexual essence, it prompts Lyotard to problematize metaphysics itself and to question the very possibility of getting to the "truth" of sexual difference: "I don't know whether sexual difference is ontological difference. How would a person *know*?" (Lyotard 1991a: 21).

Not exactly a demand for knowledge, and still less an outright denial of the tenacious hold of metaphysics on our understanding of sexuality, the question declares the uncertainty that surrounds sexual difference. Rather than attempting to resolve this uncertainty by an appeal to two autonomous sexual essences (which is Braidotti's project), Lyotard emphasizes the incompleteness of sexual identity:

> It's an accepted proposition that sexual difference is a paradigm of an incompleteness of not just bodies, but minds too. Of course there's masculinity in women as well as femininity in men. Otherwise how would one gender even have an idea of the other or have an emotion that comes from what's lacking? *It's lacking because it's present deep inside, in the body, in the mind. Present like a guard, restrained, off to the side, at the edge of your vision, present on some horizon of it. Elusive, impossible to grasp. Again*

we're back at transcendence in immanence. The notion of gender dominant
in contemporary society wants this gap closed, this transcendence
toppled, this powerlessness overcome. (Lyotard 1991a: 20–21; my
emphasis)

Redefined not as a unified presence but as *lack,* as the lack of a unity or one-
ness of being ("there's masculinity in women as well as femininity in men"),
sexual difference in Lyotard's account is undecidable and enigmatic. What is
more, to the extent that this difference is "impossible to grasp", not only
because it is precisely a difference, a lack, and therefore an absence of being,
but also because the notion of sexual difference is both immanent ("it's present
deep inside, in the body, in the mind") and elusive (it's "Present like a guard,
restrained, off to the side, at the edge of your vision, present on some horizon
of it"). It shares something of the mysterious and transcendent quality of
Braidotti's definition of sexual essence. The phrase "transcendence in immanence" conjures up the idea of something that occupies a position of excess
over meaning that cannot be reduced to representation, something that in its
essence is "unpresentable".[3]

For Braidotti, the unrepresentability of sexual essence confirms its pre-
cultural and ontological existence. Thus separating sexual essence from the
scene of representation, she locates the essential difference of woman from
man in a realm beyond politics, culture and language. Lyotard, however,
argues to the contrary that rather than being metaphysically removed
from the symbolic order of language and culture, the mysterious and, in his
account, incomplete structure of sexual difference is what mobilizes human
thought and language. In other words, it is difference, not identity, that initi-
ates meaning and desire. For Lyotard, sexual identity is irreducibly split by the
intervention of unconscious desire. He argues that sexuality isn't just a property of bodies, nor is it solely an invention of the mind, of conscious thought, it
is also, and crucially, implicated in the structure of unconscious thought.

Sexual difference isn't just related to a body as it feels its incompleteness, but to an unconscious body or to the unconscious as body. That
is, as separated from thought – even analogical thought. This difference is *ex hypothesi* outside our control. Maybe (because as Freud
showed in his description of deferred action, it inscribes effects without
the inscription being "memorized" in the form of recollection) it's the
other way around? And this difference is what initially sets up fields of
perception, and thought as functions of waiting, of equivocations, as
I've stated? This quite probably defines suffering in perceiving and
conceiving as produced by an impossibility of unifying and completely
determining the object seen. (Lyotard 1991a: 21)

77

Not easy to summarize, Lyotard's complex description of the relation between sexual difference, the body, and thought, is overdetermined by his broader concern with the philosophical question "What is thinking?" which comes back to the problem of metaphysics, and by his analysis of the limits of textual representation.[4] The key point to be grasped here, however, is that the unconscious produces a remainder of meaning that both counters the possibility of arriving at the truth of sexual difference and gives rise to thought. The split in meaning introduced by the unconscious creates a difference that is *ex hypothesi* outside the subject's control and thus makes the perceived difference of gender unable to be fully conceptualized. Lyotard states: "This difference makes thought go on endlessly and won't allow itself to be thought. Thought is inseparable from the phenomenological body: although gendered body is separated from thought, and launches thought" (Lyotard 1991a: 23).

The proposition that gender difference both "makes thought go on endlessly and won't allow itself to be thought" is encapsulated in the phrase "the irremediable differend of gender" (Lyotard 1991a: 22). Defined in his book *The differend* (Lyotard 1988) as an immanent faculty of discourse, the differend is "the unstable state and instant of language wherein something which must be able to be put into phrases cannot yet be" (Lyotard 1988: 13). It is "signalled by what one ordinarily calls a feeling: 'One cannot find the words,' etc" (Lyotard 1988: 13). Because the differend cannot be phrased or communicated in existing idioms it is necessarily a site of dispute: "a differend [*différend*] would be a case of conflict, between (at least) two parties, that cannot be equitably resolved for lack of a rule of judgement applicable to both arguments" (Lyotard 1988: xi).

There is thus no meta-discursive position from which a differend can be resolved, no way of deciding in the case of gender difference on the ontological existence of a pre-discursive sexual essence.

The significance of a gender differend for a feminist politics of sexual difference is that it allows for Braidotti's notion of the existence of an idea, or emotion, that we are essentially sexed male or female, which affects social and sexual relations, but it does not admit the fixing of this feeling in a biological, extra-discursive body, which would inevitably unify sexual identity. By bringing the excess or remainder of meaning, which Braidotti defines as essence, into the realm of language and discourse, Lyotard presents the question of sexual difference precisely as a question or contest of meaning within culture. The meaning of masculine and feminine, man and woman, becomes in consequence a matter of political debate, a site of struggle and the location of change. Moreover, if sexual difference is not ontological and if sexual identity is not autonomous and self-determining, but differential, it follows that Freud's question "male or female?" can no longer be answered with "unhesitating certainty".

The body in fiction

What would it mean, though, to question the certainty of sexual difference? And what would be the implications of doing so for feminists reading and writing about the body? *Written on the body*, published in Britain in 1992, explores the limits of humanism's belief, which feminism has largely shared, that the body is the key to unlocking the truth of sexual difference. Traditionally, humanism and feminism have located meaning in individual experience. And for feminism, at least, the role of fiction in exploring what it means to be a woman in contemporary culture has had a special importance. Arguably since the eighteenth century and certainly from the 1960s on, many of the propositions put forward in feminist theory have also been formulated in fiction by women. Mary Wollstonecraft's political treatise *Vindication of the rights of woman* (1792) was followed by her novel *The wrongs of woman: or, Maria* (1798) which is in many respects a sequel to the earlier work. And the re-emergence of the feminist movement in the 1960s was visibly accompanied by a range of best-selling semi-autobiographical fictions that chart the heroine/author's growing political awareness, principally in terms of her increased knowledge of her own sexuality and her readiness to recognize the specificity of her female bodily needs and desires.[5] Early feminist fictions therefore inevitably encouraged readers to identify with the realism of their characters' and authors' experiences; in consequence, they also defined for feminism a version of truth based on individual experience. In this respect, the sexual pronoun was supremely important: only women it was commonly believed were in a position to tell the truth about female experience. The implicit purpose of feminist fiction was to gratify the reader's demand for a resolution of the question, what does "woman" mean?

In all these respects *Written on the body* is not a typical feminist fiction. It is a love story but the narrator of the tale, who is also its protagonist, is genderless. By turns boastfully macho and beguilingly feminine the narrator flaunts its sexual undecidability. Meanwhile, by avoiding the demands of realism to "know" the truth of the narrator's sex, the fiction declares itself as a fiction, a fantastic illusion. Playing relentlessly with the reader's desire to pin down the sexual identity of the narrative voice, the novel brings into the foreground as a question the relationship between truth and experience, essence and identity. Moreover, from a feminist perspective, it reaches what is in many ways a startling conclusion: "truth", the novel declares, including the truth of what it means to be a woman or a man, to be in love, and to write about that experience, is ultimately a literary and cultural convention, and it is only that. The novel opens with a rehearsal of some of modern love's conventional clichés and metaphors.

Why is the measure of love loss?

It hasn't rained for three months. The trees are prospecting underground, sending reserves of roots into the dry ground, roots like razors to open any artery water-fat.

The grapes have withered on the vine. What should be plump and firm, resisting the touch to give itself in the mouth, is spongy and blistered. Not this year the pleasure of rolling blue grapes between finger and thumb juicing my palm with musk. Even the wasps avoid the thin brown dribble. Even the wasps this year. It was not always so.

I am thinking of a certain September: Wood Pigeon Red Admiral Yellow Harvest Orange Night. You said "I love you." Why is it that the most unoriginal thing we can say to one another is still the thing we long to hear? "I love you" is always a quotation. You did not say it first and neither did I, yet when you say it and when I say it we speak like savages who have found three words and worship them. I did worship them but now I am alone on a rock hewn out of my own body.

CALIBAN You taught me language and my profit on't is I know how to curse. The red plague rid you for learning me your language.

Love demands expression. It will not stay still, stay silent, be good, be modest, be seen and not heard, no. It will break out in tongues of praise, the high note that smashes the glass and spills the liquid. (Winterson 1992: 9)

Clearly an intertextual event (the allusions to love are overtly literary) but nonetheless special for that, the novel draws to attention the extent to which love is citational ('I love you is always a quotation'). Love's "truth" is not an extra-textual one. The novel also highlights as a convention of love in Western culture, and of that culture's literature of love, the paradoxical demand that love is experienced as a uniquely individual emotion: "yet when you say it and when I say it we speak like savages who have found three words and worship them". "You" and "I", the object and subject of desire, are universal, unsexed pronouns, but they tell a story of love in the Western world that is immediately familiar. It does not matter here that they lack a gender; the language of desire has no sexual essence.[6] It is the structure and conventions of literary love, its metaphors and clichés, with which the reader is invited to identify, not the character or essential sexual being of the protagonists. The unpresentability of love's essence, it's transcendent and elusive truth, is equally part of the convention. "Love demands expression", the narrator states, but the narrative also demonstrates the impossibility of giving full or accurate expression to love. In language, the meaning of love relies on the absence of the thing itself, which is present only in the metaphoric substitution of words: of withered grapes for loss; of "Wood Pigeon Red Admiral Yellow Harvest Orange Night" for love.

How, then, are we supposed to read this love story? As feminist? As post-modern? In terms of the realist genre that feminist writing has traditionally subscribed to, *Written on the body* is a subversive text: it does not satisfy the demand for truth-in-experience; neither does it consolidate the meaning of woman or man. I want to propose, however, that in another sense the text is not incompatible with a feminist project. This is in the sense that in its insistence on the narrative conventions and metaphors of love it opens up the degree to which even the most intimate of experiences are culturally encoded and therefore identifiable as points of change. Moreover, if the novel can be called postmodern, insofar as it withholds the certainty of a sexual truth behind the text (the signifier has no essence) and in its stress on the intertextual meaning of love, then postmodernism might also be the basis of a productive feminist sexual politics. Postmodern, here, indicates not an abdication of sexual categories but their complexification. The novel demonstrates that to disturb the certainty of the opposition male/female is not thereby to surrender meaning, it is merely to make meaning undecidable: a matter for dispute and debate. But if the meaning of love depends on narrative, speech, metaphor, what of the "body" of the novel's title? What role does it play in the love story and what are the implications of its inscription for feminism?

Louise, the narrator's lover is dying from leukaemia. In the second section of the novel she abandons the narrator in order to seek medical aid for her condition. In Louise's absence, the narrator turns to the study of anatomy in order to understand better Louise's illness, to get at her bodily truth, and to regain by proxy her lost presence. Reading at this point more like a medical textbook than a modern romance, the narrative plots the pathology of cancer across "The Cells, Tissues, Systems and Cavities of the Body"; "The Skin"; "The Skeleton" and "The Special Senses". The prose in each section is headed by short clinical descriptions of the composition of bodily parts and senses. Here are some of them:

> The multiplication of cells by mitosis occurs throughout the life of the individual. It occurs at a more rapid rate until growth is complete. Thereafter new cells are formed to replace those which have died. Nerve cells are a notable exception. When they die they are not replaced. (Winterson 1992: 115)

> Tissues, such as the lining of the mouth, can be seen with the naked eye, but the millions of cells which make up the tissues are so small that they can only be seen with the aid of a microscope. (Winterson 1992: 117)

> For descriptive purposes the human body is separated into cavities. The cranial cavity contains the brain. Its boundaries are formed by the bones of the skull. (Winterson 1992: 119)

Delivered with anatomical accuracy, but ultimately unable to further the narrator's knowledge of Louise, to unlock the secret of her attraction, these factual descriptions contrast with continuous prose running beneath them, which tells a new love story, one whose heroine is the body itself, or more exactly, the body on to which the narrator projects its desires. More meaningful as metaphor than as anatomical substance, Louise's body, which, strictly speaking, is no longer her own, is the *tabula rasa* for the narrator's inscription of an extravagant love poem. Its poetic intensity climaxes in a song of love, which is framed by a medical textbook definition of taste.

> Taste: there are four fundamental sensations of taste: sweet sour bitter and salt.

> My lover is an olive tree whose roots grow by the sea. Her fruit is pungent and green. It is my joy to get at the stone of her. The little stone of her hard by the tongue. Her thick-fleshed salt-veined swaddle stone. (Winterson 1992: 137)

Without its inscription within a poetic register, its appropriation by the language of literature and desire, "taste" only describes one of the human body's special senses; it gains meaning in this passage, however, not as pre-cultural instinct or as an innate bodily sensation but as metaphor and personification. The emphasis on the literary evades recourse to an anatomical, extra-textual truth. Metaphorized as a lover's hunger to gain absolute possession of the loved one, body and soul, taste exemplifies the force of desire, which aims to merge the difference between self and other, lover and loved one. It also demonstrates the impossibility of achieving this unity (Louise's voice is notably absent from the text). Part of this impossibility is linguistic: as speaking subjects we take up a position in language than can never be identical with the place from which the other person speaks. Moreover, we can never be absolutely certain of the object of the other person's desire, since, like our own, as Lyotard implies, the difference that produces desire is as much unconscious and conscious.

But as Lyotard also observes, that difference is additionally perceived as a property of the body.[7] Certainly, in and of its essence, Louise's body is unread: it is a body that is "written on", a body that is made weightier by the narrator's words than by flesh. But the material reality of her sexed body does not thereby fade into insignificance. The narrator's desire for Louise is shown to inhabit her flesh and in this respect sexual identity is referential: even when Louise's body is heavily metaphorized, as in the passage on "taste", it is distinctly female, at least it is for a reader familiar with the amatory codes for describing oral sex. Yet the body is also, and this, I think, is Lyotard's point, not the origin of sexual difference but its irreducible *figure*: the body, in other words, marks the limit of language's capacity for representation.

The fictive body

I have wanted to suggest that there is no inevitable incompatibility between a postmodern scepticism towards the existence of an extra-textual sexual essence, or truth, and feminism's insistence on the necessity of recognizing the existence of sexual difference. To locate language and culture as the site where meanings of the body and of sexual difference are produced, and to emphasize the consequential textual undecidability of those meanings does not inevitably entail the abandonment of the sexual opposition itself. In other words, to disturb the stability of that opposition does not equal its denial. Language is important here: although it cannot be said to be material in the sense that the body is, it does have material effects. To name a thing is precisely to give it meaning, and if that meaning goes unchallenged there follows the likelihood that it will quickly become accepted in the culture as natural, as true. Fiction is not insignificant in this process: the texts we read do affect our perceptions of the world. What is radical about *Written on the body*, it seems to me, is that it bears witness to the tenacity of the body's hold on shaping our understanding of sexual difference while simultaneously refusing to unveil its (metaphysical) truth. The body, I want to suggest in conclusion, is inscribed in the novel as the *figure* of that "truth".

The figure is a term used by Lyotard to invoke the point at which representation is put in crisis. Defined in Bill Readings' book on Lyotard as rhetoricity, as distinct from discursive signification (meaning), the figure is "an unspeakable other necessarily *at work* within and against *discourse*, disrupting the rule of representation. It is not opposed to discourse, but is the point at which the oppositions by which discourse works are opened to a radical heterogeneity or *singularity*" (Readings 1991: xxxi). The figure is a condition of representation; it points to the excess of meaning that subsists in the gap between the signifier and the signified; an excess that in its elusiveness is finally unpresentable and cannot be reduced to meaning. Functioning as the unpresentable, because it marks the outer limits of language, the "real" of the sexual body is thus permanently a site of dispute.

Lyotard argues that all representation, whether verbal or visual, is threatened by the irreducibility of the figure. It is precisely this irreducibility that marks the limit of metaphysical concepts, such as the notion of an extra-textual biological essence. It is also that which mobilizes the contest over meaning. The body-as-figure evokes the possibility, suggested by Braidotti, of an innate sexual meaning that resists conceptualization but it also, crucially, brings back the sexual referent itself as an exciting textual enigma. Not a metaphysical certainty, but a culturally contested meaning, sexual difference is in consequence an open question. The deferral of closure, not its resolution, is, I suggest, where feminism and postmodernism, fruitfully coincide.

To explain this conclusion, it is necessary to acknowledge that feminism's traditional insistence on sexual difference does not necessarily disappear in the context of a postmodern problematization of the body's fictions. What does recede is the feminist imperative to name and naturalize an *oppositional* sexual difference. Now it may happen, as Braidotti fears, that to interrogate that difference, to destabilize the sexual boundaries, denies feminism the ground on which to cement its politics, but the project of categorizing difference car-ries its own dangers: there is the danger, for example, of producing totalizing definitions of sexual difference that close the questions that feminism has also been traditionally concerned to raise. On the other hand, to privilege the undecidability of sexual difference could equally open out the possibilities for a feminist rethinking of sexual identities. It is perhaps worth stressing here that an emphasis on sexual undecidability does not automatically promote a sexual *indeterminacy* nor, indeed, does it necessarily result in political anarchy. In the abstract, these are possibilities, but in material practice the meanings raised by the undecidable are themselves highly determined in strictly defined cultural and historical situations.[8] Complete subjective autonomy is simply not possible in a culture where subjects are positioned by social class and sexual difference.

This does not mean, however, that sexual destinies are wholly determined. To recognize a culture's differential boundaries is not thereby to accept them as natural, as true. Paraphrasing Jane Gallop's words, it is possible both to assume difference and immediately call it into question.[9] Exploring the limits of what it is possible for subjects to act and speak in a culture in a way that respects the restraints on meaning in a specific historical and cultural situation but refuses to naturalize those meanings, this seems to me to be what brings together a feminist politics of change with a postmodern textual practice in a way that makes both possible and necessary to continue interrogating the body's fictions.

Notes

1. For a succinct account of Derrida's deconstructive analysis of metaphysics see the interviews "Implications" and "Semiology and grammatology" in *Positions*

(Derrida 1981: 3–36).

2. A strong mistrust of metaphysics runs throughout Lyotard's work. In brief, his argument is that metaphysical thought reduces the complexity of meaning to a culture's accepted beliefs. In this respect metaphysics is characterized by Lyotard as a form "illiteracy", which manifests itself as a lack of close reading, or in his words, a "lack of respect of severe and serene reading of the text, of writing with regard to language" (Lyotard 1991c: 199–200).

3. For an account of Lyotard's use of the concept of the "unpresentable" in painting, philosophy and politics see his essay "Representation, presentation, unpresentable" (Lyotard 1991b: 119–28).

4. Lyotard problematizes the relationship between thought and the body in terms of the question "What is thinking?" His answer is that thinking involves suffering, because it is the attempt to think beyond the "already-thought", which in turn involves exploring the point at which language is unable to contain or adequately express meaning (Lyotard 1991a: 17–18).

5. For a poststructuralist analysis of feminism's relation to semi-autobiographical fictions such as Marilyn French's *The woman's room* and Erica Jong's *Fear of flying*, see Rosalind Coward's "The true story of how I became my own person" (1989).

6. The point is made by Jacques Lacan in his controversial essay "The meaning of the phallus" (1982: 80–81) where desire is described as a residue (of meaning). For a broader discussion of the narrative structure of desire in romantic fiction, see Catherine Belsey, "Reading love stories" (1992).

7. Lyotard writes: "Finally, the human body has a gender" (1991a: 20).

8. Diane Elam draws attention to the distinction in Derrida's writing between indeterminacy and undecidability in her book *Feminism and deconstruction. Ms. en Abyme* (1994: 83).

9. Gallop writes: "Identity must be continually assumed and immediately called into question" (1982: xii).

References

Beauvoir, S. de. 1949. *The second sex*, tr. H.M. Parshley. London: Penguin.

Belsey, C. 1992. Reading love stories. *Studies in Slavic Literature and Poetics* **17**, 136–52.

Braidotti, R. 1989. The politics of ontological difference. In *Between feminism and psychoanalysis*, T. Brennan (ed.), 89–105. London: Routledge.

Braidotti, R. 1991. *Patterns of dissonance: a study of women in contemporary philosophy*, tr. E. Guild. Cambridge: Polity.

Coward, R. 1989. The true story of how I became my own person. In *The feminist reader: essays in gender and the politics of literary criticism*, C. Belsey & J. Moore (eds), 35–47. London: Macmillan.

Derrida, J. 1981. *Positions*, tr. A. Bass. London: The Athlone Press.

Elam, D. 1994. *Feminism and deconstruction. Ms. en Abyme*. London: Routledge.

Freud, S. 1991. Femininity. In *New introductory lectures on psychoanalysis*, tr. J. Strachey, vol. II, *The Penguin Freud Library*, 145–69. London: Penguin.

Gallop, J. 1982. *Feminism and psychoanalysis: the daughter's seduction*. London: Macmillan.

Gallop, J. 1988. *Thinking through the body*. New York: Columbia University Press.

Jardine, A. 1985. *Gynesis: configurations of woman and modernity*. Ithaca, New York: Cornell University Press.

Lacan, J. 1982. The meaning of the phallus. In *Feminine sexuality*, J. Mitchell & J. Rose (eds), 74–85. London: Macmillan.

Lyotard, J-F. 1988. *The differend: phrases in dispute*, tr. G. van den Abbeele. Manchester: Manchester University Press.

Lyotard, J-F. 1991a. Can thought go on without a body? In *The inhuman*. tr. G. Bennington and R. Bowlby, 8–23. Cambridge: Polity.

Lyotard, J-F. 1991b. Representation, presentation, unpresentable. In *The inhuman*, tr. G. Bennington and R. Bowlby, 119–28. Cambridge: Polity.

Lyotard, J-F. 1991c *Domus* and the megalopolis. In *The inhuman*, tr. G. Bennington and R. Bowlby, 191–204. Cambridge: Polity.

Readings, B. 1991. *Introducing Lyotard: art and politics*. London: Routledge.

Winterson, J. 1992. *Written on the body*. London: Jonathan Cape.

Wollstonecraft, M. [1792] 1989. *Vindication of the rights of woman*. In *The works of Mary Wollstonecraft*, J. Todd & M. Butler (eds), 7 vols. London: Pickering.

Wollstonecraft, M. [1798] 1989. *The wrongs of woman: or, Maria*. In *The works of Mary Wollstonecraft*, J. Todd & M. Butler (eds.), 7 vols. London: Pickering.

CHAPTER 5

Culture, subjectivity and the real; or, psychoanalysis reading postmodernity

Fred Botting

Introduction

What was culture? In these postmodern modern times similar questions consume history, reality and subjectivity. Where, once, culture, like the individual human subject and "his" history and reality, was assumed to be singular, unified and ordered, it is now rendered partial, fragmentary in construction and relative in value by the diverse challenges of class, sexual and postcolonial discourses as they have contested and pluralized its provenance and constitution. Since Lyotard (1984a) diagnosed the postmodern condition in terms of a discrediting of the grand narratives that once regulated the world, a host of specific language games have turned history into stories. Disavowing the possibility of a global, totalizing framework, the end of grand narratives has also signalled the end of a grand narrator. The privileged subject of discourse, this narrator, or the intellectual, for Lyotard (1984b) and Foucault (1977), is no longer a credible figure.

The concern with the dissolution of totalizing narratives and cultural homogeneity implies, given the dependence of individuals on symbolic frameworks for their sense of identity, the investment of particular intellectual positions in the general cultural field. Where one is threatened, so is the other, the loss of cultural unity coincident with the eclipse of intellectual authority. While the loss provides the occasion for mourning, the diagnosis of cultural disintegration as psychotic simultaneously recognizes and attempts to overcome the chaos of signification associated with postmodernity. The use of psychoanalytical terms like mourning and psychosis is not arbitrary. Psychoanalysis informs many positions that attempt to account for postmodernity. The versions of postmodern culture offered by Jean Baudrillard, Fredric Jameson and Terry Eagleton become entangled in, even as they try to escape, psychoanalytical frameworks. The complex and interimplicated differentiations proposed by Lacanian psychoanalysis between symbolic, imaginary and real registers problematize the boundaries between reality and fantasy and empha-size the operations of language in the constitution of subjectivity. The ramifi-cations of psychoanalytical frameworks are important for accounts of the hyper-real or aestheticized form of contemporary culture and subjectivity; they are, moreover, important for examining the ideological investments, the cultural fantasies, of positions analyzing postmodernity.

Psychoanalysis also suggests that the construction of culture depends on the way reality and subjectivity are formed. Baudrillardian hyper-reality desig-nates a reality of images, signs and simulations beyond the control and com-prehension of any particular subject. This general explosion and implosion of images, signs and meanings caused by new technologies and postmodern practices leads to history's decomposition into stories and subjects' dissolution: they become plural and decentred selves, their reality virtually absorbed into the image machines of technical reproduction where cultures proliferate and consume themselves. In the expansion of the sphere of culture that Jameson (1984) observes, not only is everything aestheticized, everything is also con-sumable. Postmodern pastiche delivers a historicism that commodifies the past.

While Jameson attempts to recover a radical past along with political agency and subjectivity, consumer culture continues to accelerate in a hyper-real direction absorbing subjects in a voracious eroticism of object and image. "Culture", indeed, has a biological sense, exploited by Baudrillard in the term "viral" to describe "a general tendency towards transsexuality which extends well beyond sex, affecting all disciplines as they lose specificity and partake of a process of confusion and contagion – a viral loss of determinacy which is the prime event among all the new events that assail us" (Baudrillard 1993: 7). In a "transeconomic", "transaesthetic", "transpolitical" world the viral contamina-tions of all boundaries present an image of culture that doubles (multiplies and divides), mutates and exceeds all regulation. Culture has become psychotic for Baudrillard (1993) and an object of loss for Jameson (1984) and Eagleton (1990).

The different reactions to postmodern culture, however, circulate around a locus that, following Lacan, can be called the real as it is differentiated from conventional, symbolized, reality. The real, a hole resisting all symbolic struc-tures and order, is the site of loss and anxiety, associated with mourning and psychosis. It is also, however, the site that activates calls for symbolic authority, for the erection of a signifier or paternal metaphor to regulate and repair the unity of the symbolic framework. As the question of reality and culture opens on to Lacan's theory of the real, what remains at stake, strangely given the pronouncements of his or her demise, is the position of the subject who held a dominant and central place in Western culture.

The real

Lacanian psychoanalysis differentiates between reality and the real. It is only the former that is directly bound up with language: "it is the world of words that creates the world of things" (Lacan 1977a: 65). What passes for the real world is "only a humanised, symbolised world" (Lacan 1988a: 87). Language, the symbolic order, determines the shape of lived reality, casting "a net over the entirety of things, over the totality of the real" (Lacan 1988a: 262). As an ideological form, language regulates the way reality is understood, perceived and lived as solid, natural and substantial. Althusser formulates his notion of ideology along these lines: "what is represented in ideology is therefore not the system of the real relations which govern the existence of individuals, but the imaginary relation of those individuals to the real conditions in which they live" (Althusser 1984: 39). From Althusser's Marxist perspective the real conditions, rather than the real itself, are the economic relations of capitalist production, a reality that has already been symbolized. It is the imaginary, however, that establishes individuals with an ideological and fundamentally misapprehended sense of their own unity and their natural place within a symbolized world.

The real is something else, escaping determination by both registers, something that cannot be determined, the point at which retrospective construction falters. Doubled, as Žižek observes, the real is both "*logically constructed* as a point which escapes symbolisation" and "the fullness of inert presence, positivity" (Žižek 1989: 169). It is the second sense that accords with Lacan's location of the real in direct opposition to the lack manifested in the symbolic register: "there is no absence in the real"; "the lack of the lack makes the real"; "the real is without fissure" (Lacan 1988b: 303, 1977b: ix, 1988b: 97). Without the absence, lack and fissure constitutive of the order of language, the real is seen as the locus of absolute plenitude that is lost when the living body is alienated in the imaginary otherness of the specular reflection and subjected to symbolic orders of signification. For the subject of analysis, the real is linked to the traumatic loss of plenitude. As trauma, or *tuche* – "the encounter with the real", an encounter that is "missed" since the real "presented itself in the form of that which is *unassimilable* in it" – "the real is beyond the *automaton*, the return, the coming back, the insistence of signs, by which we see ourselves governed by the pleasure principle" (Lacan 1977b: 53–5). The trauma is thus the point of origin that can never be reached, a lost beginning that is repeatedly posited and imagined in the movements of signification, a gap that is never possible to cross, which remains beyond signification, a leftover that can never be assimilated or mastered. The real is "impossible" (Lacan 1977b: 167).

Impossible though it must logically be, the real, as the effects of trauma demonstrate, has important effects on the subject's language and desire and in disclosing the fragility of symbolic and imaginary networks, their lack of absolute closure and consistency. As a traumatic return, the real engenders the repetitious production of signifiers that attempts to recover the loss, to cross the gap or fill the hole that the real opens up. Causing an insistence of signification in the process of dealing with the trauma, the real also freezes and dissolves the capacity for speech and desire. In his reading of Freud's interpretation of the dream of Irma's injection, Lacan describes

> an anxiety provoking image which summarises what we call the revelation of that which is least penetrable in the real, of the real lacking any possible mediation, of the ultimate real, of the essential object which isn't an object any longer, but this something faced with which all words cease and all categories fail, the object of anxiety *par excellence*. (Lacan 1988b: 164)

This object, glimpsed in the silence of Irma's symptoms at the back of her throat, is the symbol of castration, the "abyss of the feminine organ", the lost source from which all life emerges and from which the subject is forever severed. The object that stands in place of the real and reveals one's castration, one's alienation in signification, is called the *objet a*. The object *a*, like the real that it stands in place of, is doubled. For Lacan it "has emerged from some primal separation, from some self-mutilation induced by the very approach of the real" (Lacan 1977b: 83). It thus "serves as a symbol of lack, that is to say of the phallus, not as such, but only in so far as it is lacking" (Lacan 1977b: 103). It both marks the subject's alienation and establishes the possibility of an imaginary reconciliation at the point "where the subject sees himself caused as a lack by *a*, and where *a* fills the gap constituted by the inaugural division of the subject". But, Lacan goes on, "the *petit a* never crosses this gap": it is at this point of lack that the subject has to recognize himself (Lacan 1977b: 270). The object that fills but does not cross the gap can be anything that cannot be assimilated by the symbolic register. The object also constitutes the point at which the imaginary is knotted with the symbolic and the real.

The object *a* thus enables a "hole in the real" to be filled, enables the subject's projection of a fantasy of coherent reality at the same time as it continually interrupts the imaginary unity that is established. Both limit and excess, the *a* is not the object of desire but, Lacan states, the "object *in* desire" (Lacan 1977c: 28). The object is only linked to desire through the function of fantasy: "the phantasy is the support of desire; it is not the object that is the support of desire" (Lacan 1977b: 185). In fantasy, desire finds "its reference, its substratum, its precise tuning in the imaginary register" (Lacan 1977c: 14). The object *a* supports the fantasy which supports desire. But while it is the imaginary that gives desire its "precise tuning", it is the symbolic and its privileged signifier, the phallus or the paternal metaphor, that orientates the fantasy: the object thus takes the place of what the subject, alienated in signification, is symbolically deprived of, the phallus. It is the phallus, which binds the subject within symbolic and imaginary registers, which gives reality some coherence and consistency at the price of the subject's utter severance from "his very life", of the lack of his total and real being. Never able to fill the loss of the real, symbolic reality repeatedly returns to loss when there is no symbolic explanation that can cover it up.

There is a dynamic involved in the articulation of Lacanian registers that accounts for the relation between biological organisms and inert objects (the real), individual consciousness and identity (the imaginary) and linguistic and cultural regulation (the symbolic). Despite the priority of the symbolic register in the construction and maintenance of cultural identities, the dynamic relation means that symbolic networks are never stable in general or individual terms. The real repeatedly disrupts the smooth running of imaginary and symbolic economies with an unsymbolizable excess. The loss of particular objects can reopen the hole in the real: the death of another, loved, person opens a wound that symbolic reality cannot deal with, a loss that cannot be explained and in which subjects recognize their mortality and their lack in being. It is a loss that, initially, has no meaning and makes no sense, but that demands that the lack be filled through the reintegration of the phallus, of the signifier, in a process of symbolization that occurs in rituals of mourning.

The traumatic encounter with the real has other effects that, Lacan notes, are the inverse of mourning, producing not a reintegration of the subject and the Other but "*Verwerfung* [repudiation, foreclosure]" (Lacan 1977c: 37–8). Earlier seminars on psychosis argue that what is rejected in the symbolic reappears in the real and the hole that is opened up signals that the "Name-of-the-Father" or the phallus never reaches, in the subject's psychic economy, the place of the Other. Not accepting a place within the orders of language, the subject remains in opposition to the Other and thus in a position of instability, fluctuation and vacillation:

> it is the lack of the Name-of-the-Father in that place which, by the hole that it opens up in the signified, sets off a cascade of reshapings of the signifier from which the increasing disaster of the imaginary proceeds, to the point at which the level is reached at which the signifier and signified are stabilized in the delusional metaphor. (Lacan 1977a: 217)

The psychotic departs from all laws of signification, lost in a "cascade" in which any imaginary sense of unity or symbolic stability is lost in relation to anything but a particular delusional metaphor.

Mourning and psychosis are related in relation to the hole in the real: they both encounter "swarms of images" that "assume the place of the phallus". However, psychosis seizes upon one image without reference to the symbolic community that is the Other; mourning sets out to reintegrate imaginary and symbolic registers:

> there is nothing of significance that can fill the hole in the real, except the totality of the signifier. The work of mourning is accomplished at the level of the *logos*: I say *logos* rather than group or community, although group and community, being organized culturally, are its mainstays. The work of mourning is first of all performed to satisfy the disorder that is produced by the inadequacy of signifying elements to cope with the hole that has been created in existence, for it is the system of signifiers in their totality which is impeached by the least instance of mourning. (Lacan 1977c: 38)

Mourning is doubled in that it signifies the loss of the phallus, as organizing principle, and the desire for it. Moreover, mourning indicates that the phallus was never actually there, except as a function. Mourning recognizes the loss, unlike psychosis in which the subject substitutes any image or metaphor to fill the gap. The phallus, the imaginary point at which the subject finds its bearings and meaning in the community of others composed in relation to the Other, is thus mapped onto *logos*, the Name-of-the-Father in the Other. It is only in the interrelation of the two that meaning is produced. *Logos*, like the phallus, is not present, is not an object or a signifier that is rich with meaning. Rather, it is produced, not by subjects, as singular discrete beings, but by their relation to the system of signifiers that constitutes the possibility of their articulation. Mourning, even as it wants the filling of the hole in the real by the totality of the symbolic, leaves that system open to question and reformulation by the very act of mourning in which the hole, the loss, is recognized and the system's smooth running impeached.

Postmodern culture

The problem of the paternal metaphor remains a cultural phenomenon. Lacan's analysis of the real and the object *a* offers both a diagnosis, as it were, of postmodernity and a way of reading its effects on political and theoretical positions in terms of mourning and psychosis. Described by Jean-François Lyotard as "incredulity towards metanarratives" (Lyotard 1984a: xxiv), the postmodern condition describes a gap in the way the world is presented and lived, a disjunction between imaginary and symbolic registers in which a hole

in the real is manifested. The resulting multiplication of signifiers – the fragmented plethora of forms, styles and images associated with postmodernism –
corresponds to the "cascade of reshapings of the signifier", the "swarms of
images" and a "floating mass of meanings" that try to fill the hole in the real
which produces conditions of mourning and psychosis. Mourning appeals to
the Other, seeking a signifier that will arrest the play of meaning and unite the
social fabric with a total system of signifiers, an appeal to *logos*, to the paternal
metaphor. Psychosis rejects the paternal metaphor and the meaning that it
establishes and, separated from the Other, substitutes a delusional metaphor
that is invested with total significance.

Both mourning and psychosis, however, interrogate the function of the
paternal metaphor and the Other that prescribes law with a castrating "no"
that arrests the movement of signification. The postmodern condition militates against this metaphor, questioning the legitimacy of the *logos*: who lays
down the law, who says "no"? By what authority? What figure is empowered
to cut meaning from the meaningless play of signification and impose it on
others? Nonetheless, in many accounts of postmodernism just such a figure is
the object of desire: the missing signifier that binds the chain and produces
singular meaning as "the point of convergence that enables everything to be
situated retroactively and prospectively" (Lacan 1993: 268) is mourned or,
alternatively, foreclosed in psychosis by the substitution of a delusional metaphor, though the difference between paternal and delusional metaphors is
itself open to question. Variations of these different responses – manifested by
Eagleton, Baudrillard and Jameson – emerge in relation to the recalcitrant
object, postmodernity, that is stuck in the hole in the real.

In Terry Eagleton's *The ideology of the aesthetic* postmodernism is an object of
anxiety that necessitates an aggressive riposte in a return to older metaphors.
Eagleton exhumes the living presence of an idealized human figure as the
basis of a critique of the postmodern aestheticization. The ritual of mourning
fills the hole in the real with the recognizable figure of the human being. This
human figure functions as the point at which nature, truth, history and culture
coalesce. Culture, for Eagleton, supplements biological human nature, it fulfils
the lack in biological being, the needs that cannot be satisfied by frail individuals alone (Eagleton 1990: 410–12). Biological nature, transhistorical and universal, supplies the grounds for a moralizing position that legitimates an attack
on the advocates of postmodernism. The hole in the real is filled by the
authority of cultural meaning provided by Eagleton and guaranteed by
human nature and need.

The concern, however, is not the other, that needy, human body, for that
other as mirror image has already been unified by a fantasy that transcends
dualism with a unifying figure of Eagleton's paternal metaphor. The "we" that
dominates Eagleton's discourse is the anticipated unity of the human commu-

nity who, like Eagleton, are bound to recognize themselves in their own discourse. But that strange object called postmodernism remains the primary site of anxiety: it announces the lack of phallic authority that the position has already assumed. For, the postmodernist preoccupation with "a plurality of life-styles", according to Eagleton, "averts its eyes" from "the quite specific historical conditions" that permit such plurality and the checks and restrictions imposed on plurality "by our present conditions of life" (Eagleton 1990: 409). It is these conditions and limits that Eagleton sets out to identify and impose by way of human biology. And the limits are ultimately moral ones since aesthetics is a matter of evil. Postmodernist aestheticization, for Eagleton, is "revolted by the sight of virtue, unable to see truth or meaning as anything but pretentious shams with which human beings pathetically conceal from themselves the utter vacuousness of their existenc" (Eagleton 1990: 412). This cynicism is related to evil, a relation that legitimates the utter exclusion of postmodernism.

Postmodern mockery of human idealism, however, means that the human figure and the likeminded community Eagleton assumes and requires in order to have his position recognized is missing, a lost object. The human remains a fantasy; it is what should function as the Lacanian paternal metaphor, the figure that fills the empty space of the real with truth and meaning. But that empty space is left open by the unassimilable incursions of postmodernist aesthetics: the human can no longer occupy the place of the paternal metaphor. Postmodernism signifies that the Other is no longer what it used to be, that the very material conditions and reality that Eagleton invokes do not correspond to the human ideal. Humanism can no longer fully misrecognize itself, if it ever could, because the Other, in which the human is imaginarily located in the place of the paternal metaphor, the symbolic community, no longer recognizes it. Eagleton is left to mourn its passing, bitterly rebuking postmodernists along the way.

For Eagleton, positions such as Baudrillard's eclipse the possibility of arguments being grounded on a paternal metaphor like the human figure. They do, however, produce a particular subject in their diagnosis of postmodern forms, despite their vision of a world of excessive simulation. The subject that emerges is, like the culture that produces it, psychotic: the term is applicable, even though Baudrillard's position attacks psychoanalysis, since his writing remains, ironically, within a psychoanalytic purview. In the world represented by Disneyland, fantasy and reality emerge, for Baudrillard, as effects of simulation. Disneyland serves to produce the illusion that there is a real America beyond it, concealing the fact that all of America *is* Disneyland, that the real is no longer real. Thus Disneyland, "saving the reality principle" along the way, rejuvenates, in reverse "the fiction of the real" (Baudrillard 1983: 25). The retrospective inscription of the boundaries of fantasy and reality renders the latter symbolized, fictionalized, simulated: the "reality principle" replaces the real in a process of deferred action. There is, however, a sense of loss, tacitly expressed in the silence regarding the elusive real of psychoanalysis. In Baudrillard's account, the excess of the real re-emerges in the Other of culture, with subjectivity, abolished in regard to the Other, appearing elsewhere: lost and nostalgic, the subject remains a disillusioned spectator at the apocalyptic orgy of signification.

Baudrillard's postmodernity has no paternal metaphor to establish and regulate differences, to decide between sense and nonsense, between legitimate and improper meanings, with an enunciation of symbolic authority: it allows for no point at which signifier and signified can be knotted together to arrest the play of images and signification. Indeed, Baudrillard adopts an anti-metaphorical stance, refusing the possibility of attaining an external position of singularity: the excess of simulation has completely outstripped human capacities to discern or direct what is signified. The critique of metaphor is made explicit in Baudrillard's account of viral culture. There is no longer the possibility of a regulating signifier, no paternal metaphor, only an incessantly sliding metonymic chain of signifiers: "Today, metonymy – replacing the whole as well as the components, and occasioning a general commutability of terms – has built its house on the dis-illusion of metaphor" (Baudrillard 1993: 8). Moreover, Baudrillard's subject has no place in an utterly alien system of signification for there is no point at which meaning emerges, no joining of signifier to signified, no paternal metaphor to arrest the viral metonymic movement. The subject is left in a psychotic position, in the real: "for the psychosis to be triggered off, the Name-of-the-Father, *verworfen*, foreclosed, that is to say never having taken the place of the Other, must be called into symbolic opposition to the subject" (Lacan 1977a: 217). The subject is not alienated in the system of signification, the Other, but alienated, excluded from it in the foreclosure – or impossibility, for Baudrillard – of the paternal metaphor. Moreover, the subject also stands in opposition to the absolutely different Other, taking a place in the real.

For Baudrillard, the real is the American desert: "luminous, fossilized network of an inhuman intelligence, of a radical difference" (Baudrillard 1988: 6). Absolute in its difference, the desert's full nothingness becomes the mirror of American culture: "In this sense, for us the whole of America is a desert. Culture exists there in a wild state: it sacrifices all intellect, all aesthetics in a process of literal transcription into the real" (Baudrillard 1988: 99). This mirror of the desert-real absorbs all the symbols of culture in an image of the emptiness that underlies cultural production and regulation: natural deserts

denote the emptiness, the radical nudity that is the background to every human institution. At the same time they designate human

institutions as a metaphor of that emptiness and the work of man as
the continuity of the desert, culture as a mirage and as the perpetuity
of the simulacrum. (Baudrillard 1988: 63)

Culture, ironically, mirrors the emptiness of the subject who remains
absolutely separated from any meaningful or active place in systems of signification, possessed only by the delusional metaphor of this emptiness, this
"desertification of signs and men [sic]" (Baudrillard 1988: 63): the desert is the
metaphor, "the sublime form that banishes all sociality, all sentimentality, all
sexuality. Words, even when they speak of the desert, are always unwelcome"
(Baudrillard 1988: 71). Beyond words, the subject becomes pure excess, mirrored in the excessive totality of the real. But the very words in which this
psychosis is transcribed suggests a certain nostalgia for the Romantic metaphor, the "I", that transcendent figure of plenitude, that self always joyously
teetering on the brink of its own dissolution.

Jameson's (1984) examination of postmodernism's relationship, even com-
plicity, with the transnational networks of late capitalism mourns the loss of
an authoritative "I" as it attempts a more productive redefinition of the real.
Jameson's account accords with a Baudrillardian diagnosis of postmodernity,
but it rejects the implications because they leave no room for humans in the
process of social change: it is the active cultural and political interventions of
the critical Marxist intellectual that Jameson aims to preserve. This involves
the preservation of the past and a critique of the aesthetics of commodification. With an eye towards Baudrillard, Jameson states, "the approach to
the present by way of the art language of the simulacrum, or of the pastiche of
the stereotypical past, endows present reality and the openness of present history with the spell and distance of a glossy mirage" (Jameson 1984: 68). The
past is pastiched or "cannibalized" (Jameson 1984: 65–6); the density of the
present evacuated in the rush of superficial stereoscopic illusions and filmic
images termed the "hysterical sublime" (Jameson 1984: 76–7). The emerging
mutation of the space, or "hyperspace", of postmodern culture "has finally
succeeded in transcending the capacities of the individual human body to
locate itself, to organize its immediate surroundings perceptually, and
cognitively to map its position in a mappable external world" (Jameson 1984:
83). The unmappability of postmodern space is explained in Lacanian terms
as "the breakdown of the signifying chain", a "rubble of distinct and unrelated
signifiers" without a metaphor, or "paternal authority" to regulate and render
them meaningful for the subject (Jameson 1984: 72).

While the diagnosis of postmodern culture accords with Baudrillard,
Jameson's response and prognosis is quite different from the abandonment of
the subject in the real and the foreclosure of the paternal metaphor that
abandonment entails. Indeed, the prognosis is more in line with Eagleton's

Marxist-humanist critique of postmodernism, though without its explicit hostility and moralism. Like Eagleton, Jameson turns on the distinctly human figure of the subject, setting out to recuperate or salvage a form of radical past that has been lost in the general aestheticization of postmodern culture. To recover a radical past also involves the restoration of the "critical distance" that postmodern historicity consumes in the present and thus enables political agency and activity to intervene in processes of social transformation and change. This is not to be done by means of older forms of ideological critique and its underlying moralism; postmodern aesthetics has precluded that possibility (Jameson 1984: 85–6). What it requires is an engagement in aesthetic practices themselves, a process of "cognitive mapping". This process involves recourse to Lacan, mediated by Althusser's version of ideology as the imaginary relation of the subject to their real conditions of existence (Jameson 1984: 90). Cognitive mapping also involves a cognizant appeal to the function of Lacan's symbolic: the real (transglobal capitalism) is understood by the individual subject (imaginary) through the co-ordinates provided by the "subject-place of knowledge" (the subject-presumed-to-know located in the symbolic Other). For Jameson this Other is Marxian science, specifically the knowledge of late capitalism provided by Ernest Mandel (Jameson 1984: 91). The subject recovers itself to gain a "new heightened sense of its place in the global system" and regain, as an individual and collective being, "a capacity to act and struggle which is at present neutralized by our spatial as well as our social confusion" (Jameson 1984: 92).

Thus, the response to the postmodern hole in the real is, for Jameson, one of mourning. It requires the restitution of a paternal metaphor that can articulate the specific and global, the imaginary and symbolic. The metaphor that Jameson identifies among the symptoms of postmodern culture he diagnoses is the network of transglobal capitalism itself. For Jameson the fascination with communicational systems and computer technology is a "distorted figuration of something even deeper, namely the whole world system of present-day multinational capitalism" (Jameson 1984: 79–80). "The whole new decentred global network of the third stage of capital" becomes the metaphor that fills the hole in the real. The "truth of postmodernism" is grasped by means of "its fundamental object – the world space of multinational capital" (Jameson 1984: 92).

The symbolic fabric, ripped in the encounter with the postmodern real, is imaginarily repaired by way of the lost object and the paternal metaphor. The process of mourning, however, establishes Marxism as the symbolic order, a grand narrative towards which theorists, such as Foucault (1977) and Lyotard (1984b) have become avowedly incredulous, suspicious of the subject, the intellectual, on which it depends. The suspicion emerged in the wake of the political events of May 1968 in which left-wing leaders were seen to be complicit with the state they were supposed to be challenging. Their role was theorized by Foucault (1977), conversing with Gilles Deleuze on the function of intellectuals: the intellectual is an effect of totalizing bourgeois discourses and regimes of truth, already superfluous in the diverse political actions of the masses. Only the institutionally specific role of the intellectual as interrogator of forms of power is tenable for Foucault (1988), not the prophetic and prescriptive shaper of general political will.

This (bourgeois) intellectual, however, looms large in Jameson's revision of aesthetic practice since the restoration of the Marxist grand narrative involves an intellectual human subject. Stating, in distinct contrast to, and with an implicit rebuke of, Foucault's position, that left-wing cultural theorists have been intimidated by bourgeois aesthetic traditions, Jameson advocates the pedagogical and didactic functions of art in the aesthetics of cognitive mapping (Jameson 1984: 89). The knowing subject is not eclipsed by simulation; he or she can still, Jameson hopes, understand, direct and change systems of meaning and signification, whether they are postmodern or not. Artist and teacher, it seems, are central intellectual figures in the constitution of the new cultural model proposed by Jameson: they fulfil the function, rendered untenable in postmodern culture, of the paternal metaphor; they are subjects supposed to know. This position seems more wishful than accepted. Lyotard (1984b), for example, finds such a position untenable as he argues that not only is the intellectual dead, but that the roles of artists and philosophers are far from prescriptive or didactic: their task is, instead, to formulate questions rather than dictate programmes and answers. The aesthetic pedagogue that, for Jameson, is supposed to occupy the place of the intellectual is already, it seems, condemned to be an object of mourning.

In this return of the real, the return to the anxiety-generating hole, signification still circulates, rather than being arrested by a recognized paternal metaphor. The narrative that Jameson advocates as the truth of postmodernism remains out of reach, unrecognized by the Other, the symbolic cultural community he addresses. Indeed, it is the Other, imagined as a total and unifying symbolic system, that becomes the object of mourning. While the function of the paternal metaphor may be general, its specific significance and effects are restricted to particular cultural and institutional communities: there might be no Other of the Other, no final metalanguage, but there may well be different Others. To wish for a homogeneous and global symbolic network is, perhaps, the most aesthetic of all gestures, one that, eclipsing the virtualization of technological realities, imagines the obliteration of the real. In the contestations of postmodern culture, however, the paternal metaphor, as *logos*, truth and law, remains open to question.

References

Althusser, L. 1984. *Essays in ideology*. London: Verso.

Baudrillard, J. 1983. *Simulations*, tr. P. Foss, P. Patton and P. Beitchman. New York: Semiotext(e).

Baudrillard, J. 1988. *America*, tr. C. Turner. London: Verso.

Baudrillard, J. 1993. *The transparency of evil*, tr. J. Benedict. London: Verso.

Eagleton, T. 1990. *The ideology of the aesthetic*. Oxford: Basil Blackwell.

Foucault, M. 1977. Intellectuals and power. In *Language, counter-memory, practice*, tr. D. F. Bouchard and S. Simon, 205–17. Ithaca, New York: Cornell University Press.

Foucault, M. 1988. The concern for truth. In *Michel Foucault: politics, philosophy, culture*, L. D. Kritzman (ed.), 255–67. London: Routledge.

Jameson, F. 1984. Postmodernism, or the cultural logic of late capitalism. *New Left Review* **146**, 53–92.

Lacan, J. 1977a. *Ecrits*, tr. A. Sheridan. London: Tavistock.

Lacan, J. 1977b. *The four fundamental concepts of psychoanalysis*, tr. A. Sheridan. London: Penguin.

Lacan, J. 1977c. Desire and the interpretation of desire in *Hamlet*. *Yale French Studies* **55/56**, 11–52.

Lacan, J. 1988a. *The seminar of Jacques Lacan I*, tr. J. Forrester. Cambridge: Cambridge University Press.

Lacan, J. 1988b. *The seminar of Jacques Lacan II*, tr. S. Tomaselli. Cambridge: Cambridge University Press.

Lacan, J. 1993. *The psychoses*, tr. R. Grigg. London: Routledge.

Lyotard, J-F. 1984a. *The postmodern condition*, tr. G. Bennington and B. Massumi. Manchester: Manchester University Press.

Lyotard, J-F. 1984b. *Tombeau de l'intellectual et autres papiers*. Paris: Galilee.

Žižek, S. 1989. *The sublime object of ideology*. London: Verso.

CHAPTER 6

Adorno, Oakeshott and the voice of poetry

Andrew Edgar and Peter Sedgwick

Introduction

We intend to explore the possibility of establishing a critical relationship to the dominant position of science within contemporary culture. At the core of postmodernist thinking is the rejection of the Enlightenment project. Insofar as this project is manifest, at least in part, in the rise of the natural sciences, we share some common ground with postmodernist criticisms. However, by appealing to two Hegelian authors, the German critical theorist Theodore Adorno and the British political philosopher Michael Oakeshott, we suggest that it is possible to engage in criticism of the Enlightenment without thereby abandoning the critical and emancipatory potential inherent in the Enlightenment project itself. After introducing those themes of Hegel's philosophy that are relevant to this argument, specifically the concepts of actuality and reality, we rehearse Oakeshott's account of human culture in terms of the metaphor of conversation, and the tension he identifies between the "voices" of science and poetry. This is complemented by Adorno's account of late capitalism, and the ambiguous place enjoyed by tradition, which is at once subordinated to commodity exchange and yet remains indicative of that which is radically other to capitalism. In conclusion, we suggest that the two authors converge in a micro-politics that is quite distinct from that celebrated by postmodernism.

The Enlightenment and Hegelianism

As the co-author, along with Max Horkheimer, of the *Dialectic of enlightenment* (Horkheimer & Adorno 1972), Adorno is acknowledged by a number of commentators, such as Docherty (1993: 3), as a precursor of much postmodernist thought. Writing towards the end of the Second World War, they challenge the Enlightenment's self-interpretation as the progressive emancipation of humanity from myth and superstition, by means of scientific reason. From the perspective of Enlightenment thought, science would replace mythical and superstitious accounts of natural (and social) phenomena with scientific accounts that are open to empirical testing and verification. This ambition found its most forceful expression in positivism (not least insofar as positivism sought to reject, as meaningless metaphysics, all knowledge claims that failed to meet the criteria of empirical verifiability demanded of science). Political and economic emancipation would be realized through the increasingly sophisticated application of theoretical science and technology to the task of manipulating nature to human ends. Horkheimer & Adorno counter this emancipatory claim by arguing that scientific reason fails to emancipate itself from the mythical thinking within which it has its origins. Confident in its own superiority over all other forms of thought, Enlightenment reason is unable to recognize that which is alien to it, and specifically the (external and human) nature that it seeks to dominate, except in the Enlightenment's own formal and instrumental terms. Horkheimer & Adorno thereby anticipate postmodernism, insofar as they concur that Enlightenment thought serves to elect a single form of reason as universal, and that it thereby becomes repressive of the human subject. While the Enlightenment celebrates the entwining of knowledge and power, Enlightenment knowledge serves only to empower (or emancipate) a specific form of human subjectivity.

What separates Adorno from much postmodernist thinking is his continued commitment to the emancipatory ideals of the Enlightenment. The claim that instrumental reason is not the only form that rationality can take, and that the Enlightenment subject is not the only form of human subjectivity, is used by certain postmodernists to defend an extreme pluralism, that culminates in the glorification of a montage of diverse localities, histories, moralities, sciences and ultimately truths and realities. From Adorno's perspective, a one-sided emphasis upon difference and particularity is as problematic as the Enlightenment's one-sided emphasis upon unity and universality. Postmodernism degenerates into a relativism, such that moral, political and even scientific criticism is inhibited because that which one seeks to criticize stands within an alternative, and most importantly incommensurable, cultural location. Further, the totality of human culture itself slips from the analyst's grasp, for the totality can only ever be constituted from a particular perspective. Lyotard expresses something of this in his claim that postmodernism is characterized by an incredulity before metanarratives (Lyotard 1984: xxiv). For Adorno, the loss of a critical position allows the repressive potential within the Enlightenment (or indeed any other culture) to continue unchecked. By abandoning the Enlightenment ideals of human emancipation, postmodernism does not merely remain passive before repression, but serves the very reproduction of those repressive practices.

Michael Oakeshott is a far less obvious source of guidance in the face of postmodernism than Adorno. During much of his career Oakeshott was a somewhat marginal figure in British political philosophy. His work belongs to a conservative tradition, seemingly at odds with the predominant concerns of neo-Marxists such as Adorno, or even the post-Marxist elements of post-modernism. However, on the one hand his philosophy, like Adorno's, is steeped in the study of Hegel, and as we will suggest, it is because Hegel is such an ambiguous figure in the Enlightenment, that both Adorno and Oakeshott stand in a crucial position to both the Enlightenment and its critics. On the other hand, Oakeshott anticipates a number of postmodernist concerns, including the cultural construction of incommensurable realities. Equally, he strives to challenge notions of the identity of the human subject. What is crucial for our account, however, as with Adorno, is the potential that Oakeshott provides for engaging with the most potent aspects of post-modernist criticism of the Enlightenment project, without losing sight of that project itself, and thus without losing the potential for critical comment.

The place that Hegel plays in this strategy must be outlined. On the one hand Hegel appears to be the prime exponent of formal Enlightenment rea-son, and indeed Lyotard sees Hegel as providing one of the metanarratives that serve to legitimate modern science (Lyotard 1984: 31–7). In the *Encyclo-paedia of the philosophical sciences* (Hegel 1892), Hegel seeks to account for all creation by revealing the logical structure that underlies nature, human psy-chology and human culture. On the other hand, *The phenomenology of mind* (Hegel 1807) suggests a far more cautious project, in which absolute truth, while continually sought, is permanently deferred. Humanity can, at best, grasp truth through a series of more or less distorted images or illusions.

The problematic position of truth may be introduced through the Hegelian distinction between "reality" (*Realität*) and "actuality" (*Wirklichkeit*). "Reality" may be taken to refer to the (social and natural) world as it exists, at present and in the past. This world, which is comprehended as a determinate arrange-ment of facts, is presupposed as the subject-matter of the empirical sciences. In contrast, the "actual" refers to the perfection of reality. Hegel summarizes this by famously remarking that: "What is rational is actual and what is actual is rational" (Hegel 1952: 10). Robert Solomon notes that this "is *not* the horren-dous political statement that what is real, that is, whatever is the case, is rational and therefore right" (Solomon 1983: 275). The actual is an ideal real-ity, and as such bears a superficial correspondence to the scientific and politi-cal goal of Enlightenment reason. However, the actual is not to be achieved by a simple application of existing forms of knowledge. At his most insightful, Hegel is aware that what counts as knowledge depends upon the community in which knowledge claims are made. The imperfection of any existing society will thereby serve to corrupt both the predominant understanding of how knowledge should be acquired, and the ideal that is to be sought through the application of that knowledge. The distinction between the real and the actual is thus intended to facilitate the criticism of the real. If deployed within social science or political philosophy, it entails that the student cannot rest content with the mere description or even explanation of social reality. The profound understanding of social reality recognizes that society is inadequate to its own ideal, and thus that it can be, and indeed ought to be, otherwise than it is. The ideal stands as the Other to the community that formulates it.

The distinction between the real and the actual is as implausible in the context of postmodernism as it is in that of Enlightened positivism. While Enlightenment reason culminates in a scientific and economic culture that reproduces itself through the overwhelming affirmation of the real, the post-modern concern with a depthless (albeit fluid and mobile) surface similarly inhibits the recognition of any potential for fundamental change, or criticism. By indicating, albeit in broad terms, how the distinction between reality and actuality informs the work of Adorno and Oakeshott we will seek to demonstrate the importance of theorizing "actuality" for maintaining critical social thought in the face of a postmodernist plurality of realities.

Oakeshott and conversation

Oakeshott characterizes "civilized human beings" as inheritors "of a conversation, begun in the primeval forests and extended and made more articulate in the course of centuries" (Oakeshott 1962: 199). The unpacking of this metaphor suggests a critical intention. A conversation is characterized in opposition to the formal logic of the discourse of science. Conversation therefore does not entail a co-operative inquiry pursued towards the goal of discovering truth, or indeed to any other goal. Conversation is not "designed to yield an extrinsic profit", but is rather "an unrehearsed intellectual adventure", and is like gambling, where the reward lies not in winning or losing, but in the wager itself. Further, as there are no rigid rules governing the speculations of conversation, so there are no grounds to exclude or to rank certain types of conversationalist (Oakeshott 1962: 198). Oakeshott may be seen to anticipate not merely the postmodernist concern with openness and the transgression of boundaries, but more specifically Lyotard's search for a "dissensus" (of continued and open-ended debate) in the face of a conversational consensus or final agreement that would mark only a cessation of creative thought. Oakeshott may, however, be interpreted as cautiously but firmly outlining a Utopian image of human society. Conversation marks the anticipation of the actual in real society. As we will demonstrate below, he develops this by finding its fullest manifestation in artistic activity.

Oakeshott claims that the civilized conversation has become "boring" in contemporary society, for it has come to be dominated by the voices of science and politics (Oakeshott 1962: 202). More emphatically, a conversation dominated by a single voice is a form of barbarism (Oakeshott 1962: 201). While for Oakeshott science must participate in the conversation, its current domination, and more significantly the culture that legitimates that domination and serves to exclude alternative voices, fundamentally falsifies civilized human existence. In effect, positivistic philosophies serve to deny the non-teleological (and qualitative) activity that must ground the judgemental and teleological, and this denial is crucial to the new barbarism that threatens human civilization.

Oakeshott's critical position may be explicated by considering the account he gives of the relationship between the knowing subject and the known object. (Again, in his emphasis on the construction of reality, and the embeddedness of the human subject in particular social relations of knowledge and practice, Oakeshott anticipates key postmodernist themes.) Oakeshott's criticism of contemporary society focuses on the manner in which the relationship between subject and object has been distorted or forgotten, and thus upon the manner in which the reality of the known object is constructed. Oakeshott expresses the subject–object relationship through the concepts of "self" and "non-self". The self is presented as the primordial activity of "imagining", which is to say, the generation of images (Oakeshott 1962: 204). The images that are made and recognized are images of the subject's environment or non-self. Neither self nor non-self exist independently; rather, each generates the other. The images (and even the material) of the non-self do not pre-exist the self, and nor does the self exist as some potential or substance prior to the activity of imagining a particular portion of the non-self. Reality is not prior to self or non-self, but is "a world of experience within which self and non-self divulge themselves to reflection" (Oakeshott 1962: 204). This entails that the nature of the self (and not just the non-self) is dependent on the mode of imagining in which it is engaged at any given moment.

Oakeshott focuses on three principle modes of imagination: science, practical activity and poetry. Each is an idiomatic voice, and necessary participant in the conversation of human civilization. The idiosyncrasy of these voices is most acutely expressed in the assertion that they are fundamentally incommensurable to each other. Oakeshott illustrates this by suggesting that to "speak of H_2O as 'the chemical formula for water' is to speak in a confused manner", precisely insofar as the activity of science ("H_2O") is confused with practical activity ("water") (Oakeshott 1962: 222). A conversation cannot then be held strictly between voices, for they each talk in a unique language, and in that the reality of the non-self is constructed through that language, each talks about a unique reality. Yet, Oakeshott does not rest with the sterility of mere incommensurability. Incommensurability does not inhibit creative movement between voices, although a conversation can move from one voice to another only insofar as the modes of imagining supersede one another. (For example, an unattainable object of desire may become a mere object of contemplation, so that the practical voice gives way to the poetic; or initial wonder may be focused into scientific curiosity, and thus the poetic gives way to the scientific.) In such successions, an image that has been constructed in one context is transferred to another. While the image may be constant, the reality to which it refers changes, as the relationship between self and non-self changes (Oakeshott 1962: 223 and 238). The idea of voices succeeding each other is developed by presenting each voice as an escape (or in Oakeshott's own Enlightenment terminology, "emancipation") from the conditions that determine the idiom of the other voices (Oakeshott 1962: 239–40).

The three principal voices may be considered in more detail. In science, the self orientates to the non-self in terms of the latter's status as fact. The language in which scientists communicate, and in which the images of the real world are constructed, is restricted by the demands of mathematical measurement. The world of science is thus a world *sub specie quantitatis* (Oakeshott 1962: 212–16). This account is coherent with the postmodernist criticism of the Enlightenment. As Docherty expresses this:

> A mathematical consciousness thus produces the world, not surprisingly, as mathematics. So a desired knowledge of the world is reduced to the merest *anamnesis* [recollection], in which the consciousness never cognizes the world as it is, but rather *recognizes* the world as its own proper image and correlate. (Docherty 1993: 6)

If barbarism is the domination of a single voice, and most significantly in the present age the voice of science, this entails the quantification, not merely of the natural world, but also of the human community. In effect, pure domination by science would impoverish the language available for the human community, and reduce conversation to mere social administration.

Oakeshott effectively identifies two forms of practical activity that may be characterized as the technical-practical and the moral-practical, respectively. In technical activity the self has the specific goals of seeking pleasure and avoiding pain. The non-self is a means to the self's end, in a relationship characteristic of the domination of nature. This may entail the failure of the self to recognize the human non-self as another subject. In contrast, the moral attitude entails what Oakeshott terms the "approval" or "disapproval" of images. The self situates itself as an equal member of a community of selves. Socialization into a moral community is ultimately constitutive of the human's identity as an agent, for the human comes to consciousness in a world illuminated by a moral practice and as a relatively helpless subject in it . . . There is no agency which is not the acknowledgement of a moral practice, and no moral conduct which is not an exercise of agency. (Oakeshott 1975: 63)

Participation in the community therefore entails that the subject must engage in moral practice. Some will perform better than others, and there may be substantive differences according to gender, age and other social divisions, but no-one can choose to renounce the practice altogether. Moral practice provides a cement for the human community, and a bulwark against the Hobbesian extremes of individual desire (Oakeshott 1962: 206–12). The openness and diversity that Oakeshott attributes to moral practice does not, however, appear to provide a viable alternative to postmodernist relativism. This alternative comes, more radically, through the voice of poetry.

Poetic activity is characterized by the irrelevance of questions of facticity or utility. Pleasure and approval are similarly inappropriate. The non-teleological activity of contemplation is concerned with its images only insofar as they give what Oakeshott terms "delight" (Oakeshott 1962: 216–22). Oakeshott's aesthetics centres on the disinterestedness of this poetic activity. As such, the language of poetry is distinct from all other languages in not being "symbolic". Characterizing poetry through a deliberate paradox, as a language without a vocabulary, he rejects any aesthetic theories that would reduce the images of art not merely to referents or allegories but to the expression or imitation of any more primitive images (be they emotions or physical objects). Poetic images are not governed by rules (be they akin to the rules of a game or of an economy), and they are not tools for some extrinsic purpose (Oakeshott 1962: 234–5). Poetry is thereby presented in negative terms, in distinction from all other acts of imagination. (One may suggest that Oakeshott's account is reflexively structured. Just as poetry evades representation, so Oakeshott's account of poetry respects that evasion.) Oakeshott does not merely oppose the voice of poetry to other activities, but rather suggests that the voice of poetry expresses an antipathy between scientific and practical (including moral) activities and civilized society itself. The incommensurability of the voice of poetry is thus of another order to the incommensurability that exists between the scientific and practical voices, and it is in this other order that the critical ground of Oakeshott's project lies.

Contemplative activity is unique, in that, while it bears within itself the very pattern of civilized life, it can never of itself constitute the basis for a total life. (There is no *vita contemplativa*, Oakeshott claims.) Oakeshott's summary comment that poetry "is a sort of truancy, a dream within the dream of life, a wild flower planted among our wheat", is acutely understated (Oakeshott 1962: 247). Society may indeed continue without poetry, but such a society (even given the precondition of a moral life) is a false, or barbaric, society. Barbarism is the end of conversation, while poetry is conversation's epitome. It may be suggested that the difficulty of articulating precisely what Oakeshott means by the voice of poetry stems from the Utopian intention of poetry. Poetry, through its close correspondence with the mode of civilized society itself, in that both are essentially free, open and purposeless activities, is an anticipation of a perfected society. The incommensurability of the poetic voice is thus the incommensurability that exists between a perfect society and the corruption of existing society. Poetic activity is the moment of actuality, pitted against the reality of mundane social existence. It is the struggle to articulate an ideal that exceeds real's capacity for representation and imagination. In terms of social science, what this entails is that poetry remains open to the voice of the Other, of that which is repressed in contemporary social formations. An approach to cultural theory that listens to the voice of poetry thereby avoids the positivistic tendency of merely representing reality, and the postmodernist concern with surface. The substance of such an approach may be worked out through reference to Adorno's criticism of contemporary capitalism.

Adorno and tradition

It may be noted that Adorno's analysis of society is firmly rooted within Marxism, and what may be seen as the modernist (and thus Enlightenment) project of late-nineteenth-century sociology (Adorno 1969–70, 1987). On the one hand, Adorno seeks to retain the critical potential of Marxism, not least in that Marx's analysis of commodity fetishism provides him with a model of critical analysis. Similarly, he draws on the work of Durkheim and Weber in developing an account of capitalism. On the other hand, insofar as the *Dialectic of Enlightenment* (Horkheimer & Adorno 1972) questions the Enlightenment concept of historical progress, it also undermines any formulation of historical materialism that is premised on the presupposition of progress, or any sociological project that presupposes the unambiguous role of the social sciences in the emancipation of humanity.

If the work of Marx, Durkheim and Weber serves the analysis of modernity, then Adorno may be seen to propose an analysis of a postmodern society, in the sense of a social formation that exists after modernism. While contemporary society is still to be analyzed in terms of capitalism, it is a late capitalism, specifically insofar as the progressive and emancipatory potential of Marx's capitalism has been stifled. This society is characterized in terms of the domination of exchange value and the mathematical quantification of science and technology in all areas of social life. The commodity's use-value, that in early capitalism represented a moment of subjective freedom and qualitative uniqueness, for it represented the grounds upon which the consumer freely chose or rejected a commodity, is undermined by what Adorno calls the "culture industry". The consumer in late capitalism does not choose freely, but only within the limits dictated by advertising and the leisure industries. Conversely, the revolutionary tension posited by the young Marx between the forces and relations of production is released, for modern administrative and management techniques bind together the two sides within a single systematic totality. While class conflict is not thereby eliminated, its manifestation and practical articulation is curtailed. Adorno's model of contemporary society is ultimately Oakeshott's world *sub specie quantitatis*.

The quantifying approach of Enlightenment science is mirrored in, and serves to reproduce, the transformation of (qualitative) use-value into (quantitative) exchange-value in commodity exchange. The exclusive emphasis on data that can be subjected to quantification, or that can be deployed to the ends of the existing economic and administrative systems, serves the reproduction of reality, at the expense of the potential of the society to be otherwise. The reduction of qualitative difference to quantitative difference, such that the calculation of exchange-value becomes the dominant principle of all bourgeois thought, does violence to the human subject by objectifying it. Both the value that the subject gives to the object in consumption, and the subjectivity that is incorporated into the object in its production are concealed, as they come to appear to be inherent properties of the object itself, independent of the human subject and human society. The possibility of changing the object (and ultimately of changing human society) is thereby undermined, for the dominant culture of rational administration is incapable of acknowledging subjectivity, and thus that which is fundamentally different from the system, as anything other than an irrational and idiosyncratic irrelevance (Adorno 1978: 69–70). Late capitalism is underpinned by the continual scientific and administrative affirmation of the real. Postmodernist thinking is powerless in response to this. By positing itself as incommensurable to Enlightenment reason it leaves itself defenceless against marginalization as mere subjective idiosyncrasy. At worst, it serves to legitimate what passes for subjectivity (in the administered choice of consumer goods) as genuine subjectivity. Baudrillard's hyper-reality, while bearing close comparison with Adorno's work on the culture industry as an analysis of contemporary consumer culture, ultimately has no resources to recognize and mark the falsehood of the society it describes. Critical practice thus collapses into an active participation in a system one cannot, in any case, escape.

Adorno himself is typically seen as expressing resignation over the possibility of changing late capitalism, and thus resignation at the consequent failure of all forms of resistance. Oakeshott avoids the deepest pessimism of Adorno's vision, principally by making the moment of moral practice, in which the human non-self is acknowledged as a fellow self, irreducible. In Adorno's vision of contemporary capitalism, even this moment has been superseded by positivistic science and technology. Adorno may be seen to respond to this condition through an analysis of tradition, that at once engages with the problem of writing history (in an ultimately static society, and after the undermining of metanarratives of progress) and serves to fuse Oakeshott's moral practice with the Utopian and critical voice of poetry.

Adorno observes that the term "tradition" suggests a process of more or less intimate and personal transmission between individuals and generations (Adorno 1977: 310). Tradition, as a defining characteristic of pre-industrial society, constitutes a network of substantive obligations and social competences. Adorno thereby situates Oakeshott's moral practice in pre-Enlightenment communities. In late capitalism, however, traditionally constituted moral practices provide only the semblance of qualitative subjectivity in an otherwise quantified, and formal, social structure. This occurs because tradition is itself subject to the administrative process of positivist science, and thus facilitates the intrusion of rational administration into moral practice. The moral self becomes an illusion, ultimately insofar as tradition is merely functional to the reproduction of the existing social system. In sum, Adorno entertains a possibility that Oakeshott overtly denies: that a society could remain viable despite the substantive exclusion of the moral practical voice. However, by entertaining the possibility of a barbaric society, Oakeshott suggests that society can continue despite the conditions of civilization having been withdrawn. It is here that his project once more coincides with Adorno's, and diverges from postmodernism. For Oakeshott, the denial of the voice of poetry is characteristic of barbarism; for Adorno, while barbarism is grounded in the quantification of the subject, it is poetry that must generate a moment of resistance to barbarism. The judgement of barbarism remains anathema to postmodernist relativism.

Adorno's alternative to Oakeshott's account may briefly be outlined through consideration of the antinomy that lies at the heart of his essay on tradition: nothing should be invoked from tradition, for such invocation serves the justification of a false society; and yet if anything from the past is forgotten, this opens the way to inhumanity (Adorno 1977: 315). From the positivistic viewpoint of the voice of science, tradition is that which contemporary society has surpassed. From one perspective, it is old-fashioned or out-moded. It is a part with the idiosyncratic and subjective. However, in a society characterized by quantification and objectification, the traditional may be deployed as the simulation of subjectivity and quality. It is at this point that the historicism characteristic of postmodernism may be noted. Jameson defines historicism, with specific reference to the development of postmodern architecture, as "the random cannibalization of all the styles of the past, the play of random stylistic allusion" (Jameson 1984: 65–6). Coherent with the rejection of the possibility of writing a grand historical narrative, the surface features of the past may be appropriated, sundered from their original historical and social contexts. History is thereby reproduced through pastiche. For Adorno the naïvety and seeming randomness of such a montage technique is already suspect. He suggests that a carefully administered tradition can be appropriated and applied "like putty" to capitalist society, giving illusory reassurance against the atomization of contemporary society (Adorno 1977: 312).

The mere appeal by the poet and artist to this condoned past subordinates her or him to the demands of capitalism. While Oakeshott's voice of poetry may remain incommensurable to positivistic science, a simulation of poetry may serve purely economic ends. More specifically, attempts at restoring the past conceal the fact that the traditional material resists restoration to what it once was (Adorno 1977: 316). Paradoxically for postmodernism, appropriation falsifies the past, making it too readily commensurable with the present. While the popularity of nostalgic images of market places and half-timbered houses may be indicative of a yearning for a better life (and thus of the contemporary betrayal of the Enlightenment hope), more significantly such images sanitize the past, stripping it of actual inhumanity and sacrifice. To forget this suffering, and to fail to recognize it in the material drawn from tradition, or to suppose that the suffering has been redeemed in the Enlightened equality or postmodernist consumerism of contemporary society, is to betray both the past and the present. In Oakeshott's terms, it is to fail to recognize the human subject in the non-self. Adorno's antinomy may therefore be seen to focus on the problem that the recall of the past submits the past to the sway of reality. For Adorno, the moment of actuality in the past is the moment of unacknowledged suffering and of a yearning for something other. This is lost to positivism and postmodernism alike.

The redemption of this moment of actuality from the corruption of tradition is crucial. Adorno identifies certain "significant traditionalists" within early-twentieth-century German literature. These include Stefan George, his followers and Hugo von Hofmannsthal (Adorno 1977: 315). The profound traditionalist does not, like proponents of a postmodernist heritage industry, merely strip images from their context (Adorno 1977: 313). Rather, tradition is turned against the expectations of contemporary society by revealing, as already hidden within the object, its alienness and distance from the present. Adorno thus champions those who throw ephemera, and that which has been neglected, overruled or judged to be "antiquated", against the orthodox demands for immortality, or permanence, within the traditional canon (Adorno 1977: 317). Adorno thereby questions the inherent meaningfulness of aesthetic tradition, and thus of history itself, as forcibly as the postmodernists, insofar as the rules governing the construction and articulation of historical and practical images are disrupted. For Adorno, this culminates in the "absurdity" of Beckett's theatre (Adorno 1977: 318). The disruption is how-ever not brought about by the mere absence of rational order as suggested by postmodern montage. The disruption is disciplined through a recognition of the depth of the actual, in opposition to the mere surface of the postmodernist real. The voice of poetry is the voice of the suffering Other, and is found, not in great works or accepted standards of excellence, but in the aesthetic trans-formation of the mundane and ephemeral remnants of moral practice.

The politics of everyday life

Culture can perhaps be characterized in terms of the manner in which humanity constitutes both its environment and itself. We have attempted to explore Oakeshott's and Adorno's negotiation of a critical stance towards a society that they see as being constituted through the domination of a narrow conception of science and scientific activity. Both have therefore been seen to share postmodernism's suspicion of Enlightenment reason and the consequent domination of nature. They do not, however, abandon the Enlightenment project itself. Certain trends within postmodernist culture, celebrating differ-ence and surface, become congruent with the very social and technological administration that is the epitome of Enlightenment reason. In contrast, we suggest that Oakeshott and Adorno yield a micro-politics of a quite distinct sort to that championed within postmodernism. For both authors the under-standing and constitution of the particular is to be sustained only through a critical relationship to a universal. We suggest that this may be grasped in the Hegelian relationship of the real, as the fragmentary surface of contemporary society, and the actual, as a critical depth and potential present within it.

For Oakeshott, the voice of poetry struggles to articulate the actual, in the eternally unsatisfied aspiration to a more genuine form of social practice. The weakness in Oakeshott's approach lies in the danger that focusing on the voice of poetry alone permits a degeneration into a stoic aesthetic, itself akin to some postmodernist theorization of the sublime. Radically incommensurable poetic images have no determinate relationship to a society *sub specie quantitatis*. Adorno maintains a moment of universality through a philosophy of suspicion. He assumes that all surfaces, however attractive, are underpinned by a repres-sive depth. The apparent fragmentation and subjectivization of society is thus rejected in favour of a theoretical model of total administration. Finding him-self before the macro-structure of society in the same position of impotence as the postmodernist, albeit that Adorno can acknowledge and begin to theorize this position, we have suggested that his later work, at least, sees him with-drawing into a politics of everyday life. The actual is articulated through an aesthetic reappropriation of mundane and local practices. In contrast to Oakeshott's account of the voice of poetry, the aesthetic is not a pure free play, but is concretely grounded. The voice of poetry thus comes to infuse moral practice, convicting the human agent of his or her own falsehood, and so articulating at once human suffering and an aspiration to a better society.

References

Adorno, T. W. 1969–70. Society. *Salmagundi* **10–11**, 144–53.

Adorno, T. W. 1977, Über Tradition. In *Gesammelte Schriften*, vol. X, 310–20. Frankfurt: Suhrkamp.

Adorno, T. W. 1978. *Minima moralia*. London: Verso.

Adorno, T. W. 1987. Late capitalism or industrial society. In *Modern German sociology*, V. Meja et al. (eds), 232–47. New York: Columbia University Press.

Docherty, T. (ed.) 1993. *Postmodernism: a reader*. Hemel Hempstead, England: Harvester Wheatsheaf.

Hegel, G. W. F. [1892] 1952. *The logic of Hegel*, 2nd edn. From the *Encyclopaedia of the philosophical sciences*, W. Wallace (ed.). Oxford: Oxford University Press.

Hegel, G. W. F. [1807] 1967. *The phenomenology of mind*, tr. J. B. Baillie. New York: Harper & Row.

Horkheimer, M. & T. W. Adorno 1972. *Dialectic of enlightenment*. London: Allen Lane.

Jameson, F. 1984. Postmodernism, or the cultural logic of late capitalism. *New Left Review* **146**, 53–92.

Lyotard, J-F. 1984. *The postmodern condition: a report on knowledge*. Manchester: Manchester University Press.

Oakeshott, M. 1962. The voice of poetry in the conversation of mankind. In *Rationalism in politics and other essays*, M. Oakeshott (ed.), 197–247. London: Methuen.

Oakeshott, M. 1975. *On human conduct*. Oxford: Clarendon Press.

Solomon, R. C. 1983. *In the spirit of Hegel: a study of G. W. F. Hegel's phenomenology of spirit*. Oxford: Oxford University Press.

CHAPTER 7

Representing AIDS:
the textual politics of health discourse

Karen Atkinson and Rob Middlehurst

Introduction

Debates around postmodernism raise a number of intriguing issues for those
of us involved in interdisciplinary approaches to critical textual analysis. At a
time when we are witnessing the recasting of cultural studies to make better
use of the conceptual tools of linguistics (see Johnson 1987, Montgomery &
Allan 1992), there also exists a considerable amount of discussion amongst language researchers regarding the most appropriate way to engage with cultural
theory (see Fowler et al. 1979, Kramarae et al. 1984, Chilton 1985, 1988,
Fairclough 1989, 1992, 1993, Fowler 1991, Cameron 1992, van Dijk 1993). It
is in recognition of these recent developments that we seek to introduce for this
chapter an interdisciplinary approach to the study of texts, one which makes
several key linkages between cultural and literary theory, on the one hand, and
the critical study of discourse, on the other hand. In this way, we aim to redress
the failure of much postmodernist analysis of language to attend to linguistic
specificity.

Questions regarding the manufacture and institutional legitimation of social
inequality, together with how counter-power challenges these forces, are
axiomatic as prioritized concerns in the critical theorization of culture. In
contrast, the attention paid to such socio-political issues in language studies
has been relatively minimal. Since the late 1970s, Critical Linguistics (CL) has
sought to account for how language functions ideologically through texts. A
wide variety of studies have been undertaken of different types of texts, all of
which render explicit the implication of language in relations of power and
resistance. Significantly, however, even here scant regard has been given to the
fact that texts are multiply read and their meanings negotiated, even resisted.
The discursive contestation of meaning has been largely ignored, and CL has
consequently been criticized for neglecting how discourse itself is an integral
part of the dynamic struggle for socio-political and cultural change.

More recently, those researchers engaged in Critical Discourse Analysis (CDA) have been paying closer attention to how issues of power and resistance inter-relate with the ways in which texts work. Fairclough (1993: 135) explains that CDA aims:

> to systematically explore often opaque relationships of causality and determinism between (a) discursive practices, events and texts, and (b) wider social and cultural structures, relations and processes; to investigate how such practices, events and texts arise out of and are ideologically shaped by relations of power and struggles over power; and to explore how the opacity of these relationships between discourse and society is itself a factor securing power and hegemony.

In recognizing ideological conflict as being discursively constituted, CDA attempts to show how "texts" are inextricably linked with the social relations of signification indicative of the society within which they are produced and consumed. Research studies have engaged with the task of explicating the precise mechanisms by which the forces of hegemony underpin "preferred" definitions, how narratives structure the popular inflection of "common sense" and how discourses work to "legitimize" or "naturalize" the iniquitous social divisions of class, gender, race, ethnicity, sexuality and so forth, within complex matrices of power.

The materiality of meaning as a site of struggle is nowhere more apparent than within the "linguistic battlefield" (Callen 1990) of HIV and AIDS. By the end of September 1994, the number of AIDS cases recorded in the UK totalled 9,865, and those known to be infected with the HIV virus had reached 22,581.[1] The state, after announcing in 1986 that £20m was to be set aside for public health education, began its information campaign the following year by way of media advertisements and a promise to send an information leaflet to every home in Britain. In a tone that was to characterize government-sponsored HIV and AIDS information campaigns for quite some time, television advertisements forebodingly warned of the risks to health through "tombstone" and "iceberg" imagery. Right from the outset then, the scene was being set for HIV and AIDS to be ideologically constructed in particular ways.

The culture of AIDS discourse

Theorizing the cultural politics of AIDS discourse in the context of recent debates about postmodernity is important to understanding how relations of power, resistance and language are ideologically entangled. In this section, we offer a brief, and thus necessarily selective, overview of several studies pertinent to the larger politicization of AIDS discourse. In so doing, we are also providing a basis for our own textual analysis of health promotion materials that follows in the subsequent section.

Several works highlight how AIDS constitutes a site for a discursive struggle for meanings. For example, one of the earliest and most influential studies that drew critical attention to specific linguistic features of AIDS discourse is Susan Sontag's essay "AIDS and its metaphors". This work complements an earlier essay "Illness as metaphor" which was based on Sontag's own experience of suffering from cancer. Implicit in Sontag's argument is that language, especially meanings encapsulated in metaphors, construct our representations of the world of experience (Ortony 1979, Lakoff & Johnson 1980). Both of her essays seek to elucidate and to provide a liberation from the constraints of "metaphoric thinking" (Sontag 1991: 3).

Specifically, Sontag (1991: 179) argues that AIDS needs to be "much better understood and, above all, treatable . . . much in the way of individual experience and social policy depends on the struggle for rhetorical ownership of the illness: how it is possessed, assimilated in argument and in cliché". She claims that the metaphors associated with AIDS "cannot be distanced just by abstaining from them. They have to be exposed, criticized, belaboured, used up" (Sontag 1991: 179). Although she is also critical of the authoritarianism and the "state-sponsored repression and violence" inherent in what she calls "the medical model of the public weal", she is eager for "the military metaphor" of illness, associated with discussions of cancer as well as of AIDS, to be "retired" (Sontag 1991: 179–80). It "overmobilises . . . overdescribes, and it powerfully contributes to the excommunicating and stigmatizing of the ill" (Sontag 1991: 180). Her recommendation for the military metaphor is: "Give it back to the war-makers" (Sontag 1991: 180).

Callen (1990), in discussing the "linguistic battlefield" (Callen 1990: 174–5) of AIDS, observes that the language in play is "like a house of cards" since it is based on presumptions and doubts in response to alternative presumptions. Given that current medical knowledge about AIDS and HIV is necessarily and inevitably speculative and exploratory, he is particularly critical of the ways in which "beliefs" may be circulated as "truths" and how lexical collocation muddies the informational waters.[2] For instance, he draws attention to the fact that medical opinion differs on the precise nature of the assumed link or "correlation" between HIV and AIDS, yet these differences are seldom reported in a way that is sensitive to their attendant complexities.

Koestenbaum (1990) discusses how the "spectres" and "moral panics" associated with plagues and epidemics in the past have currently resurfaced in discourses of AIDS. "Because language is multiple", he argues, "the word 'AIDS' always means more, and differently, than we intend. There is no possibility of an independently elected language; every word is stained by community"

(Koestenbaum 1990: 166). The term "community", as employed within this context, is clearly an equally contested site *vis-à-vis* AIDS discourses. Grover (1990), in examining the connotations of the word when used to differentiate "homosexuals" from "heterosexuals", claims that it "conveniently . . . reduce[s] the troubling diversity of humankind to a single stereotype or scapegoat" (Koestenbaum 1990: 153). She notes that, particularly since the mid 1960s in the United States, "community" has been most frequently invoked as an oppositional term negatively identifying a local, ethnic, racial or political variant in relation to the "mainstream". In response, gays themselves have sought to reappropriate the term. Foucault's (1981: 100–102) notion of the "tactical polyvalence of discourses" aptly describes how "community" has been strategically co-opted as part of a "reverse" discourse. Homosexuals are speaking for themselves, demanding the right to define "normalcy" using the same lexicon by which "mainstream" institutions seek to label them as "deviant".

Unravelling the complex dynamics by which cultural, especially sexual identities are evaluated, Patton (1990) charts the semantic derogation of terms previously defined as "positive". She discusses its resultant consequences for health intervention in the United States following the "heterosexual AIDS scares" triggered by the death of Rock Hudson in 1985. The effects were very real, she argues, since it perpetuated the denial of homosexuality and drug use outside the identified "communities":

> Once the "public" could no longer ignore the presence of AIDS, educational projects were split into "public" education and "community" education, with each group getting its own special message. "Public" was no longer those who had managed to keep AIDS at a distance and became instead, those people "not at risk". "Risk group" terminology broke down under protest from the minority communities, who soon discovered that the once-empowering word "community" would now be equated with "risk group" . . . The selection of information now depended on an individual's perception of membership in either the "public" or a "community", a change in nomenclature which retained the confusion between difference and risk. (Patton 1990: 101)

In the context of these discussions of AIDS and political action by individuals and groups in the "public sphere", postmodernist cultural theory's playful "agonistics" and "language games" appear self-indulgent and politically irresponsible. Patton argues persuasively for the crucial role of language and "symbols" in enabling oppressed individuals to assert their identity and to organize themselves politically, advocating that AIDS activists should relentlessly pursue their speech (Patton 1990: 122, 131). While Patton does pay due attention to the central and dynamic role of discourse in cultural politics, her work also lacks an analysis of textual specificity.

Recent work by Lupton (1994), however, redresses this problem by using CDA (see earlier) as a technique to examine Australian news texts on AIDS. Making interdisciplinary linkages across cultural and media studies, medical anthropology and the sociology of health, she shows how discourses, in describing and categorizing the world, "gather around an object, person, social group or event of interest, providing a means of 'making sense' of that object, person, and so on" (Lupton 1994: 28–9). Moreover, she remedies the inattention paid by postmodernists like Lyotard and Baudrillard to the relationship between discourse and ideology by arguing, in turn, that discourses are unavoidably ideological in being concerned with representing particular versions of "reality" (of the world, of perception and experience). They inevitably highlight some aspects and diminish, or even silence, others. Ideologies, she claims, "contribute to and shape the formation of discourses: in fact, discourses can be considered the realisation of ideologies, the constellation of practices and verbal products by which ideologies are expressed, produced and reproduced" (Lupton 1994: 29).

This larger, societal inflection of AIDS discourses is addressed by two recent studies by members of the Glasgow Media Group which concern the news media reporting of HIV/AIDS. Miller & Williams (1993: 126) consider the ways in which the agendas related to HIV/AIDS coverage have "shaped media-source interaction from the point of view of the source as well as the reporter". In relation to "who does the telling", they discuss how the Health Education Authority and voluntary sector organizations (e.g. ACT UP, Outrage!, Stonewall, the Terrence Higgins Trust) are engaged in a discursive contest where the construction of popular representations of AIDS/HIV is a complex and dynamic process outside of the control of any one organization. Following this point, but paying closer attention to specific texts, Beharrell (1993) examines the content of press coverage of AIDS, exploring the similarity and diversity of reporting in tabloids and broadsheets. He argues that in order to understand how content is determined, analysis must give due recognition to the contextual fluidity of the marketing, political and professional forces that help to establish the parameters of a news report's narrative.

In the next section, we set out to analyze a variety of health promotion texts, both "mainstream" and "alternative". It is our intention to address the textual specificity of this ongoing discursive struggle to *naturalize* certain ways of speaking the "reality" of HIV and AIDS.

The politics of textuality

The corpus of texts we selectively analyze here is comprised of, first, two early official publications, *AIDS: some questions and answers* (Department of Education and Science (DES) 1987) and *AIDS: don't die of ignorance* (Department of Health and Social Secutiry (DHSS) 1987); secondly, two more recent "mainstream" publications, *Guide to a healthy sex life* (Health Education Authority (HEA) 1992) and *Safer sex for gay men* (HEA 1989); and thirdly, two "alternative" texts, *Smack in the eye* (Lifeline 1990) and *Information about AIDS/HIV for men who have sex with men* (Cardiff AIDS Helpline 1994). These publications differ significantly from each other in a whole variety of ways, and our analysis below is by no means exhaustive. Rather, what we draw attention to is how the dynamic ideological contestation of politicized meanings across and within AIDS discourses is evidenced textually.

The official publications

A critical textual analysis of two official documents, *AIDS: some questions and answers* (DES 1987) and *AIDS: don't die of ignorance* (DHSS 1987), provides several insights into how the "common sense" of hegemony (Gramsci 1971) is being interwoven *vis-à-vis* AIDS discourses. An overarching political and ideological agenda gets realized in a number of ways, not least through *who* speaks and *how* the reader is positioned. As might be expected, there is a striking difference between the "mainstream" and "alternative" guides on HIV and AIDS. Significantly, these former publications are typical of the "top-down" approach to health education in which a disembodied authorial voice sets itself up as "expert" knower, transferring information "down" to a homogeneous set of supposedly passive recipients of knowledge. There is a disregard of society as legitimately diverse and polyvocal, which textually marginalizes particular sections of "the community" (see above) whose lifestyles are inconsistent with the *normalcy* of the social, especially sexual mores being described. Both of these official texts decentre and peripheralize those who do not constitute the "ideal" audience.

This process is apparent right from the outset. The foreword of *AIDS: some questions and answers* (DES 1987) (hereafter ASQA) explicitly positions young people as "subordinate" receivers of knowledge from those in positions of power:

> The information and guidance offered in this booklet are intended to help teachers in schools in dealing with questions about AIDS and in formal teaching about it. We hope it will be used by lecturers, youth workers and parents. The main objective must be to present sound, factual information in a straightforward and balanced way.

The fact that young people may resist being interpellated as school pupils, members of the local youth club or as their parents' offspring is not recognized as being an issue. Although *AIDS: don't die of ignorance* (DHSS 1987) (hereafter ADDI) calls attention to how the government is taking seriously its responsibility to educate "the nation", to reach *all* audiences ("This leaflet is being sent to every household in the country. It is about AIDS"), eleven lines later, we find out exactly who its intended readers actually are: "So if you have children, think carefully what they need to know. Whether you approve or not, many teenagers do have sex and some may experiment with drugs" (DHSS 1987).

For HIV and AIDS information, teenagers are thus beholden to their parents who are imbued with the responsibility of defining their needs, and who are encouraged to deliver their "advice" interwoven with platitudes about "appropriate" social and sexual behaviour.

Strategically locating HIV and AIDS education within moralizing rhetoric is consistent with a larger political agenda here. Specifically, reappropriating the "safer sex" message from grassroots gay organizations (Patton 1989) and enshrining it in discourses of "objectivity" and "facticity" hegemonically attempts to re-articulate the New Right's "family values" morality within discourses of health concern. To illustrate, ASQA continues in its opening foreword:

> Teaching the facts about AIDS is an obvious aspect of health educa-
> tion. But there are serious moral and social issues as well. Children
> and young people need to be reminded of their responsibilities both to
> themselves and to other people. *They need to be reminded of the values and
> virtues of family life* . (DES 1987; our emphasis)

The disembodied authorial voice thus becomes a technique for party political propaganda. HIV and AIDS education is only to be "intertextually" (see Fairclough 1989) expressed through discourses of high moral censure. The hijacking of health promotion offers a way in which to ideologically define standards of social and sexual "normalcy".

Having sought to define the parameters of the HIV and AIDS education message like this, both texts "fittingly" reprimand those individuals or groups who resist traditionalist mores. For instance, in ASQA, "homosexual" premodifies "males" to identify a category of persons differentiable from those engaging in "*normal* heterosexual intercourse" (DES 1987: 7; our emphasis). Intertextually drawing on "preconstructed" (Pêcheux 1982) expressions of gay sexuality as deviations from "good healthy practice", the ideological make-up of the audience (as "hetero-" and thereby "normal") is discursively constituted. Accordingly, what such a perspective risks is that those who take pleasure in gay sex, for whom homosexual practice is defined as "normal", can be effectively distanced from the text and its message.

119

What's more, paralleling what Patton (1990) argues above, the textual demarcation of "homosexuals" as a negatively perceived monolithic social group to which one belongs or doesn't, demonstrates a naïvety to the complexity of identity politics (what behaviours and with what frequency, for instance, defines "homosexual"?). Such is the wont to interweave moralizing rhetoric about "abnormal" sexuality with HIV and AIDS health education, that the diversity of male-to-male sexual practice goes ignored. And, in a section which, ironically, promises a focus on the risks to homosexual men ("Are homosexuals particularly at risk?"), the juxtaposition of clauses and ambiguous phrasing allow the linguistics of blame to come into play:

> As it appears that homosexual intercourse has been of major significance in the transmission of HIV in this country, particular care needs to be taken in dealing with the subject of homosexuality, especially in schools. (DES 1987: 4)

Allocation of blame doesn't stop there. The final paragraph of the same section oddly ends with identifying another politically "convenient" scapegoat, pejoratively labelled "drug *mis*users" (DES 1987; our emphasis). Responsibility for the spread of AIDS is similarly laid at the door of those who decide to be non-monogamous. The high moral voice is textually evident as the avoidance of promiscuity (defined as having sex with anyone but your partner) is interwoven with the "safer sex" message. "Beliefs" are circulated as "truths" and in bold print ASQA warns, "The message is clear: do not be promiscuous" (DES 1987: 8). ADDI similarly follows this line of argument, advising, "It is safest to stick to one faithful partner" (DHSS 1987). Perpetuating the metaphor of AIDS as some kind of retributive disease (Sontag 1991), it goes on to forebodingly exhort, "if you do have sex with someone who is not your usual partner, not only might you become infected, but you may also infect your partner when you return home" (DHSS 1987).

On other levels too, the early government publications may serve to marginalize and distance those whose lifestyles lay outside the remit of what is defined as "acceptable" social behaviour. The lexis typically used, for example, is clinically "unifying" (Bakhtin 1981) when employing vocabulary such as "semen", "sexual intercourse", "anal sex", "vagina", "penis", and unobtrusively in a footnote in smaller case letters, "urine" and "faeces". Format-wise, both publications follow a highly formalized "question-and-answer" style. The authorial voice sets its own agenda and prioritizes its own questions to be answered in light of its preferred definitions of the realities of HIV and AIDS. The officially sanctioned norms of morality, epitomized by the promotion of monogamy and the "nuclear family", are represented textually via this centralizing mode of address.

The "alternative" publications

This attempted displacement of dissonant voices by "unifying" official AIDS discourses is matched by a "reverse" discourse (Foucault 1981) in the "alternative" publications distributed by localized community groups. As might be expected, these differ significantly, both in terms of mode of address and style, as they seek to dialogically contest the presuppositions and moral censuring typically promulgated by official texts. Lifeline's *Smack in the eye* (1990) (hereafter SITE) speaks directly to the drug-using subculture of young adults, while the Cardiff AIDS Helpline (1994) (hereafter CAH) leaflet explicitly identifies itself as "for men who have sex with men". In contrast with the interpellative appeals that characterize the official texts discussed above, these "alternative" texts articulate the realities of HIV and AIDS in a language other than that of reprimand and retribution.

In organizing the narrative elements of their messages, both SITE and CAH draw on discourses that are significantly more grounded in the everyday experiences of the particular subcultures they are directing themselves to than those of the official documents. Official definitions of "normalcy", "appropriate behaviour" and "risk", as well as the idealization of the "traditional nuclear family", are countered through the explicit recognition of sexual diversity, both in terms of how many partners are slept with and the wide-ranging nature of sexual practice. In contrast to ASQA and ADDI's high moral call for (heterosexual) monogamy, here "pleasure" is reappropriated and redefined (often in celebratory terms) in relation to sexual variety. To illustrate, in the CAH leaflet, listed alongside "rimming" (anus-licking) and "water sports" (involving urination), having sex with more than one person is described as "Group Fun". Instead of the morally censuring "drug misusers " (DES 1987), taking drugs in the CAH leaflet is positively connotated by the premodifier "recreational". Such a practice is also contextually located to be part and parcel of the wider pleasure picture. Only here is using drugs situated in relation to other aspects of social enjoyment:

> If you go out cruising and use recreational drugs or drink as an important part of that, think about what that allows you to do. Does it allow you to talk to people, to have really good sex . . . or to take risks you wouldn't have done otherwise? Drugs damage your immune system particularly smoking and drinking. (CAH 1994)

Broadening the category to include smoking tobacco and drinking alcohol (disregarded in early official definitions of what constitutes "risky behaviours"), drug-using is related to the larger question of immunity more generally. In such a way, discourses of blame are avoided, the audience addressed can find familiarity with the social picture being painted, and the message of "safer practices" is potentially more persuasive. That this has been effected in real terms has been discussed by Gilman (1992) who points out that:

> Evaluative interviewing has shown that drug users perceive the production of "Smack in the eye" as a positive step by the Lifeline Project to "take sides" with them. If the target audience for health education messages "trust the messenger" they are more likely to "trust the message". (Gilman 1992: 144)

At the level of lexis too, the "alternative" publications strategically interpellate their readers. There is a vernacularizing of HIV and AIDS information: an interweaving of advice with "street talk", a verbal inventiveness that is invested with the politics of cultural activism. Official clinical terminology surfaces and brings with it a sense of medicalization, but insofar as it clashes with the resistant forces of colloquial language, it is reaccentuated as part of the "alternative" discourse. Alongside "sperm" then, we find "cum"; instead of "faeces", we read "shit". A repertoire of informal vocabulary is employed including "cocksucking", "piss", "tripping", "wanking", "fucking" (CAH); "arse", "dick" and "shagging" (SITE). In this way, the health promotion message is articulated without moral condemnation, its "common sense" intertwined into the very "ordinariness" (Pêcheux 1982) of the language it attributes to its audience.

This attempted democratization of AIDS discourses is similarly realized through the format of these publications. In contrast to the formal question-and-answer mode of ADDI and ASQA, SITE's health education is delivered in adult comic-book style. Deliberately intended to be attention-grabbing and instantly familiar to the subculture of drug-users identified as needing advice, it is distributed without charge (thereby answering, in part, Patton's (1990) call to politicize AIDS discourse by cultural activism). The marked parallels with other well-known adult comics like VIZ is, of course, no accident, and a similar "sending-up" of characters occurs. For instance, Tough-Shit Thomas and Grandpa Smackhead Jones act as vehicles for "safer practices" advice. Specifically, HIV and AIDS information is articulated through character voices that mix colloquial language use and humorous stereotypical clichés. Here again, the employment of "youth talk", like Bakhtin's (1968) folksayings, anecdotes and street songs, contributes to the heteroglossia and "carnival" of AIDS discourses.

In "Pumping iron", a comic strip parodying the macho world of weight-training, Tommy informally greets his friend who has just arrived at the gym with "right Lenny, bit cold out ain't it?" In a similar vein, a second comic strip ("Waiting for my man") speaks to the heterosexual female readership of SITE. When Mandy negatively comments on the libido-losing effect of using condoms with her partner (who actually turns out to be macho-man Lenny, intertextually transposed from the previous strip), her friend Sharon colloquially admonishes "what's she like! Use your imagination kid!" Rather than the disembodied authorial voice articulating what is right and wrong, SITE delivers its health education through character-to-character interaction, and in such a way avoids lecturing its audience. Moreover, advice about what constitutes "good practice" gets voiced by black characters in both comic strips, thereby attempting to counter early racist discourses of blame for the spread of HIV (see Patton 1990: 77–97).

By positing well-rehearsed arguments against using condoms into the words of some characters, and countering these points by other characters, popular myths surrounding HIV and AIDS are being deconstructed. This is not to deny, however, that certain other ideological presuppositions are being perpetuated, even reinforced. For instance, although the pejorative labelling of women who use condoms is strongly refuted by Sharon, who says "using condoms don't mean you're a slag. Just sensible", the intertextual reliance upon discourses of derogation is, in itself, sexist. Similarly, when Lenny rationalizes his decision to share a syringe in order to pump 50 mg of deca-durabolin into his body ("I'm only going into the muscle Pete"), the advice given corrects one piece of misinformation while, in collocating "AIDS" and "virus" ("makes no difference! If you share other people's equipment you could pick up hepatitis or the AIDS virus"), it reinforces another one.

Noticeably, the strategic use of humour in SITE contrasts vividly with the grim warnings issued by the 1987 official publications. In "Pumping iron", we have a comic parodying of Lenny and Tommy as epitomes of muscled machoism ("You've got to be hard Tommy, I run to Blackpool with a fridge on me back before breakfast just for fun, me . . . Go on, smash an iron bar into me guts . . . won't feel a thing"). In "Waiting for my man", Mandy humorously complains "but it's still a bit of a passion-killer wrapping his dick in clingfilm". Bakhtin's notion of "carnivalisation" – how official discourses are undermined by unofficial ones – is clearly in evidence here. For Bakhtin (1968), laughter brings an object up close and draws it "into a zone of crude contact where one can finger it familiarly on all sides". This "familiarity", he argues, liberates our perspective. "Crude contact" with the object enables us to:

> turn it upside down, inside out, peer at it from above and below, break open its external shell, look into its center, doubt it, take it apart, dismember it, lay it bare and expose it, examine it freely and experiment with it. (Bakhtin 1968: 23)

Moreover, laughter, according to Bakhtin, "demolishes fear and piety before an object", it is "a vital factor in laying down that prerequisite for fearlessness without which it would be impossible to approach the world realistically" (Bakhtin 1968: 23). In recognition that the anxiety and defensiveness generated by the earlier official publications may have prompted a dismissal of the message itself, Lifeline textually employs laughter to effectively realize what Bakhtin describes. In describing how Lifeline chose to intentionally mark itself as different from previous official texts, Gilman (1992: 142) notes: "The humour of the comic format clearly distances the messages contained within it from the standard serious messages which create such defensiveness."

Health Education Authority publications

In later government-funded publications, it is textual evidence of these more "alternative" strategies which demonstrates most saliently the extent to which official AIDS discourses have sought to appropriate the "ordinariness" (Pêcheux 1982) of meaning. Many regional Health Education Authorities, currently charged with the responsibility for health promotion, have intertextually drawn on a range of devices from the likes of documents such as SITE and CAH leaflets. A close textual analysis of this material highlights several key features of this ideological shift to re-articulate the "common sense" of HIV and AIDS discourses within certain normative frameworks.

The *Guide to a healthy sex life* (HEA 1992) (hereafter GHSL) and *Safer sex for gay men* (HEA 1989) (hereafter SSGM), both published in Wales, have clearly been produced as responses to a perceived need to make the "unitary" language of the official texts more informal. Through the incorporation of sex-slang and humour, the moralizing tone typically inflected by earlier official texts is dramatically reduced. In addition, a more sensitive understanding of the potential audience is apparent. In GHSL, for example, the advice is represented as part of a wider concern with healthy sexual practices generally: "today sex is more accepted as a normal part of our lives" (HEA 1992: 5). Deliberate care is taken to avoid the categorization or "ghettoization" of HIV and AIDS as distinct "problems". In contextually locating them as just one aspect of health promotion, the discourse is invested with a more positive tone. Here, once again, elements of the "carnivalesque" surface, particularly through the use of brightly coloured comic drawings. One cartoon character, pointing at the male genitals on an authoritative anatomical illustration while checking his own by peering down his underpants, is obviously not a doctor or academic on a raised dais; he is a clownish caricature. In such a way, the "objectivity" of the "official" discourse is subverted or, after Bakhtin (1968), made "low". Arguably, we are being presented with a levelling between the educator and those being educated.

SSGM is similarly positive in its mode of address and public idiom. Rather than addressing a decontextualized "ideal" reader, the text immediately focuses on how to practically negotiate "safer sex" in real encounters as a shared concern of both partners ("By playing safe you are teaming up together to protect each other"). Acknowledging the problematic nature of doing this ("talking it through takes careful handling"), the guide suggests adopting particular strategies, both discoursal ("say something straight-forward and simple like 'Have you got a condom? If not, I have'") and practical (by describing "safer sex activities"). Lexically, SSGM also demonstrates an attempted, albeit rather coy, willingness to use colloquial language. So while the more characteristic features of official discourse are still very much in evidence, there exists a recognition of the need to speak the language of the reader, and this "ordinary" language is allowed in certain instances to surface. For example, bracketed after "anal intercourse", we read "often called fucking"; similarly, "masturbation" is followed by "often called wanking"; "pre-ejaculatory fluid" is glossed as "pre cum", and "digital intercourse" is acknowledged as the euphemism for a practice "usually called fingering". In contrast to the early official publications discussed above, then, these later guides textually demonstrate a more frequent use of "street talk", humour and visually attractive formats in an attempt to reach their intended audiences.

At a national level, it is interesting to note how HEA information campaigns are continuing to attend to "polyvocality" (Bakhtin 1981) and sexual diversity. Not only can we now see an advert that photographically follows the progress of a young female–male couple from first kiss to sexual intercourse, we can also read one in which a black-and-white photographic image depicts two male hands clasping one another, and is captioned: "If a married man has an affair, it may not be with a woman." Moreover, at the time of writing, the HEA appears to be having some success in keeping the moralizing prescriptivism of its funding body (the Department of Health) in check. A government ban on the sexually explicit *Your pocket guide to sex* (Fisher 1994) has been overturned recently, thereby leading the author, Nick Fisher, to seize upon its marketing potential by including the phrase: "The book the Government tried to ban!" on its front cover. Fisher describes in his introduction to the book the extent to which the HEA has shifted in ideological terms, commenting that: "[they] knew what they wanted . . . something spunky and punchy . . . something full of facts and information; . . . with advice about safe sex. It had to be sexy, unpatronising" (Fisher 1994). The cultural politicization of HIV and AIDS discourses continues apace.

Concluding remarks

Our analysis has endeavoured to show, first, how two official AIDS-related leaflets distributed in 1987 attempted to naturalize "traditional moral standards" in the framing of their message. The mode of address of these respective texts sought to prohibit sexual diversity or plurality and, moreover, to re-articulate "pleasure" within the realm of monogamy and the "nuclear family". We have also examined the textual strategies employed in "alternative" publications distributed by localized community groups, detailing how the health promotion message attempts to effectively connect with their audience; specifically, through the use of humour and informal discourse. Finally, we mapped the partial re-appropriation of these same strategies by the Health Education Authority, arguing that this shows a progressive step forward *vis-à-vis* the ideological re-conceptualization of HIV and AIDS by official organizations.

In conclusion, then, we would like to remark on several different directions future work on the textual politics of HIV and AIDS discourses could proceed to develop. It is apparent to us that far more attention needs to be paid to how HIV and AIDS discourses are produced within particular institutional contexts. Research needs to consider, for example, how certain ideological presuppositions about the audience are "encoded" in the course of manufacturing public health documents within the parameters of state policy frameworks. Given that these institutional arenas are themselves sites of discursive contestation, work needs to be undertaken into how official discourses are constructed *vis-à-vis* these contending institutional interests.

Secondly, we would like to call for further work to be undertaken on the role discourse plays in naturalizing and de-naturalizing the ideological reproduction of relations of dominance. We have attempted to show that by reading texts "against the grain", critical analyses can discern some of the ways in which the public contest over the realities of HIV and AIDS is being waged. In general, the definitions of "discourse" that tend to be taken-up in postmodern cultural theory are far too all-encompassing to be of use to the analyst interested in deconstructing particular texts. While the type of discourse analysis undertaken by postmodernists often offers important insights, securing textual evidence for its claims is typically given scant attention. The time is therefore ripe for closer integration of critical discourse analysis with the work of cultural theorists such as Bakhtin, Gramsci and Foucault.

And finally, we wish to pinpoint the need for further cultural research on the heterogeneous processes by which the representation of HIV and AIDS discourses in different texts is "consumed" by distinct audiences. In arguing for a text-centred approach, we have nevertheless tried to avoid stating how the texts in question would be read by the (imagined) reader; instead, we have sought to highlight, after Bakhtin (1968, 1981), how the "dialogic" quality of language ensures that meaning is the product of the reader's dynamic negotiation of the text. Much of the research on audience readings of HIV and AIDS representations has sought to determine their "effectiveness" or "impact" on public attitudes. We envisage a conceptual strategy that would draw upon other approaches, particularly those of ethnography (see Atkinson & Coffey, this volume), in order to help us explicate how texts are embedded in the social relations of their use. In this way, then, the textual materiality of health promotion discourses as they circulate across society will be explicitly linked to the broader contest for power over what can and what cannot be defined as the "reality" of HIV and AIDS.

Notes

1. Source: Public Health Laboratory Service, as reported in *The Independent*, 6 November 1994.
2. Watney (1989: 65–8) notes:
   The simple distinction between a virus and a syndrome is entirely obscured as soon as the phrase of "the AIDS virus" is used. At the same time, however, this phrase establishes a basis from which the equally inaccurate notion of "the AIDS carrier" can be advanced. Thereafter, a discourse comes into being that draws on a rich historical legacy that summons up the all-too-familiar imagery of contagion and plague . . . Instead of "AIDS carriers" we should be talking of people with HIV infection. Instead of "the AIDS virus", we should be talking of HIV.

References

Aggleton, P., G. Hart, P. Davies (eds) 1989. *AIDS. Social representations and social practices*. Sussex: Falmer Press.

Bakhtin, M. M. 1968. *Rabelais and his world*. Cambridge, Mass.: MIT Press.

Bakhtin, M. M. 1981. *The dialogic imagination*. Austin, Texas: University of Texas Press.

Beharrell, P. 1993. AIDS and the British press. In *Getting the message: news, truth and power*, J. Eldridge (ed.), 210–49. London: Routledge.

Callen, M. 1990. AIDS: the linguistic battlefield. In *The state of the language*, C. Ricks & L. Michaels (eds), 171–81. London: Faber and Faber.

Cameron, D. 1992. *Feminism and linguistic theory*, 2nd ed. London: Macmillan.

Cardiff AIDS Helpline (CAH). (1994). *Information about AIDS/HIV for men who have sex with men*. Cardiff: CAH Publications.

Chilton, P. (ed.) 1985. *Language and the nuclear arms debate*. London: Pinter.

Chilton, P. 1988. *Orwellian language and the media*. London: Pluto.

Department of Education and Science (DES) 1987. *AIDS: some questions and answers*. London: HMSO.

Department of Health and Social Security (DHSS) 1987. *AIDS: don't die of ignorance*. London: HMSO.

Fairclough, N. 1989. *Language and power*. Harlow, England: Longman.

Fairclough, N. 1992. *Discourse and social change*. Cambridge: Polity.

Fairclough, N. 1993. Critical discourse analysis and the marketisation of public discourse: the universities. *Discourse and Society* **4**, 133–68.

Fisher, N. 1994. *Your pocket guide to sex*. London: Penguin.

Foucault, M. 1981. *The history of sexuality: an introduction*, vol. I. London: Penguin.

Fowler, R. 1991. *Language in the news*. London: Routledge.

Fowler, R., B. Hodge, G. Kress, T. Trew, 1979. *Language and control*. London: Routledge.

Gilman, M. 1992. Smack in the eye! In *The reduction of drug-related harm*, P. A. O'Hare, R. Newcombe, A. Matthews, E. C. Buning, E. Drucker (eds), 137–45. London: Routledge.

Gramsci, A. 1971. *Selections from the prison notebooks*. New York: International.

Grover, J. Z. 1990. AIDS: keywords. In *The state of the language*, C. Ricks & L. Michaels (eds), 142–62. London: Faber and Faber.

Health Education Authority (HEA) 1989. *Safer sex for gay men*. Health Promotion Authority for Wales (Cardiff).

— 1992. *Guide to a healthy sex life*. Health Promotion Authority for Wales (Cardiff).

Johnson, R. 1987. What is cultural studies anyway? *Social Text* **16**, 38–80.

Koestenbaum, W. 1990. Speaking in the shadow of AIDS. In *The state of the language*, C. Ricks & L. Michaels (eds), 163–70. London: Faber and Faber.

Kramarae, C., M. Schulz, W. O'Barr 1984. *Language and power*. London: Sage.

Lakoff, G. & M. Johnson 1980. *Metaphors we live by*. Chicago: University of Chicago Press.

Lifeline 1990. *Smack in the eye: bumper fun album*. Manchester: SITE Publications.

Lupton, D. 1994. *Moral threats and dangerous desires: AIDS in the news media*. London: Taylor & Francis.

Miller, D. & K. Williams 1993. HIV/AIDS information: agendas, media strategies and the news. In *Getting the message: news, truth and power*, J. Eldridge (ed.), 126–42. London: Routledge.

Montgomery, M. & S. Allan 1992. Ideology, discourse and cultural studies. *Canadian Journal of Communication* **17**, 191–219.

Ortony, A. (ed.) 1979. *Metaphor and thought*. Cambridge: Cambridge University Press.

Patton, C. 1989. Resistance and the erotic. In *AIDS. Social representations and social practices*, P. Aggleton, G. Hart, P. Davies (eds) 237–51. Sussex, England: Falmer Press.

Patton, C. 1990. *Inventing AIDS*. London: Routledge.

Pêcheux, M. 1982. *Language, semantics and ideology*. London: Macmillan.

Sontag, S. 1991. *Illness as metaphor and AIDS and its metaphors*. London: Penguin.

van Dijk, T. 1993. Principles of critical discourse analysis. *Discourse and Society* **4**, 249–83.

Watney, S. 1989. The subject of AIDS. In *AIDS. Social representations and social practices*, P. Aggleton, G. Hart, P. Davies (eds), 64–73. Sussex, England: Falmer Press.

CHAPTER 8
News, truth and postmodernity: unravelling the will to facticity

Stuart Allan

Introduction

Much of the current research on the ideological effectivity of news discourse, whether it concerns the array of televisual sounds and images of the news broadcast, the utterances of radio news talk or the printed words of a daily newspaper, has sought to prioritize for enquiry the problem of "objectivity". Attention often focuses on the dynamics by which certain types of institutional voices, having been nominated as sources of *newsworthy* statements, are routinely processed *vis-à-vis* the news frame at the expense of other, less *authoritative* voices. A characteristic feature of the attendant theoretical projects is the presupposition that the notion of "ideological manipulation" is methodologically inadequate when seeking to explicate a given news account's (hierarchical) inflection of politicized meanings. The conceptual space previously allocated to the term "dominant ideology" is now largely occupied by new formulations, particularly ones that emphasize the *hegemonic* aspects of the *ruling* or *legitimate* definitions of "reality" available for interpretation by news audiences.

In this chapter, I want to draw attention to the extent to which this key conceptual shift away from the "dominant ideology thesis" to a (usually Gramscian) conception of "hegemony" has recurrently allowed residues of the earlier, arguably modernist analytical frameworks to persist. It is my contention that researchers anxious to retain the theoretical category "objectivity" in order to demonstrate how one particular news account is more biased in the support of hegemony than another one are usually relying upon certain empiricist notions of "reality" to support their claims that are untenable. Specifically, where these researchers implicitly assume that journalists possess the capacity to symbolically *translate* "the world out there" (the world beyond our immediate experience) in an "objective" manner, the ensuing critique of "news bias" is frequently restricted to considering the degree to which this reality has been *distorted* in the resultant news narrative. Given that the very notion of "news bias" implies that, by definition, the existence of an "unbiased" news account is possible, this recourse to the concept of "objectivity" is not advantageous in either conceptual or strategic terms.

While it is indeed the case that the resultant forms of academic analysis have often proven to be insightful, this chapter will argue that recent debates around the issue of postmodernism have succeeded in highlighting the need to radically recast this line of enquiry. Arguably one of the most elusive terms circulating in public discourse, "postmodernism" is only rarely discussed in relation to news media studies in a sustained or rigorous fashion. More often than not, it is invoked in this context to describe those modes of thought that deny the existence of an *objective* reality outside of the various *subjective* accounts of it being routinely manufactured by journalists. For this and other reasons, it is usually regarded as a pejorative term, one that stands as a convenient Other to those accounts that seem to be simply acknowledging the obvious: namely, that there is such a thing as "reality" and it may be presented to the news audience in a "literal" manner. This chapter is organized to privilege this conceptual disjuncture in such a way as to encourage an alternative stance, that is, one that recognizes several important advances made in and through postmodernist forms of critique, yet nevertheless retains at its centre a commitment to a critical approach to theorizing culture.

The limits of common sense

In looking to explore a series of issues germane to the problem of "objectivity" in the context of recent interventions around the question of postmodernism, I first want to highlight for discussion the very *common sense* of journalistic assumptions or "gut instincts" about what constitutes the *factual* in relation to the incessant institutional pressures (temporal and spatial) associated with processing the "raw material" of the social world in discursive terms.[1] Critical enquiries into how certain (usually institutional) "voices in the news", acting as "primary definers" or "authorized knowers" of occurrences typified as news events, are mobilized to demarcate "what counts as news" recurrently bring to the fore this issue of common sense and its *naturalization* in and by the "news frame".[2] In my view, however, far too often the descriptions of how news discourse naturalizes a common sense of existing social divisions and hierarchies are relying upon rigid, zero-sum formulations of "hegemonic domination". The very *taken-for-grantedness* of the "social order" is usually linked, in turn, to ill-defined conceptions of how hegemony *conceals* or *masks* the *true* nature of power relations from the news audience. Consequently, I would argue that these types of analysis generally fail to adequately account for the indeterminacies or contradictions implicated in a news text's inflection of reality or, in the terms I wish to introduce here, the materiality of its *will to facticity*.[3]

The problem of how to unravel this common sense of facticity is, in my view, one of the most troublesome aspects of recent academic investigations into the politics of news discourse. Accordingly, in seeking to define the space for a "critical discourse analysis" of news texts, I want to proceed to problematize the underpinnings of those formulations of "naturalization" typical of much of this research (once again, extensive use is usually made of Gramsci's writings on "hegemony"). It is my intention, in the first instance, to extend the proposition that the social relations of re-articulating the "facts at hand" are structured in hierarchies of definitional power (especially in relation to credibility, topicality and relevance) by considering certain productive dimensions of news discourse. A number of questions arise once we ask how best to render analytically visible the invisibility of truth-claims embedded in a *factual* account of *reality* as they work to ostensibly displace the charge of "subjective bias" in the name of "objective, impartial reporting". Of particular interest here is this inscription of the "hard" news account's *will to facticity* within the movement to contest, revise and reformulate the polysemic quality of meaning within the ideological limits of "that which is known to be true". I will argue that this strategic shift away from modernist conceptions of news language as a singular, entirely unified instrument is crucial, as a critical discourse analysis of the will to facticity must account for the codification of a complex matrix of power struggles being played out at the level of the *naturalization* or *depoliticization* of truth-claims about *reality* in news stories.

First, then, I offer the observation that critical investigations of this naturalization process, when electing to draw upon a notion of "hegemony" derived from the writings of Gramsci (1971), frequently do so without acknowledging the importance he attached to the effectivity of language when theorizing the "solidity of popular beliefs" or "common sense". A much broader category than ideology, here common sense signifies the uncritical and largely unconscious way of perceiving and understanding the social world as it organizes habitual daily experience. Gramsci suggests that far from being a strictly arbitrary (or "unorganic") *individual* elaboration of systematically coherent concepts about "reality", common sense is to be identified as "a cultural battle to transform the popular mentality and to diffuse the philosophical innovations that will demonstrate themselves to be historically true *to the extent that they become concretely – i.e. historically and socially – universal* " (Gramsci 1971: 348; emphasis added). It follows that to proffer a range of insights into the inflection of these logics in the language of news narratives, it is practical for a critical discourse analysis to reaffirm the epistemological value of the related proposition that researchers look beyond the *validity* of the content of "ideas" or "popular beliefs" so as to consider the cultural practices implicated within them.

131

In other words, to the extent that the notion of "common sense" is transformed into a totalizing concept, its explanatory power will be diminished. In
my view, any definition of common sense which elides the temporal and spatial specificity of its material force in and through ideas has failed to ask a vital
question: namely, whose common sense is being defined as *natural, obvious* or
inevitable? To prepare the ground for a sustained critique of the will to facticity
as it is actualized, to varying degrees, in news accounts, we need to further
qualify several of the operative assumptions underlying this modernist conception of how popular conceptions of "reality" help to reinforce a range of
hegemonic norms constitutive of "the truth". Here it is the Gramscian view of
language as both a "living thing" and a "museum of fossils of life and civiliza-
tions", where words "absorb" and "carry with them" meaning or ideological
content, which needs to be further elaborated upon so as to elucidate the
effectivity of common sense. If, after Gramsci, "the fact of language is in reality a multiplicity of facts *more or less* organically coherent and co-ordinated"
(1971: 349; emphasis added), it follows that the unity of news discourse, always
provisional, must be actively negotiated by both writer and reader alike.

A newsworker, in order to avoid unnecessary explanations of "reality" while
preparing a "hard" news account (as opposed to "soft" or "human interest"
news; sub-typifications include: "developing", "continuing" and "spot" news;
see Tuchman 1978, Fishman 1980, Ericson et al. 1989), has to assume that the
reader will share a similar "background knowledge" or "frames of reference"
about "how the world works" (see Gitlin 1980, van Dijk 1988, Clayman 1990,
Bell 1991, Eldridge 1993,). Common sensical presuppositions, far from being
fixed in temporal and spatial terms, are in a constant state of renewal: "new
ideas", as Gramsci notes, are always entering daily life and encountering the
"sedimentation" left behind by this "contradictory, ambiguous, chaotic aggregate of disparate conceptions" (1971: 422–3). Still, his subsequent contention
that common sense be theorized as the site upon which "dominant ideology"
is inflected leaves to one side a conceptual difficulty of serious import for our
purposes here, namely the problem of how to identify the mechanisms by
which the very legitimacy of "the historically true" is "fought out" at the level
of signification. It would appear that to effectively develop a conception of
news discourse as a provisionally unified nexus of *factual* truth-claims about
reality, this schematization of the "aggregate of disparate conceptions" as being
ultimately reducible to the efficacy of "dominant ideology" needs to be recast.

Another troublesome tendency indicative of certain "borrowings" from
Gramsci's writings about "hegemony" concerns the (often implicit) assertion
that common sense *necessarily* functions to preserve through these processes of
naturalization a prefigured dispersal of power relations across the social field.
Even those approaches to common sense that ascribe to it a heterogeneous nature often tend to retain a highly restrictive view of this dynamic such that

common sense comes to represent an amalgam of ideologies coincidental with the interests of a ruling class or bloc. Where Gramsci, in my view, sought to stress how common sense may be theorized as a complex and disjointed "infinity of traces", and as such never simply identical with a class-based ideology, for these approaches to news discourse the effectivity of "popular consciousness" is often narrowed to the point where it may be explicitly or implicitly defined as "untruthful" or "false".

Moreover, the pivotal matter of how it is that "voluntary" compliance with the demands of common sense varies in intensity from truth-claim to truth-claim is frequently reduced rather ambiguously to the (preconstructed) class position of the reader. Analytical arguments then arise as to whether these processes of depoliticization occur in the "first" or "last" (overdetermined) instance of ideological reproduction, while the specific dynamics by which contradictory conceptions of the social world (distinct responses to problems "posed by reality") are regulated within news language as being indicative of common sense remain largely unexplored. Hence the need to consider the extent to which the discursive investment of certain words with common sense, with an authority *outside of history* ("currently enjoying widespread acceptance", "as is generally agreed", "the popular mood", "according to public opinion" and so forth), is contingent upon a re-articulation of *the truth* across the domain of *the factual* "news frame".

In my opinion, then, a shift of emphasis is required in order to accentuate the very normative dynamics in and through which the intentional possibilities of news language are being expropriated by newsworker and reader alike. After all, to prioritize the routinized processing of those statements made by institutional voices recognized by newsworkers as being conversant in the preferred ways to speak of "reality" is, at the same time, to centre the ways in which their (implicit) claims to newsworthiness work to exclude alternative voices (those of the Other) as existing outside the realm of the factual.[4] News discourse may therefore be theorized as being *stratified* in the forms that carry its meanings according to, first, the statements of the institutional voices that the journalist weaves into (objectified) *newsworthy facts* or truth-claims, and secondly, the setting of *correct* or *reasonable* limits via identificatory mechanisms to police the meaning of the truth-claims available for the news account's (implied) reader to negotiate.[5]

In light of the discussion to this point, it would seem that the professional procedures or "strategic rituals" (Tuchman 1978) employed to secure *impartial* statements from *accredited* sources simultaneously promulgate a series of inferential practices that are constitutive of the news account's authorial voice (or, more specifically, its mode of address and public idiom). The correlative argument that these truth-claims are riddled in contradictions and indeterminacies similarly constitutes an important step forward. This is particularly so to the extent that investigations may avoid falling into a deterministic trap whereby a single, unitary "meaning" is *necessarily* manifest in the identificatory mechanisms by which certain subject positions are "preferred". In contrast with those approaches that are reliant upon a linear formulation of hegemony, then, I would suggest that a critical discourse analysis cannot succeed in any endeavour to ascertain either the "intended" message or the "dominant reading" of a given news account. Rather, as hegemonic meanings can never be established conclusively or "once and for all", we may perhaps best proceed by elucidating the effectivity of partial fixations precisely as they are re-articulated across the boundary between "reality" and the Real.

Reporting reality

The problem of defining precisely what constitutes "reality" is hardly a new one, yet the different ways it has been taken up in the (often acrimonious) debates around "the postmodern" is rather startling. Formulations of "reality" as an *empirical fact* to be located outside of the social relations of signification are often sharply counterpoised against those formulations of "reality" as a *cultural construction*. Angry charges of "unreconstructed positivism" are routinely met with accusations that "everything is being reduced to discourse". This chapter, in attempting to theorize the very common sense of what I am calling "the will to facticity" in news discourse, seeks to intervene in this dispute by rethinking the logic that underpins this problematic in the first place.

Here I wish to engage with Žižek's (1989, 1990) approach to the problem of "reality", one derived, in part, through a Hegelian reading of Lacan (see Botting, in this volume, for a more detailed discussion). Briefly, Žižek argues that "reality" may be distinguished from the "Real" where the latter is:

> the rock upon which every attempt at symbolisation stumbles, the hard core which remains the same in all possible worlds (symbolic universes); but at the same time its status is thoroughly precarious; it is something that persists only as failed, missed, in a shadow, and dissolves itself as soon as we try to grasp it in its positive nature. (1989: 169)

In other words, the Real is the "empty space" that cannot be inscribed in any symbolization of reality; ". . . it in itself is nothing at all, just a void, an emptiness in a symbolic structure marking some central impossibility" (Žižek 1989: 173). In order to highlight the contingent nature of any claim to "objectivity", then, analyses must discern that which threatens to disrupt it, that is, they need to show that it is the very impossibility of this claim that is being effaced. It follows from Žižek's thesis that any claim to "objectivity" is dependent upon the effacement of that which it denies, namely the power relations that anchor its articulation of "reality" as a *translation* of the Real. Once analyses acknowledge how claims to "objectivity" are caught up in the ineradicability of power relations defining what is to be included and what is to be excluded as being constitutive of "reality", then the ideological traces of that which eludes or escapes this symbolization (the Real) will be rendered visible. "Objectivity" is thus a political construction, the will to its accomplishment being socially contingent upon the changing power relations that make this affirmation of *truth* as the *unfolding of reality* ostensibly possible.

In seeking to render problematic the naturalness or obviousness of this discursive accomplishment, facticity itself needs to be recognized as constituting a provisional configuration (marred by occasional moments of disruption) of rules or conventions governing the news text's invocation of narrative and ideological closure *vis-à-vis* the Real. Here I want to propose that we move beyond the question of a vocabulary of newsworthiness, where one set of terms or lexical descriptions is more "biased" than another set, so as to consider the particular regimen of *what can and should be said* (Pêcheux 1982). The precise inflection of which is reliant upon the intervention of the (actual) reader in relation to the (ideal) one embedded in the account's authorial voice. Accordingly, by privileging for enquiry the disjuncture between the reader assumed or implied in a news account's authorial voice and the living, breathing individual engaged in the work of making it signify, a critical discourse analysis of news could in this way provide insights into the materiality of facticity that various renderings of the "dominant ideology" thesis have, in the past, virtually precluded from discussion.

To clarify, the ideal knowing subject for news discourse, as implicitly configured in the mode of address and public idiom of an account typified as "hard" news, will actively negotiate the "preferred" authorization of the Real as a *correct, reasonable* or at least *plausible* reflection of external reality.[6] News frames, constitutive of (and by) a set of normative conventions, govern the reader's expectations: indeed, as noted, the disruption of common sense is itself a recurring storytelling code in "hard" news accounts. Each account must therefore be organized to confront the accusation that its multiple meanings (and the *natural, logical* subject positions they project as being *truthful*) are not equally obvious to all who will encounter them. That is, while the text's conditions of existence and possibility (its embeddedness in common sensical explanations of the Real) effect certain material constraints upon the range of "choices" available at the level of the self-evident, there is always the danger that the reader will "choose" not to accept the preferred inflections of common sense on offer.

Once this reader has elected (not necessarily on a "conscious level") to "turn against" the news account's appropriation of the Real, he or she is initiating a form of concrete struggle against "*ideological evidentness on the terrain of that evidentness*, an evidentness with a negative sign, reversed in its own terrain" (Pêcheux 1982: 157; emphasis added). This "trouble-making" subject, detecting that this very "evidentness" is characterized by conflict and incongruity, refuses to identify with the obviousness of the meanings in play. However, and this point is crucial, a struggle over "evidentness" at this level transpires without calling into question the ideological authority of news discourse: that is, its capacity to faithfully *reflect* reality. Instead, the will to facticity may fail only when a reader takes up an antagonistic or *non-subjective* position by denying the evidentness of meaning without remaining complicit with it: he or she may then succeed in displacing the pull of the news account's interpellative strategies as a re-articulation of the Real (Pêcheux 1982: 159–68). Attention therefore turns to examine the contours of the normative logics of the will to facticity precisely as it is subject to modification in the perpetual struggle to affix the protean limits within which *proper* sense can be made of the Real *at the constant risk of its own disruption* (see also Montgomery & Allan 1992).

A conceptual dilemma emerges at this point, however, regarding how to theorize the naturalization of a news account's meanings if, in analytical terms, these meanings must be framed in relation to the backdrop of other commonsensical discourses marked not only in the news account itself, but also in the personal, inter-textual experiences of the reader. Here we may elaborate upon Pêcheux's observation that "words change their meaning according to the ideological positions held by those who use them" (Pêcheux 1982: 111) by accentuating how each of the statements processed in the final account is itself a locus of disputes, the "meaning" of which is conditioned by the degree to which it strikes a resonance with the reader's everyday experiences or praxis. A critical enquiry will need to highlight the conditions or "strings" attached to this naturalization of meaning so as to draw attention to the proliferation of subject positions constructed by news discourse via the mobilization of "the reader" as an ideological configuration, that is, how this configuration fosters a particular way of relating to the text as a factual representation of the Real. The obviousness of the rules of *what can and should be said* may then be distinguished by looking not only at the "content" of news language, but also at the restrictions or prohibitions that regulate its productivity. For critique to speak the ostensibly unspeakable, the socially situated logics of facticity shaping that which may be nominated as appropriate or pertinent over that which is unsuitable or irrelevant, like the typifications reinforced by normative appeals to newsworthiness, will need to be disentangled precisely as they secure the reciprocity of news language (and with it the authorial voice) with ordinary, everyday discourse.

It is the very *ordinariness* of the "will to facticity", however, that makes it difficult, in analytical terms, to discern the complex set of practices working to produce, circulate and police the boundaries of truth-claims within the circumscribed limits of the factual. Herein lies a further dilemma for a critical discourse analysis of news: namely, how to conceptualize the setting of these normative limits? How to distinguish the perpetual struggles transpiring over the concrete realignment of the rules of inclusion and exclusion in continuity with this invocation of the self-evident? Discursive conflict, a principal component of newsworthiness, clearly does not ensure that equal prominence will be given to "both sides of the story". Rather, as has been documented in the pertinent research, a politics of truth is emergent in the types of routine, professional judgements being made by newsworkers engaged in the work of first "gathering" the *facts* caught in the "news net", and then arranging them hierarchically *vis-à-vis* a news frame and narrative. The normative criteria being brought to bear to govern the authentication of these newsworthy voices, and the interpretative procedures that sustain them, help to set down the rules of objectivity for both writer and reader alike as they each "create" a sense of facticity. Consequently, if it is accepted that the "reality of the world out there" cannot be isolated nor removed from the social relations of signification, then it follows that the re-articulation of the Real must be theorized as it acquires its meaning in precise conjunctural (spatial and temporal) contexts (see Adam 1990, 1994, Laclau 1990, Nicholson 1990, Lefebvre 1991, Allan 1994). That is, the issue of "objectivity" needs to be addressed precisely as the reader engages with the *obviousness* of the news text's regulation of "truth".

The unruliness of the Real

In my view, to enlarge the scope of our enquiry so as to encompass a more nuanced understanding of this process of regulation, a new emphasis needs to be placed on news discourse as it confronts the (usually unspoken) Others that shape its conditions of existence and possibility (Foucault 1977, 1980). Such a line of enquiry will affirm that there is nothing *natural* about this process of naturalization: each truth-claim is in "dialogue" (Bakhtin 1981) with others articulated previously, only a limited number of which may be defined as *truthful*. Insofar as the naturalness of this hierarchical alignment of meaning with the Real is problematized, then, "objectivity" may be itself recognized as a potential point of antagonism where the invocation of common sense will be called into question. Here, the "logical consistency" the reader expects of a "hard" news narrative, particularly how she or he finds in its resolution a "sense of completion", highlights not only the question of plausibility but also the politics of closure.

In order to make a news account exhibit traces of this ideological discord, it is first necessary to explicate its orchestration of diverse truth-claims precisely as it is marked by this conflict to affix or naturalize a particular hierarchy of meaning in relation to the preferred inferences of the Real being generated via a news frame embedded in the "here and now" (see also Adam, this volume). The language of "hard" news may thus be advantageously theorized as being under constant threat of collapse as the particular voices it holds in tension are themselves fraught with the contradictions of dialogue. The narrative ascendancy of one voice over another, as affirmed by the news frame, is constantly shaken by the collision of ideologies mobilized to efface the traces of their own effectivity. Consequently, in looking to prioritize for critique a particular news account's appropriation of common sense at the expense of its Other (non-sense), and in this way its conditions of existence and possibility, this thesis that news language is dialogically shaped by the potential negotiation of the intended addressee is crucial. News theorized as a "field of possibilities" (Bakhtin 1981) regulates the limits within which it can be read *properly* with recourse to common sense, yet these limits are subject to the social contingency of a *reciprocity of perspective* existing between newsworker and reader (once again, even if this reciprocity, having been negotiated as possible, is nevertheless refused: see also Connell 1992).

This condensation (Lacan 1977) of divergent relations of reciprocity within a dialogic framework, specifically those requisite to the accomplishment of facticity, is itself fraught with tensions engendered by what may be described here as the "unruliness of the Real". The inflection of an *acceptable* range of statements to anchor a particular appropriation of the Real is constrained not only by a need to reaffirm certain meanings of "news sense" with the (actual) reader, but also, as noted above, by the need to secure for this reader a symbolic invocation of the preferred or ideal (implied) reader with whom he or she is to be asked to identify. "An ideology is really 'holding us'," Žižek writes, "only when we do not feel any opposition between it and reality – that is, when the ideology succeeds in determining the mode of our everyday experience of reality itself" (Žižek 1989: 49). To enhance the probability that this appropriation is achieved (once again, marked by ongoing resolution and resistance) as being obvious to all, the news account must therefore speak the Real in a way that appeals to the intended reader to recognize the relevance of its authorial voice as meaningful and familiar. That is, when making its most direct call upon the reader, news discourse has to seize hold of the very ordinariness of commonsensical discourses of the Real and order them coherently in relation to the interests it attributes to the (ideal) reader immanent at the level of the news frame.

And yet, this appropriation never fully succeeds. Here I want to suggest that the *coherence* of news discourse as a factual configuration of "truth", conditional as it is on the condensation of certain partial interpellations (political, economic, racial, sexual, familial, ethnic, religious, regional, aesthetic and so forth), is inextricably linked to the "fixity" of this lexicon of facticity being mobilized to re-articulate the Real. It is up to the reader to make a news text "coherent", to fill in the "gaps" marked by that which has been left unsaid. If common sense provides a multiplicity of (inchoate) conceptions of "reality" from which the individual is "free to choose", this invocation of "truth" nevertheless entails an implicit reaffirmation of the modes of subjectivity that make possible not only the recognition of its *logical* assemblage of facts but also, in the same instance, the denial of the Other (the unruliness of the Real) from the "sense" of the news account.

Researchers may thus take as their point of conceptual intervention the coercive constraints delimiting the range of these "choices" apparent in the textual moment precisely as they absolve the threat of non-sense. This is not to suggest that the individual is not at times aware, or indeed even sceptical of these constraints, only that no other possible alternative is likely to be demarcated as being *obviously appropriate* within the realm of common sense as a locus of subject positions (the discursive incorporation of which is marked by complexity, differences and contradictions). The ideological *jouis-sense* of common sense, the enjoyment-in-sense proper to ideology described by Žižek (1989), needs to be theorized as being held in suspension across the constraints produced by the mode of address precisely as it is (dialogically) embedded within the news account's narrative and the reading relations it fosters or invites as self-evident.

In this way, we are able to radically extend the Gramscian claim that social praxis is essential for common sense as "organic cement" to *solidify* by exploring, in turn, whether it is not also the case that it simultaneously marks the seams along which it may ultimately be cracked and broken. The effectivity of ideology is best theorized, Žižek (1989: 45, 83) contends, not as a means to offer us a point of escape from our reality, but to make us complicit in the concealment of the surplus-enjoyment proper to the ideological form where social reality is itself an escape from the Real. Although it may appear to *mirror* reality through its selective appropriation of ordinary speech, news discourse provides an objectified Real expurgated of contradiction. A *proper* (realist) network of truth-claims about the Real has to be projected as replete or final "in light of the facts". News discourse holds up for inspection the "unruliness of the Real" only to the degree necessary for a narrative logic, itself characterized by discursive conflict, to be set down. If "every news story has two sides", then "truth" must be rendered recognizable to the reader in a way that is *legitimately* "balanced".

This is not to suggest, however, that newsworkers (ostensibly seeking to process "all the facts fit to print") will not occasionally confront certain "awkward" truth-claims in the course of negotiating routine contextual pressures. Awkward, that is, in the sense that certain presuppositions about the Real may potentially be called into question should the "storyness" of the narrative, and thus the normative rules governing its concrete appropriation of common sense, be explicitly acknowledged in the final text. Accordingly, for a news narrative about the Real to be sustained as a *translation* of the Real, the news account has to implicitly deny that it is indeed an "account", that the news, no matter how *true*, is a "story". The partiality of the various truth-claims being mobilized, together with their inconsistencies, need to be regulated in such a way that the *rational* inferences to be drawn by the reader from this translation of a "news event" will not denote, in turn, that ideology structures the social "reality" itself.

The will to facticity is, in this way, caught up in the news account's elaboration of an authorized set of positions to "read" the Real, one that is organized so as to repair the various emergent cracks and fissures constraining the deployment of the news frame within the realm of the obvious. The reader, in order to "make sense" of the Real, must engage in the complex work of "reading between the lines", and yet to transgress these lines is to destabilize the normative logics of the news frame. Crucial to this process of aligning the (actual) reader with the (ideal) reader configured in the news text's public idiom, therefore, is the act of explaining the precise nature of the (transitory) crises engendered by the lacunae or silences of common sense in such a way that the account's preferred points of engagement are privileged *vis-à-vis* its inscription of the "will to facticity". The resultant range of inferences about the Real encouraged by the text, and the contradictory interests they presuppose, demarcate what is and what is not *common* about common sense. Only those "facts" consistent with the dictates of the authorial voice are likely to "command the field", yet even then the danger that the rationale underpinning these preferred points of engagement will be attenuated or broken is always present. In endeavouring to centre for critical enquiry the news account's implicit denial of the very impossibility of its re-articulation of the Real, therefore, much greater emphasis needs to be placed on the openings, gaps and closures emergent within its normative appeal to the (ideal) reader, as well as to the unauthorized Others which compromise its efficacy.

A question of imperatives

Over the course of this chapter, I have argued that a critical enquiry into the very *obviousness* of common sense as it is inflected in and by "hard" news accounts will have to identify the rules delimiting the dialogic play of truth-claims about "the world out there". These truth-claims, through their very discursive configuration, imply a series of prohibitions regarding the forms of social knowledge about "reality" that can be generated and subsequently called "factual". It has been suggested that for the subsequent reification of this normative "gap" between "reality" and the domain of significations to be sustained, certain modernist notions of "truth" and objectivity have to be shared, or at least implicitly recognized, by newsworker and reader alike.

Moreover, I have contended that the materiality of what I have termed "the will to facticity" is contingent upon the newsworker's appeal to a common frame of reference or shared ideological schemata with both the news source and the assumed reader. The larger effect of this, in narrative terms, is the capacity to position each *fact* in alignment with another one so as to construct a larger factual value for the account itself. The rules of facticity are set to ensure that the principal relationships between the ideological elements in motion follow the contending imperatives of the news frame such that the resultant narrative structure will reinforce the interpellative claim that "these are the real facts", "this is what is at issue" and "this is how to make sense of reality". Clearly, the will to facticity implicated in the various operationalized notions of newsworthiness in play is of crucial importance when looking to investigate the ways in which "hard" news accounts encourage or invite an authorized range of subject positions (the signification of which is not fixed in advance), while simultaneously denying as irrelevant any non-authorized assemblage.

This is to propose that a news text's authorized appropriation of the Real is conditioned not simply by ideological repression, but also by the projection of its opposite (constitutive of the discursive Other) in accordance with the dictates of the truthful. The winning of the reader's acceptance of the text's claims as appropriate, such that no alternative claim seems reasonable, is tied to the successful inflection of the Real as a unified totality contained within the "facts of the matter". If these truth-claims are at their most rigid where the risk of contradiction is most profound, the very "obviousness" of the common sense at stake becomes the basis for the "over-rapid historicization" (Žižek 1989) of the "hard" news account's articulation of "reality". That said, however, once a mode of enquiry elects to seize upon the effectivity of the truth-claims by prioritizing for critique precisely that which is dismissed as *too obvious to be spoken*, the normative limits of factual speech, and consequently the politics of its signification, will be brought to the fore for further examination.

I would argue, therefore, that in order for a critical discourse analysis of the will to facticity to achieve its aims, we need to succeed in rendering problematic the conditions of existence and possibility upon which the "truthful meaning of the text" is made to rest (its situation within "what everyone knows"). Next, we need to proceed to elucidate the regulatory effects these discursive relations imply for the complex array of contending truth-claims aligned within the codified rules of "objectivity". Researchers may, in this way, grapple with the vital question of precisely why it is that specific configurations of truth are being commonsensically framed by newsworkers as factual, as opposed to simply asserting that the demonstration of a correspondence between hegemonic interests and a particular news narrative should in itself constitute a satisfactory exegesis of ideological effectivity.

Notes

1. Recent attempts to theorize news as discourse have succeeded in developing a variety of insights into the question of the ideological effectivity of news accounts (see, for example, Bruck & Allan 1987, van Dijk 1988, Fairclough 1989, Bell 1991, Fowler 1991, Montgomery & Allan 1992). When employing the term "news discourse", allowances need to be made for significant differences in the types of reading strategies audience members associate with various news media and, moreover, how the related texts are negotiated across the "public" and "domestic" spheres of everyday life. Here, for example, the status of television as the most authoritative or truthful source of news (as is often argued on the basis of various public opinion surveys) becomes an important question for further enquiry. See also Nicholson (1990) for a consideration of the "maleness" of different affirmations of "objectivity". Finally, for an alternative reading of "objectivity", one which in defending the common usage of the term appeals to the tenets of modernism, see Lichtenberg (1991).

2. News frames, as Gitlin (1980) argues:

   are persistent patterns of cognition, interpretation, and presentation, of selection, emphasis, and exclusion, by which symbol-handlers routinely organize discourse, whether verbal or visual. Frames enable journalists to process large amounts of information quickly and routinely: to recognize it as information, to assign it to cognitive categories, and to package it for efficient relay to their audiences. Thus, for organizational reasons alone, frames are unavoidable, and journalism is organized to regulate their production (Gitlin 1980: 7; see also Hopper, this volume).

3. Here it should be noted that facticity, as the outcome of a series of discursive imperatives engendered through newswork, is a relatively recent development. Various historical examinations have suggested that the advent of professionalism amongst both British and North American journalists took place largely in the final decade of the last century, while the general invocation of "neutral", "objective" journalism would not be a common practice until the 1920s (see Schudson 1978, Tuchman 1978, Schiller 1981, Hallin 1986). Similarly, see Winston's (1993) discussion of US television in the late 1940s and the "naturalization" of news presentation: "Achieving the clear ideological advantage of transparency", he writes, "was television news' first and arguably greatest triumph" (Winston 1993: 181). The "transparency" of academic discourse, including this chapter and its implicitly "factual" claims, might serve as an interesting counterpoint for discussion.

4. As Ericson et al. (1989) point out, "the reality of news is embedded in the nature and type of social and cultural relations that develop between journalists and their sources, and in the politics of knowledge that emerge on each specific news

beat" (Ericson 1989: 377). Regarding this question of source competition, Schlesinger (1990) argues that due consideration should be given to:

> the processes whereby sources engage in ideological conflict *prior to or contemporaneous with the appearance of definitions in the media.* [We need to ask] questions about how contestation over definitions takes place *within* institutions and organisations reported by the media as well as the concrete strategies pursued as they contend for space (1990: 68).

5. An important feature of news stories in general, writes Dahlgren (1992), is that they generate their own "worlds":

> It could be suggested that the more intense the narrative coherence, the less imperative is the referential function to an external reality for meaning to be conveyed . . . [Moreover,] there seems to be a limited number of basic patterns and variations, which are endlessly repeated. The news is in some ways, at least in part, familiar. Narratives have ingredients which culturally competent audiences can readily recognize and classify . . . One can say that "storyness" both enhances and delimits the likely range of meaning (1992: 15).

The extent to which "hard" news accounts implicitly deny this "storyness" will be addressed at a later point in the discussion.

6. As will be shown, this emphasis on "negotiation", as opposed to the often mechanical notion of "interaction" found in some related formulations, is directly tied to the problem of the *reciprocity of perspectives* between newsworker and reader. Interestingly, while our discussion here is limited to "hard" news, Fiske (1992) argues that:

> the last thing that tabloid journalism [the US publications *Weekly World News* and the *National Enquirer* are cited as examples] produces is a believing subject. One of its most characteristic tones of voice is that of a sceptical laughter that offers the pleasures of disbelief, the pleasures of not being taken in (1992: 49).

For news (in general) to be pleasurable, and thus *popular*, he maintains, it needs to provoke conversation: "it is by taking up and recirculating the issues of news orally that the people construct aspects of the public sphere as relevant to their own. The oral recirculation of news is a typical way of re-informing it into popular culture" (Fiske 1992: 57).

References

Adam, B. 1990. *Time and social theory.* Cambridge: Polity.

Adam, B. 1994. *Timewatch: the social analysis of time.* Cambridge: Polity.

Allan, S. 1994. "When discourse is torn from reality": Bakhtin and the principle of chronotopicity. *Time and Society* **3**, 193–218.

Bakhtin, M. 1981. *The dialogic imagination.* Austin, Texas: University of Texas Press.

Bell, A. 1991. *The language of news media.* Oxford: Basil Blackwell.

Bruck, P. & S. Allan 1987. The commodification of social relations: television news and social intervention. *Journal of Communication Inquiry* **11**, 79–86.

Clayman, S. E. 1990. From talk to text: newspaper accounts of reporter-source interactions. *Media, Culture and Society* **12**, 79–103.

Connell, I. 1992. Personalities in the popular media. In *Journalism and popular culture*, P. Dahlgren & C. Sparks (eds), 64–83. London: Sage.

Dahlgren, P. 1992. Introduction. In *Journalism and popular culture*, P. Dahlgren & C. Sparks (eds), 1–23. London: Sage.

Eldridge, J. (ed.), 1993. *Getting the message: news, truth and power*. London: Routledge.

Ericson, R. V., P. M. Baranek, J. B. L. Chan 1989. *Negotiating control: a study of news sources*. Toronto: University of Toronto Press.

Fairclough, N. 1989. *Language and power*. Harlow, England: Longman.

Fishman, M. 1980. *Manufacturing the news*. Austin, Texas: University of Texas Press.

Fiske, J. 1992. Popularity and the politics of information. In *Journalism and popular culture*, P. Dahlgren & C. Sparks (eds), 45–63. London: Sage.

Foucault, M. 1977. *Language, counter-memory, practice*. Ithaca, New York: Cornell University Press.

Foucault, M. 1980. *Power/knowledge*. New York: Pantheon Books.

Fowler, R. 1991. *Language in the news: discourse and ideology in the press*. London: Routledge.

Gitlin, T. 1980. *The whole world is watching: mass media in the making and unmaking of the new left*. Berkeley: University of California Press.

Gramsci, A. 1971. *Selections from the prison notebooks*. New York: International.

Hallin, D. C.. 1986. *The "uncensored war"*. Oxford: Oxford University Press.

Lacan, J. 1977. *Ecrits: a selection*. New York: W. W. Norton.

Laclau, E. (ed.) 1990. *New reflections on the revolution of our time*. London: Verso.

Lefebvre, H. 1991. *The production of space*. Oxford: Basil Blackwell.

Lichtenberg, J. 1991. In defence of objectivity. In *Mass media and society*, J. Curran & M. Gurevitch (eds), 216–31. London: Edward Arnold.

Montgomery, M. & S. Allan 1992. Ideology, discourse and cultural studies. *Canadian Journal of Communication* **17**, 191–219.

Nicholson L. J. (ed.), 1990. *Feminism/postmodernism*, London: Routledge.

Pêcheux, M. 1982. *Language, semantics and ideology*, tr. H. Nagpal. London: Macmillan.

Schiller, D. 1981. *Objectivity and the news*. Philadelphia: University of Pennsylvania Press.

Schlesinger, P. 1990. Rethinking the sociology of journalism: source strategies and the limits of media-centrism. In *Public communication: the new imperatives*, M. Ferguson (ed.), 61–83. London: Sage.

Schudson, M. 1978. *Discovering the news*. New York: Basic Books.

Tuchman, G. 1978. *Making news*. New York: The Free Press.

van Dijk, T. A. 1988. *News as discourse*. Hillsdale, New Jersey: Lawrence Erlbaum Associates.

Winston, B. 1993. The CBS evening news, 7 April 1949: creating an ineffable television form. In *Getting the message: news, truth and power*, J. Eldridge (ed.), 181–209. London: Routledge.

Žižek, S. 1989. *The sublime object of ideology*, London: Verso.

Žižek, S. 1990. Appendix: beyond discourse-analysis. In *New reflections on the revolution of our time*, E. Laclau, 249–60. London: Verso.

PART II
Recasting cultural politics

Introduction to Part II

In this, the "twilight" of postmodern cultural theory, each of the contributors to this section of the book seeks to address the vitally important issue of what a critical approach to culture should look like tomorrow. In the spirit of inter-disciplinarity, the respective chapters presented here address a specific set of concerns pertinent to this complex problematic. Each contribution endeavours to highlight, from its particular vantage point, the conceptual, methodological and strategic implications of a particular configuration of cultural practice. At stake is the need to rise to the challenges posed by postmodern cultural theory without, at the same time, getting caught up in theoretical modes of argument to the point that "the play of truth claims" comes to signify little more than the "anything goes" ethos of relativism. Accordingly, the shared objective here is to disrupt the array of assumptions that underpin the discursive logics of postmodernism such that, when and where possible, we may proceed to recast its potential for engagement, action and reflexive responsibility within a critical framework.

The first chapter of this section, Glenn Jordan and Chris Weedon's "The celebration of difference and the cultural politics of racism", offers an examination of two characteristic features of "postmodern" societies: the celebration of difference and the cultural commodification of Otherness. Specifically, in looking at how the "postmodern age" markets lifestyles and bodies as commodities, Jordan and Weedon suggest that whereas many of the choices available to the postmodern consumer are innocuous, the consumption of racial difference is not. They proceed to investigate how "Western" representation, celebration and commodification of Black bodies and Black culture relate to long established traditions of "Western" racism. In this way, they demonstrate why it is the case that questions of culture cannot be divorced from questions of power and history.

145

Taieb Belghazi's chapter, entitled "Cultural studies, the university and the question of borders", similarly takes up the theme of Otherness in a radical manner. Cultural studies itself is centred for examination here, with Belghazi defining it as an ambivalent theoretical and political space situated across the shifting borders of contending academic discourses. In his view, this ambivalence is an enabling condition for oppositional thought, one which, on the one hand, repudiates monolithic thinking and, on the other, subverts the Kantian model of the university where fields of study are frequently rigidly demarcated. These and related points are illustrated through a consideration of Derrida's text, *Mochlos*, as well as through a discussion of "travel theory" as it pertains to the relocation of cultural studies in Morocco. The primary trajectory of this chapter's argument is that the discursive practices of academic discourse need to be deconstructed with the aim of opening up new terrain for pedagogical challenges to the institutionalization of cultural studies.

This question of how best to redefine the project of cultural studies is addressed from a different vantage point by Brian Doyle in his chapter "Changing the culture of cultural studies". Doyle makes a case for shifting the emphasis within the broad interdisciplinary Field of cultural, media and communication studies beyond the limits of "pure critique" so as to secure the basis for an affirmative approach not only to studying culture but also to developing useful cultural "skills". He argues that recent work in media studies and sociology that attempts to trace new connections between academic work, social systems and the psychological dimensions of self, groups and organized cultures is important here: especially the work of Anthony Giddens. In addition, Doyle suggests that the Transactional Analysis tradition provides not only a useful analytical model for cultural theory, but also an exemplification of what might count as "good cultural practice". In his opinion, the difficult work of establishing a fresh agenda for critical cultural theory will involve changing its *own* cultural orientations as much as its methodologies and theoretical frameworks.

The cultural construction of "the self" is also at issue in Cynthia Carter's chapter, entitled "Nuclear family fall-out: postmodern family culture and the media". This chapter's discussion commences with the assertion that there currently exists a considerable gap between the *idealized* family form (the "nuclear family") represented in much of our mass media content and the ways in which we are currently organizing our personal lives. Despite significant changes in the social structures of human relationships over the past few decades, she argues, it is still possible to discern a cultural politics of *normalcy* whereby a specific configuration of "the family" is being naturalized as *proper* and *correct* (the "traditional family values" of much right-wing rhetoric being a case in point). This apparent contradiction is explored via a critical assessment of recent cultural studies research on "familial ideology", with special attention given to discourses about the "postmodern family". It is Carter's conviction that cultural theorists must seek to develop a new, explicitly moral language capable of disrupting the ideological purchase of the very *normalcy* of "the family".

Memories of "the self" in relation to "the family" are one of several related themes considered in the next chapter by Timothy Robins, entitled "Remembering the future: the cultural study of memory". Robins traces the implications of a recent turn in cultural theory towards the exploration of how the constitution of subjectivity is accomplished through forms of storytelling. He points out that this conceptual shift has encouraged not only a redefinition of "memory" as an object of investigation, but also a re-evaluation of how "remembering" and "forgetting" operate as political practices. Particular attention is given to the ways in which several key issues raised in the 1970s and early 1980s in debates between Gramscian and Foucauldian perspectives around the concept of "popular memory" have recently re-emerged in autobiographical and ethnographic studies. While such cultural studies of memory have provided useful accounts of the continuity and discontinuity of lived experience, Robins argues, future work needs to be even more reflexive about the re-appropriation of memories by institutions located across the cultural field.

The cultural politics of remembering English rural life are centred for examination in the next chapter, entitled "Imagining Nature: (re)constructions of the English countryside", by Samantha Humphreys. Starting from the thesis that our conceptions of what is "natural" or "unnatural" play a major role in our definitions of the world about us, Humphreys seeks to render problematic the very *naturalness* of various distinct discourses about "the environment". She proceeds to consider the implications of the claim that our current ecological crisis actually arises from the ways we have of distinguishing between "Nature" and "Culture", that is, between the "natural" and "human" worlds. It is her contention that while many cultural theorists have prioritized our need to acknowledge our place – as humans – within "Nature", not enough attention has been paid to the way that "Nature" forms part of the human world. In an attempt to rectify this problem by allowing us to see the extent to which "Nature" is itself recreated by human ideologies, Humphreys engages in a cultural critique of the English rural mythology and its historical (re)constructions of the natural countryside.

Discourses of "technology" are recurrently articulated in sharp contrast with those about "nature", a central theme of the next chapter by Brian Winston, entitled "Tyrell's Owl: the limits of the technological imagination in an epoch of hyperbolic discourse". According to Winston, there is a "basic litany" about technological change that isolates it from its cultural, political and economic contexts so as to position it, in turn, as being somehow "irresistible". In effect,

147

he suggests, this is the rhetoric of those who erroneously believe technology to be the determining factor in such change. This chapter thus argues that by putting technology, specifically the information technologies currently converging to create "super-highways" and "virtual realities", back into these contexts, it will be shown that technological change is far from being irresistible. At issue, then, is the need to deconstruct this "basic litany" precisely as it obscures this fact behind what Winston describes as "a smoke-screen of overheated, hyperbolic discourse shared by 'technological determinism', both scientific and populist, as well as some strands of 'postmodernist' thinking".

The cultural specificity of technology is also at the heart of the next chapter by Hughie Mackay, entitled "Technological reality: cultured technology and technologiized culture". This chapter discusses the centrality of technology to everyday life and culture in the "postmodern era" – at work, in the home, in education and in entertainment. In looking to develop a critique of the prevailing orthodoxies of "technological determinism" and the "information society thesis", Mackay outlines key approaches within the broad "social shaping of technology" school: labour process, social constructivist, systems and actor-network theory. Next, the argument is made for a redefinition of the cultural studies approach to technology, one which moves beyond a focus on the *origins* of technology so as to consider its actual *consumption*. It is Mackay's contention that information and communication technologies constitute vital elements of "postmodern culture", thus the study of culture needs to consider the technological dimension of culture while, at the same time, the study of technology needs to take account of the cultural specificity of technology.

Barbara Adam in the final chapter of this section, "The temporal landscape of global/izing culture and the paradox of postmodern futures", seeks to explicate the temporal processes of "global culture". In the first instance, this chapter takes as its focus the mutual implication of "self" and "other", "local" and "global", "nature" and "culture", as well as the "material" and "immaterial". Using the question of temporality to organize the conceptual logic of her argument, Adam proceeds to identify several of the more pronounced weaknesses of the concept of "postmodernism" which become apparent once analyses endeavour to confront the contemporaneity of "globalized culture". The aim of this project, she suggests, is to find a basis for a critical praxis and engagement with "the future": specifically, to outline a theoretical source for political commitment more appropriate than the modernist discourses of "objectivity" and "mastery", on the one hand, and the postmodernist language of "relativism" on the other hand. Adam thus concludes this volume by arguing that the need to take account of the future and responsibility for posterity constitutes an inescapable moral imperative for cultural theory after postmodernism.

CHAPTER 9

The celebration of difference and the cultural politics of racism

Glenn Jordan and Chris Weedon

So, the range available to the contemporary palate is potentially wider than ever before, stretching from international fast food (Wimpy, McDonalds, Pizza Express) to the widespread discovery of post-Empire culinary tastes (Indian and Chinese cooking) and macrobiotic diets. (Iain Chambers 1986: 49)

The fundamental shift in mood that the Post-Modern world has brought is a new taste for variety. (Charles Jencks 1989: 55)

Yes! Everyone seems to be clamouring for "difference", only too few seem to want any difference that is about changing policy or that supports active engagement and struggle. (bell hooks 1991: 54)

This chapter looks at two key features of "postmodern" societies: the celebration of difference and the commodification of Otherness. The "Post-Modern Age" is the age of diversity, choice and the proliferation of tastes. Virtually anything I can imagine, seek or desire is available in the international capitalist market place. If I want to complement my CD collection of Beethoven and Wagner with Amazonian folk music, that is not a problem. If I wish to purchase "African-look" clothes by a Parisian designer, I need only consult those who know. If I have a taste for food from the Far East, I can easily find it in my small Welsh village. If I desire a house that is simultaneously "classical" and "modern", my cheque-book can make my dreams come true. If I wish to change the way I look, I simply consult *Yellow pages* . . .

The world is at my fingertips – in my local supermarket, on my multi-channel television set, on the billboards that confront me as I drive in to work. My dreams are my reality. My credit cards are my solace.

149

I, the solitary consumer, can fulfil all of my desires. I can transform all of my wishes into pleasures – if the price is right.

"Pluralism", Charles Jencks says, is "the 'ism' of our time". Our era – i.e. the era of those of us who live in late capitalist societies – is one in which "Everyman becomes a Cosmopolite and Everywoman a Liberated Individual" (Jencks 1989: 7). This is the message I receive daily – from television, magazines and advertisements, from my relatives, my friends and the eager faces of insatiate consumers.

I, the Bourgeois Subject, am free to buy. My only constraint is my ability to pay.

Postmodernism celebrates plurality, heterogeneity, difference. And I, the seduced consumer, can shop for difference. (Thanks to the new electronic media, I can often make my choices without even leaving the comfort of my home.) Ours is a world in which images and fantasies are packaged and sold more often than loaves of bread and containers of milk. (As Marx said, the commodity is a strange, mysterious thing.)

Today's Descartes: *I consume. Therefore, I am.*

Within the endless stream of commodities on offer in the international capitalist market of the "Post-Modern Age" are symbols and fantasies of racial Otherness. It is sometimes assumed that People of Colour – Black and Brown bodies, minds, character and culture – are despised in the dominant representations of race in Western culture, i.e. that racism works *only* by suppression, domination and exclusion. We wish to suggest, as Foucault undoubtedly would, that the reality is otherwise: Blackness, for example, is often *celebrated* in the dominant – that is to say, racist – culture, especially by those in the dominant group who regard themselves as liberal, avant-garde and/or cosmopolitan.

The celebration of racial and cultural difference is a marked feature of the radical twentieth-century avant-garde (both modernist and postmodernist) in the West. We look at this phenomenon and ask whether "postmodern" celebrations of the Blackness have transcended the legacy of classical racism which secretly (but nonetheless insidiously) permeated earlier modernist celebrations. Our questions, put simply, are these:

– Isn't the Cosmopolitan often inadvertently a Racist?
– How innocent is shopping for difference (that popular pastime of the "Post-Modern Age")? Doesn't this particular recreation often reproduce – again, inadvertently – racist imagery and fantasy?

Let us begin to answer these questions by probing into the popular culture of the area in which we (the authors) live. Later, we explore this same theme through a case study of life in an Ivy League American town.

Shopping for difference: case study 1

The back page of the *Cardiff Post*, our local free weekly newspaper, consists of a section called "Meeting Point: Voice Link". Voice Link is "a completely confidential personal message service" which any member of the public may use, at any hour of the day or night, to find that special someone. If you are interested in advertising yourself, there are only two small steps involved: you write out a short message, consisting of twenty words or less, for publication in the next issue of the paper, and you leave an audio-recorded message with Voice Link for your prospective Mr or Ms Right. If you are interested in contacting those who have advertised themselves, you have two choices. On the one hand, you may use "the new browse service". This service divides the advertisers into eight groups – Men 18–30, Men 30–40, Men 40–55, Men over 55, Women 18–30, Women 30–40, Women 40–55, Women over 55 – with each of the groups having a specific telephone number. For 39 pence (60 cents in US currency) per minute cheap rate, or 49 pence (75 cents) per minute at all other times you can listen to a selection of advertisers in your chosen category. On the other hand, if you would like more targeted choice, you can directly phone specific advertisers – or rather their recorded message – using their Voice Link number. If you find someone – an advert and a voice – that interests you, you can phone up and leave them a personal recorded message. The advertiser then listens to your message and chooses whether to contact you more directly.

My desires have been manufactured and channelled. And you are the recipient.

That is how the service works. Below is a sample, taken almost at random, of some adverts from one week (1 September 1994).[1] Please read them closely, noting what is offered and sought.

> **CARDIFF** male, 30's, seeks large, cuddly lady, age and looks not important. Cardiff.
> **ATTRACTIVE** curvaceous, mature student, 38, divorced, seeks intelligent, articulate, sensitive, attractive male. Am I being too optimistic? Barry.
> **LOVING** caring widow, finding life lonely, wishes to meet lonely, caring widower, 60–70, to share holidays & long evenings together & make most of what's left. Llanishen.

SINGLE male, 30, coloured, looking for females, prefer large lady for long relationship, genuine ad, genuine replies only.

ATTRACTIVE slim blonde, alternative male, 36, vegetarian, single parent, interests, self-sufficiency, sharing, male/female equality, fun, seeks gentle loving female soul mate. Clwyd.

WELSH gentleman, widower, 68, retired company director, solvent, fit, seeks lady, 48–65, affectionate, immaculate grooming, interests, wining, dining, travel, no ties. Leominster.

CARDIFF female, blonde, blue eyed, 35, in need of handsome, respectable guy, 30–35, to put laughter back into life. I own house & car, am told that I'm pretty. Cardiff.

REASONABLY good looking, but slightly overweight male, 30, N/S [i.e. non-smoker], wishes to meet young lady, slim, 20–30, for nights out/in, possible relationship. Penarth.

FEMALE 18, blond [*sic*] & fun loving, seeks hunky black guy, 18–25, must be exciting & enjoy music & clubs. Cardiff.

What is so interesting about Voice Link? Why discuss it in an essay on postmodern culture and the commodification of difference?

First, this is a genuinely *popular* service, in both senses of the word: it is widely used by ordinary people and it is affordable to them (i.e. compared to dating agencies, video services, etc.). It is also quick: you submit your advert and it appears in the next issue; you wish to hear the voice of your dreams and there you have it, present in your ear. Voice Link is an example – admittedly not the best – of cultural democracy at work. Such services are becoming increasingly accessible to ordinary people – eventually the mode will surely be interactive video – as a result of advances in media technologies. Variegated pleasures are becoming more and more affordable.

Secondly, the voice you hear is a *recorded* one. Now, obviously, this helps to protect people from being abused or exploited but it also points to a central feature of contemporary societies: societies of the so-called "Post-Modern Age" are societies in which face-to-face communication has been increasingly replaced by communication through media. We live in a world in which, more and more, one encounters other human beings through media images, recordings and so forth.

My friends and lovers are images and voices. We meet through billboards, televisions and computer screens.

You claim that my world is not Real, but it is you, not me, who has been conned. For I, the "Post-Modern Age" Subject constituted through today's common sense, know reality when I see it.

Thirdly, the service is *localized* – virtually all of the adverts are from Cardiff and the South Wales valleys – but the mailing address is in London. My local, community-based service, which caters exclusively to my needs, turns out to be a national (or international?) capitalist corporation. The global masquerades as the local. And I am seduced.

You say the tape recorded message is for No One In Particular but I experience each sensual word as stated only for Me.

Our Motto: WE AIM TO PLEASE!

"Lonely-hearts" columns have a long history. However, and this is the fourth point, we now have, in the "Post-Modern Age", lonely-hearts columns with a difference.

Name your lifestyle, your desires, and I, the invisible hand of the free market, will gladly supply your needs.

This is the late capitalist market place with its *infinite choices* (or as infinite as our respectable local paper will allow):[2] What would you like? An older man? A younger one? A cuddly lady? A blonde? A handsome man? A divorcée? A mature student? A home owner? Someone with a good sense of humour? A smoker? A disco goer? A Welsh speaker? A "new man"? A vegetarian? Or is it "a hunky black guy, 18–25", who is "exciting" and enjoys music and nightclubs?

Our fifth and main point here is that this shopping for difference is *a means by which we can all advertise and consume – not just ordinary commodities but also lifestyles and bodies – according to taste.*

The "Post-Modern Age" allows, indeed encourages, *the consumption of difference and Otherness.* Through music, dance and style, through sexual fantasy and sexual reality, I, the lonely heart alienated and frustrated in the late capitalist city, can encounter the Other. Even if I live in an all-White community, I can use the capitalist market place and the electronic media to encounter a hunky Black male (or an exotic brown-skinned female). Whether the encounter is via sexual fantasy or reality makes little difference. Either way it brings me pleasure.

I have watched with envy as Black people laughed and danced. I will place an advert and find a dark-skinned partner.

I have longed so long for a dark penis inside me that I only achieve orgasm by fantasizing in Black and White.

Most of the choices available in the "postmodern" capitalist market place are innocent ones. The consumption of racial difference, however, is not. Why not?

The answer to that question is the concern of the remainder of this chapter. Let us continue by examining another case of shopping for difference, leaving Cardiff and the South Wales valleys for Ivy League Town, USA.

Shopping for difference: case study 2

Fascination with the racialized Other has long been a feature of Western culture. Some of this fascination has been in the form of caricature – of American Indians as tomahawk-wielding savages, of Australian Aborigines as Stone Age nature-people, of Arabs and Muslims as vicious and threatening, of people of African descent as hypersexual, uncivilized and intellectually backward . . . On the other hand, Westerners have long celebrated "primitive" cultures, especially African and Oceanic art and rituals, as a source of authentic, elemental creativity and power. Indeed, much of modern Western art precisely emerged out of a (not always positive) dialogue with the Other.[3]

Similarly, it would be wrong to assume that White standards of beauty allow no space for non-White beauty. Besides the attraction to blondes and other White angels, there is a long tradition of fascination with "exotic" Women of Colour. For example, during slavery – which is to say, during 75 per cent of the time that people of African descent have been in the New World – "specific African tribes gained a reputation for having women who made attractive concubines for their masters" (Drake 1987: 80). For generations, in Brazil, Spanish America and the French Caribbean there was a cult of the mulatto. "Mixed-race" women, themselves the product of interracial sexual relationships (and of White male rape), were – and often still are – prized for their exotic and erotic appeal. These women occupy a central place as objects of (usually White) male desire in a social and cultural system where females are ranked and classified according to their use-value.

But that was all long ago. Things are very different now. We, Cosmopolitans of the "Post-Modern Age", are miles away from such racist and sexist nonsense. Unlike our predecessors, we are open to encounters, even intimate encounters, with the Other.

Below is testimony from bell hooks, the American feminist cultural critic, who, like us, has noted how different things are in this, the "Post-Modern Age":

> While teaching at Yale, I walked one bright spring day in the downtown area of New Haven, which is close to campus and invariably brings one into contact with many of the poor black people who live

nearby, and found myself walking behind a group of very blond, very white, jock type boys . . . Seemingly unaware of my presence, these young men talked about their plans to fuck as many girls from other racial/ethnic groups as they could "catch" before graduation. They "ran" it down. Black girls were high on the list, Native American girls hard to find, Asian girls (all lumped into the same category), deemed easier to entice, were considered "prime targets". Talking about this overheard conversation to my students, I found that it was commonly accepted that one "shopped" for sexual partners in the same way one "shopped" for courses at Yale, and that race and ethnicity was a serious category on which selections were based. (hooks 1992a: 23)

In her discussion of this incident in "Eating the other" (an insightful essay on the cultural and sexual politics of race and racism), bell hooks points out that the expression of open desire on the part of White men for sex with Women of Colour breaks a long established, rigorously enforced taboo. While White men in the USA have a long history of sexual relations with Women of Colour – including the violations of Black women's bodies that were part of everyday life under slavery – this has virtually never been a publicly acceptable practice. Today, among the privileged, highly educated, young White men of America's elite colleges, *racial difference has been reinscribed as cultural diversity and pluralism.* But does this mark a real change in attitudes?

The "Post-Modern Age" practice of "shopping" for racial and cultural difference, whether in the form of style, music or sexual partners, suggests that such differences have become commodified. But what is it exactly that has been commodified? What are the differences that young White male students at Yale and young White females in South Wales wish to consume? What meanings are attributed to the bodies of Women and Men of Colour – from Michael Jordan to Tina Turner – in order that they should become desirable icons? These are questions to which we will return.

Openness to difference and the question of power

In "Post-Modern Age" societies, symbols of "cultural diversity" – including Black bodies – have become highly profitable commodities. Young people from London to Tokyo sport the symbols of urban, Black American culture. In Britain and some other western European countries, blues sounds and James Brown recordings form the soundtracks for up-market television commercials. School children in Britain hanker after Michael Jordan T-shirts and Michael Jackson records. White men, not Black youth, are the leading consumers of Black rap music.

155

Black American music and style are all around us. Black bodies are never far away.

The commodification of difference in contemporary society is closely linked to more general, often celebrated features of "postmodern" societies – specifically, their apparent openness to difference. As White Western meanings and values with their Eurocentric narratives of history and culture have been increasingly decentred – actually or apparently? – in academic life, so it is in the arena of popular culture, where the celebration of difference occurs predominately via variegated commodities that are marketed and consumed. The "Post-Modern Age", like postmodernist theory, seems to offer a context that allows historically excluded voices – those of women, People of Colour, dominated minorities – to be heard.

Yet does openness to difference, whether in studies of history and culture or in culture as it is lived, signify a real change in power relations?

In the wake of postmodernism, theorizing difference has become a crucial issue in theorizing culture. A range of ways of seeing difference have become commonplace in cultural analysis – from Derrida's concept of *différance* as a structuring principle of language to ideas of difference as an effect of the play of the signifier to appeals to plurality and diversity. Such theorizing has often led to a concentration on *culture as textuality* at the expense of considerations of *questions of power*. Race and racism are a case in point.

We, however, refuse to separate questions of culture from questions of power (and of History). Thus, we are concerned with how Western representation, celebration and commodification of Black bodies and Black culture relate to long-established traditions of Western racism. What, we ask, are the implications of this for theorizing difference?

Strong, graceful and super-sexual: the commodification of Black male bodies

In the West, people of African descent are represented, first of all, as bodies – as physical and emotional beings (as compared, say, to intellectual beings). In hegemonic and popular discourses, in modern and postmodern systems of representation, the Black is strong, powerful and, on the dance floor, football field and basketball court, a smooth mover.

The South Wales blonde is right. If she wants an exciting companion for music, dancing and clubs, she should seek out the Darker Brother.

Perhaps the most spectacular current example of the contemporary fascination with Black bodies is the Michael Jordan phenomenon.

Before him, it was O. J. Simpson. And, before him, Muhammad Ali. And before him, Willie Mays. And before him Joe Louis. And before him . . . the Black African slave.

As we write this essay (in the mid 1990s) Michael Jordan, basketball superstar with the Chicago Bulls, is the most famous athlete in the world – and thought by many to be the best. Nike markets Air-Jordan shoes, Chevrolet markets a Michael Jordan car (complete with his signature on the outside and on the dashboard), teenagers all over the world wear Michael Jordan on their chests, his restaurant is the most famous in Chicago, corporations pay millions of dollars to have his name associated with them . . . Michael Jordan's image is virtually everywhere. As Michael Dyson argues in his essay "Be like Mike? Michael Jordan and the pedagogy of desire", Jordan "has attained unparalleled cultural status because of his extraordinary physical gifts, his marketing as an icon of race-transcending American athletic and moral excellence and his mastery of a sport which has become the metaphoric centre of black cultural imagination" (Dyson 1993: 64).

Over the last few decades, basketball has moved from its position as a largely Black American sport into the mainstream of American life and its icons – foremost among them Michael Jordan – have become the heroes of White as well as Black America and beyond. Sport has long played an important affirmative role in the lives of Black Americans, offering the possibility of success and recognition denied them in other areas of life. It has served as what Dyson calls "a way of ritualizing racial achievement against socially imposed barriers to cultural performance".

In short, black sport activity often acquired a heroic dimension, as viewed in the careers of figures such as Joe Louis, Jackie Robinson, Althea Gibson, Wilma Rudolph and Arthur Ashe. Black sports heroes transcended the narrow boundaries of specific sports activities and garnered importance as icons of cultural excellence, symbolic figures who embodied social possibilities of success denied to other people of color. But they also captured and catalyzed the black cultural fetishization of sport as a means of expressing black cultural style, as a means of pursuing social and economic mobility. (Dyson 1993: 66)

For his Black fans, Jordan offers an image of a Black athlete who has achieved wealth, fame and respect beyond their wildest dreams. (The same was true of O. J. Simpson, which is why his downfall has been experienced as a personal crisis and loss by so many African-Americans.) For his White fans he is, perhaps above all, a Great American Hero. Yet the emphasis on physique, style, performance and sporting prowess, which characterizes media representations of Michael Jordan and other Black American superstars, reaffirms long established myths about Black bodies. Moreover, the importance of style and performance is part of a more general commodification of these aspects of Black character and culture.

We all know Black people are only physical. They are super-athletes and super-studs. And I, the White shopper for difference, love it!

For centuries Black bodies, male and female, have been Objects of Fascination, if not envy, for many White people – as dancers, musicians, athletes and fantasy lovers. In "My Negro problem – and ours" (Podhoretz 1963), an interesting, self-reflexive essay, Norman Podhoretz makes the following confession:

Just as in childhood I envied Negroes for what seemed to me their superior masculinity, so I envy them today for what seems to be their superior physical grace and beauty. I have come to value physical grace very highly and *I am now capable of aching with all my being when I watch a Negro couple on the dance floor, or a Negro playing baseball or basketball.* They are on the kind of terms with their own bodies that I should like to be on with mine, and for that precious quality they seem blessed to me. (quoted in hooks 1992b: 96; emphasis added)

White people have been known to spend hours on end trying to learn to dance like Black people, to move as they do on the basketball court or football field.

In contemporary Western youth culture, the Black body, especially the Black male body, has obtained a kind of mythical status. This is the continuation of a long tradition – but with a difference: whereas from the sixteenth to the nineteenth century "it was this black body that was most 'desired' for its labor in slavery", today "this body . . . is most represented in contemporary popular culture as the body to be watched, imitated, desired, possessed" (hooks 1992a: 34).

Why is the Black body, especially the young, athletic Black male body, so highly regarded and imitated? Because of the cultural politics of race and the marketing abilities of modern capitalism. "Blackness" – Black culture, Black bodies, Black character – stands, in the Western (that is to say, White) imagination, as a primitive sign of wildness. And this is arguably as true today as it was 200 years ago. "It is the young black male body that is seen as epitomizing this promise of wildness, of unlimited physical prowess and unbridled eroticism"

Figure 9.1   Dancing in "Tiger Bay", late 1940s
(Bert Hardy/Hulton Deutsch Collection).

(hooks 1992a: 34). We all know, thanks to the never-erring brilliance of common sense, "that black people have secret access to intense pleasure, particularly pleasures of the body" (hooks 1992a: 34). Because I am in search of the path to pleasure, I must seek an encounter with those who are its guardian. Hence, I offer myself to the Other.

Super-stud: the myth of the Black penis

What are Black male bodies? They are not only the super-athletic, they are also the super-sexual. The sexualized imagery of the Black male is constantly packaged and sold – more than ever, as it turns out, in our "Post-Modern"

159

(but, unfortunately, not "Post-Racist") Age. The Black stud is a recurrent feature in Hollywood films, from the "Blaxploitation" films of the 1970s to *Miami Vice* and the films of Eddie Murphy and Spike Lee. Black male singers and entertainers, perhaps most of them, sell this imagery: reggae stars, rap stars, Prince, Michael Jackson, James Brown, B. B. King . . . The over-sexed, smooth dancing Black male with half a voice stands a good chance of making money – especially if he can manage to incorporate a gyrating pelvis into his stage routine.

Black men, after all, have exceptionally large penises – this idea has been around for hundreds of years and, especially in the eighteenth and nineteenth centuries, has received varying degrees of scientific legitimacy. Here is a quote from a book published in London in 1799, entitled *An account of the regular gradation in man, and in different animals and vegetables; and from the former to the latter* (White 1799), by Dr Charles White:

> That the PENIS of an African is larger than that of an European has, I believe, been shewn in every anatomical school in London. Preparations of them are preserved in most anatomical museums; and I have one [i.e. a pickled African penis] in mine. (quoted in Jordan 1969: 501)

Since Dr White was both a careful scientist and the proud owner of a pickled Black penis, we do not dare to question his authority.

Below is a more recent statement of the large penis thesis. This passage was published in 1948 by a French author, Michel Cournot, in his book *Martinique*:

> The black man's sword is a sword. When he has thrust it into your wife, she has really felt something. It is a revelation. In the chasm that it has left, your little toy is lost. Pump away until the room is awash with your sweat, you might as well just be singing. This is *good-bye* . . . Four Negroes with their penises exposed would fill a cathedral. They would be unable to leave the building until their erections had subsided; and in such close quarters that would not be a simple matter. (Cournot cited in Fanon 1968: 120)

The predominate myth regarding Black male bodies is not so much that they are endowed with exceptionally large penises, although this *is* part of it. Rather, it is that the Black man possesses a powerful body with a superhuman sexual appetite – an unquenchable drive for ravenous, aggressive sex – and that he/it lusts particularly after White women (especially blondes?).

The image of the strong, infinitely virile Black male hunk seeking to ravish White women is powerful indeed. Here is some interesting evidence from psychiatric interviews conducted *c.* 1950 with White women in France by the

West Indian psychiatrist Frantz Fanon:

> There is something in the mere idea, one young woman confided to me, that makes the heart skip a beat. A prostitute told me once that in her early days the mere thought of going to bed with a Negro brought on an orgasm. She went in search of Negroes and never asked them for money. But, she added, "going to bed with them was no more remarkable than going to bed with white men. It was before I did it that I had the orgasm. I used to think about (imagine) all the things they might do to me: and that was what was so terrific." (Fanon 1968: 112)

The mere thought brought on an orgasm . . . Her fantasy is enough. My world, I thankfully and proudly say, is even better than that of the honest French prostitute. I live in the "Post-Modern Age" where fantasies are sold like *Coca-Cola*. Mine is predominately a hyper-real world, a world in which I, like you, do not distinguish between the realm of illusory appearances and the realm of fact.

Is my hunky, exciting, sexy Black man real or illusion? The question does not arise.

An irony

It must be said that the cultural construction of Black bodies as a zone of Pleasure is, in America, Britain, France and other racist societies, somewhat ironic.

> *Truth:* Regarded fetishistically in the psycho-sexual racial imagination of youth culture, the real bodies of young black men are daily viciously assaulted by white racist violence, black on black violence, the violence of overwork, and the violence of disease and addiction. (hooks 1992a: 34)

Concluding reflections

Racism is a cultural politics, producing its effects in the conjoined spaces of culture, power and subjectivity. The history of attitudes to, and practices upon, Black bodies in the West is closely intertwined with the history of racism. Racism makes aesthetic and moral judgements about different categories of bodies and phenotypes: some facial features are considered more attractive than others, some ethnic or racial groups are viewed as more interesting and sensual than others.

Racism in its cultural forms has more often than not functioned as a justification of brutal practices of exploitation, exclusion and genocide. Certain unpleasant facts must never be forgotten: the Black bodies consumed by sharks in the Middle Passage, the Australian Aborigines and American Indians hunted like dogs, the Jews exterminated in the heartlands of modern civilization . . .

This side of racism, however, has not been the topic of this chapter. Our concern has been to show that, as cultural politics, racism makes certain claims about the Body (about beauty, ugliness, sexuality) and about Culture and Character (about what different categories of people are like); and to suggest that core aspects of the cultural politics of racism are reproduced in the "cosmopolitan" capitalist market place of our "Post-Modern" world.

What are the implications of our investigation? What does it suggest about theorizing difference in the wake of the "Post-Modern Age" and postmodernist theory? Surely the crucial point is that it is not adequate to theorize difference merely as plurality, the play of the signifier or as an effect of cultural diversity. Difference, like "free choice", in racist and sexist societies is an effect of power.

Postmodernist theory offers a framework from within which to question long-established Truth, narratives of History and the exclusion of marginalized and oppressed groups from the institutions that define what we are and how our society should be. It has the potential to raise fundamental questions about concepts and perspectives that conflate categories like race and culture or sex and culture. Nonetheless, if we do not focus on the material interests and structures of power that produce cultural meanings and values – on the power structures of racism and sexism (and other such oppressions) – our re-theorizing of culture in the light of postmodern theories of difference will remain a liberal enterprise that leaves existing material relations of exclusion, oppression and even brutality intact.

To celebrate cultural diversity without attention to the construction of this diversity is to leave long-established racist assumptions, integral to both the history and present of Western societies, unchallenged.

Take, for example, the two stories of shopping for difference with which we opened this chapter. In the first case – that of the 18 year-old blonde desiring an exciting Black male – we would argue that, despite the fact that she probably knows next to nothing about racism, she has reduced her prospective companion to music, dance and exciting times, i.e. to a kind of racial caricature.[1] In the second case – that of White American boys shopping for brown-skinned exotics – we would suggest that the desire to experience sex with women from a large number of racial and ethnic backgrounds marks a re-formulation of a perversely racist, if unconscious, set of assumptions about

Women of Colour that draw on the classic racist patterns of belief about Black and Asian bodies. They include assumptions about higher levels of sensuality, superior sexual knowledge and exotic sex.[5]

The commodification of racial difference in this "Post-Modern Age" – our era in which there are new ways of consuming Otherness – appears to offer White people alternatives to crises of identity that many of them experience in contemporary Western societies. bell hooks argues that these crises, "especially as experienced by white youth, are eased when the 'primitive' is recouped *via* a focus on diversity and pluralism": "the Other can provide life-sustaining alternatives" (hooks 1992a: 25–6).

But does this "postmodern" fascination with the Other mark a real change? Does it indicate an end to the binary opposition White/Other, that insidious relation of domination and oppression in which White Power is always privileged whatever disguise it may wear? Does it signal the development of real respect for Others which might herald an end to racism? Don't hold your breath.

> *The Final Word:* To make one's self vulnerable to the seduction of difference, to seek an encounter with the Other, does not require that one relinquish forever one's mainstream positionality. When race and ethnicity become commodified as resources for pleasure, the culture of specific groups, as well as the bodies of individuals, can be seen as constituting an alternative playground where members of dominating races, genders, sexual practices affirm their power-over in intimate relations with the Other. (hooks 1992a: 23)

Notes

Some parts of this essay are included in Chapter 9 of our book, *Cultural politics: class, gender, race and the postmodern world* (Jordan & Weedon 1995).

1. There were a total of 128 "Voice Link" messages in the 1 September 1994 edition of the *Cardiff Post*. We have chosen a sample of nine.
2. The choice of partners would have been even greater if our lonely-hearts column had been published in, say, Amsterdam, Berlin, Paris, New York or San Francisco rather than in highly respectable South Wales. If you write, "**KINKY** male seeks companion for bondage, must have own handcuffs", our local paper will kindly refuse to print your message.
3. See Chapters 9, 10 and 11 of Jordan & Weedon (1995). Also see Rubin (1984).
4. The fact that some young (and even old) Black males do not object to being reduced to such stereotypes does not make this sort of practice any less dangerous. Arguably, it makes it more so.
5. An excellent discussion, from a very illuminating historical perspective, of many of the issues raised in this chapter is contained in Jordan (1969).

Bibliography

Chambers, I. 1986. *Popular culture: the metropolitan experience*. London: Methuen.

Dixon, T. 1905. *The clansman: an historical romance of the Ku Klux Klan*. London: Heinemann.

Drake, St. C. 1987. *Black folk here and there*, vol. I. Los Angeles: Centre for Afro-American Studies, University of California, Los Angeles.

Dyson, M. E. 1993. Be like Mike? Michael Jordan and the pedagogy of desire. *Cultural Studies* **7**, 64–72.

Fanon, F. 1967. *The wretched of the Earth*. Originally published in 1961 as *Les damnés de la terre*, tr. C. Farrington. London: Penguin.

Fanon, F. 1968. *Black skin, white masks*. Originally published in 1952 as *Peau noire, masques blancs*, tr. C. Lam Markmann. New York: Grove Press.

Gilman, S. L. 1992. Black bodies, White bodies: toward an iconography of female sexuality in late nineteenth-century art, medicine and literature. In *"Race", culture and difference*, J. Donald & A. Rattansi (eds), 171–97. London: Sage in association with the Open University.

hooks, b. 1991. Critical interrogation: talking race, resisting racism. In *Yearning: race, gender, and cultural politics*, 51–5. London: Turnaround.

hooks, b. 1992a. Eating the other. In *Black looks: race and representation*, 21–39. London: Turnaround.

hooks, b. 1992b. Reconstructing Black masculinity. In *Black looks: race and representation*, 87–113. London: Turnaround.

Jencks, C. 1989. *What is postmodernism?* London: Academy Editions and New York: St. Martin's Press.

Jordan, G. & C. Weedon 1995. *Cultural politics: class, gender, race and the postmodern world*. Oxford: Basil Blackwell.

Jordan, W. 1969. The bodies of men: the Negro's physical nature. In *White over Black*. London: Penguin.

Maurer, E. 1984. Dada and surrealism. In *"Primitivism" in 20th century art: affinity of the tribal and the modern*, W. Rubin (ed.), 535–93. New York: Museum of Modern Art.

Podhoretz, N. 1963. My Negro problem – and ours. *Commentary*.

Rose, P. 1989. *Jazz Cleopatra: Josephine Baker in her time*. New York: HarperCollins.

Rubin, W. (ed.) 1984. *"Primitivism" in 20th century art: affinity of the tribal and the modern*. New York: Museum of Modern Art.

Thorpe, E. 1989. *Black dance*. London: Chatto & Windus.

Turner, T. 1987. *I, Tina: my life story*. New York: Avon.

White, C. 1799. *An account of the regular gradation in man, and in different animals and vegetables; and from the former to the latter*. London: C. Dilly.

CHAPTER 10

Cultural studies, the university and the question of borders

Taieb Belghazi

> I want to suggest a different metaphor for theoretical work: the meta-phor of struggle, of wrestling with the angels. The only theory worth having is that which you have to fight off, not that which you speak with profound fluency. (Stuart Hall 1992: 280)

In this chapter, I argue for a relocation of cultural studies as an ambivalent border space, one that does not apprehend culture merely as *heimlich* "with its disciplinary generalisations, its mimetic narratives, its homologous empty time, its seriality, its progress, its customs and coherence" (Bhabha 1994: 136). I propose, instead, a reappropriation of the history of this field as a shifting battleground for conflicting positions where no point in time is made sacro-sanct, a historical articulation of disparate domains of language use, or, as Hall (1992: 278) puts it, "a set of unstable formations 'centered' only in quotation marks". In my reading, emphasis will be laid on cultural studies as *unheimlich*, for "to be distinctive, significatory, influential and identifiable, it has to be translated, disseminated, interdisciplinary, international, interracial" (Bhabha 1994: 137). Cultural studies would be, on this account, a challenge to the understanding of culture in terms of authenticity; it would no longer be viewed as the embodiment in one language of an undivided people. In other words, I want to counter the nativist approach that resorts to a mythical past in order to affirm an undivided, "pure" origin. In this chapter, then, I shall draw on the writings of scholars who tend to work outside the cultural frame that has traditionally defined and delimited cultural studies.

Travelling theory: the Moroccan example

In a country like Morocco, the site of this chapter's production, cultural stud-ies could hardly be considered to be a matter of Moroccan cultural workers

"catching up" with their Western colleagues, reproducing the hegemonic relations that prevail in, say, "Commonwealth studies". Rather, it necessitates the
construction of what Edward Said (1983) calls "travelling theory", which considers the changes that theory undergoes as it moves from one intellectual
location to another. An example would be the transformation of the notion of
reification used by Lukacs (the Hungarian Marxist) when it is re-interpreted
and re-appropriated in France as "homology" by Lucien Goldman (Said
1983: 226–47). Cultural studies has "travelled" well and has engaged with
concerns and methodologies that are at odds with its British origin. It is worth
noting, for instance, that the studies of the conditions of indigenous popula-
tions, in societies such as the USA, Canada and Australia, where power is held
by Whites, have opened up new horizons for cultural research.

Such a "relocation" of cultural studies has the potential to both water down
its richness and potency, as well as to energize it, or to empower it with new
and different meanings. As Robbins (1992: 66) suggests:

In the name of "travel," the academy can either be condemned as a
place of drowsy rootedness and inactive belatedness, or, on the contrary, it can be defended as the one place – really a non-place – where
criticism can be truly itself: non-totalizing, perpetually alert and self-
critical, pure.

In any case, it is the cultural worker's awareness of the complex predica-
ment of uprooted cultural studies that helps to bring about his or her theoretical vigilance and critical potential.

An understanding of cultural studies in terms of travelling theory is of particular interest in the Moroccan context, since there has always been a powerful trend among Moroccan intellectuals to conceptualize scholarship as a site
of travel and to perceive uprootedness as inextricably linked to dissent. Thus,
when schools were founded in the fourteenth century during the reign of the
Merinid dynasty, one of the most outstanding scholars of the time, Cheikh
Abili, objected to them on the ground that they tied scholars to particular
places and made them dependent on the authorities which paid them (Al
Wancharissi 1981: 479).

Two major consequences follow from this re-reading of cultural studies in
terms of travel. On the one hand, as Clifford (1992: 101) argues, "the organic,
naturalising bias of culture – seen as a rooted body that grows, lives, dies, etc –
is questioned. Constructed and disrupted historicities, sites of displacement,
interference, and interaction come more sharply into view." In my view, this
reading of culture would benefit from grammatology as it teaches that it is
impossible to locate an originary moment of full presence that can be set off
from its reinscription in time. On the other hand, cultural studies provides the

166

basis to generate a politics that is not grounded in a high court of appeal that adjudicates between different claims, but rather in a methodology that is aware of its own provenance.

The understanding of cultural studies in terms of travel would imply, for example, that the Centre for Contemporary Cultural Studies at Birmingham would no longer simply be the "ground from which travelling departs and to which it returns" (Clifford 1992: 114). It should be noted in this respect that spatial contraction, the global simultaneity arising from technological changes as discussed by Virilio and Baudrillard (1987), renders the traditional distinction between departure and arrival a difficult one to sustain. According to Virilio, ours is the time of "dromologie" or "the logic of race", when everything arrives without necessarily having to depart – a point Baudrillard elaborates in *The ecstasy of communication*:

> Just as we have reached the limits of geographic space and have explored all the confines of the planet, we can only implode into a space which is reduced daily as a result of our increasing mobility made possible by aeroplanes and the media, to the point where trips have already taken place. (Baudrillard 1987: 39)

The proliferation of sophisticated media technology has, in a sense, led to the homogenization of world culture, but the heterogeneity of culture persists because media images take on a variety of meanings depending on the ways in which audiences in different locations interact with them.

Abdelkebir Khatibi, one of the most thought-provoking cultural workers in Morocco, rejects as theological the notion of unity (*wahda*), deployed as "a community principle" within one country or as a means of "rallying all moslems in the framework of an Oumma [nation]" (Khatibi 1993: 9). In order to keep abreast of these changes in world culture, Khatibi has emphasized the necessity of internationalizing research; that is to say, of opening it up to different methods and styles. He wants Moroccan cultural workers to reject sterile rootedness that generates all sorts of foundational thought and to approach the study of culture as a hybrid discursive space. One of the elements of analysis he proposes to approach is "the dissymmetrical plurality between various areas of knowledge", that is, what he calls "the bi-code" that permeates Moroccan society. This bi-code is particularly important, Khatibi (1988: 98) argues, because of Morocco's multiple and heterogeneous linguistic scene, because of the close "proximity between the sacred and the secular, the national and the foreign, the same and the other." For Khatibi, the bi-code constitutes the condition of possibility for a mode of thinking that departs from entrenched theoretical positions. It also facilitates dialogue as a mode of doing cultural studies. The aim is not the liberal ethic of diversity where, as Bhabha

(1992: 62) suggests, Fish's "interpretive communities" try to keep the conversation going. Nor is it Rorty's linguistic metaphor of political culture, "the consensual overlapping of 'final languages' which allow 'imaginative' identification with the other, so long as certain modes – kindness, decency, dignity are held in common" (Bhabha 1992: 62), nor even, after Habermas, a noise-free "ideal speech situation". In other words, cultural workers need to be aware of the power relations involved whenever they engage with their own and other cultures.

A second element of Khatibi's cultural theory is the focus on what he calls "the interval between knowledge and technology". Here, he considers the ways in which dramatic transformations in mass communication technologies are affecting popular culture. For Khatibi (1988: 98), it is crucial that we understand this conjuncture not as a "purely academic interdisciplinarity, but an active production, a memory in becoming". Research, he insists, should not be a matter of lamenting the degeneration of "popular" culture as a result of the recent technological changes, but should view the transformation Moroccan culture is undergoing as the time to reject any search for monolithic unitary thought and to promote, instead, ambivalence as an empowering strategy in the treatment of culture.

An obvious objection to this line of argument would be that cultural studies cannot assert itself as an impure liminality for it can only operate within the constraints of the Moroccan university. I would argue, however, that the Kantian model of the university as the site of determinate spheres on which such an objection would be premised is no longer tenable, and that the changes experienced by the universities in Morocco could be the condition of possibility for a reconceptualization of cultural studies. In order to illustrate this point, I would like to turn to Derrida's text "Mochlos" (Derrida 1992) where he discusses "The conflict of faculties" by Kant, widely considered to be the founding text of the modern university. This text was written after the King of Prussia had decided to censor some of Kant's writings.

Cultural studies in the context of university research

As Derrida (1992) points out, Kant's text has a continuing relevance to ongoing debates about the university, its relation to the state and the function it is called upon to fulfil. Very briefly, Kant distinguished between philosophical pronouncements – which are constatives – and the royal utterances which are performatives, since they carry the force of law that goes with someone who has authority. Kant also made a distinction between higher faculties – law, medicine and theology – and the lower faculty which refers to philosophy. He subdivides the latter faculty into two departments: the historical sciences which consist of history, geography, linguistics and humanities, and the purely rational sciences which consist of pure mathematics, pure philosophy and the metaphysics of nature and morals. The lower faculty has the task of judging the theoretical validity of any given law, medical procedure or ecclesiastical statute, while the higher faculties – bureaucratic extensions of state and church – are responsible for keeping the domains separate without in any way impeding the capacity of philosophy – the lower faculty – to make its judgements.

It is this policing of boundaries that cultural studies disrupts. No wonder, therefore, that it has been criticized by those who consider themselves to be the custodians of spheres of study whose objects and methodologies cultural studies plunders impudently. Stuart Hall (1980) gives us an example of the sanctity of borders when he recounts one of the responses to the opening of the Centre for Contemporary Cultural Studies at Birmingham where a letter from two social scientists threatened reprisals if cultural studies crossed territorial boundaries, "overstepped its proper limits and took on the study of contemporary society (not just its texts), without proper scientific (that is quasi-scientific) controls" (Hall 1980: 21). It is with this tension in mind that I would suggest that Derrida's intervention is so important.

In "Mochlos", Derrida (1992: 6) highlights the difficulty of holding hard and fast distinctions between the various spheres demarcated by Kant. He points out that the notion of responsibility which Kant evokes in order to preserve the "inviolability" and the "purity" of the various spheres is more problematic today. He insists that contemporary academics work in a context where the notion of responsibility is pushed to the background. This is the reason that prompts him to say, in turn, that "we feel bad about ourselves" (Derrida 1992: 7). His view is that "those who feel good about themselves are perhaps hiding something, from others or from themselves" (Derrida 1992: 7). Interestingly, Derrida considers the destabilization of Kant's rigid boundaries from an ethical perspective. He is not engaging in the type of project that is (in my view wrongly) ascribed to him by anti-deconstructionists. In other words, he shows once again that deconstruction is not a mere textualism; on the contrary, as he puts it in "Mochlos",

> Deconstruction is limited neither to a methodological reform that would reassure the given organisation nor, inversely, to a parade of irresponsible or irresponsibilizing destruction, whose surest effect would be to leave everything as it is, consolidating the most immobile forces of the university. (Derrida 1992: 23)

Futhermore, Derrida's discussion of the various aporias running though Kant's text hinders any attempt to view "Mochlos" as a kind of nostalgia for a time when spheres of knowledge were defined as mutually exclusive.

According to Derrida (1992: 10), the "western university", which is "a very recent construction or artifact" is "finished". Here, Derrida is not simply indulging in the type of apocalyptic discourse that has been holding sway in English departments over the last two decades. Rather, his point follows from his observation that the Kantian model of the university is no longer operative. Kant's aim, as Derrida points out, has been to adjudicate between various university departments and to arrange those departments in a hierarchical order. On Kant's reading, the centres of research lying outside the university could pose no serious threat to the university. This, however, is no longer the case: today border conflicts between university and non-university research centres are not uncommon. Both lay claim to the production and transmission of knowledge (Derrida 1992: 14). That is to say that the relation between the university and its other has changed. Whereas in Kant's time, it was perhaps possible to keep the research centres on the margins of the university, "Today, in any case, the university is what has become the margin" (Derrida 1992: 14) and some members of the university have joined these centres and started "irritating the insides of the teaching body like parasites" (Derrida 1992: 15).

Kant, of course, tried to eradicate parasiting. He viewed the political authorities as a safeguard against border crossings. He even went so far as to tell the King of Prussia that he is true to what he preaches, in the sense that his writings are addressed to a minority of scholars who share his specialism, and that those writings could have no impact on the populace who would not be able to understand them anyway. For this reason, then, there was no need to censor his work. By way of an example, Kant pleads not guilty to the charge of harming people's religious faith and practice through his book *Religion within the limits of reason alone* (Kant 1960), since ordinary people cannot understand it. It is, Kant argues, "an unintelligible and closed book, a mere debate between Faculty scholars, of which the public takes no notice; the faculties themselves, to be sure, remain, to the best of their science and conscience, free to judge it publicly" (quoted in Derrida 1992: 19).

Nowadays, the Kantian argument would be ill-advised for all who seek to attract funding from decision makers. Robert Young (1992), in his contribution to the discussion of Derrida's "Mochlos", points out the paradoxical situation in which British theorists find themselves. Set on protecting their disciplines against persisting "government cuts", he tells us, they have to invoke the view of usefulness and relevance that in intellectual terms, they wanted to attack (Young 1992: 113). These theorists present cultural studies as "a bridge between theory and material practice" (Grossberg et al. 1992: 6) and as an antidote to the pessimistic view held by some literary scholars who in "considering how little impact the humanities have had on the development of world affairs and how little public attention has been paid to the professional humanists, have decided to forget about the ills of humanity and concentrate on their well-being" (Kecht 1992: 2).

My reading of cultural studies goes against this utilitarian and instrumental-ist approach to knowledge which simply tries to keep abreast of the market forces. This position is aptly described by Lyotard:

> The old principle that the acquisition of knowledge is indissociable from the training (*Bildung*) of minds or even of individuals is becoming obsolete and will become even more so. The relationship of suppliers and users of knowledge to the knowledge they supply and use is now tending, and will increasingly tend to assume the form already taken by the relationship of commodities they produce and consume – that is, the form of value. Knowledge is and will be produced in order to be sold, it is and will be consumed in order to be valorised in a new pro-duction: in both cases, the goal is exchange. (Lyotard 1984: 4)

Asserting itself as a transgressive force, however, cultural studies refuses to be considered as a mere commodity. It subverts the traditional perception of knowledge in terms of a simplistic correspondence and affirms the inextricable link between the knowledge it offers and power, without lapsing into a stand where "anything goes" for there will always be what Hall calls "an arbitrary closure" (Hall 1992: 278). Cultural studies reinflects, reshapes and destabilizes the traditional disciplinary distinctions, because fixed borders would imply, as Derrida says, critical dogmatism. Thus, Khatibi (1988) calls for the explora-tion not only of the institutional divisions that exist within the Moroccan uni-versity, but also those that persist between various areas of knowledge and which remain "unthought", such as "the question of bilingualism" or the sepa-ration of religion from the secular (Khatibi 1988: 98). According to Khatibi, the analysis of these various divisions is an important condition for establishing bridges between different areas of knowledge and for transforming the Moroc-can university.

Furthermore, it is important to note that the borders on which cultural workers place themselves are neither secure nor definite. "Borders", as Abdul. R. Jan Mohamed (1992: 103) puts it, "are neither inside nor outside the terri-tory they define but simply designate the difference between the two." For Mohamed, cultural workers are committed interventionists and not simply "'sitting' on the border; rather, they are forced to *constitute themselves as the border*" (Mohamed 1992: 103). Their position is a marginal one, in Bhabha's sense (1990: 4) "not the space of celebratory, or Utopian self-marginalisation". Instead cultural workers intervene and displace what modernity has taken for granted: "progress, homogeneity, cultural organicism, the deep nation, the long past – that rationalise the authoritarian, 'normalising' tendencies within cultures in the name of the national interest or the ethnic prerogative". In the case of Morocco, Khatibi (1983) also affirms marginality as a prerequisite for non-repressive thinking: "thinking which does not draw its inspiration from its poverty is always elaborated to dominate and to humiliate; thinking which is not in the minority, marginal, fragmentary, and incomplete is always thinking of the ethnocide" (Khatibi 1983: 18).

On this account, it follows that cultural theorists working in English departments need to unsettle the view of the curriculum as something that has a trans-historical validity, namely as a collection of texts whose "literariness" is what justifies their selection in the first place (Zavarzadeh & Morton 1991: 10). Similarly, they need to reject what Spriggs (1972: 222) calls "the frozen syllabus" and instead work towards a permanent de-stabilization of the institutional boundaries of the English department. Furthermore, the traditional role of the teacher as "a midwife of truth" also needs to be rejected in order to adopt what Giroux (1992) calls a "border pedagogy". By this she does not simply mean the encounter of students with a multitude of cultures, but equally a recognition of the fragility of identity "as it moves into border lands crisscrossed with a variety of languages, experiences, and voices" (Giroux 1992: 209).

Allow me to conclude, then, by suggesting that as cultural theorists we need to revise and remake cultural studies on a daily basis; it is not a field endowed with stability. Cultural studies is, in my view, best thought of as an *event* in the Foucauldian sense; that is to say, as *a happening that escapes the homogenizing influence of narrative*. As an "event", therefore, cultural studies resists subsumption and subordination, and encourages, in turn, its own constructing culture. That is to say, in Fanon's terms, cultural studies is "the occult zone of instability where people dwell" (Bhabha 1990: 128) and, I would add, constitutes a means of travel.

References

Al Wancharissi, A. A. 1981. *Al Mi'ar Al Mu'arrab wa al jami' Al Mugharab: 'An Fatawi Ahl Ifriquia wa al Andalus wa al Maghrib*, vol. II. Morocco: wizarat Al Awqf wa Al Choon Al Islamiya.

Baudrillard, J. 1987. *The ecstasy of communication*, tr. B. C. Schultz. New York: Semiotext(e).

Bhabha, H. (ed.) 1990. *Nation and narration*. London: Routledge.

Bhabha, H. 1992. Postcolonial authority. In *Cultural Studies*, L. Grossberg, C. Nelson, P. Jones (eds), 56–66. London: Routledge.

Bhabha, H. 1994. *The location of culture*. London: Routledge.

Clifford, J. 1992. Travelling cultures. In *Cultural Studies*, L. Grossberg, C. Nelson, P. Jones (eds), 96–116. London: Routledge.

Derrida, J. 1992. Mochlos. In *Logomachia*, R. Rand (ed.), 3–34. Lincoln, Nebraska: University of Nebraska Press.

Giroux, H. 1992. Resisting difference: cultural studies and the discourse of critical pedagogy. In *Cultural studies*, L. Grossberg, C. Nelson, P. Jones (eds), 199–212. London: Routledge.

Grossberg, L., C. Nelson, P. Jones (eds) 1992. *Cultural studies*. London: Routledge.

Hall, S. 1980. Cultural studies and the centre: some problematics and problems. In *Culture, media, language: working papers in cultural studies, 1972–79*, S. Hall, D. Hobson, A. Love, P. Willis (eds), 15–48. London: Hutchinson.

Hall, S. 1992. Cultural studies and its theoretical legacies. In *Cultural studies*, L. Grossberg, C. Nelson, P. Jones (eds), 277–86. London: Routledge.

Kant, I. 1960. *Religion within the limits of reason alone*, tr. T. M. Greene and H. H. Hudson, edited by T. M. Greene, H. H. Hudson, J. R. Siber. New York: Harper & Row.

Kecht, M. R. 1992. The challenge of responsibility: an introduction. In *Pedagogy is politics: literary theory and critical theory*, M. R. Kecht (ed.), 1–21. Urbana and Chicago: University of Illinois Press.

Khatibi, A. 1983. *Maghreb Pluriel*. Paris: Denoël.

Khatibi, A. 1988. Capter des signes Techniques. *Signes du Présent* **1**, 97–8.

Khatibi, A. 1993. *Penser le Maghreb*. Rabat: Sner.

Lyotard, J-F. 1984. *The postmodern condition: a report on knowledge*. Manchester: Manchester University Press.

Mohamed, A. R. J. 1992. Worldliness, – without world, homelessness – as home: toward a definition of the secular border intellectual. In *Edward Said: a critical reader*, M. Sprinker (ed.), 96–120. Oxford: Basil Blackwell.

Robbins, B. 1992. The East is a career: Edward Said and the logics of professionalism. In *Edward Said: a critical reader*, M. Sprinker (ed.), 48–73. Oxford: Basil Blackwell.

Said, E. 1983. Travelling theory. In *The world, the text and critic*, 226–47. Cambridge, Mass.: Harvard University Press.

Spriggs, J. 1972. Doing English literature. In *Counter courses*, T. Pateman (ed.). London: Penguin.

Young, R. 1992. The idea of Chrestomathic University. In *Logomachia*, R. Rand (ed.), 99–126. Lincoln, Nebraska: University of Nebraska Press.

Zavarzadeh, M. & D. Morton (eds) 1991. *Texts for change: theory/pedagogy/politics*. Urbana and Chicago: University of Illinois Press.

CHAPTER 11
Changing the culture of cultural studies

Brian Doyle

Introduction

The new Field of media, cultural and communication studies was initially founded upon a critique of traditional academic disciplines. It took as its central objective the uncovering of the illusory and ideological character of what passes as "real", both in academic discourse and the world at large. As a result "reality" all but disappeared as a *positive* reference point from studies of contemporary culture. This has now become a great impediment to further growth and development.

If it is to move beyond reliance upon a purely sceptical stance, the Field requires a grounding in some sense of cultural and communicative reality or authenticity. In the past, the stability of the Field was thought to be guaranteed by some objective conception of social relations (often derived from Marxism) or by a cognitive or epistemological stance sustained by Grand Theory. More recently, the former has been shaken by political events, while the latter is crumbling under postmodernist assaults. Somewhat paradoxically, in parallel to the weakening attachment to any grand critical narrative has come the firm establishment of media, cultural and communication studies within higher education institutions – a stabilizing process for which the received approaches to culture and communication have left its practitioners ill prepared. Indeed, the retreat from "reality" and from the making of new realities, has limited the options available within the new Field for defining its *own* culture and possibilities of tradition making.

It is my view that the Field and its practitioners have much to gain both professionally and personally from a theoretical engagement with the diverse forms of social organization with which research of this kind ought to be concerned. A number of recent discussions of media studies have suggested ways in which the scope of academic work might be redrawn with respect to its literary and sociological dimensions as well as to the task of preparing students for the contemporary post-college world.[1] I wish to extend further these proposals and suggest a transformation of the whole Field of media, cultural and communication studies particularly by examining potential contributions from such areas as psychoanalysis, social psychology and organizational studies. In arguing for this transformation, I shall draw particularly upon the work of Eric Berne, Claude Steiner, Gibson Burrell & Gareth Morgan and the recent work of Anthony Giddens.

Currently, the methodological and theoretical models that define the Field are not well suited to attending seriously to the cultures of groups, families, organizations and institutions, or indeed to individuals within cultures. It is my contention that, with the injection of some new emphases, media, cultural and communication studies could gain a new sense of purpose and direction. The emphases for which I am arguing all focus on a unified understanding of the relations between the intrapersonal, interpersonal and institutional dimensions of culture and communication. Furthermore, I want to suggest that the establishment of such a new sense of purpose and direction would require also the building of a new culture for the Field itself, a process for which the available paradigms offer little guidance.

Culture and Transactional Analysis

The usual candidate for linking the intrapersonal with the interpersonal dimensions of culture and communication has been "psychoanalysis". However, the purely theoretical version of psychoanalysis that has been appropriated within the Field has shed that crucial emphasis on change and "cure" which has always been at the centre of a complex and multi-faceted tradition.[2] In contrast, I wish to argue for the value to the Field of those post-Freudian approaches – most notably Transactional Analysis (TA) – which have heretofore been dismissed as "ego psychology" or simply "humanism". The arguments against such approaches have been well rehearsed within a critical cultural studies framework through a critique of intentions, needs, values and self as sources of social meaning and action. The counterbalancing strengths have rarely been noticed. For example, TA offers a well-tried approach to instigating practical change, developing options and problem solving, by providing a firm basis for distinguishing between authentic and inauthentic communicative transactions. This tradition has matured over the three decades since Eric Berne began to develop a distinctive post-Freudian approach which he called "social psychiatry", and continues to carry a strong social and cultural emphasis to this day.[3]

In my view, TA provides an analytical and practical "tool kit" that is better adapted to the needs of the contemporary Field than the versions of

175

psychoanalysis that have usually been preferred, especially when related to current sociological work on "self-identity" that I discuss below. Increasingly, Lacanian appropriations of Freud have maintained a level of abstraction that has militated against any applications to the implementation of actual cultural change. In contrast, rather than identifying cultural change with a somewhat dislocated process of "positioning subjects in discourse", a transactional approach generates options for changing actual communicative processes (both verbal and non-verbal) in which "subjects" (I would prefer "people") participate while being engaged in specific goal-oriented projects.[4] A transactional emphasis offers ways of relating individual experiences to cultural dynamics while allowing a role for "agency" in communicative processes. This approach is also firmly grounded in locatable judgements about authentic thought, feelings and actions. It allows the dynamics of family of origin (as the fundamental locus for the construction of self-identity) to be related to subsequent group identifications (using such concepts as Berne's "imago"). Finally, TA draws upon a vocabulary that is accessible to most people, and thus provides an important ("lay") antidote to the abstruse ("expert") language of much cultural studies discourse. For example, the key concepts of "Parent", "Adult" and "Child" refer to observable ego states, i.e. identifiable combinations of thinking, feeling and behaving, rather than standing as purely theoretical abstractions in the manner of Superego, Ego and Id, or the even more distantiated notion of "subjectivity".

Cultural analysis would benefit from such a way of dealing with the structured patterns of communicative transaction in which cultures are actively reproduced by actors engaging in both authentic and inauthentic attempts to satisfy needs for recognition or "stroking". This is not the place to elaborate further upon the theories and methods characteristic of TA. Suffice it to say that concepts like "cultural scripting", "lifescript", "ego states" and "drivers", offer ways of both classifying and actively changing cultures, as is evidenced through decades of work with families, organizations and groups as well as individuals. In general, TA opens out for examination and alteration, forms of culture that link processes within families of origin with those in organizations and other groups. This is achieved by maintaining a focus that encompasses broad cultural dynamics, inner dialogue, and unfinished business left over from decisions made in childhood; TA also reveals how specific cultural script themes are drawn upon in our attempts as biographical and social persons both to complete our childhood projects and to avoid confronting the painful aspects of our emotional worlds.

The lived relations of culture

As I have already suggested, such a transactional approach to culture and communication seems fruitfully to link with recent developments in social theory. In his latest work Anthony Giddens (1991; see also 1987, 1990, 1992) offers valuable insights into the lived relations between the three factors mentioned above: the key cultural script themes of the modern age; the inner and outer transactions (or dialogue) through which we construct our self-identities; and the unfinished business left over from our childhood socialization. Like Berne (1963), albeit using a different terminology, Giddens suggests that, while the scripts by which we (unknowingly) live may be negotiated biographically and psychologically, they are at the same time socially and culturally constituted. Thus, I would suggest that Giddens's conception of the relations between the main constituents of contemporary culture and the projects involved in constructing self-identities, could usefully be developed alongside TA, within the cultural studies Field so as to assist its transformation in the directions I propose below.

Giddens argues that the characteristically "modern" spheres and dimensions of society and culture have thoroughly undercut the traditional habits and customs that in the past provided a measure of cultural and psychological authority and certitude. In the long process of global and local reshaping, ways of individual living as well as institutional practices have come under the dominating influence of industrial capitalism and its specific controls over violence and surveillance. These influences have provided cultural analysts as well as lay participants with new tasks. If lay participants are faced with new existential challenges, it is the task of analysts to understand and identify effective ways of dealing with these changes at the level of personal experience as well as collective and institutional thought and behaviour. The analysts of media, culture and communication could benefit greatly from a perspective of this kind that invites a mode of understanding, and action, that is not just adapted to, but also able to transcend, these new realities.

At the heart of this order of "late modernity" Giddens finds mechanisms adapted to the constant reflexive monitoring of organized social activity that extend also into the intimacies of the self. As a result of the powerful influence of such mechanisms we are all faced at the level of our own deepest experiences with a dynamic in which doubt has replaced certitude and multiple sources of authority have replaced traditional beliefs. The modern global reorganization of space and time is itself interlaced with our senses of self-identity, since fundamental human experiences have been appropriated, sequestered and disembedded from local foundations and repackaged as global abstract and expert systems. For example, the sophisticated reflexive institutional mechanisms associated with medicine and health, money and goods, symbols and life-planning, all increasingly provide the building blocks for constructing our self-identities.

While discussing these abstract systems, Giddens frequently writes in terms of "culture", yet this term does not receive the direct analytical attention in his writing as it does within media, cultural and communication studies. Nonetheless, I believe that his work suggests that the study of culture must confront the dialectical relations between global institutional trends and the reflexive making of self-identities not only as an *object of analysis*, but also in our *subjective negotiations* within the Field of study itself. However, one problem immediately suggests itself. This results from the fact that cultural studies has itself been shaped by the very process that Giddens describes. As with other abstract systems, cultural studies contributes to processes by which experience is increasingly monitored, packaged and re-embedded in people's lives, and like other abstract systems it tends to detach culture from morality and self-actualization. This is why I am suggesting a role for such projects as TA that are directly concerned to engage at a most practical level with existential meaning, morality and processes of self-development, self-growth and self-actualization. Without the injection of this kind of emphasis it will be very difficult for the Field to provide its teachers and researchers as well as students with the kinds of intellectual, emotional and practical skills that are required to deal effectively with contemporary life.

Giddens provides a detailed and complex discussion of these issues to which I have not done justice here. However, my main aim is to draw out some of the implications of his discussion for the identification of the key tasks facing cultural studies today. I have already mentioned Giddens's emphasis on the need to forge links that will confront the detachment of moral and existential issues that has resulted from the sequestration of experience by abstract systems. The building of such links should involve active reflexive projects of the self that can provide sources of authority and trust in the world of risk inherent in modern abstract systems. The current emphasis on a critique of the positioning of subjects cannot provide the basis for such projects. Instead, the Field should address the tasks of documenting, understanding and skilling people to deal with the dimension of doubt that forms the general existential horizon of modern cultures. Once again, this will require a firmer transactional base. At the most general level, cultural studies needs to supplement the existing emphasis on uncovering ideology and exploitation with what Giddens calls a "life-politics" embracing a propositional ethos of self-growth or social self-actualization. In order to achieve this in practice, the Field will need to focus upon the points at which such cultural script themes impinge upon and merge with everyday practical involvement in personal as well as cultural change.

Giddens provides an extremely valuable typology of cultural script themes which, under the conditions of late modernity, all of us are forced to confront;

Table 11.1

(a)	unification	fragmentation
(b)	powerlessness	appropriation
(c)	authority	uncertainty
(d)	commodified experience	personalized experience

and which can be identified as the dynamic cultural forces most likely to inhibit the process of self-actualization. There are four of these, each of which can be identified in terms of a pair of polar opposites (Table 11.1).

Each of these can be seen as a "script" theme that provides a cultural horizon against which the business of identity-formation and transformation must take place within late modern cultures, initially within the "family-of-origin", and subsequently within other organized cultural settings. The problem is that such apparently "natural" horizons can be experienced as offering the only range of options available for dealing with emotions as well as thought and action.

(a) This first opposition represents the pressures towards the (apparently opposed but actually related) poles of compulsive and rigid traditionalism, on the one hand, and the sense of a fragmented and false self that works against the reconstruction of our narratives of self-identity on the other hand. Thus families (or similar social groups) are, for example, forced to confront this polarity at a most intimate level as a dialectic between traditional rigid patriarchal forms and weak permissiveness.

(b) In the second set of extremes pressure is either towards seeking after omnipotence or alternatively towards experiencing a sense of engulfment that militates against personal and cultural empowerment. The path to be negotiated here may seem limited to the options of total dependency or a repression of emotion.

(c) The third parameter is indicative of the pressures towards a choice between dogmatic authoritarianism and immobilizing doubt. This, in fact, tends to inhibit autonomy, flexibility and wise counsel, and may encourage a culture of oppositional critique rather than imaginative innovation.

(d) The polarities identified in this fourth set are, at one extreme, the pressures towards narcissistic self-display (particularly through psychological investment in commodities) and, at the other, an over-individuated withdrawal from the involvement of self in culture. This works against effective projects of self-actualization by means of "healthy" or intimate communicative transactions (both intrapersonally and interpersonally).

The dynamic underlying all of these dichotomies is indeed the one that I am suggesting must be confronted directly by – and within – cultural studies. This is the cultural and institutional as well as personal process of "screening off"

179

the fundamental issues that human existence poses for us within a technically competent but morally arid environment. While abstract systems may seem to cocoon us from ontological insecurities, they cannot easily provide psychological protection against the threat of personal meaninglessness that is brought on at moments of critical change.

If these script themes were systematically confronted at theoretical, methodological and (especially) practical levels, the result could be a revitalization of the whole Field of media, cultural and communication studies on the basis of an existential and moral grounding in cultural and communicative reality and authenticity. Clearly, I am calling for something more than a new piece of Grand Theory: in my view, we need to shift our focus from abstract theory to forms of "applied work" that place a crucial emphasis on the making of new cultural realities. Also, I am suggesting that the place to start this process is in generating new options within the Field for defining the Field's *own* culture, including options for remaking its own tradition and its "vocational mission". Cultural studies need no longer continue that retreat from concrete experience and active experimentation that has encouraged in practitioners (including students) a sense of alienation from their own options for living and change.

The culture of the self

Currently cultural studies emphasizes the difficulties, even the impossibility, of significant change at the levels of self and culture. It is unfortunate that, in foregrounding the process of "positioning subjects", the Field has largely ignored the means by which it is possible to generate useful options, make informed decisions about one's own conditions, and instigate desirable changes. It is my contention that we need to develop modes of study that provide the means for students to build links between their own subjective experience and patterns of communication and cultures that are active in the world at large. The Field could offer a pedagogy that enhances authenticities and positive actions rather than alienating people from their own capacities and the capacities of their peers. A new culture for cultural studies could then be built upon the competences needed to negotiate the range of cultural pressures and challenges faced both within and beyond the college, home and workplace.

What then is to be the agenda for generating new options for "reality" within the Field? As I have suggested, of greatest importance is the making of a new culture for the Field itself. However, closely following this is the need to develop ways of bringing this altered educational culture to bear upon ways of thinking, feeling and behaving in the wider world; perhaps through a pedagogy which positively embraces the task of developing capacities for "self-

Table 11.2

Regulation	Radical change
Status quo	Fundamental change
Social order	Structural conflict
Consensus	Modes of domination
Integration and cohesion	Contradiction
Solidarity	Emancipation
The actual	The potential
Subjective	Objective
Labels	Empirical fact
Quality	Quantity
Experience	Reality
Decisions	Natural order

management" and other "cultural skills" as applied both to interpersonal and technological processes.[5] This would necessitate adopting considered answers to questions such as: What kinds of cultures are worth aspiring to? What would constitute adequate conceptions of cultural "health" or vitality? How is the cultural approach best adapted to building effective links between education, personal development and senses of community?[6]

In answering such questions it is important to get some overall sense of the range of methodological and theoretical models within the Field, particularly with a view to attending to areas thus far excluded. Some time ago, Gibson Burrell & Gareth Morgan (1979) suggested two parameters which can be used to map out the key areas of thought and methodology within sociological and organizational studies. Using as their intersecting parameters "social order" (in a spectrum from regulation to conflict) and "social reality" (ranging between inner subjective and outer subjective domains) (Table 11.2), they have identified four distinct paradigms: "radical structuralism", "functionalism", "interpretive" approaches and "radical humanism" (Figure 11.1). Each of these paradigms is characterized by a distinctive frame of reference, mode of theorizing and processes of operation. Work within the functionalist paradigm seeks essentially rational explanations of social processes, where society is seen as a network of empirical facts that can be measured. In contrast, work within the interpretive paradigm attempts to understand the world as it is at the level of subjective experience. Here, society is seen as a network of shared assumptions or meanings. Within the radical humanist framework, the objective is to overthrow and transcend the limitations of the existing social order through changes in consciousness (and, possibly, unconscious processes), where forms of consciousness and ideology are seen as fundamental social forces. Finally, the radical structuralist paradigm, while concerned also with social change,

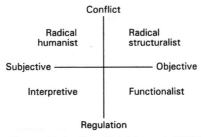

Figure 11.1   Burrell & Morgan's (1979) four paradigms.

seeks means of change at the level of social structures. In this case, society is seen as a set of fundamental conflicts that are rooted in political and economic processes.

The same parameters can be used to chart the Field of media, cultural and communication studies. Using this framework, it can be seen that in focusing upon large power structures, the Field has developed strengths in the structural and functional domains. In addition, with respect to more ethnographic approaches, a significant body of work has been produced that uses interpretive modes. However, the fourth quadrant has been all but dismissed within the Field. At the least it has been seen as reducible (in the final instance) to a form of "radical structuralism". Anything resembling "radical humanism" has largely been attacked as a mere ideological form. The word "humanist" itself has become inadmissible within most cultural studies discourses because, like "community", it is seen as politically contaminated.

The result of this omission is of some importance for the culture of cultural studies itself. The disciplinary culture has not allowed a space for building a sense of community within the Field, or any sense that the Field ought to link personal to collective "needs". This has, in turn, inhibited serious attention to the cultures of groups, organizations and institutions, and indeed individuals within cultures. It is interesting, therefore, to consider how the approach I have been advocating might bear upon the discipline itself. What kind of "family of origin" might be posited as most resembling the culture of cultural studies? A healthy, flexible, adaptable and emotionally as well as intellectually fulfilling one? Or, a culture dominated by rigidity, dogma and a repressive attitude to dissent and emotional expression? No doubt there are traces of both to be found. However, this very thought prompts questions about what is to count as "cultural expertise" or "know-how". The skills of critique and deconstruction will no doubt continue to have a place within the Field. But, what kind of culture is primarily concerned with revealing how others are ideologically contaminated? I would suggest that it is no longer desirable to hold up this kind of culture as a desirable pedagogic and professional model to which others might aspire. A review of the strengths and weaknesses of the cultural approach is now overdue. Such a review could make an important contribution to the extension of what is valuable about the "cultural" emphasis into areas beyond the traditional categories of nation, class and subculture.

In conclusion, my own agenda for the Field is an attempt to move beyond the constrictions of a pure emphasis on "critical theory". This could be developed under five headings, which no doubt will seem to some as representing a new kind of humanistic profanity:

1. *The recovery of authenticity.* This involves that we allow for and encourage an authentic engagement between self and culture. The objective is to develop a living and potent sense of the sources and creative energies of the self, and of how these capacities can effectively be used within a range of cultural arenas. In achieving this it would be necessary to move beyond cognitive critique to engage directly with options for communicative change and development. Within the TA tradition this would be formulated in terms of the achievement of personal autonomy within a culture based on "I'm OK, you're OK" principles, and which valued "script-free" and "game-free" living. For Giddens, it might involve developing a life-politics grounded in personal and cultural growth and actualization.

2. *The building of a cultural studies community.* With the recovery of alienated subjectivity it ought to be possible to link personal and professional life with the sense of a common (but diverse) cultural studies project to which whole-hearted and trusting commitment could be given. Both TA and the ideas I have associated with Anthony Giddens could play their part in moving beyond a stance of doubt (and indeed its mirror opposite, certainty) so as to engage in a common moral, existential and political project.

3. *Developing an expanded pedagogy.* Here, my suggestion is that, with the establishment of such a sense of personal and professional community, new initiatives would be developed that extended the range of work with peers, students and other interested parties – work that illustrated the practical value of the contribution of a cultural approach to wider processes of education. This would require of "experts" within the Field a strong commitment to the acquisition as well as sharing of practical cultural and personal skills – and, indeed, a commitment to developing effective "lay" forms of discourse.

4. *Theoretical and methodological developments.* The area in most urgent need for development seems to be that identified above as "radical humanism" where there is a commitment to the kind of radical change that emphasizes subjective and cultural processes as much as structures. There are ample opportunities for work within the Field to address options for serving those human needs not satisfied by critique, contestation and

183

problem-identification. This would require a more existentially grounded conception of "persons" than is currently favoured within the Field, and here again work in both the TA tradition and recent social theory has a good deal to contribute.

5. *Validating the cultural emphasis.* It will be important to agree means for validating the strengths available from a specifically cultural approach for the improvement of communication in families, groups and organizations, and for the active making of new institutions. While such validation would play an important role in establishing a positive professional standing for the Field, perhaps it would be of even greater importance in contributing to the development of strong and humane links between "expert" technical worlds and the fundamentals of existential, moral and – ultimately – cultural values.

Notes

1. Donald (1990), Durant (1991). However, these writers are working against the trend to establish "critical theory" as the defining feature of the Field, as represented, for example, by Brantlinger (1990), Turner (1990) and Easthope (1991)). In contrast, I am following Kolb's example (1984) in assuming that all learning involves experience, reflection and application as much as theory and model building.
2. Easthope (1991) provides perhaps the most extreme example of this narrowing of emphasis.
3. The broader cultural emphasis is most evident in Berne (1963) and Steiner (1974). More recent examples of relevant applications of TA are to be found in Hay (1991) and Hewson & Turner (1992).
4. For a discussion of the sociology of the "project" see Jaques (1976: 101–2) and Giddens (1987: 104).
5. As well as teaching the capacity to "manage" in the vocational sense discussed by Donald (1990) in relation to Connell & Hurd's conference paper (1989), I wish to encourage provision in the Field for teaching skills in "managing" a range of cultural situations, and indeed "self-management" (see Pedler & Boydell (1990) for example).
6. For contrasting views on the value of the concept of community see Bellah et al. (1988), Peck (1988), Cooke (1990) and Hay (1991).

References

Bellah, R. et. al. 1988. *Habits of the heart: Americans in search of themselves.* London: Unwin Hyman.
Berne, E. 1963. *The structure and dynamics of organisations and groups.* New York: Ballantine.

REFERENCES

Brantlinger, P. 1990. *Crusoe's footprints: cultural studies in Britain and America*. London: Routledge.

Burrell, G. & G. Morgan 1979. *Sociological paradigms and organisational analysis: elements of a sociology of corporate life*. London: Heinemann.

Connell, I. & G. Hurd 1989. Cultural education: a revised program. *Media Information, Australia*, 23–30.

Cooke, P. 1990. *Back to the future*. London: Unwin Hyman.

Donald, J. 1990. Review article. *Screen* **31**, 113–18.

Durant, A. 1991. Noises offscreen: could a crisis in confidence be good for media studies? *Screen* **32**, 407–28.

Easthope, A. 1991. *Literary into cultural studies*. London: Routledge.

Giddens, A. 1987. *Social theory and modern sociology*. Cambridge: Polity.

Giddens, A. 1990. *The consequences of modernity*. Cambridge: Polity.

Giddens, A. 1991. *Modernity and self-identity: self and society in the late modern age*. Cambridge: Polity.

Giddens, A. 1992. *The transformation of intimacy*. Cambridge: Polity.

Hay, J. 1991. *Transactional analysis for trainers*. New York: McGraw-Hill.

Hewson, J. & C. Turner 1992. *Transactional analysis in management*. Bristol: The Staff College, Coombe Lodge.

Jaques, E. 1976. *A general theory of bureaucracy*. London: Heinemann.

Kolb, D. A. 1984. *Experiential learning: experience as the source of learning and development*. Englewood Cliffs, New Jersey: Prentice-Hall.

Peck, M. S. 1988. *A different drum*. London: Rider.

Pedler, M. & T. Boydell 1990. *Managing yourself*. Aldershot, England: Gower.

Steiner, C. 1974. *Scripts people live*. New York: Bantham.

Turner, G. 1990. *British cultural studies: an introduction*. London: Unwin Hyman.

CHAPTER 12

Nuclear family fall-out: postmodern family culture and the media

Cynthia Carter

Introduction

"The image of the perfect nuclear family with mother, father and 2.4 children", claims the *Daily Express*, received a "battering" in the recently published 1992 General Household Survey. These "official figures" tell us that the most common household in Britain (over one third of all living arrangements) now consists of a married or cohabiting couple with no children. The next most common arrangement, also representing around one third of all households, is that of single people living on their own. Framed as a "worry" for the Conservative government's "Back to Basics" policy, the *Daily Express* also notes that the increase in the number of single parent families has "more than doubled" over the past two decades, and that marriage is on the decline.[1] What is one to make of these statistics? It seems to me that they clearly point to a large gap between what is being held up as the *ideal* family form (nuclear) by the mass media and the ways in which people are actually organizing their personal lives. At the very time when conservative rhetoric has become most virulent about the maintenance of "family values", members of the British public appear to be choosing alternative (non-nuclear) forms of household configurations in record numbers.

This chapter engages in a cultural critique of contemporary family forms, arguing that despite what on the surface may appear to be radical changes in the structures of human relationships, the *normalcy* of the "nuclear family" (with breadwinning father, stay-at-home mother and two children) still claims a strong ideological purchase for many people. A number of studies now uneasily report that regardless of the fact that growing numbers of people find themselves living in what used to be known as alternative family formations out of choice, many feel a strong sense of nostalgia for the "normal nuclear family" (Press 1991) or remain certain that this form of familial configuration is ultimately preferable to the ones in which they find themselves (Stacey 1992).

186

In this chapter I want to tease out this contradiction through a conceptual engagement with several recent research efforts that have attempted to theorize the pervasive and resistant character of "familial ideology" across distinct genres of popular media texts. Much of the cultural studies research on the family has analyzed the position of women within the "nuclear family", with most studies attempting to ascertain the extent to which the media contribute to the (re)production and naturalization of traditional roles for women within the "nuclear family" formation. In seeking to denaturalize the cultural politics of normalcy in relation to the "nuclear family", however, it seems to me that this research is often able to do little more than document examples of how media representations, or the use of various media (particularly within the household), work to reproduce this normalcy (problematic as those processes might be). Given this apparent theoretical *cul-de-sac*, some may be tempted to point to recent household statistical surveys as proof of the failure of the media to successfully "interpellate" (Althusser 1971) growing numbers of people into the ideology of the "nuclear family". The result of such thinking may be a celebration of the "postmodern family" as a potent symbol of this refusal.

In this chapter I argue, in contrast, that it is not only important to problematize the notion of the postmodern family but also to show that we need to adequately address the complex reasons for the continuing affective purchase of the "nuclear family" in popular cultural representations. Informing my critique, therefore, is the view that cultural studies researchers must now turn their attention to the task of developing a new "moral language" (Weeks 1991) and a set of community values (Giddens 1993). One of the aims of such a project would be to establish the parameters of a new *ethical pluralism* which assumes that human happiness and *normal* family life are not necessarily synonymous. Through the creation of new spaces for the exploration and critique of the gendered structure of the media, researchers might then be better placed to contribute to the articulation of a new, progressive cultural politics.[2]

Wither away "nuclear family"

Before engaging in a discussion of the notion of postmodern families and their import for cultural studies research, I will briefly outline what I mean by "familial ideology" and the politics of the "normal family". For our purposes here, familial ideology will refer to a system of beliefs and material practices organized to appropriate a particular family arrangement or unit as hegemonic. Specific social positions, particularly those of class (middle class), race (White) and sexuality (heterosexual), are hierarchically aligned with, or deemed equivalent to, that which is considered to be "normal" or "typical". Bernardes, for example, characterizes familial ideology as "that varied and multi-layered system of ideas and practices which holds 'The Family' to be a natural and universally present feature of all human societies, an 'institution' which is positively functional and the basis of morality" (Bernardes 1985: 279). For Barrett (1980), familial ideology is rooted in biologism, in which women are defined in terms of their anatomy and are, therefore, somehow *naturally* dependent on men. Thus, familialism projects the role of the adult male as that of the head of the household, the individual ostensibly defined by *nature* as the one responsible for providing the family with the necessary degree of economic security, as well as its code of moral discipline, to ensure its survival as a unit. Further, Weeks (1991) describes the family as a "variable set of relationships, between men and women, adults and children, shaped and structured by uneven power relations, whose unity is historical and ideological rather than natural" (Weeks 1991: 228).

It is precisely at the point where the *normal* "nuclear family" is reduced to a *natural fact* that the politics of normalcy come to the fore. As various feminist examinations have indicated (Barrett 1980, Barrett & McIntosh 1982, Gittens 1985, Davidoff & Hall 1987, Collier et al. 1992, Thorne 1992), the concept of the "nuclear family" as the norm is a relatively recent development, having first developed in Europe during the last century alongside the rise of industrial capitalism and the bourgeoisie. Hence the need, in my view, to recognize the historical contingency of normalcy as a discursive configuration. Donzelot's genealogical study of the discursive construction of the "nuclear family" in France over the past two centuries, for example, demonstrates how it is clearly not a static and unchanging social institution, but rather an "uncertain form" that is made intelligible only when analyzed through the "system of relations it maintains at the socio-political level" (Donzelot 1979: xxv). Thus, for Donzelot, the normal family is the complex (always provisional) product of ongoing social processes through which certain preferred definitions of the ideals or the promise of family life have been constructed and policed. Popularized notions of the "nuclear family" as normal, consistently rationalized in terms of a larger normative role in the maintenance of public order, are thus implicated in the effectivity of concrete political and economic interests. Familialism needs to be theorized, then, in a way that accounts for its historical (temporal and spatial) specificity: the precise mechanisms by which it structures a certain delimited sense of what *should* constitute contemporary family life that is always changing. For this reason, Barrett (1980) concludes that critical researchers should perhaps cease referring to the *family*, as it does not exist other than as an ideological construct.

It is my intention here, then, to discern the contradictions implicit in the ideological construction of normalcy associated with the "nuclear family" in media representations of family life. As will be shown, feminist inquiries into the effectivity of popular forms of entertainment are centring for investigation certain marginalized cultural products that have, until recently, all but eluded sustained analytical treatment. In the next section I will focus on radio talk by providing an evaluative assessment of various studies that draw upon distinct conceptual and methodological approaches. In subsequent sections, I discuss the cultural dynamics of familialism as it pertains to television and romance narratives using the same organizing principle.

Radio and the rhythms of everyday life

Feminist researchers concerned with the study of radio talk have noted how developments in this medium have been closely linked to the establishment and expansion of the market research techniques used to understand audience tastes. Much attention has been given to the issue of how radio directs its audience towards the consumption of advertised products. In the early days of commercial radio in North America, for example, market research quickly established that the female, domestic consumer made the vast majority of all household goods purchases. As the range of choice for consumer goods expanded, and advertising became a multi-million dollar industry organized largely to establish brand loyalty, corporations were keen to develop radio programming that would deliver this female audience to the advertisers. In the commercialized environment of North America, radio soap opera developed as a genre of women's fiction which worked, in turn, to reaffirm the "nuclear family" as the key base of national economic prosperity (Cantor & Pingree 1983, Allen 1985).

Textual analyses in this area have examined how the narrational structure of soap opera on commercial radio actually works to secure the loyalty of the female listener. This process is thought to hinge on making her involved on a personal and direct level with a programme on a regular basis. Having positioned, in discursive terms, the female listener as the object of the mode of address, she was then "interpellated" (Althusser 1971) as the consumer for the family, both in the programme itself and in the advertisements that followed it. The equivocation of this role for women with *normalcy* was anchored, at the same time, by the authority of the narration as it instructed the female audience to assume their *natural* or *proper* responsibilities.

Investigations into current audience "uses" of radio have observed that the medium often plays a key role in helping women to structure the structureless character of domestic labour. Here the context of radio listening within the isolated, private sphere of the home has been examined, as have certain structural features of radio discourses that women are invited to identify with as *feminine domestic subjects*. Radio, it is suggested, can provide time boundaries that may be used to mark the passage of the day, thereby offering women a greater sense of control over their work processes (Hobson 1978, 1980). At the same time, however, the *maleness* of these programming structures may also work to reinforce the presupposition that "women's place is in the home", engaged in domestic duties rather than "real work". These discourses serve not only to re-assure women who have *chosen* to work in the household that their decision was the *correct* one because that is where they *belong* but also tend to reinforce a sense that women's experiences are collectively and identically felt by millions of others (although feelings of isolation and loneliness are only rarely acknowl-edged). Thus, the sexual division of labour in the household serves not only as a private, familial interest, but also as a "noble responsibility" to the nation at large (Coward 1985).

This brief discussion of various approaches to the study of radio helps to illustrate the extent to which this medium contributes to the (re)construction and naturalization of traditional roles for women within the "nuclear family". While this research has provided many interesting insights, I am often left with the sense that the familialized discourses of the media are sometimes granted a greater effectivity than is due. Still, critiques such as these ones are particularly helpful to the degree that they make apparent the ideological work of the media. As various critics have pointed out, however, such research often fails to adequately account for the extent to which media audiences negotiate their ways around such discourses. The "nuclear family" does have a privileged place amongst various discourses in the media – I would not want to challenge that point, yet how do we then connect such insights to the growing disjunc-ture between a longing to be part of a *happy* "nuclear family" and family life in postmodern society?

Filming femininity

Feminist research on gender and the "nuclear family" within film studies usu-ally focuses on a consideration of specific film texts. Much of this work draws upon psychoanalytic concepts and categories to articulate its insights into the discursive construction of gendered identities. Modleski, for example, has sought to discern how popular narratives function to contain and structure cer-tain "feminine anxieties" and fantasies around personal life and the "nuclear family" (Modleski 1982: 29). She contends that popular film narratives often operate to establish barriers between women's desires and their realization, in discursive and ideological terms, by focusing on anticipation as an end in itself. Consequently, she advances the thesis that women are encouraged to find order in a sense of place within the domestic sphere, a logic that reifies the "nuclear family" as the legitimate point of identification for them, and the source of their emotional and financial support (Modleski 1982: 88–90).

The conceptual tools of psychoanalysis have also been employed with the aim of substantiating the claim that women somehow prefer the *symbolic* satisfactions provided by media texts over the *real* satisfactions intrinsic to their everyday lives. For example, films centred on the theme of romantic love, it has been argued, are often used against women in order to domesticate them (Doane 1987). Romance seems to offer women a place for the expression and recognition of feminine sexuality that is outside of the constraints and expectations of marriage and domestic labour. Still, the patriarchal conventions of the romance narrative work to define and regulate sexual difference, ultimately recuperating feminine sexuality within a heterosexual, domestic norm. Thus, the (heterosexual) "romantic myth" ultimately rests on a contradiction between what it promises women and the actualities of domestic experiences, thereby posing a potential threat to the hegemony of traditional family life.

Byars's (1988) research in Britain suggests that most mainstream cinema narratives of the 1950s worked to reinforce, in addition to a hierarchically divisive set of class and "race" relations, a dominant ideology of the "nuclear family". At the same time, however, unruly heroines of the family melodramas, designed primarily for female audiences, often represented threats to the prevailing familial ideology by opening up certain subject positions used to negotiate or oppose the preferred form of narrative closure (see also Coward 1985, Mulvey 1986). Femininity, in this way, becomes a contested terrain (a product of discourse). Here the focus is limited to the textual construction of femininity, contained within the safe confines of the "nuclear family". While more recent research efforts in feminist film studies have undertaken ethnographic investigations into the relationship between film texts and female audiences (see Pribram 1987, Livingstone 1988, Schroder 1988, Stacey 1988, Brown 1990, Nightingale 1990), the effectivity of familialism in film texts is primarily framed in terms of particular isolated instances of unruly heroines in specific film texts.

Television and the domestic sphere

Several researchers have noted the importance of the "family audience", with women being encouraged to identify with the "housewife" who cooks, cleans, looks after children and maintains a youthful, "unhousewifely" appearance so as to remain sexually attractive to her husband. They argue that part of the effectivity of television images and messages lies in a fetishistic re-articulation of women in the home regardless of their actual living arrangements, thereby providing them with certain idealized forms of identification that are impossible, by definition, to achieve.

Kaplan (1987), analyzing contemporary television soap opera, argues that these types of narratives are often organized in order to engage the viewer in explorations of personal life so as to inscribe them in particular ideological frameworks in relation to "the family" as an idealized construct. Soap operas, principally written for and watched by female audiences, work to construct a "moral consensus about the conduct of personal life" (Brunsdon 1981: 35). The narrative strategies they employ tend to highlight areas of "feminine competence" within the "nuclear family household", once again recurrently defined as women's *proper* sphere of influence based on their "natural" abilities.

Even the ostensibly liberal or progressive programmes such as *thirtysomething*,[3] can evoke what Probyn (1990) calls a *new traditionalism* whereby women (and men) are urged to return to the traditional family values (here attractively repackaged in order to be more appealing to audiences in the 1990s). "New traditionalism", not surprisingly, still offers up the home as women's natural or "biologically driven" choice of workplace identification (Probyn 1990: 152).[4] Significantly, *thirtysomething*'s narrow focus on the "normal family" becomes conflated, in ideological terms, with society. The significance of this move is that the public sphere, organized around certain collective forms of identification where individuals and their families are socially located, is textually denied.[5]

David Morley's ethnographic study, *Family television* (1986) continues to this day to be regarded as a path-breaking investigation of television audiences. Morley attempts to grapple with how certain programme types, family position and cultural background, when articulated together, create a schemata of familial dynamics and viewing behaviour. More recent research in this field signals the growing development of this type of endeavour (see Gillespie 1989, Morley & Silverstone 1991, Press 1991). Still, much of the research on television, while providing a wider understanding of how it is used by audiences within the *naturalized* setting of its habitual site of consumption, the household, is nevertheless largely descriptive. In other words, it fails to address how people actually understand their familial position within the household. Additionally, while Morley's (1986) work, in particular, takes some pains to signal the limitations of its sample base in terms of a wider generalization of its findings, there is still an underlying assumption that "family" is to be understood primarily in its "nuclear" configuration.

Romancing narratives

Feminist analyses of the production and consumption of romance fiction have supported the view that the "fantasy world of romance" consists of certain images of women that bear little resemblance to the "everyday experience of real women engaged in wage-labour" (Harrison 1978, Jensen 1984). The narrative logics mobilized within these texts frequently serve to offer justification for the isolation of women into low-status positions, usually where they have little job autonomy and poor pay. The types of recurrent images found in romance fiction are said to reproduce the common-sense beliefs that women are not committed to their work. Married women, for example, are presented as being free to choose whether they want to work or not, often "choosing" to do so strictly for social reasons or for "pin money", not because they need a liveable wage. Concomitantly, women are also seen to represent a "sexy distraction" for men in the paid labour force, thereby providing an escape from the serious work at hand.

A variety of textual analyses have sought to render problematic the social construction of romantic ideology itself. Romantic ideology is often understood here as a class-based relation within which women are differentially positioned as sexed subjects within the sphere of (re)production – primarily *biological* reproduction. However, while romantic ideology is based on the assumption of women's subordination and dependency upon men for their material needs, it often acknowledges the material conditions and contradictions of women's lives, although usually in certain circumscribed ways. A recurring pattern of handling narrative tension concerns the contrary pulls of romance and career where, increasingly, the heroine does not always "end up with her man". Instead, she finds herself enjoying the rewards of a successful career. Despite such developments, the central tenets of the ideology of romantic love are only rarely challenged within such narratives. Instead, according to much of this research, the narrative is usually sustained through certain discursive limits placed on what is *acceptable* sexuality (heterosexual), courtship, lovemaking and so forth.

In seeking to contextualize these themes, some researchers have argued that the continuing appeal of the romance genre may best be accounted for through a rigorous consideration of women's actual reading practices. If, in the past, researchers tended to view romance readers as an undifferentiated mass who took the same meanings and pleasures from these texts, more recent ethnographic research (Radway 1984) has highlighted the ways in which readers "use" media products in highly differentiated ways. These findings have prompted, in turn, a reappraisal of the extent to which any institutional or textual research strategies provide a satisfactory understanding, on their own, of contemporary cultural practices.

Clearly, much research needs to be done on the ideological effectivity of romance narratives, as well as the ways in which readers negotiate the meanings of these texts. After all, we still do not have a clear sense of the extent to which familial discourses of romance are taken up or rejected by their readers. Moreover, we need to make more explicit the questions of how readers negotiate ideologies of romance within the context of "postmodern family life". It is this issue of the "postmodern family" as a conceptual problematic for cultural studies research that I wish to address in the remaining sections of this chapter.

Postmodern families – same difference

As I noted above, current statistical trends around the organization of family life suggest that we are witnessing the end of the primacy of the modern, nuclear family, and the beginning of what some critical family studies researchers describe as the postmodern family (Cheal 1991, Stacey 1992, Bernardes 1993). For Stacey, the term "postmodern family" means "competing sets of family cultures" (1992: 93). In other words, she argues with reference to the United States:

> No longer is there a single culturally dominant family pattern, like the modern one, to which the majority of Americans conform and most of the rest aspire. Instead, Americans today have crafted a multiplicity of family and household arrangements, which we inhabit uneasily and reconstitute frequently in response to changing personal and occupational circumstances. (1992: 93)

The diverse and fluid character of contemporary family life thus challenges the norms of modernity. As Stacey contends, the "teleology of modernization narratives that depict an evolutionary history of the family" (Stacey 1992: 94) is being recast. Still, she cautions, the postmodern family is not a new model of family life. Rather, it is characteristic of a particular phase in the history of the modern family, one during which the concept of progress has collapsed (Stacey 1992: 94).

Depending on one's political allegiances, of course, the arrival of the postmodern family may either signal a key point of political resistance to the confining nature of its predecessor, or the failure of the modern family to weather the storms of feminist and other radical challenges to its primacy. For researchers of the political Right in Britain, such as Sheila Lawlor of the right-wing Centre for Policy Studies, the collapse of the traditional family represents a victory for "a feminist ideology" that aims to banish men from women's lives (cited in Roberts 1993: 16). Commentators such as Lawlor firmly believe that the traditional (nuclear) family is the historical cornerstone of society. For example, Ferdinand Mount, author of *The subversive family* (1982) and policy adviser to former British Prime Minister Margaret Thatcher, has argued that the nuclear family embodies the *timeless nature* of biological duties of care provided by women in the *natural* family. The political response to the unwelcome breakdown of the nuclear family has been characterized by a call for a return to traditional family values ("Back to Basics") from political conservatives, as well as from some political figures on the political Left (see Abbott & Wallace 1992).

Anxieties over the demise of the "normal family" are interrelated, according to Weeks (1991), in three important ways. First, in this era of rapid social and economic change, women, in particular, are facing the double burden of increasing responsibility for care in the community, while encountering growing economic pressures to participate in the paid labour force. Secondly, the very changes taking place in terms of household composition are in fact increasing the emotional significance of the traditional family. This intensification of the emotional aspect of family life is at once positive in that it helps to create a sense of stability and belonging for many people, yet it may also "act as the fulcrum for the generation of violence against women and against children" (Weeks 1991: 220). Finally, family diversity itself is the basis for what Weeks calls the "question of value". That is, while demographically families are changing their structure and composition, what is crucially at stake is how family values will change, and, more importantly, what people see "ought to change" to provide support for both individual and collective needs (Weeks 1991: 221). I share Weeks's view that this is the backdrop against which we now have to come to terms with contemporary discourses on "the family". Most importantly, it would appear that the desire for a return to "traditional family values", for commentators on both the political Left and Right, lies in its provision of a

> symbolic focus for the resolution of personal and social problems that might otherwise seem intractable. The reality might actually be quite different as affluence, social dislocation and social policy continue to undermine these very values. Nevertheless "the family", with its powerful myth of harmony and personal integration and fulfilment, retains a powerful appeal. (Weeks 1991: 221)

Accordingly, the degree to which the arrival of the postmodern family epitomizes a popular refusal to accept current ideological arguments that tend to favour the "normal" or "traditional" family as the ideal and its attendant values is open to question. However, for those who are encouraged by the notion that the postmodern family represents the embodiment of radical challenges to the primacy of the "normal" nuclear family, Giddens cautions that we must not confuse the current situation of family diversity with the disintegration of the ideological purchase of this "traditional" family form. Instead, he suggests that because conservative philosophy has placed such an emphasis on individual responsibility over community solidarity, "it's quite possible to argue that parents and children might in some circumstances be more, rather than less, responsible and interdependent than before" (Giddens 1993: 20). Nevertheless, rather than retreat into the seemingly safe cocoon of "traditional family values", Giddens challenges radical critics of the nuclear family to reconstruct personal and community values so as to re-establish a continuity of the generations with a collective sense of responsibility and care for one another.

New agendas for cultural studies

Weeks (1991) has powerfully argued that attempts to redefine "the family" over the past few decades to include diverse family formations have broadened the term "family" to a point where it has almost become meaningless as a sociological categorization. The primary outcome of this exercise, he suggests, is that it has allowed us to avoid challenging the discourse of "normal" family life. This research, suggests Weeks,

> takes for granted the discourse of family life, and simply incorporates every other form of workable life-style into it. Against this, it is important to stress that not all household patterns can be called families, whatever their "family-like" qualities. On the contrary, there exist a plurality of relational forms that are regarded by many as both legitimate and desirable that are different from any recognisably familial pattern. (Weeks 1991: 227)

What, then, is the significance of this claim for cultural studies research? It would seem that the only terms we presently have to describe our most "passionate loyalties" have been constructed within the language of "family relationships". Without a language to make sense of the current diversity of human relationships, we *naturally* fall back into a search of "the security of what we know, or believe, to be secure and stable, a haven . . . where those who feel besieged may find protection" (Weeks 1991: 227). This failure, argues Weeks, signals a conceptual "poverty of thought" regarding language in relation to *non-family forms*. Thus, for cultural studies this means that rather than engaging in research that only documents the postmodern family in its many different forms, we need to consider taking up Weeks's challenge to "develop a new "moral language". Such a language would be able to come to terms in a reasoned way with the variety of social possibilities that exist in the [post]modern world, to shape a pluralistic set of values which is able to respect difference" (Weeks 1991: 230).[6]

In my view, the construction of this "moral language" (Weeks 1991), and with it "personal and community values" (Giddens 1993), will help to create a greater sense of collective responsibility and care. Media research that does not address the actuality of current human relationships is working to reproduce the very power relations it otherwise seeks to deconstruct. How can we commence with the project of creating spaces from which to challenge the ideological purchase of contemporary media representations of "the family" without first denaturalizing the cultural dynamics of familial ideology that underpin so many of our own assumptions as cultural theorists?

Notes

1. Thorne (1992) suggests that the conservative "defense of the family" sits uneasily between the logic of individualism and "family-based nurturance". Conservatives tend to view the family as a *retreat* from the exigencies of the *market place*. Care-giving and nurturance are undermined by the structures of capitalism. Yet, rather than challenge capitalism and patriarchy, those who defend the *family* "demand that the family, and women, make up for everything the indifferent and hostile outer world refuses to do" (Thorne 1992: 24; see also Morgan 1991).
2. "Ethical pluralism", as described by Weeks (1991), does not mean that we accept all forms of human social organization. Instead, he suggests, we need to explore and critique

   the principles that make a pluralistic society possible: a common acceptance of the value of diversity and choice; a sensitivity to the power relations that hinder and inhibit the fulfilment of individual needs, and above all, an avoidance of the proselytizing zeal of those who believe that they have the key to the good life. It does not mean that "the family" is redundant or that it can contribute nothing to individual or social well-being. But a true pluralism must begin with the assumption that happiness and personal fulfilment are not the privileged prerogative of family life. (1991: 230–31)
3. *thirtysomething* was one of American television's first attempts, in the mid 1980s, to connect with the "yuppie" television audience. It featured a group of people, aged somewhere in their thirties, living in Philadelphia, who had been in college together in the late 1960s or early 1970s. This group of liberal individuals is constructed as one that was typical of those involved in student activism at the time, and it explores how their idealism has been tempered by the onset of middle age. The key areas explored in its stories are relationships, careers, family and friends. At the end of the series in 1992, one of the main characters (who had one of the most stable marriages in the series) parts company with her husband to pursue a career in New York (he leaves Philadelphia to further his career in California) stating that she just cannot do the "family thing" any more.
4. Even if "normal nuclear family" life is often depicted as turbulent and contradictory, this is not to suggest that these are the only family forms currently represented on television in North America or Britain. On the contrary, on

American television, familial primary groups, or *surrogate families* (postmodern?), are found in the workplace (*NYPD blue, Nurses, Murphy Brown, Homicide: life on the street*), in a community (*Cheers, Northern exposure*), or are presented as extended/reconstituted families (*Grace under fire, Frasier, Roseanne*). That said, however, these familial groups are often defined as *substitutes for the real thing*.

5. As Bonner & du Gay (1992) point out, this argument seeks to collapse "a sociopolitical 'outside' onto a famialized and domestic 'inside', promote 'enterprise', 'consumerism', and individual responsibility for success or failure to achieve – that is, to provide for 'the family'" (1992: 87). The "normal" family is made responsible for providing the institutional infrastructure (nursery, health care, education, leisure) for individual family members, in addition to its older responsibilities for the generational transmission of wealth and "traditional moral values" embodied by the "nuclear family". The logical conclusion of this argument, then, as former British Prime Minister Margaret Thatcher declared, is that there is no longer such a thing as *society*, only individuals and their families.

6. Several Black feminists have rightly criticized research on familial ideology, pointing out that White feminists have often failed to understand the crucial role of the Black family in providing women (men and children) with protection against the racism of White-dominated societies (see Amos & Parmar 1984, Trevedi 1984).

References

Abbott, P. & C. Wallace 1992. *The family and the New Right*. London: Pluto.

Allen, R. 1985. *Speaking of soap operas*. Chapel Hill, North Carolina: University of North Carolina Press.

Althusser, L. 1971. Ideology and ideological state apparatuses. In *Lenin and philosophy and other essays*, 127–88. New York and London: Monthly Review Press.

Amos, V. & P. Parmar 1984. Challenging imperial feminism. *Feminist Review* **17**.

Barrett, M. 1980. *Women's oppression today*. London: Verso.

Barrett, M. & M. McIntosh 1982. *The anti-social family*. London: Verso.

Bernardes, J. 1985. "Family ideology": identification and exploration. *Sociological Review* **33**, 275–97.

Bernardes, J. 1993. Responsibilities in studying postmodern families. *Journal of Family Issues* **14**, 35–49.

Bonner, F. & P. du Gay 1992. Representing the enterprising self: *thirtysomething* and contemporary consumer culture. *Theory, Culture and Society* **9**, 67–92.

Brown, M. E. (ed.) 1990. *Television and women's culture: the politics of the popular.* London: Sage.

Brunsdon, C. 1981. "Crossroads" – notes on soap opera. *Screen* **22**(4), 32–7.

Byars, J. 1988. Joan Collins and the wilder side of women: exploring pleasure and representation. In *Female spectators: looking at film and television*, E. D. Pribram (ed.), 102–11. London: Verso.

Cantor, M. & S. Pingree 1983. *The soap opera*. Los Angeles: Sage.

Cheal, D. 1991. *Family and the state of theory*. Toronto: University of Toronto Press.

Collier, J., M. Z. Rosaldo, S. Yanagisako 1992. Is there a family? New anthropological views. In *Rethinking the family: some feminist questions*, B. Thorne & M. Yalom (eds), 31–48. Boston: Northeastern University Press.

Coward, R. 1985. *Female desires: how they are sought, bought and packaged*. New York: Grove Press.

Daily Express. Nuclear family fall-out: two's company as couples choose life without children. 26 January 1994, 15.

Davidoff, L. & C. Hall 1987. *Family fortunes: men and women of the English middle class 1780–1850*. London: Hutchinson.

Doane, M. A. 1987. *The desire to desire: the woman's film of the 1940s*. Bloomington, Indiana: Indiana University Press.

Donzelot, J. 1979. *The policing of families*. London: Hutchinson.

Giddens, A. 1993. Dare to care, conserve and repair. *New Statesman*, 29 October, 18–20.

Gillespie, M. 1989. Technology and tradition: audio-visual culture among south Asian families in west London. *Cultural Studies* **5**, 226–39.

Gittens, D. 1985. *The family in question*. London: Macmillan.

Harrison, R. 1978. Shirley: relations of reproduction and the ideology of romance. In *Women take issue: aspects of women's subordination*, Women's Studies Group, Centre for Contemporary Cultural Studies, University of Birmingham (eds), 176–96. London: Hutchinson.

Hobson, D. 1978. Housewives: isolation as oppression. In *Women take issue: aspects of women's subordination*, Women's Studies Group, Centre for Contemporary Cultural Studies, University of Birmingham (eds), 79–95. London: Hutchinson.

Hobson, D. 1980. Housewives and the mass media. In *Culture, media, language*, S. Hall et al. (eds), 105–14. London: Hutchinson.

Jensen, M. A. 1984. *Love's sweet return: the harlequin story*. Toronto: The Women's Press.

Kaplan, E. A. 1987. Feminist criticism and television. In *Channels of discourse*, R. Allen (ed.), 211–53. London: Routledge.

Livingstone, S. M. 1988. Viewers' interpretations of soap opera: the role of gender, power and morality. In *Television and its audience: international research perspectives*, P. Drummond & R. Paterson (eds), 83–107. London: British Film Institute.

Modleski, T. 1982. *Loving with a vengeance: mass-produced fantasies for women*. London: Methuen.

Morgan, D. 1991. Ideologies of marriage and family life. In *Marriage, domestic life and social change: writings for Jacqueline Burgoyne (1944–88)*, D. Clark (ed.), 114–38. London: Routledge.

Morley, D. 1986. *Family television: cultural power and domestic leisure*. London: Comedia.

Morley, D. & R. Silverstone 1991. Communication and context: ethnographic perspectives on the media audience. In *Qualitative methodologies for mass communication research*, K. B. Jensen & N. W. Jankowski (eds), 149–62. London: Routledge.

Mount, F. 1982. *The subversive family: an alternative history of love and marriage*. London: Jonathan Cape.

Mulvey, L. 1986. Melodrama in and out of the home. In *High theory/low culture: analysing popular television and film*, C. MacCabe (ed.), 80–100. New York: St. Martin's Press.

Nightingale, V. 1990. Women as audiences. In *Television and women's culture: the politics of the popular*, M. E. Brown (ed.), 25–36. London: Sage.

Press, A. 1991. *Women watching television: gender, class and generation in the American television experience.* Philadelphia: University of Pennsylvania Press.

Pribram, E. D. 1987. *Female spectators: looking and film and television.* London: Verso.

Probyn, E. 1990. New traditionalism and post-feminism: TV does the home. *Screen* **31**(2), 147–59.

Radway, J. 1984. *Reading the romance: feminism and the representation of women and popular culture.* London: Verso.

Roberts, Y. 1993. We are becoming divorced from reality. *New Statesman*, 24 September, 16–19.

Schroder, K. C. 1988. The pleasure of *Dynasty*: the weekly reconstruction of self-confidence. *Television and its audience: international research perspectives*, P. Drummond & R. Paterson (eds), 61–82. London: British Film Institute.

Stacey, J. 1988. Desperately seeking difference. In *The female gaze: women as viewers of popular culture*, L. Gamman & M. Marshment (eds), 112–29. London: The Women's Press.

Stacey, J. 1992. Backward toward the postmodern family. In *Rethinking the family: some feminist questions*, B. Thorne & M. Yalom (eds), 91–118. Boston: Northeastern University Press.

Thorne, B. 1992. Feminism and the family: two decades of thought. In *Rethinking the family: some feminist questions*, B. Thorne & M. Yalom (eds), 3–30. Boston: Northeastern University Press.

Trevedi, P. 1984. To deny our fullness: Asian women in the making of history. *Feminist Review* **17**, 37–52.

Weeks, J. 1991. Pretended family relationships. In *Marriage, domestic life and social change: writings for Jacqueline Burgoyne (1944–88)*, D. Clark (ed.), 213–34. London: Routledge.

Women Studies Group 1978. *Women take issue: aspects of women's subordination.* Centre for Contemporary Cultural Studies. London: Hutchinson.

CHAPTER 13

Remembering the future: the cultural study of memory

Timothy Robins

Introduction

The last decade has seen a growing interest in memory as a site where public and private identities are constructed. Where the discipline of psychology has tended to define memory as a product of the biological or cognitive processes of the individual, cultural studies has conceptualized memory as a product of social processes whereby the past is represented through cultural forms.

My aim in this chapter is to trace the ways in which a variety of cultural theorists have differentially constituted memory as an object of study and to examine the different implications of these respective accounts for remembering and forgetting as a political practice. These studies seem to me to be characteristically postmodern in their shared concern with the narrativity of culture and cultural explanation. Still, their emphasis on the active part individuals play in the process of self-narration and self-creation directly challenges the passivity that seems to be inherent in postmodern conceptions of the human subject as a product of positioning within discourse. Furthermore, I suggest that they begin to meet the need to account for how the fragmented subject of postmodernity is held together to produce the subjective experience of continuity as well as discontinuity.

My starting point, introduced in the next section, is the writings of Michel Foucault, Colin MacCabe and the Birmingham University-based Popular Memory Group. I suggest that these works provide a framework for understanding the more recent approaches to memory. Moreover, in my view, they also help to demonstrate the ways in which different conceptualizations of ideology and discourse have correlative implications for a politics of memory, and for the status of identity as a lived experience.

Foucault, "Screen Theory" and the Popular Memory Group

Michel Foucault (1975: 25) first spoke of a "popular memory" in an interview with the editors of the film journal *Cahiers du cinéma*. The editors discussed with Foucault the proliferation of "retro-style" films such as *Lacombe Lucien* and *Night porter* which, they argued, represented the populace as collaborators with the Nazi regime in occupied France. The editors suggested that, with the recent election of Giscard d'Estaing and the death of Gaullism, a hidden right-wing history was emerging that would deny the existence of any popular struggle against the Nazi regime.

Foucault discussed this process in terms of a struggle over "popular memory", defined by him as accounts of the past produced in oral or written forms by those denied access to the production of published historical accounts. Television and cinema were among those institutional apparatuses which sought to disseminate official histories in order to take possession of popular memory in an act of control and administration. He suggested that this had led to a "*re-programming* of popular memory, which existed but had no way of expressing itself. So people are shown not what they were, but what they must remember having been" (Foucault 1975: 25).

Reprinted in the *Edinburgh '77 Magazine*, this interview with Foucault appeared alongside articles that continued a debate from the film journal *Screen* about the "progressive" potential of realism as a form of representation. These articles explored the relationship between history and memory. Academic Colin MacArthur argued that the BBC television series *Days of hope*, dramatizing the rise of the British Labour Movement between the introduction of conscription in 1916 and the General Strike of 1928, demonstrated that the conventions of social realism were capable of producing progressive, radical forms of drama that exposed the conflicts and contradictions of power interests inherent in society. In contrast, Colin MacCabe argued that there existed a dominant, classic realist textual form that was inescapably bourgeois and which overdetermined the viewing experience (MacCabe 1981a,b). Following Lacan and Althusser, MacCabe theorized the audience as a unified subject position produced by a process of "ideological misrecognition". In the case of film and television, this imaginary identity subsumed representations of conflict and contradiction.

The significance of this debate for film and television studies, particularly for realism as a form of representation, has been well documented (see Fiske 1987 and Moores 1993 for recent accounts). Here, then, I will draw out the ways in which a politics of memory was implicated in the discussion. MacCabe's (1981b) response to MacArthur directly challenged the Left's conceptualization of memory and the subject of history. Interestingly, he extended his critique of the imagined identity implicit in the hierarchical gaze of the cinema audience to that of the hierarchical gaze of historians. MacCabe noted that the empiricism inherent in the Left's search to uncover a past created a chain of similar imaginary identities. This included an identity between present representations and the past events which they claimed to transparently reflect; a unity of class subjects that celebrated an unchanging, essentialist truth of working-class experience; and a class memory "such that the features and positions of the working class are given for all time" (MacCabe1981b: 317–8).

To substantiate his counter-position, MacCabe combined the Marxisms of *The 18th Brumaire of Louis Bonaparte* and Walter Benjamin with Freud's account of remembering and forgetting as an active process; he argued that class identities and experiences should be seen as continually re-inscribed through struggles in the present. He also maintained that since remembering linked the past and the present in a chain of cause and effect, it created a misrecognized identity within the individual psyche "confirming men [*sic*] in an imaginary relation to the present" (MacCabe 1981: 316). Indeed, MacCabe ultimately dismissed the possibilities of memory for a "progressive" politics in order to call for a politics of forgetting!

Foucault's conceptualization of a popular memory remained undeveloped by MacCabe, perhaps because his interview offered a politics of memory that was more open to Marxist historicism. Although Foucault wondered if "the Marxist analyses aren't victims to some abstractedness of the notion of liberty" (Foucault 1975: 28), his discussion produced an account of repressed and obstructed personal and public knowledge that could be assimilated into concerns with writing histories "from below". Consequently, it was left to the self-styled "Popular Memory Group" at the University of Birmingham-based Centre for Contemporary Cultural Studies to answer MacCabe's criticisms and develop popular memory as an object of study and a political practice. In *Making histories*, Johnson & Dawson (1982) provided a conceptual sketch of popular memory as a potential field of study, Bommes & Wright (1982) provided an early critique of national heritage as conceived by the National Heritage Act, while Davies et al. (1982) gave an account of the memoirs, biographies and autobiographies of early-twentieth-century feminist activists.

Unlike MacCabe, Johnson & Dawson (1982) asserted a positive role for realism as a way of knowing and a form of representation. They argued for a research project that would bring together structural and cultural readings of memory. Structural readings would treat oral and autobiographical representations as texts while recognizing that such conventional accounts also signify, are produced by, and are understood with reference to, a knowable reality that exists beyond the text. Cultural readings would analyze the ways in which memory was enacted in everyday life as performance and became transcribed with the values and conventions of that life. These cultural features "are not simply the product of individual authorship; they draw on general cultural repertoires, features of language and codes of expression which help determine what may be said, how and to what effect" (Johnson & Dawson 1982: 229).

Although the Popular Memory Group made only passing reference to the work of MacCabe and the *Days of hope*, they too were concerned that the empirical assumptions underlying the methods of oral and working-class histories reproduced a passive model of memory that became "a completed process, representative of a past which is itself dead and gone and therefore stable and objective"; a model in which memories are "the sedimented form of past events, leaving traces that may be unearthed by appropriate questioning" (Johnson & Dawson 1982: 211). Instead, they suggested that memory must be seen in terms of an *active past–present* relationship (thereby echoing MacCabe) so as to suggest that memories exist as traces that are continually re-worked in the present. This need for an active model of memory is further revealed in their critique of oral history projects. Johnson & Dawson argued that, by attempting to produce a transparent representation of the past through controlling cultural determinates as if they were confounding variables in an experiment (a process in which memories as objects remained unchanged), oral historians validate the historian as expert and remove individuals and memory from the cultural conditions in which they are constituted.

The Popular Memory Group, despite sharing Foucault's concerns with the relationship between power and knowledge, as well as MacCabe's concerns about the conceptualization of memory by Left historians, proceeded to relocate popular memory onto the more recognizable cultural studies terrain mapped out with reference to Althusser (1971) and Gramsci (1971). This introduced the possibility of contestation in the relationship between the media and memory. They argued that media and heritage institutions should be understood as "historical apparatuses" (echoing Althusser's concept of Ideological State Apparatuses) as they produce a "dominant memory" that attempts to win consensus over the way the past is understood. Memory, defined as representations of the past, is produced in a double articulation: in struggles between popular memory and dominant memory in the "public sphere", and between the forms of public representation and the contesting forms of memory, including letters, photograph albums and personal memorabilia, that were produced in the "private sphere".

The Popular Memory Group also insisted that self-knowledge, a consciousness of the conditions of existence that produced the experience of individuality within the psyche, had a positive and useful political function. A political project of "knowing thyself" also necessitated an account of what self there was to be known. Here, unsurprisingly, the group took up Gramsci's rather than Foucault's answer to the question "What is Man?" They also echoed

Raymond William's (1992) discussion of "individual" creativity to argue that the psyche is constructed like society as "an ensemble of relations" and, crucially, as "a series of active relationships" (Johnson & Dawson 1982: 236). Critical remembering was, therefore, the means by which individuals might "become self-conscious about the formation of common-sense beliefs" (Johnson & Dawson 1982: 214). Individual memories, constructed from social relations and cultural forms, needed to be understood in terms of their implication in more general collective struggles and identities. Rather disappointingly, however, the Popular Memory Group did not pursue the construction of memory at the level of the psyche nor did they provide a method for the critical process of self-remembering.

Recent work in cultural theory has provided more personal accounts of remembering and forgetting and their function in forging the continuities of identity from contradictory subjectivities. This work has often been from feminist and pro-feminist perspectives that locate memory as part of personal-political projects, thereby producing accounts of the production of gendered subjectivity in order to find resources for personal and social change. As I intend to show, these approaches also highlight the difficulties inherent in MacCabe's and the Popular Memory Group's conceptualizations of memory.

Haug, Jackson and Steedman: memory work and the narrative construction of subjectivity

Female sexualisation (Haug 1987), a collection of essays by a Hamburg and West Berlin-based socialist feminist collective, usefully engages in a dialogue with Foucault's conception of power as a productive force, one that constructs identities through institutional practices. As the collective point out, since Foucault "allows neither for active subjects nor for any potential self-determination, both appear dispensable in projects for class and sexual liberation" (Haug 1987: 204). Here, the collective explores the active participation of individuals as "human subjects" in the relationship between culture and memory with particular reference to the construction of gendered identity. Their "memory-work" is a collective practice combining theoretically informed criticism with methods such as storytelling, the evocation of emotion and the examination of cultural resources such as language and pictures. Their aim, as explained by editor Frigga Haug, is in understanding how their bodies have become sexualized. At stake is the need to produce resources for liberation from "heteronomy" or the "alien determination" of patriarchy (Haug 1987: 18) that has shaped their memories into taken-for-granted patterns of thought and feeling; a mode of remembering that "plasters over the cracks" in personal history to create a "fantasized harmony" (Haug 1987: 69).

The collective's approach is thus distinct from the autobiographical method; the latter being based on a "theoretically untenable presupposition" that assumes childhood and adolescence are part of a logical sequence of cause and effect culminating in the adult personality. Despite this, the collective still holds that past experience such as moments of resistance to male authority are obtainable through memory once they have overcome the obstacles of patriarchal culture which causes these experiences to be forgotten. However, this leads the collective to see memory as an active process only in terms of the blocks placed in front of the recollection of past experiences, "elements of resistance" (Haug 1987: 40) which are always contained in identity. The ways of remembering provided by the dominant culture work only by "censorship" (Haug 1987: 58) and "repression" (Haug 1987: 48) or by transporting "alien" qualities into their selves (Haug 1987: 61).

Clearly, then, critical remembering combines emotions and self-reflexive theorizing to access omitted experiences. Still, the members of this collective do not see memory as actively constructing even those experiences. Instead, critically informed remembering frees memory from the biases of dominant culture, thereby allowing us to see "events in the past in new and more or less unprejudiced ways" (Haug 1987: 47). Thus, while the collective does not share social psychology's split between the individual psyche and society, I suggest it does see memory's relation to social practices and cultural formations in terms similar to those of social psychology. That is, where social and cognitive psychology see the social as a source of confounding variables, for the collective it is the site of confounding social practices and ideologies.

David Jackson (1990) is confronted by a related set of problems in his critical autobiography *Unmasking masculinity*. In this text, Jackson seeks to identify a "typical" masculine narrative form that shapes public autobiographies of male careers. Jackson acknowledges that this form has also acted to organize his own psyche. This closed narrative form, amongst other features, organizes events into an "ejaculatory narrative rhythm" (Jackson 1990: 230) of ascending action leading to climactic achievement. This identification of "masculine" and "feminine" narrative forms is based on Fiske's (1987) discussion of gendered television. Fiske's account synthesizes a wide range of material to draw up a correspondence between popular idealizations of masculinity and femininity and the structure of stories. Jackson argues that narrative forms become masculine and feminine through their location within the gendered division of labour and other patriarchal practices in capitalist society. He explains, therefore, that this critical examination and reshaping of his masculinity has been, in part, made possible by social and bodily crises in his life that removed him from the "public sphere" dominated by masculine work and placed him, instead, in the "domestic sphere" with its more open work regimes. He argues that this relocation at the social level is represented in the

text of his book and partly accounts for his ability to challenge the determinations of masculine narrative forms and reading formations.

There are a number of problems which Jackson's account shares with the
work collected by Haug. For example, in making realist appeals to social practices beyond the narrative forms that constitute their subjectivities, Haug's and
Jackson's respective texts rest on monolithic conceptions of patriarchy and the
division of labour. Recent research on media audiences reveals Jackson's assertion of the relationship between work patterns, viewing practices and gender is
over-generalized (see, for example, Ang & Hermes 1991). In the end, what
seems to mesh narrative forms and reading practices to gendered identities are
the metanarratives in the stories provided by Marxism, socialist-feminism and
cultural studies itself. It is precisely this issue that is addressed by Carolyn
Steedman in her book *Landscape for a good woman.*

Steedman's (1986) text engages in a feminist literary practice of self
consciously using generic conventions to make visible their "socially and politically conservative discourses" (Cranny-Francis 1990: 19). She extends this
practice to expose the conservatism in some discourses of feminism and cultural studies. Specifically, Steedman employs the metaphors of room and landscape conventionally used by feminist literature (see Horner & Zlosnik 1990)
to explore the possibilities and limitations for the self within patriarchal society.
She then reveals, in turn, the limitations of these metaphors at work within the
stories of cultural studies, in particular the northern working-class landscape of
Hoggart's *The uses of literacy*. In part, she finds Hoggart's implicit nostalgia for
a working-class past produces the passivity and unchanging working-class
experience that MacCabe felt was an inevitable effect of memory. Interestingly, Steedman argues that this impoverished landscape is partly the product
of a Marxism that can only conceive of working-class consciousness as an
undifferentiated mass consciousness and a cultural studies that has "celebrated
a kind of psychological simplicity in the lives lived out in Hoggart's endless
streets of little houses" (Steedman 1986: 7).

Like Haug and Jackson, Steedman sees consciousness as a product of narrative and actively produced through telling stories. She uses the narrative conventions of history, biography, autobiography, psychoanalytic case study and
other forms of storytelling to create a more complex psychology and to
produce specific truth effects and subjectivities. From her position as a social
historian, she presents a historical narrative that represents an empirical,
material, objective world; "this is a book about *things* (objects, entities, relationships, people)" (Steedman 1986: 23). Steedman notes that autobiography rests
on similar empirical truth-claims and uses this form of narrative to offer up
her working-class past as evidence: a wealth of background detail on the
1950s. These details not only particularize the otherwise "profoundly a-historical landscape" (Steedman 1986: 16), but also provide evidence (such as the

failure of her father's authority within the home) to challenge theories of patri-archy and working-class struggle.

Nevertheless, Steedman notes that while for the historian the possibilities of refutation are endless, the autobiographer shapes events into a story with an end. This effects a closure on time, knowledge and the self. In this way, autobi-ography is similar to a psychoanalytic case study which is set in the "here and now" and ends in the figure of the subject, who produces a sense of self by tell-ing their story in their "own time". Still, a psychoanalytic case study has a different chronological and epistemological configuration to that of an autobi-ography. As Steedman explains, within a psychoanalytic case study "truth and order do not matter in the same way. If the events are falsified, the reader still ends up with the same story in the end: the individual's account of how she got to be the way she is" (Steedman 1992: 125). Therefore, Steedman uses meta-phor to transport objects of history and autobiography into the conventions of the psychoanalytic case study. Within this structure these objects no longer have the same epistemological status. The historical narrative allows her to give a complexity to her childhood, but when this periodizing and particular-izing is placed within the psychoanalytic narrative the childhood she recounts becomes the childhood of her *imagination*.

Landscape for a good woman demonstrates that history and psychoanalysis are different forms of political understanding: at issue is precisely what is to be defined as political, what is the material basis of that politics and what form political action should take. The difficulty for Steedman is that the two narra-tive forms do not just allow different things to be included as evidence, they constitute the nature of that evidence. Throughout *Landscape for a good woman* we see how the different conventions of history and psychoanalytic case study exist in tension with each other, tensions that remain unresolved. What is particu-larly useful about her account, in my view, is that while it attends to the narra-tive production of subjectivity through memory, it also shows a concern with the cultural, performative and contingent aspects of memory. So, for example, Steedman shows that the act of writing history, of constructing historical narra-tives, produces historical consciousness while also recognizing that the power of interpretation, of making sense of the stories presented in the book, rests with the story-taker. It is the readers who can use their own historical understanding to piece together a linear historical narrative from the complex forms of repre-sentation in *Landscape for a good woman*. As she notes, "I could write it backwards indeed, and you would still know it happened forward" (Steedman 1992: 50).

Steedman's insistence on the marginality of her story, of her observations of a landscape from the edges, challenges the Popular Memory Group's concep-tualization of a politics of self-knowing which must search for a wider rep-resentativeness (see Marcus 1987). Seen in this way, the particularism of Steedman's landscape would simply be reduced to an ideological effect of dominant memory. Steedman therefore criticizes the Marxist and feminist realism informing many structural readings for their general assumptions about what has been "hidden" from history. Not only does her life story fail to produce the representativeness demanded by such accounts, but her text would suggest that the impoverishment of working-class history is a product of a poverty of materials, an irrecoverable and unknowable absence. However, by setting her sights on the past, Steedman brings into view a more homogeneous, more passive landscape than she might desire; an industrial landscape of mass employment with all the familiar landmarks "traditionally" examined by British cultural studies. At the same time, the present in which that point of view is produced remains unexplored.

Here, I want to briefly highlight one recent attempt to widen *Landscape for a good woman's* horizons. Ganguly's (1992) study of the remembrances of members of a postcolonial community in the United States pinpoints the need to attend to the question of nationalism. While exploring the way postcolonial subjects produce a sense of identity through narratives, Ganguly exposes the limitations of narrative as a way of conceptualizing subjectivity. She argues that such approaches tend to understand the lives of "others" only as metaphors and have an existence "only as a narrative genre or as the endlessly deferred product of signifying processes" (Ganguly 1992: 128). Whereas Steedman (1986) addresses ethnicity only in the exoticized figure of a transitory Hindu student lodger in her mother's house, Ganguly uses ethnography to demonstrate that "others" exist not at the margins or as transitional objects but as concrete presences in "our" midst. Significantly, then, Ganguly's (1992) work makes use of a Foucauldian understanding of the body as a site of power and resistance, particularly his discussion of "technologies of the self" in order to argue that "the self is like a technology . . . which, at any given moment, articulates a series of *realized* relationships" (Ganguly 1992: 129).

Remembering the future

My selective engagement with several key aspects of the cultural study of memory has not identified a single memory project. Memory has been constituted as a different object of study with different political functions within different academic discourses. There are, however, certain commonalities shared by the writers discussed above: namely, a concern with seeing memory as a process through which identities are constructed or re-constituted in the present by actively articulating a relationship with the past. Alongside this is an anti-essentialism concerned with understanding subjectivity as socially constructed, while allowing for the individual to be recognized as a site for personal and social change.

The Gramscian project of attaining historical consciousness by constructing an "inventory" of trace elements of the past (which have, in turn, been deposited in the self), is faced with the problem of reproducing a passive conception of that very past, that is, a model of memory based upon a reified division between self and society. For example, following Gramsci, the Popular Memory Group wrote, "memories of the past are, like all common-sense forms, strangely composite constructions, resembling a kind of geology, the selective sedimentation of past traces" (Johnson & Dawson 1982: 211). This suggests that to construct an inventory, the rememberer becomes an archaeologist of self-knowledge. Memory-work, in this way, becomes spade work; we dig down through the geological strata in search of lost causes – the bedrock on which the present has been built. This metaphor of "inventory" is also shared by certain approaches within cognitive psychological research where memories are regarded as objects held in a storehouse. Here the process of memory is understood as the search for indications of how the storehouse is organized and the mechanisms by which memories are sorted and retrieved. This, too, gives little sense of the active process by which memories themselves may be modified or re-constituted in the act of remembering.

A critical memory project based on the work of Foucault is faced with a different set of difficulties. Foucault (1988: 18), in yet another recasting of his work, said that he was concerned with two understandings of the production of subjectivity: technologies of power, "which determine the conduct of individuals and submit them to certain ends or domination, an objectivizing of the subject" and technologies of the self, "which permit individuals to effect by their own means or with the help of others a certain number of operations on their own bodies and souls, thoughts, conduct, and way of being, so as to transform themselves in order to attain a certain state of happiness". His account of memory as a technology of power was presented in *Discipline and punish* (Foucault 1986) which extended Nietzsche's assertion that the function of punishment was a means of creating memory in its account of the creation of a corporeal identity. Here, the human subject is not a product of ideological misrecognition; instead, identity is made material within the disciplinary regime of the panopticon that acts on the body to establish a causal continuity.

The advantages of seeing identity as something other than ideological misrecognition are set off by the difficulties of conceptualizing resistance to such institutional regimes where self-knowledge is productive of power. Foucault's later turn to technologies of the self scarcely resolves the difficulties of appropriating his work within the concerns of those wishing to conceptualize "knowing thyself" as a political project. In the course of investigating the history of sexuality, Foucault (1988: 22) traced the ways Christian morality prioritized the project of knowing thyself above what ancient Greek and Roman texts presented as a complementary set of practices and injunctions to

"Take care of yourself." Foucault's reading of the works of the Stoics gives memory and remembering a central function in the care and transformation of the self. However, although Foucault understood memory as a process of self-subjectivization in relation to moral injunctions, and as a resource for change, he was certainly not proposing a project based on "knowing thyself" (a task which, he argued, Christianity came to prioritize to the exclusion of caring for the self). Indeed, Christianity and Marxism, he suggests, share a rejection of "cultivating the self" as a morally justifiable project. There are also parallels between Christianity's demands to "know one's self" in order to renounce that self, and Marxist-informed approaches to memory that see self-knowledge as the first step in renouncing individuality in favour of collective identities. Needless to say, this demand for wider "representativeness" not only renounces individual cultivation of the self, but also produces a distinctive politics of memory.

Accordingly, this approach highlights a crucial disjunctive *vis-à-vis* the formulations introduced above by Haug (1987), Jackson (1990) and the Popular Memory Group (Bommes & Wright 1982, Davies et al. 1982, Johnson & Dawson 1982). For these cultural theorists, it is the task of remembering events and elements of subjectivity that have been repressed by dominant ideology which is central to a critical project. This process, drawing in part on Althusserian Marxism, similarly entails a forgetting of any unified sense of identity (dismissed as an "ideological misrecognition") as well as any events or elements deemed to be "unrepresentative" of the social conditions and collective identities recognized as relevant to political action. In addition to this "burden of representation", therefore, there is a related "burden of memory". Individuals are criticized either for forgetting material they have never known, or for failing to possess a memory expansive enough to encompass social conditions the limits of which have yet to be specified.

MacCabe's prioritization of a politics of forgetting is the result of a similar critique of identity as the product of ideology. Instead of a popular-memory, his account suggests to me the need for a counter-memory, a political practice that would operate against the memory's function in the construction of such imaginary unities. This emphasis is also apparent in *Landscape for a good woman*, which ends with Steedman calling for a politics that will consign her stories to the dark. In this manner, I would suggest that Steedman moves away from the poststructuralist concerns of MacCabe towards that strand of postmodernism that is suspicious of all forms of representation; a strand that does not search for more complex ways of seeing, but for ways of not being seen; for ways of escaping institutionalized forms of being by non-representational practices such as silence and disappearance. In this way, Steedman identifies a further burden for popular memory; namely, that it can only exist in tension with dominant memory and, therefore, can have no independent existence or agenda.

Given that the cultural theorists discussed above provide multiple (and contradictory) accounts of how memory "works", what matters are the possibilities for future change engendered by their respective conceptualizations of the politics of remembering and forgetting. Here, I want to suggest that there is a need to move away from the task of "essentialism spotting", as it leads the cultural study of memory to start from the lived experience of continuity and identity only to dismiss that experience as "misrecognition". Instead, there is a need to recognize identity as a resource for resistance and change. As Larrain (1994) has recently pointed out, "identity is not so much what one is as what one wants to be". To understand memory as produced through stories is to recognize this important future orientation, for stories contain a past, present and future relationship in which the end is implicit in the beginning and the beginning is a product of the present. This recent move towards conceptualizing memory in terms of a life story or project, in my view, marks the entry of existential concerns on to the agenda of a cultural critique.

References

Althusser, L. 1971. *Lenin and philosophy and other essays.* London: Verso.

Ang, I. & J. Hermes 1991. Gender and/in media consumption. In *Mass media and society*, J. Curran & M. Gurevitch (eds). Sevenoaks, England: Edward Arnold.

Bommes, M. & P. Wright 1982. Charms of residence: the public and the past. In *Making histories: studies in history-writing*, R. Johnson et al. (eds), 253–301. London: Hutchinson.

Cranny-Francis, A. 1990. *Feminist fiction.* Cambridge: Polity

Davies, T., M. Durham, C. Hall, M. Langan, D. Sutton 1982. "The public face of feminism": early twentieth-century writings on women's suffrage. In *Making histories: studies in history-writing*, R. Johnson et al. (eds), 302–24. London: Hutchinson.

Fiske, J. 1987. *Television culture.* London: Routledge

Foucault, M. 1975. Film and popular memory: an interview with Michel Foucault. *Radical Philosophy* **11**, 24–9.

Foucault, M. 1986. *Discipline and punish: the birth of the prison.* London: Penguin.

Foucault, M. 1988. Technologies of the self. In *Technologies of the self: a seminar with Michel Foucault*, L. H. Martin, H. Gutman, P. Hutton (eds). London: Tavistock.

Ganguly, K. 1992. Migrant identities: personal memory and the construction of selfhood. *Cultural Studies* **6**, 127–50.

Gramsci, A. 1971. *Selections from prison notebooks.* London: Lawrence & Wishart.

Haug, F. (ed.) 1987. *Female sexualisation: a collective work of memory.* London: Verso.

Horner, A. & S. Zlosnik 1990. *Landscapes of desire: metaphors in modern women's fiction.* Hemel Hempstead, England: Harvester Wheatsheaf.

Jackson, D. 1990. *Unmasking masculinity: a critical autobiography.* London: Unwin Hyman.

Johnson, R. & G. Dawson 1982. Popular memory: theory, politics, method. In

Making histories: studies in history-writing, R. Johnson et al. (eds), 205–52. London: Hutchinson.

Larrain, J. 1994. *Ideology and cultural identity: modernity and the Third World presence*. Cambridge: Polity.

MacArthur, C. 1981. Days of hope. In *Popular television and film*, T. Bennett et al. (eds), 305–9. London: British Film Institute/Open University.

MacCabe, C. 1981a. Realism and cinema: notes on Brechtian theses. In *Popular television and film*, T. Bennett et al. (eds). London: British Film Institute/Open University.

MacCabe, C. 1981b. Memory, phantasy, identity: "Days of hope" and the politics of the past. In *Popular television and film*, T. Bennett et al. (eds), 314–18. London: British Film Institute/Open University.

Marcus, L. 1987. "Enough about you, let's talk about me". Recent autobiographical writing. *New Formations* **1**, 77–94.

Moores, S. 1993. *Interpreting audiences: the ethnography of media consumption*. London: Sage.

Steedman, C. 1986. *Landscape for a good woman: a story of two lives*. London: Virago.

Steedman, C. 1992. *Past tenses: essays on writing, autobiography and history*. London: Rivers Oram Press.

Williams, R. 1992. *The long revolution*. London: Hogarth Press.

CHAPTER 14

Imagining Nature: (re)constructions of the English countryside

Samantha Humphreys

Nature is perhaps the most complex word in the language. (Raymond Williams 1988)

In 1984, Charles Jencks wrote that postmodernism had begun at 3.32 pm on 15 July 1972 with the destruction of the Pruitt-Igoe housing scheme in St Louis, Missouri (Jencks 1984: 9). At that time Jencks owned a townhouse in London. Indeed, so spectacular was the internal decor of this house that it was featured in the April 1985 edition of *House and Garden* (cited in Ley 1989). Taking his inspiration from the natural world, Jencks had designed a house that displayed a consistent and self-conscious programme of natural and cosmological iconography. By way of an example, four rooms representing each of the seasons revolve around the central Sun Stair. In a perfection of detail, the Sun Stair itself has 52 steps and three rails (Sun, Earth and Moon) that rotate upwards in a spiral motion (Ley 1989: 55).

Remarkable though this may be in terms of imagination, attention to detail and, at a practical level, construction, I tell you about it not as some triumph of design and engineering but rather because of its ideological significance. In the postmodern world (a world where Nature may be celebrated through artificial reconstruction) we are denied the metanarratives of magic or religion, so that we must find some other commodity that "remains worthy of celebration in a secular age" (Jencks 1985, cited in Ley 1989: 55). As Ley explains, this has often taken the form of nostalgia for the past or appeals to populist sentiments (Ley 1989: 54). For Jencks, however, the solution lies not within the human world at all but with Nature.

If the world in which we live is a postmodern one it is also one where every day, and in every conceivable way, Nature is manipulated, the "natural order" of things altered, sometimes irrevocably. Environmentalists have linked this to the way we have established a dichotomous understanding of the human and natural worlds, creating an absolute distinction between Nature and Culture, and privileging the latter over the former so that we do not care what we do to our planet (see, for example, Griffin 1989). Nevertheless, while the rhetoric of environmental change tends to call to mind images of fast-disappearing rain-forests, water pollution and global warming, it is not hazards such as these ones that I wish to consider here. Important though they are, they seem some-how to be abstract problems for which it is easy to disclaim responsibility – to argue that they are caused by us as a species but not us as individuals.

There are other, more elemental ways in which we – as individuals – violate Nature. Consider not just the obvious fact that we have created for ourselves a predominantly artificial world (a world of cities, brick houses, cars, television sets and Sun staircases; a world where the very term "culture" seems to auto-matically and inevitably exclude Nature), but also the literal ways in which we have altered natural processes and phenomena – for example, by damming and diverting rivers, even redefining how a river should look. As Cosgrove (1990: 3) explains:

> The geometrical precision of an aqueduct signifies the engineer's vision of water flow, a bounded channel form that has become the common conception of how even a natural river should appear. In Europe, in other long-settled regions subject to large-scale administra-tion, and increasingly across the world, rivers do indeed appear this way in the landscape: linear features clearly defined by banks and levees, their flow regulated and largely predictable – in short, tamed. Today we find it hard to say what a natural river might look like [because] along with the landscapes through which they once so freely flowed, they have all been controlled and engineered.

There is thus a paradox to be found in our attitudes to Nature, to the natu-ral world. We reserve the right to define what constitutes a "natural" situation or occurrence yet, at the same time, ideas of the natural commonly serve as a yardstick, the conceptual standard against which we can measure notions of normality and "properness". "Natural" is not only the way things were but also the way things should be, the correct and customary way ("it's only natu-ral you should feel like that"). It is this seemingly contradictory relationship between ourselves and Nature (a relationship where our very ideas of "the natural" may themselves be *un*natural) that I wish to explore in this chapter. In particular, I will be considering the (mis)conceptions of Nature that we can detect in discourses and ideologies of the English countryside and, specifically, in articulations of the "rural myth".

Rural mythologies

The first question I shall be addressing is what exactly is meant by the "rural myth". There are various answers to this, but essentially it is the way that urbanized and industrialized England, even now, is *recreated as a rural nation*. It is the "pretence that the Englishman [*sic*] is a thatched cottager or country squire at heart" (Hobsbawm 1968, quoted in Wiener 1981: 46), the belief that somewhere "at the far end of the M4 or the A12 there are 'real' country folk living in the midst of 'real' English countryside in – that most elusive of all rustic Utopias – 'real communities'" (Newby 1979: 14). It is, in short, the sense that the countryside is somehow special – the feeling that life is better, the people kinder, and the existence "truer" there – although actually the rural myth is considerably more complex than just this basic eulogy of country life. In fact, there are several different strands within it that can be summarized under three main headings.

First, the rural myth is based on a fundamentally *dichotomous understanding* of the world, establishing an unconditional distinction between "natural" and "artificial", rural and urban, past and present; it privileges one – the rural past – over the other – the urban present – in an anti-urban and anti-modern discourse. Secondly, both distinct and leading on from this first point, the rural myth is highly *selective* in its portrayal of the countryside. The inherent bias that prioritizes rural over urban (and past over present) is thus embodied in accounts of the countryside that present it in unambiguously glowing colours. Thirdly, it is important to note that the rural myth does not exist in isolation; rather it *co-exists* alongside other versions/visions of the countryside. Hence, as Newby (1979: 13) writes, images of the "serene, idyllic existence, enjoyed by blameless Arcadians happy in their communion with Nature" must be placed alongside those of "a backward and isolated world where boredom vies with boorishness".

To examine the first and most important of these points, the rural myth combines specifically pro-rural discourses with those that are explicitly anti-urban and anti-modern. A simple dichotomy is established with, on the one hand, all that is natural (rural, old and good) and, on the other, all that is urban, new and (therefore) bad. In this way, it relies on a misrepresentation (a particular, biased image) of the urban as well as the rural, of the present as well as the past. Indeed, it relies on a misrepresentation of the whole process of social change, seeing it as a simple transition from one to the other, rather than understanding it in its full complexity. Considering this in more detail, then, images of the countryside as peaceful, tranquil and beautiful obviously form an integral and dominant theme of the rural myth. However, comparison is also implied here and expressed in the idea that rural life is somehow better and more "real" than urban life; this too forms a central characteristic

216

of conventional romantic attitudes towards the countryside. Hence the rural myth combines certain images of the city as well as the country, for if the rural is good, then the urban is bad.

In fact, these two aspects of the rural myth are inseparable, two sides of just one coin. As Williams (1993) suggests, in the title as well as the text of his book *The country and the city*, it is only with reference to one that we can understand the other. More specifically, Short (1991: 5) writes that wilderness can only be understood in conjunction with, and in opposition to, notions of cultivation. In isolation, either term is useless and thus

> in hunting and gathering societies there was and is no distinction be-
> tween wilderness and the rest of the environment. Since there is little
> or no cultivation or domestication of animals all land is uncultivated,
> all animals are wild . . . [and t]here is no central dichotomy between
> cultivated and wilderness. (Short 1991: 5)

Similarly, "countryside" is an empty term – meaningless because it includes everything – unless there is something other than countryside, against which it can be compared. By definition, therefore, the rural myth must include notions of urban (artificial) as well as rural (natural) life.

It must also, however, contain an anti-modern element. While this is per-haps less obvious, the rural myth nonetheless needs to be understood in the context of processes of urbanization, industrialization and democratization. In other words, it needs to be understood within a framework of transition, since its development can be seen as a direct result of change. In basic (though over-simplified) terms, over the last two or three centuries the processes of urbani-zation and industrialization, and the associated changes within English society and culture, have inspired a sense of loss, a nostalgia for the past. The rural myth can thus be seen as a response to "unease about the crudities of the mod-ern age and scepticism about the amorality of modern living . . .[which] spurred an increasing urgency among intellectuals to find England's roots" (Rich 1990: 213). Because of the uncertainties and ambiguities associated with "modern life", this search took them not forwards, but backwards. Hence, the countryside became "the perfect past to the imperfect present and uncertain future" (Short 1991: 31), and the rural myth was born. Like postmodernism itself then, this particular vision of the countryside appears bound to the past even if promising hope for the present: our one bright dream for the future becomes our one bright dream from and of the past.

Moreover, this myth of the countryside has been created in an essentially urban society. Specifically, the celebration of the countryside often comes not from those who live there (and who therefore experience the reality of country living), but from those divorced from the land, who then view or remember it freed from the restraints of reality – that is, those who are free to re-imagine it, to recreate it as myth. The rural myth thus presents images of country life and Nature that have been divorced from reality, and reflected through the fact of urban experience and memory. As Short (1991: 57) writes:

> Britain is one of the most urbanized and industrialized countries in the world and has been for almost 150 years. This fact is the pivotal point of any analysis of its environmental ideologies. Notions of wilderness, ideas of countryside and urban attitudes are constantly refracted through this unique historical experience and particular social configuration.

It is only possible for us to understand the historical construction and cultural significance of the rural myth if we recognize both its urban context and its misrepresentations of English (rural and urban) lives. This is vital, for it is only through understanding contending definitions of reality that we can come to see the myth, and hence understand how ideas of rurality have been so well placed to offer a readily accepted alternative vision of England at the very time that the nation is, in practical terms, losing its rural identity.

Here then, we come to see the fundamental contradiction that lies at the heart of the rural myth: it is created specifically *by* an urban society *for* an urban society and yet revolves around the idea that rural life (which is based on a fundamental misrecognition of what rural life actually entails) is more "real" than urban life (which is, in fact, the physical reality of life for many). However, this is perhaps not quite the paradox that it might seem at first: like all illusions the rural myth can only be maintained from a distance and hence even while the experience and memory of life may be urban for the majority of the population, it is not the *reality* of that life which is incorporated within the rural myth. Rather, the *image* is everything, and individual memories and experiences (of urban and industrial centres, or of the "reality" – the hard work and perhaps isolation – of rural life) become subsumed under cultural reconstructions of the countryside. With both the production and consumption of representations of "the rural" thus divorced from actual experience, or actual memory, images of the countryside can be circulated *en masse*: those with no personal memories or experiences of the countryside can simply "borrow" from the range of cultural (re)constructions presented to them, can share in the universal (and universally available) memories and experiences on offer. Still, if the rural myth is based on a dichotomous understanding of the world, and on misrepresentations of rural and urban, past and present, then it is also *selective*.

Imagining Nature

Having examined the historical conditions and ideological implications of this myth, I now wish to explore the images of the rural that it encapsulates, and the image of England that it has served to create – that is, the visions of Nature that it both enshrines and engenders. We have already seen that it is, in fact, a complexly constructed account of the natural world and its associated values that the rural myth paints. However, not only is it selective in the sense that it has chosen rural past over urban present, but also in the way in which it has prioritized certain images of the rural over others. In particular, as a variety of authors note (see, for example, Howkins 1986: 64–5, Short 1992: 2), it has tended to create an image not of the whole of rural England, but rather the south. In the same way that a simple (but false) dichotomy was established between urban and rural, there emerged a similar contrast between north and south. Shields (1991: 229–31) suggests that the former became seen as a predominantly urban and industrial landscape populated by "rough working classes" and incorporating "windswept countryside", while the latter, "an equally imaginary region", was recreated as a combination of "pastoral landscape" and "civilisation". Thus it is village greens, wheat fields, and church spires in the distance and not the "stark and empty" landscapes of the north which inspire. This can perhaps be linked to traditional ideas of what "good" countryside should look like. Short (1991: 15) explains that up until the seventeenth century, bleak or rugged scenery was seen as unappealing, and "in 1657, the English poet Andrew Marvell (1621–78) wrote of mountains as ill-designed excrescences that deform the earth and frighten heaven".

Even though later centuries saw a re-evaluation of the classical perspective, this traditional thinking was nonetheless retained, to some extent, in the rural myth – which is, after all, a dream of a *cultivated* (and therefore safe) Arcadia, a dream of rustic peace, security and tranquillity, rather than awe-inspiring, untamed (and therefore dangerous) "wilderness". It is here that it is important to note that the rural myth, which developed in the eighteenth century and has persisted into the nineteenth and twentieth centuries, is not necessarily synonymous with the attitudes to Nature in general that developed at the same time. Romantic poets may have transformed mountainous landscapes that had earlier been dismissed as unworthy of attention into "a symbol of a divine force, a thing of beauty and a point of contact with the infinite" (Short 1991: 16), but the rural myth idealizes a different kind of Nature – that is, an essentially artificial Nature, where the presence of "humanity" is evident rather than obscured. Both redefinitions of the rural world may have the same impulses driving them, and may share the same idea of Nature as a source of inspiration, but it is clear that in the rural myth, this inspirational Nature has been translated into a more domesticated vision.

Additionally, there is another sense in which the rural myth has privileged certain ideological discourses over other ones: by excluding the "real-life" aspects of country living, such as labour, poverty and unemployment. Wohl (1984: 301), for example, points to discrepancies between visual appearance and lived reality, noting that " old cottages of thatch struck the Victorians as the perfect picture of rustic simplicity and bucolic delight, as they do us today, but the nineteenth-century reality was that most of them were hopelessly old, with oozing floors, porous walls and roofs that leaked". The twentieth century reality may jar uncomfortably with the surface image in a similar way. For example, evidence of labour has frequently been subsumed beneath superficial and aesthetic aspects of the countryside, so that the "rest" rather than "work" dimension to rural life has been emphasized. As Williams notes, "a working country is hardly ever a landscape. The very idea of landscape implies separation and observation" (1993: 120).

Thus, by creating a rural England that is essentially translated into images of pretty scenery and/or local communities, the "real" aspects are ignored; we rarely see the negative elements, or the hard work involved in country life. This is not to say that we are not made aware of the fact that "country folk" must work hard, for industry and honesty are traits associated with "clean country living", and we know (because the rural myth tells us that it is so) that it is their hard and diligent work that allows those who live in the country to reap the many – and varied – fruits of their labours. Nonetheless, work is painted in a positive light, even (and perhaps especially) when its difficulty is stressed; it becomes subfused, in Short's words, in "a good, green light – but an ideological light which can obscure as well as ornament the object of analysis" (1992: 4).

The rural myth thus presents us with an England where "real-life" country people – and the lives they lead – are simultaneously present and absent. On the one hand, we see the hard (but well-rewarded) work, the small villages and quaint cottages, and on the other, we see the land as landscape, "devoid of tangible, breathing humans with their own aspirations and problems" (Short 1992: 4). Paradoxically, however, the images presented to us are all the more human for that: we have already seen that the English countryside celebrated within the rural myth is not composed of great, barren landscapes or desolate moors and wastes, but country hamlets and neat, enclosed fields, where signs of human inhabitation are obvious. The rural myth thus offers again and again a social, rather than a natural, countryside; the land becomes a place where Nature and humans can co-exist in a state of perfect harmony, rather than vying with each other for supremacy. If one does have to win, however, then it is ultimately the human (that is, tamed), and not the natural (untamed) influence which is prioritized. As we have seen, the rural myth may be informed by attitudes to Nature, but it is a reworked Nature, defined in an essentially human image, so that the England it creates is, above all, a safe and happy England.

The Nature of Culture

Nevertheless, alternative visions of our land do exist (it is perhaps significant that "land", like "country", refers both to the rural world and the nation as a whole; see Short 1991: 34); the positive images of the countryside articulated within romantic discourses are open to challenge. For example, within the rhetoric of migration, we can detect very different attitudes towards both country and city life from those embedded within the rural myth. Smout (1990: 60, 81–2), in particular, identifies what might be termed an urban or anti-rural myth which, at an ideological level, may inform the decision to migrate: rural areas are seen as isolated and backward, inhabited by narrow-minded and dull "country bumpkins" and lacking the "range of people" and facilities that towns and cities can offer, so that the countryside is defined in increasingly negative terms and migration occurs. Thus, if the rural myth is both dichotomous and selective, then it is also just one of several visions of the countryside open to us; in short, even where romantic discourses are prioritized, they nonetheless *co-exist* with other, less idealized images and representations of Nature.

In spite of this, however, the images of England, of the natural world, offered within the rural myth have proved very strong and enduring. This can be seen very clearly in the attitudes to environments, gardens and "leafy" suburbia, which Howkins (1991: 229–32), for example, details. In a historical context, Thompson (1993: 169) suggests that the "suburban garden . . .was desired in a straightforward way because it was a piece of tangible evidence, however minute, that the dream of being a townsman [*sic*] living in the country was something more than just an illusion". Considering this in more detail, it is possible to see in the plans and designs of the nineteenth and early twentieth centuries (when the virtues of the English countryside were being extolled within both elite and popular culture as at no other time) just how effective the ideological reconstruction of England as a rural nation has been.

The suburbs may have offered "some small reminder of rural life" (Thompson 1993: 170), but their popularity did not simply *reflect* contemporary images of the countryside – rather it contributed to the active *renegotiation* of those images. As Howkins (1991) explains, it might have been the obvious appeal of mythical and idyllic representations of the countryside which persuaded people to move to the suburbs, but those who responded to this appeal were in turn crucial to the (re)invention of "English" rural life. In tree-lined avenues and houses with gardens (their own, neat, "slice of England"), such individuals set about capturing more fully the traditions of rural England: "when the first generation of suburbanites moved to the new 'village' of Bedford Park they built a village inn, suitably half timbered and called it 'The Tabard' and erected a maypole to celebrate their village festivals in Tudor dress" (Howkins 1991: 231). In this way they created, as well as recreated, the rural past.

Moreover, this creation and recreation of the countryside was evident not only in the desires of suburban families for gardens or "rustic porches" (Howkins 1986: 73), nor with the designers who attempted to incorporate green parks into housing plans (see Thompson 1993: 169), but in all aspects of life. Howkins (1986, 1991), for example, points to the increased numbers of people who joined rambling or cycling clubs, and the creation of societies such as the National Trust (established in 1894 to preserve England's cultural – that is, rural – heritage) as well as the emergence of those small groups of people who attempted to "go back to the land", living in small communes, "at one" with the natural world. Ideas of the rural were thus incorporated into popular culture as well as popular aspirations: forms of entertainment as diverse as Gray's *Elegy* (1750), music-hall songs dating from the 1890s, and the post-World War Two radio serial, *The Archers*, all took "the 'country', the 'rural scene' as a space demanding interpretation for a predominantly urban audience", and all contain some aspect of idealization of the countryside (see Laing 1992: 133– 51). Books, postcards, songs and societies, all sharing a romantic sense of English identity and rural values, abounded.

Today, we still see the countryside packaged and repackaged as a cultural commodity. Access to the rural world, whether literally (through travel, organized excursions or institutions such as the National Trust) or second-hand (through books, television programmes and art) is ensured and, because the images presented can be carefully selected to show a very specific and appealing countryside, the rural myth persists. Specifically, as "the countryside" as home or place of work has become something outside the everyday experience of most people, the reality of the rural world has consequently been subsumed beneath an imagined romantic myth whereby any sense of dissatisfaction and uncertainty associated with modern urban life is mitigated through a coherent discourse of rural stability and tranquillity. The countryside has been transformed into a dream of a neat, domesticated Nature, and Nature itself has in turn been transformed into neat, domesticated images of the countryside. The rural myth thus shows us the countryside not as it is, but rather as we see – and create – it.

In this way, we see that Nature and Culture are not so far apart after all, and we must therefore begin to question accounts of the relationship that suggest otherwise. This applies not just to those people who consistently undervalue the natural world, but also to those who see it as superior to the human one.

Jencks (1984), for whom Nature rather than Culture promises to be the only commodity "worthy of celebration in a secular age" and even environmentalists who tend to be "prejudiced for furry animals and against machines, for green plants and against concrete" (Kaufman 1992: 54), are cases in point. If Nature and Culture are inextricably connected then this is not just because we as humans are part of the natural world but also because there is a human element to what we call Nature. In fact, Nature is not always natural at all.

References

Cosgrove, D. 1990. An elemental division: water control and engineered landscape. In *Water, engineering and landscape*, D. Cosgrove & G. Petts (eds), 1–11. London: Bellhaven Press.

Griffin, S. 1989. Split culture. In *Healing the wounds: the promise of ecofeminism*, J. Plant (ed.), 7–17. London: Green Print.

Howkins, A. 1986. The discovery of rural England. In *Englishness: politics and culture, 1880–1920*, R. Colls & P. Dodd (eds), 62–88. London: Croom Helm.

Howkins, A. 1991. *Reshaping rural England: a social history 1850–1925*. London: HarperCollins.

Jencks, C. 1984. *The language of post-modern architecture*, 4th edn. London: Academy Editions.

Kaufman, W. 1992. Confessions of a developer. In *Finding home: writing on nature and culture from Orion Magazine*, P. Sauer (ed.), 38–55. Massachusetts: Beacon Press.

Laing, S. 1992. Images of the rural in popular culture 1750–1990. In *The English rural community – image and analysis*, B. Short (ed.), 133–51. Cambridge: Cambridge University Press.

Ley, D. 1989. Modernism, post-modernism, and the struggle for place. In *The power of place: bringing together geographical and sociological imaginations*, J. A. Agnew & J. S. Duncan (eds), 44–65. London: Unwin Hyman.

Newby, H. 1979. *Green and pleasant land? Social change in rural England*. London: Hutchinson.

Rich, P. 1990. The quest for Englishness. In *Victorian values: personalities and perspectives in nineteenth century society*, G. Marsden (ed.), 211–25. Harlow, England: Longman.

Shields, R. 1991. *Places on the margin: alternative geographies of modernity*. London: Routledge.

Short, B. 1992. Images and realities in the English rural community: an introduction. In *The English rural community – image and analysis*, B. Short (ed.), 1–18. Cambridge: Cambridge University Press.

Short, J. R. 1991. *Imagined country: society, culture and environment*. London: Routledge.

Smout, T. C. 1990. *A century of the Scottish people 1830–1950*. London: Fontana Press (first published 1986 by William Collins).

Thompson, F. M. L. 1993. The rise of suburbia. In *The Victorian city: a reader in British urban history, 1820–1914*, R. J. Morris & R. Rodger (eds), 149–80. Harlow, England: Longman.

Wiener, M. J. 1981 *English culture and the decline of the industrial spirit 1850–1980.* London: Penguin.

Williams, R. 1988. *Keywords.* London: Fontana.

Williams, R. 1993. *The country and the city.* London: Hogarth Press (first published 1973 by Chatto & Windus).

Wohl, A. S. 1984. *Endangered lives: public health in Victorian Britain.* London: Methuen (first published 1983 by J. M. Dent).

CHAPTER 15

Tyrell's Owl: the limits of the technological imagination in an epoch of hyperbolic discourse

Brian Winston

Technological determinism

Both the feature film *Blade runner* and its source, Philip K. Dick's novel *Do androids dream of electric sheep?*, create a world in which all animals except humans are virtually extinct. However, technology provides electronic substitutes virtually indistinguishable from living beings in compensation. The chief villain of these texts, variously called Eldon Tyrell in the film and Eldon Rosen in the book, is in the business of engineering exceptionally human-like androids known as "replicants".[1] He is immensely rich, living in quarters Babylonian in their palatial spaciousness where, most prominently, an owl is kept. In the book, a character called Rachael Rosen discusses the beast with Dick's hero, the policeman Deckard:

> "Look at the owl", Rachael Rosen said. "Here, I'll wake it up for you."
> She started towards a small distant cage, in the centre of which jutted up a branching dead tree.
> "There are no owls", he started to say. "Or so we've been told . . . It's artificial," he said, with sudden realisation; his disappointment welled up keen and intense.
> "No." She smiled. (Dick 1982: 36)

As Deckard muses in the book: "A major manufacturer of androids invests its surplus capital on living animals" (1982: 36).[2]

The point is that a world of illusion, which Dick understood very well, did not necessarily mean a world without capitalist economic relations. It is the rich who have the real owl. The poor person makes do with an artificial substitute. Put like this, Dick's insight is unexceptional for was it not ever thus? But in the context of today's debate about the converging technologies of computing, telephony and imaging, the insight is crucial. For, in short, in a world of

225

virtual realities, who (for example) will get to wear the VR helmet and all the other sensory stimulators to visit the beaches of Vanuatu; and who will get to visit those beaches the old-fashioned way – in the flesh?

In other words, when considering the impact of technology it is absolutely necessary to keep the realities of all our socio-cultural-economic arrangements – including their dynamics – in mind. It is not enough simply to look at technology and its dynamic and assume, in a deterministic fashion, that because a technology exists or is possible its diffusion is therefore inevitable. As Raymond Williams puts it:

> The basic assumption of technological determinism is that a new technology – a printing press or a communications satellite – "emerges" from technical study and experiment. It then changes the society or the sector into which it has "emerged". "We" adapt to it, because it is the new modern way. (Williams 1989: 120)

Yet, as Williams further points out, all technical study is actually a product of the society "undertaken within always existing social relations and cultural forms, typically for purposes already in general foreseen" (Willaims 1989: 120). Technology and technological innovations have little social significance *of themselves*; it is only when, as Williams puts it, the technology "is selected for investment towards production" (Williams 1989: 120) that it becomes important. This crucial selection, however, is not technologically determined. Rather, it is a response to actually existing socio-cultural conditions, patterns of usage, markets, political conditions and so on.

The dominant technological determinist vision masks the complexities of these processes in a peculiarly disabling way. Instead of understanding that technologies are only introduced into society insofar as their radical potential for disrupting existing relations and forms is suppressed (Winston 1986: 23), we are encouraged to believe that the impact of the technology is inevitable and irresistible. Thus a senior British Labour Party spokesperson can write: "Technological changes are *driving* different sectors of the industry – newspapers, television, telephony, video, computers, cable and satellite – closer together" (Mowlam 1994: 24; emphasis added). It is as if the logic of capitalist concentration were no longer a factor in such developments. Even to talk of all these enterprises and devices as an "industry" is already perhaps selling the pass, losing an insight – and this from the Shadow Secretary of State responsible for formulating alternative, supposedly socialist, policy.

It is in this way that a belief in the "driving" power of technology becomes disempowering to those holding it. Such a belief tells us, in effect, that nothing can be done; that those who own and exploit the technology are as much in its power as those who are exploited by it. It cannot be resisted and therefore neither can they. This is, of course, nonsense. Nevertheless, in 1993 for example, Rupert Murdoch, one of the world's most powerful media moguls, was arguing exactly in this way. Because of his satellites, he told his shareholders, he was unstoppable. Early in 1994, however, he was in Beijing removing offending channels from those same satellites at the order of communist China's rulers. Had he disobeyed, they would have closed him down by simply declaring satellite receiving dishes illegal. In a world where BBC detector vans can spot televisions inside houses, dishes are very easy to control. (In Malaysia, Murdoch's satellite is already banned by this means on cultural grounds.)

Murdoch's problem was that he (apparently) started to believe his own technological determinist rhetoric. In one sense this is not surprising since such rhetoric is everywhere. It is at its most frenetic in debates about technologies which, unlike satellite television, do not yet quite "exist" but are in the process of "emerging" from the laboratory.

> "What does it feel like?" . . .
>
> "Slippery, hard chunks of something fairly light, packed loosely", I reported.
>
> "That's virtual ice in a virtual bucket." She adjusted a slider control on the screen: "And this is virtual ice and molasses." I felt the molasses, instantly, in my hand. I'll always remember that as a particularly weird moment in my personal history of reality. (Rheingold 1992: 312)

This is not fiction but a report of an actual demonstration taken from one of the many populist accounts of the wonders of converging digital technologies currently available. What is crucial here – and is crucial in all such technological stories that daily bombard us in the media – is a failure of journalistic cynicism, revealed in this instant by Howard Rheingold's truthfulness. "Slippery, hard chunks of something", he reports. Most of us touching ice know it is ice. He knows it is virtual ice when he is told it is, just as he knows it is molasses when he is so informed.

This incident is utterly typical. Virtual reality is nowhere near as "real" as its proponents (such as Rheingold) claim. It cannot even for the most part yet match the mimetic power of the century-old technology of the cinema. The images it presents to the eye – like those of current computer games – are, at best, somewhat crude approximations of the cinematic. Yet, since "reality" (we are told) is only a question of more computing power, this sort of failure is endlessly glossed over.

Similar glosses can be documented with all of the possibilities currently subjected to the technological determinists' hyperbolic discourse. Take fibre optics. Almost daily, headlines promise massive broadband (e.g. full-motion, high-resolution television) capacity delivered to the home by this technology which can pass many thousands of signals down wires typically described as being "no thicker than a human hair". Thousands of channels of television and a host of other services are promised. Now, one can make many arguments against the viability of this vision. We have already tried systems with a mere hundred channels and people do not want them. We cannot conceivably finance production for a system of thousands of television channels which would meet culturally determined audience expectations of what television programming ought to be. When we add channels our experience is that they produce only minutes more of viewing per household and therefore exist at the margins of the entertainment system. There are many more arguments along these lines.

The point here is that the fibre-optic system is nowhere near ready to provide such a system in the first place. What is almost never discussed is the fact that signals passing through fibre-optic wire cannot for the moment be switched – directed to their ultimate destinations – without being expensively downloaded on to more conventional wires with much more limited capacity. This is why the fibre-optic network exists in the real commercial world of telecommunications only at main trunk line level or in discrete local area networks.

Technological determinists tend not to be halted by such observations. The question of developing a switch, although it requires new technology and not just refinements of existing solutions, is deemed to be only a matter of time. Yet the hyperbole of the current discussion surrounding fibre optics ignores this crucial lacuna. An essential bit of the engine supposedly *driving* "convergence" simply does not exist yet in any viable form.

Let me say again: we are here talking about the technology itself – the actual hardware – not what the technological determinists dream are its implications and possibilities.

The "basic litany"

It is quite easy to see how Howard Rheingold, the very model of a technological determinist, helped by the prompting of a friendly VR pioneer, begins to slide down a slippery slope of hyperbole. The possibilities offered by these technologies – from the outer reaches of musings about VR through the endless reporting about the Internet and on to the immediate policy issues surrounding everything from channel provision to media cross-ownership – all engender an unthinking hyperbolic "basic litany" (Panko 1984: 232).

This litany is made all the more powerful because these visions are supported and enhanced by cutting-edge social theorizing, that is: postmodernism. Instead of an intellectual situation where the outer reaches of sociological, philosophical and literary theory question the progressivist assumptions of science and technology, today such theory deeply supports those assumptions, at least in this area. (Even the Greens, the most overtly anti-progressivist political grouping, are not against the Internet or electronic "cottages", for instance.) In fact, postmodernism can be said to be in cahoots with technological determinism.

This does not necessarily imply an intellectual welcome for the developments of science and technology. One can regret these developments, even believe them to be catastrophic, and still have a technological determinist vision. This, remember, requires only a belief that "we" adapt to the technology. It makes no value judgement as to whether such adaptation is a good or bad thing. The point is that "high" theoretical technological discourses and "high" theoretical humanistic discourses share an *Umwelt* and, moreover, they share it with "low" popularizing discourses.

The result is a peculiar testament to the persistence of the science/humanities divide in our culture, for technologists are, for the most part, neither adept at nor trained for refined understanding of social relations and cultural forms. The humanists, for the most part, do not understand how the technology works for the same reasons. Thus one party cannot fathom how television "operates" in a social sense and why, in that sense, we might not need or want thousands of channels, while the other does not realize that the technologists have not yet got the switch to provide those channels anyway.

Of course, I am not here dismissing all current "high" theory on the basis that the theorists are ignorant of science. Such an ignorance, even were it to be universal, could not preclude the possibility of stimulating and significant discussion. And, anyway, not all theorists are ignorant. For instance, Donna Haraway (by training a scientist rather than a humanist, it must be admitted) uses the image of the cyborg – "creatures simultaneously animals and machine" to explore the outer limits of technology (Haraway 1991: 149). Analyzing current developments on the road to Dick's "replicants", she isolates "three crucial boundary breakdowns" that have taken place in our time – that between animal and human, that between animal-human (organism) and machine, and that between the physical and non-physical. However, because she is concerned with the political ramifications of these breakdowns for socialism and feminism, she grounds her discussion in a complex field of phenomena ranging from animal rights campaigns, through to quantum mechanics and the uncertainty principle, and on to electronic miniaturization. The electronic developments are thus placed in a "thick" description (to use the Geertzean term) of society. Technological determinism then emerges as but "one ideological space opened up by the preconceptions of machine and organism as coded texts through which we engage in the play of reading and writing the world" (Haraway 1991: 152).

Haraway is the scientific-literary exception who proves the rule: most post-modernist discussion of technology, however much concerned with the condition of the human self in this technologized world, is actually as dis-empowering as the most populist of technological determinist rants. Primarily this is because technological ignorance blunts postmodernist readings not only of machine and organism but also of social relations and cultural forms in general. The essential point is that postmodernism has, as Haraway points out (1992: 152), "a Utopian disregard for the lived relations of domination" under capital. The result is this "basic litany" about technology which can be summed up thus:

> The newly proliferating electronic technologies of the Information Age are invisible, circulating outside of the human experiences of space and time. That invisibility makes them less susceptible to repre-sentation and thus comprehension at the same time as the technologi-cal contours of existence become more difficult to ignore – and all of this is occurring during a lengthy period of diminished economic ex-pectation . . . There has arisen a cultural crisis of visibility and control over a new electronically defined reality. (Bukatman 1993: 2)

There are a number of problems with this all-too-typical formulation. First there is the language of change: "newly proliferating electronic technologies". What does "newly" mean? These base technologies – television, telephony, computing and digitalization – were all in existence ("demonstrated in the metal", as the engineers say) before 1950. Telephones worked by 1880, television by the early 1930s. Digitalization, the key to the current phase of development, was demonstrated as a technique in 1938. A computer ran a factoring programme in 1948. And the convergence of these technologies, via telephony, has gone on as each has come on-stream.

If one adds gestation periods, one can note that the essential architecture of the computer was first articulated in 1837, the physics of the solid-state elec-tronic device were outlined in 1879, the idea of television was patented in 1884, and the basic mathematics of digitalization theorized in 1928. Indeed, if one were to conceptualize these developments as starting with the physical exploration of electromagnetic phenomena in general one could say that they have been coming on-stream for the better part of two centuries – or even four.

So what has been "proliferating" recently? Certainly not television screens and telephone wires which have been diffused for decades. The cable tele-vision system has been building since the late 1940s. As for digital devices in the home, they are not yet as ubiquitous as analog television and telephones despite being introduced in 1974 (Atari Video Game), 1976 (Apple II Computer) and 1978 (CDs). It is therefore two decades since this "new" three-pronged domestic "proliferation" of the digital began. Secondly, the "cultural crisis of visibility" also seems to me to be more apparent than real. This "crisis" is occasioned by the mysterious invisible internal workings of these technologies that circulate "outside of the human experiences of space and time" supposedly making them "less susceptible to representation and thus comprehension".

What does it mean to say these technologies circulate "outside of the human experience of space and time"? Is this because electronic reactions are instantaneous and unseen? So is human neural activity: does this mean, say, that Rheingold's sensation of VR cold is, because instantaneous and unseen, beyond his experience? Palpably not. As much the same point can be made about the observation that the physical site of such reactions is impossibly small or (perhaps) large. This is true also of both subatomic and astro-physics – but these are fields understood, and indeed constructed, by humans called physicists.

Equally obfuscating is the point that these technologies cannot be easily represented. On the contrary, in fact, these devices are all *designed*; they begin as blueprints, drawn by human beings. What is really being said here is that humanists cannot understand the conventions of this representation and therefore it does not exist for them in any meaningful way. This is like saying the Cyrillic alphabet makes Russian less susceptible to comprehension which is true – but only to those who cannot read it. To elevate such a failure into a "cultural crisis" is hubristic.

The vision of "crisis" in this articulation of the basic litany cannot be sustained even if it is taken to refer specifically only to "cyberspace" as the site of this putative destruction of human-scaled time and space.

Cyberspace is a concept created by William Gibson in another seminal science-fiction text of the 1980s, *Neuromancer* (Gibson 1984). However, Gibson imagines that if the human brain could access the "space" between computers by directly "jacking in" to a terminal, it would understand that space as space and time as time. In fact, Gibson imagines cyberspace as a built environment to be negotiated as if by a human voyager. Thus one computer's databank looks like an "Aztec pyramid" (Gibson 1984: 105); another computer program is "a black-mirrored shark thing . . . a wingless antique jet, its smooth skin plated with black chrome" (Gibson 1984: 228).

> Case had the strange impression of being in the pilot's seat in a small plane. A flat dark surface in front of him suddenly glowed with a perfect reproduction of the keyboard of his deck . . . Headlong motion through walls of emerald green, milky jade, the sensation of speed beyond anything he'd known in cyberspace. (Gibson 1984: 256)

There is a measure of cognitive dissonance at work here. Scott Bukatman, whom I have rather unfairly chosen as the articulator of this pervasive litany, clearly understands that cyberspace (as conceived of by Gibson) has human-scale time and space, albeit "turbulent and discontinuous" (Bukatman 1993: 205). It is just that this insight is not related to the opening basic litany position he adopts in his work.

In the same way, Bukatman's initial nod towards the "real" world, which is actually experiencing "a lengthy period of diminished economic expectation", somehow does not really impinge on his apparent understanding of the concept of the "Information Age". With its invisible and uncontrollable technologies, this epoch suggests that material productivity has ceased to exist as a key determinant of human life. The only commodity that matters is, supposedly, commoditized information – as if humans can live by bytes alone. It is through such conceptualizations that, for instance, the main means of electronic communications comes to be labelled "The Information Superhighway" when in fact, since charges are levelled to enter on to it, it would be, ideologically at least, more illuminating to refer to it as an "Information Toll Road". "The Information Age", as a descriptor of the present epoch, does not really have much to do with information as such. Rather, it describes the processes whereby production in metal (or primary extraction or agriculture) are exported from the West into areas where such activities produce more effective rates of return on capital.

All this is not to say that the ignorances of scientific discourse implicitly displayed in the basic technological determinist litany of postmodernism are not culturally significant. They are, but not in ways particularly meaningful for a general discussion of the human condition – much less the human sense of self – in the late twentieth century. What is happening, rather, is a flowering of the old absurdities of the gulf in our intellectual life between the two realms of science and the arts.

Failing to imagine postcapitalism

I have used the basic litany as articulated by Bukatman not because he is an unthinking technological determinist but exactly because he is an extremely astute and illuminating critic. His acceptance of the litany is, therefore, a sort of symbolic measure of how deeply the disabling uni-dimensional visions of technological determinism have penetrated current critical understandings, even at their best and brightest.

The result of this penetration can be thought of as "noise", disturbing and, indeed, frustrating our ability to assess these technologies and develop the most effective policies for their exploitation. That is why, it seems to me, on occasion novelists such as Dick and Gibson offer a richer and more textured vision of how these technologies might diffuse through society and with what effects. The touchstone here is how capitalist enterprise itself is represented in both fiction and non-fiction texts. For the most part, technological determinists are silent on this. Dick and Gibson are, of course, astute critics of late capitalism but this aspect of their work is almost the first thing to go when they are taken up by either film makers or other writers and commentators.

In the film of *Blade runner*, for instance, not only do the great corporations of the late twentieth century survive, but they survive with their logos unchanged. These, prominently displayed as advertisements decorating the film's much-admired street sets, eloquently speak to the persistence of capitalized formations and indeed suggest some species of eternal life for them. The logos become like national costume. They are locked in time. Just as national costume concretizes the entire national state so too do these advertisements concretize the entire capitalist system – a triumph perhaps for product placement in a feature film but a major, and ideologically charged, failure of imagination. This ideological failure is then augmented by critics. Bukatman, who sees both *Blade runner* and *Neuromancer* as central in prefiguring cyberpunk texts, has nothing to say about this aspect of the film in his extensive analysis of its implications for our understanding of "the precepts of the postmodern aesthetic" (Bukatman 1993: 130).

On the other hand, in *Neuromancer*, Gibson has his hero Case, who rides at one point in a "Mercedes", nevertheless discover "an antique Sony" and explore a space yacht made by "Dornier-Fujitsu". The luxury mark persists, the popular mark is outdated and the logic of capital concentration brings Germany and Japan together. But then, such sophisticated play is not surprising in one who could write (with Bruce Sterling, Gibson & Sterling 1991) *The difference engine*, an erudite alternative history of nineteenth-century Britain in which Babbage's steam-driven computer is not just thought of in 1837 but built at that time. The consequences of this include streamlining in design ("line streaming"), computer viruses on Jacquard loom punch-cards and Lady Ada Byron (in reality the poet's daughter and Babbage's intellectual companion) outlining Gödel's incompleteness theorem in mathematics (in reality published in 1931) to a scientific meeting in 1855.

For the most part, technological texts and analyses ignore the economic and the political. This is a persistent failing. In *2001: a space odyssey* much was made of the fact that a space shuttle was operated by PanAm, a corporation, one can now note, which did not actually survive after 1991. It was destroyed by the application of neoliberal (that is, revived nineteenth-century) economic theory – "deregulation".

What is even more surprising is that the failure of technological imagination embraces the technological itself. In *Blade runner*, as in many other science-fiction works, there are airborne cars. Logic would dictate that such a technology demands total automation, but in fact the vehicles are still piloted manually. There are some aspects of contemporary life the (masculine?) imagination finds very difficult to let go. A future without driving seems to be one such aspect. (It can be said, though, that this is exactly what Jean-Luc Godard proposes in *Alphaville*. There, today's automobiles are presented as continuing into the future unchanged – except that they have no drivers.)

We are exposed to a constant stream of technological assessment/forecasting at every level, from the popular press to high cultural theory. Almost all of it fails to contextualize what might happen tomorrow in the light of what is happening today, that is: our current socio-cultural, political and economic realities. Instead we have a concentration on uni-dimensional projections of technological change. These lead to a *Boy's Own* wish list for airborne racers, android sex dolls and computers as cocoons, the whole graced with marginalia of jargonized philosophizing about what all this supposedly means to our identity as human beings. The hyperbolic discourse suggests "terminal identities" whereas the realities, could we keep them clearly in mind, suggest a continuation of the human subject under capital – business, and I mean business, more or less as usual.

So busy have the technological determinists been preparing us for the wonders of electronic owls that we are blinded as to the real reasons that might bring us to ever need such things.

Notes

1. For reference to the film, I use the Director's Cut (1991) rather than the film as released (1982).
2. In the film the exchange is slightly different:
   "Do you like our owl?" asks Rachael Tyrell – her surname altered to match the villain's. "It's artificial?" queries Deckard. "Of course it is," she replies. Deckard: " Must be very expensive." Rachael: "Yes."
   There is, though, an ambiguity here. "Rachael" is not as she seems and one can believe that, therefore, neither is the owl. In the film, but not in the book, we very rapidly learn that Rachael herself is artificial – Tyrell's latest type of "replicant". And the owl, at least as it appears in the film, is real – alive – since at the time the film was made (1982) real owls were easier to come by than fully-practical (to use the film industry's term-of-art) electronic ones.

Films

Alphaville, une étrange aventure de Lemmy Caution (1965), 98 mins. Producer, André Michelin; director/screenplay, Jean-Luc Godard; cinematography, Raoul Coutard; music, Paul Misraki; with Eddie Constatine, Anna Karina, Howard Vernon, Akim Tamiroff and Laszlo Szabo.

Blade runner (1982, 1991), 118 mins/112 mins. Producer, Michael Deeley; director, Ridley Scott; screenplay, Hampton Francher and David Peoples; cinematography, Jordan Cronenweth; special effects, Douglas Trumbull; design, Syd Mead; music, Vengalis; with Harrison Ford, Sean Young, Rutger Hauer, Edward James Olmos and Darryl Hannah.

2001: a space odyssey (1968), 141 mins. Producer/director, Stanley Kubrick; screenplay, Stanley Kubrick, Arthur C. Clark; cinematography, Geoffrey Unsworth; special effects, Walley Veevers, Douglas Trumbull; design, John Hoeslie; music, Richard Strauss et al.; with Keir Dullea, Garry Lockwood, William Sylvester, Daniel Richter and Douglas Rain.

References

Bukatman, S. 1993. *Terminal identity: the virtual subject in post-modern science fiction.* Durham, North Carolina: Duke University Press.

Dick P. K. 1982. *Do androids dream of electric sheep?* New York: Ballantine.

Gibson, W. 1984. *Neuromancer.* New York: Ace.

Gibson, W. & B. Sterling 1991. *The difference engine.* New York: Bantam.

Haraway, D. 1991. *Simians, cyborgs and women: the reinvention of nature.* London: Routledge.

Mowlam, M. 1994. Paper tigers. *New Statesman and Society*, 9 September, 24.

Panko, R. R. 1984. Office work. In *Office: technology and people,* vol. II, 207–34. Amsterdam: Elsevier.

Rheingold, H. 1992. *Virtual reality.* London: Mandarin.

Williams, R. 1989. *The politics of modernism.* London: Verso.

Winston, B. 1986. *Misunderstanding media.* London: Routledge & Kegan Paul. Cambridge, Mass.: Harvard University Press.

CHAPTER 16

Technological reality: cultured technology and technologized culture

Hughie Mackay

This chapter consists of three parts. First, I discuss the centrality of technology to contemporary society in a number of key arenas – at work, in the home, in education and in entertainment. Secondly, I outline and evaluate recent work in sociology and cultural studies which has been concerned to theorize this technologization of everyday life and culture; I argue that we need to draw together approaches which have focused on the *production* of technology with those which have focused on its *consumption*. Thirdly, I discuss some key issues which new information and communication technologies raise for understanding culture in the postmodern era.

Modernity and technology

Any history of modernity has to accord a central place to the role of technology and its accompanying technocratic spirit. Western modernization has been characterized by an increasing reliance on technology, and by the emergence of a view which sees technology as the driving force of history. The predominant narrative of the Enlightenment has been of the progressive and boundless possibilities of scientific and technological progress through mastery of the natural world. The permeation of social life by technology, however, has been most dramatic in recent years; the very word "technology" was not used with anything like its contemporary meaning until the twentieth century, and its use in this form was not widespread until after the First World War. Today, however, the term is unavoidable, with technology very much to the fore, though for many it carries less positive connotations. People entrust their lives to ever more complex technologies that offer luxury, efficiency and security. At the same time, people fear technology for dehumanizing their lives, for its control and its dangers. The notion that technology is synonymous with progress has been challenged by Hiroshima, Bhopal, Chernobyl and Challenger;

increasingly, technology is seen as the problem rather than the solution, to be avoided rather than embraced. The growth of concern for environmental issues has contributed substantially to a loss of support for the notion of technology as the progressive human mastery of over nature. Either way, however, for good or ill, technology remains central to the discourse of modernity.

New technology is pervasive and increasingly central in our everyday lives and practices. In asserting this, it is important to distance myself from the usual way in which new technology and the burgeoning social order are conceived – in terms of the "information society thesis". According to this dominant orthodoxy, new technology is leading us towards a new form of society, in which greater leisure, equality and human satisfaction are to be the outcomes. Such a positive – and normative – view of the future (which, incidentally, is propagated by writers of a variety of political persuasions) is rather different from my analysis and from the experiences of many people today.

At work, new technology has been the instrument of rationalization and restructuring, and has been attributed with causing job loss and the routinization, or de-skilling, of labour. A huge body of labour process literature has been concerned with demonstrating whether or not one can sustain the argument that new technology inevitably leads, in the long run, to the de-skilling of work (Knights & Wilmott 1990). New technology is also crucial to achieving cultural and organizational change within enterprises: the shift from Fordist to post-Fordist forms of organization – including flatter hierarchies and the globalization of operations – is inconceivable without the computer and telecommunications technologies to enable and sustain such structures and activities. At the same time, we have witnessed the emergence of the information sector – in which, it is argued by proponents of the "information society thesis", a majority of the workforce is now to be found. We have seen the technologization of just about every sector of the economy, from retailing to the culture industries. Finally, new technology has been deployed to enable new forms of homeworking, which have broken down spatial and temporal boundaries between home and work.

The past eighty years or so have witnessed the most remarkable technologization of the home. My grandparents – quite typically for people of that generation – were brought up in houses with almost no services or technologies – no electricity or gas, and a tap in one room; they had a multi-purpose stove, which heated the room space, heated the hot water, and was, in addition, their cooker. Some 80 years later, Western homes are bristling with technology: infrastructure (electricity, gas, heating and running water), appliances (including the washing machine, refrigerator, deep freezer, dishwasher, oven, hob, electric kettle, sandwich toaster and, in North America in particular, many more such gadgets) and a panoply of leisure technologies and services (radio, television, audio tape recorder, video cassette recorder, compact disc player and home computer, and, most recently, multimedia, video on demand via the telephone line, and shopping by TV – to name but a few). Technology, in short, has invaded the home; and our daily lives – in terms of both domestic work and leisure – have become largely synonymous with our operation and enjoyment of technologies.

In education, too, we have seen the rapid influx of technology. Technology was designated one of the seven foundation subjects in the national curriculum, a culmination of the rise to pre-eminence of Information Technology (IT) in education in the 1980s. During this decade, IT in education was conceived largely in terms of computer literacy. The initial initiative to get microcomputers into primary schools was promoted (and funded) by the Department of Trade and Industry (rather than Education), and most schools devoted enormous proportions of their non-salary budgets, and monies raised by parents, to the purchase of computer equipment. IT was a most remarkable priority in curriculum and budgetary terms, at a time when it was of no proven educational utility. Despite the rhetoric of interactive and pupil-centred learning, most of the practice in this early era of IT in education involved software of little educational worth, and the grandiose claims that were made for IT in education were largely unfulfilled. Never before had a new technology generated such massive demands for educational restructuring; there was no similar scale of calls for electricity or motor car literacy. IT, in other words, has been unique among educational innovations.

Few areas of entertainment remain unaffected by new technology. IT can be seen as being at the core of recent drastic changes – from the interactive multimedia without which a heritage organization finds it hard to attract visitors, to the growing range of "brown goods" produced by the emerging global culture organizations. No matter how we measure it, these developments are vast – be it satellite television in India, or computer games in the UK. Taking the latter, the industry dwarfs the pop music industry, and is growing much faster. Video and computer games head the list of toy sales, and are predicted to be the main growth area of toys through the 1990s, with market penetration in the UK still only 15%, compared with 50% in Japan, despite the ever-increasing rate of sales (160% between 1990 and 1991). Nintendo's GameBoy was the best-selling toy in 1991. An equally dramatic picture is painted if we look at hours of usage, or any other measure of the place of computer games in the culture of young people today; for a whole generation of them, video games have superseded popular music as their main form of entertainment.

How, then, are we to understand the recent and pervasive technologization of culture and society? One argument is that the root cause of this technological explosion is the range of technical developments that have taken place – in particular, miniaturization, integration of circuits, fibre optics, satellite and other elements of digital data storage, manipulation and transmission. Such developments, it is argued, have led to far-reaching changes across the full range of social arenas; this is the argument of "technological determinism", meaning the notion that technology is the *main* determinant of social change; technological developments take place in some sort of asocial (or external to the social) sense; technologies then have *effects* on the social. Technological determinism is "the single most influential theory of the relationship between technology and society" (MacKenzie & Wajcman 1985: 4). This is not simply an academic point, but of immense cultural significance: most key managers and politicians probably see technology in a determinist way. The implications of such an approach to technology are far-reaching, and deeply embedded. The notion of autonomous technology is a key part of modernist thought. Technological determinism assumes a causal connection between technological and social progress. It presents technology as artefactual, neutral and inevitable; it perpetuates the idea that it is something beyond and without culture, a matter best dealt with by engineers; it thus denies that technologies are profoundly cultural. It positions us in a passive relationship to technology: technological development is going to happen anyway, it suggests, so to resist it is to stand in the way of inevitable progress, while all that we can do about technology is to mitigate its worst excesses. It thus diverts our attention from questions of *choice* in relation to technology, and from issues of who controls, or benefits from, these developments.

In contrast, and from a variety of theoretical perspectives, there is a growing body of work that has demonstrated how technology is social *not just in its effects, but in its origins too*. Specific technologies embody the social forces that lie behind their development, and these elements of the social – including, for example, particular systems of thought – are encoded, or represented, in specific technological artefacts. This has been the focus of the emerging sociology of technology. I shall presently introduce the various approaches of sociologists to technology.

The technologization of everyday life

Work in the labour process tradition has investigated empirically how the social relations of capital are built into specific technologies (Braverman 1974). Most of this work has focused on the conflict of interest, under capitalism, between the profits of capital and the wages of labour. The level of wages is in large part determined by the replaceability of labour, which, in turn, is related to the skill level of a particular occupation. There is a substantial body of work which demonstrates how, in specific instances, the introduction of new technology leads (or does not) to the de-skilling of work. This, it is argued, is precisely the *rationale* for the development of specific technologies. That new technologies routinize work, make it less demanding, more boring and less satisfying, rather than being an unfortunate consequence, is, precisely, the intent behind their development. Later labour process work has focused on such issues as the diversity of managerial strategies and organizational cultures, and acknowledges that reducing labour costs through de-skilling work is one of many possible strategies for management.

A more micro-focused body of literature in an altogether different tradition provides further approaches to the "social shaping of technology". Three schools on the micro side can be identified: first, the social constructivist approach draws on the new Sociology of Science, the Sociology of Scientific Knowledge (SSK) (see also Hopper, this volume). In this approach, scientific facts, rather than the unfolding to humanity of the natural laws of the universe, are seen as socially constructed. Also, in the same vein, social constructivist approaches to the study of technology have argued that technological artefacts, like scientific knowledge and despite their physical obduracy, are socially constructed (Pinch & Bijker 1984, Bijker et al. 1987). They investigate how "relevant social groups" define problems, exercise closure and thus shape technological forms. Secondly, the network, or systems, approach sees system builders – inventors, engineers, managers and financiers – creating and presiding over new technological systems; people, organizations, disciplines and technical artefacts become part of a "seamless web" (Hughes 1986). Third, actor-network theory differs from social constructivist accounts in that it collapses any distinction between the "technical" and the "social", between animate and inanimate. Both, it argues, are "heterogeneous elements" in the development of technological systems. Rather than talking about humans constrained by technologies and technologies embodying the social circumstances that gave rise to them, it argues for the possibility of dissolving the categories of human and non-human (Callon 1986, Law 1987). This approach has led to some interesting debates about the implications for sociology of ceasing to privilege the human world, and applying its approaches to the non-human as well (Woolgar 1985, Johnson 1988).

Military technology provides a remarkably clear illustration of the broad thesis that technology is socially shaped, and thus constitutes an exemplary challenge to the dominant orthodoxy of technological determinism. Take the example of the PC in education. It is true that all of the elements of this technology (for example, integrated circuits and moves towards miniaturization) are the products of the US's Department of Defense Research and Development (and, indeed, in the early days of their development, the same body's procurement was also responsible for the vast bulk of the market for such products). The end product of such enormous investment was then applied, or transferred, to the business sector. Finally, it was "dumped" – quite literally, in the economic sense, in that there was a dual pricing policy – on the education sector. In education, we were told to find some purpose for a technology that had been developed, in essence, for purposes of national defence. We can reasonably assume that, with the task of developing an educational technology and the US Department of Defense's R&D budget, one would have come up with a rather different box of tricks from the PC for an educational technology.

Most "social shaping of technology" accounts suggest that the story is finished when the technology is off the drawing board, or, at least, when it has been constructed. We can, however, extend the argument in that technology is socially shaped not just at the point of its conception, invention, development and design, but, also, throughout its entire life-cycle, its styling, marketing, consumption and later life. Thus I would argue for a wider definition of the "heterogeneous elements" (Law 1987) of which a technology is composed – to encompass both marketing and the "work" of consumption (Miller 1987), in acknowledgement of the active role of consumers in the development of technology. In fact most technologies never stabilize in the way that so many constructivist accounts suggest.

A focus on the full cycle of the technology helps us to understand technology in developing countries, where technology is generally imported rather than designed. With the design stage simply not present, approaches that focus on the origins of a technology have nothing to offer. Further, the impact of a given technology in such a country often differs from its impact in the developed world. Thus a different form of technology can be identified through investigation of its take-up in a different cultural context. One might add that this emphasis should be of interest to environmentalists, given that the full life-cycle could encompass the life of a technology after the end of its use by its initial consumer, and, indeed, its use by humans (see Kopytoff 1986).

Recent work in media and cultural studies points us to the ways in which technology is social in its consumption, as well as in its production (Silverstone & Hirsch 1992). The effect and importance of a technology is not inscribed in its design. It is certainly the case that design constrains the uses to which technology may be put; but, for example, it is no more built into integrated circuits that adolescents spend most of their leisure time observing video depictions of violence, than it is that video cameras detect murderers as well as allow state surveillance of a population's activities. In other words, while technologies *do* fulfil the intentions of those involved in their development, they also lead what David Noble (1984: 325) has called a "double life", which both conforms to the intentions of their designers and which works behind their backs with unintended consequences and unanticipated possibilities. There has emerged recently a body of work that has investigated the diversity of ways in which technologies are appropriated by their consumers, and the factors – class, gender, race and geography – which structure such consumption (see Moores (1993) for a review of this work). This research, however, has been carried out with little reference to the "social shaping of technology" paradigm. It seems strange that there has been so little work that has linked the two sides of production and consumption (Mackay & Gillespie 1992); exceptions are the work of Ruth Schwartz Cowan (1987) on the stove, Wiebe Bijker (1992) on the fluorescent light and Cynthia Cockburn & Susan Ormrod (1993) on the microwave.

This work is particularly valuable for demonstrating that consumption is of *meaning* not just utility. There is no shortage of technologies to which the notion of meaning has been absolutely central: Arnold Pacey (1983) discusses some good examples. The Eiffel Tower *did* nothing, but was famous as a symbol of human achievement and as an expression of national pride; the Concorde air-liner is rather similar; the *Autobahnen* and the Volkswagen car in Germany in the 1930s had enormous symbolic significance; and in the USSR, at the same time, scale was everything and heavy industry, apart from any possible func-tional value, was symbolic of Soviet power. And a whole series of mechanical devices, particularly the steam engine, have constituted symbols of progress. My point is that technologies are shaped not only by some functional intent, but also – to a greater or lesser degree – by the meanings that they carry. This applies to a technology's form, its marketing and advertising, and its consump-tion and use. We can thus extend the constructivist notion of "interpretative flexibility"; it is not confined to the initial stage of a technology but takes place, in addition, at all of its later stages and throughout the life-cycle of the technol-ogy. Thus, the notion that technologies carry a symbolic significance can be applied to the initial, design, stage of a technology as well as to its later con-sumption. This means technologies are imbued with cultural meanings and communicate much more than a use-value (Hill 1988). Each stage of the life of a technology is inherently symbolic and it is with regard to this symbolism that the role of designers is crucial.

The common-sense view of design suggests that form follows function – that the appearance of an artefact reflects what it has to do. But such a linkage is generally very loose – as the diversity of forms for a given function testifies. Daniel Miller (1987) gives as an example the enormous diversity of glass bottles in a shop, each with an identical function. Adrian Forty (1986) rejects both common-sense and conventional histories of design as an autonomous, aesthetic, creative activity. He argues instead, using Loewy's famous "Lucky Strike" cartoon as an example, that the work of designers consists of drawing on prevailing ideologies and encoding, or representing them in artefacts. The meanings that actors hold of a technology are not infinitely amorphous and free-floating, but are structured, in a complex variety of ways. In other words, the meanings of the artefact held by "relevant social groups" are not unrelated to broader sets of ideas, or ideologies.

My argument is *not* that meaning is necessarily separable from function: a fast car includes both a fast engine (function) and suitable stripes on the body-work (symbol), and it is both that the consumer is consuming. Victor Papanek (1971) points to the irrelevance of the function versus aesthetics debate (aesthetics or forms are themselves an element of function more or less important depending on the type of object); nor can the aesthetic elements of a technology be demarcated from its functional elements. Finally, of course, functionality itself is a cultural phenomenon, rather than being implicit in a given artefact. My point is that in understanding technology design (as well as marketing and consumption – in other words the full range of arenas in which we can identify social and cultural processes that shape the technology), we need to be aware of the symbolic as well as the functional dimensions of technology.

To sum up so far, I have discussed the crucial contemporary significance of technology for some key areas of the social; and have outlined a range of approaches to theorizing technology. I have argued for an approach that deals with the notion of technology as symbolic as well as functional; and as culturally shaped through its full life-cycle, from conception to consumption. Finally, in the next section, I discuss how a focus on new information and communication technologies as culture can help us to understand some crucial features of the (post)modern era.

The culture of technology

Important features of postmodern theorizing include addressing the crisis of technological rationality as well as the decisive role of electronic information and communication technologies and large technological systems. There is no shortage of areas that could be discussed in this context.

First, new technology is implicated crucially in processes of globalization. The globalization of production and culture is dependent on the development and availability of a range of contemporary information and communication technologies. As globalization develops, these technologies become more significant to our understanding of the processes at work in the restructuring of the economy and culture across time and space. Secondly, technology is central to questions of identity and subjectivity. We can look at this in a whole variety of ways – for instance, the implications for identity of the consumption of information and communication technologies in the home. More radically, Mark Poster (1990) has argued that electronically mediated communication disperses the subject, dislocating it temporally and spatially. Where is the self if located, asks Poster, in fragments of personal data circulating, beyond our control, in computer systems? In this analysis, new technology changes the constitution of the self, and presents databases not as an invasion of privacy, but as a multiplication of the individual. Thirdly, we can take the example of language and patterns of thought – and their relationship to prevailing technologies. Valentin Volosinov (1973) argues that culture is constituted through language. One of my colleagues who is attributed with writing frequent and lengthy "streams of consciousness" is referred to as having done another "core dump" when he circulates yet another of his rambling papers; another colleague refers to his brain – perhaps in the context of it not working today as well as it might – as his "RAM"; and there are many other examples of terms that were developed in relation to computers that humans now quite readily apply to themselves and their activities – "output", "interface" and "networking", for example (Bloomfield 1989, Barry 1991). Given that the concepts with which we make sense of the world are constituted in language, such practice indicates a profound shaping of culture by technology.

Fourthly, information that was once readily accessible has become the preserve of the corporate affluent. Libraries, for example, charge for the on-line services in which information is now to be found. Even our names are bought and sold; personal signifiers have become commodities (Poster 1990). As well as the *commodification* of information, we are witnessing the rise to pre-eminence in contemporary culture of information. Information has become a privileged term, and with it an information processing, or procedural, mode of thought is emerging (Roszak 1988). Fifthly, surveillance is a major dimension of modern societies (Giddens 1990), and is scarcely explicable without reference to technology. Surveillance is exercised through a range of technologies: private databases that are used largely for credit-checking; banks, which track our consumption expenditure and movement; state databases (police, immigration, tax, health, social security, births and deaths, council tax and numerous others) and other technologies (laser listening devices, optical character recognition of vehicle registrations on roads, video cameras in public spaces, telephone listening, etc.). Together, these allow the vast gathering, storing and processing of information. The state now knows *about* its citizens – their lifestyles, activities and thoughts – in a way which has been unparalleled in history. (The work of Michel Foucault (1980) obviously takes this analysis further. He goes beyond the physical technology in his focus on the constitution of truth through discourse. His concern is with the penetration of bodies by non-physical surveillance. In other words, discourse can substitute for physical technology as a mode of surveillance.) Finally – and this is what many of the above points touch on – with new technology we are witnessing the dissolving of so many crucial categories. Technology has become more transparent; it has changed from being direct and physical. Production activity, for example, has become more distanced from humans, more hands-off; muscle, smell and movement are being replaced by VDUs, keyboards, switches and lights. In this process common understandings are challenged: what is property, what is physical, what is tangible, and where is it?

Clearly, then, electronic media alter patterns of social interactions. They do not merely expand or multiply face-to-face communicative interactions, but change the structure and conditions that underlie symbolic exchange, eliminating the context and changing the relationship of transmitter to receiver; they enable us to wander around the globe, without moving our body, dramatically shrinking the world in time and space (Meyrowitz 1985). The development of new technologies has implications for questions of authorship, originality, copyright, reproduction and regulation – whether we look at pornography by satellite or computer art. Take, for example, the changing form of pop music production. Nowadays music is generally taped on separate tracks, some of it from a synthesizer, without being performed in a totalized form: the "original" is made by an engineer combining the tracks. The product is, in a sense, a copy that has no original; the performance exists only in its reproduction.

At the time of writing, considerable media attention is being focused on computer networks. The "Information Superhighway" seems to be on the verge of eclipsing the "Information Society" as the focus of technologically determinist accounts of contemporary information and communication technologies. The Internet with its millions of connected computers – and 35% of households in the USA have a home computer and 10% a modem – enables users to find others who share their interests, however specialist or bizarre these may be. Newspapers in the USA are already producing electronic editions; in the UK the *Daily Telegraph* and others are available on the Internet. The virtual community of the Internet, in cyberspace, spans – and shrinks – the globe; yet cyberspace has no location. No-one owns the Net, and no-one controls it; its spirit, or culture, is of mutual co-operation. As such it represents a challenge to the academy (which, ironically gave rise to the Net) as the source or location of learning and discovery; and to forms of publishing and notions of authorship. Electronic communication has a range of implications for power and interpersonal communication, in that it masks differences of status, charisma, rhetorical capacity, gender and race. Personal friendships, conviviality and community, it is argued, can be re-created in the electronic global village (Rheingold 1994).

Virtual reality is one step beyond the virtual community. It involves the computer-generated simulation of our world; reality is transformed as one enters cyberspace. The technology is claimed to allow the smooth transfer from imaginary to real and back again. Identity in cyberspace, it is argued, can be a matter of freedom and choice: identities can be selected and discarded at will, allowing new, mobile and exploratory identities; subjectivity is dispersed as the subject is dissolved and fragmented. Virtual existence involves transcendence and liberation from the material world, as reality itself comes to be generated by computers (Rheingold 1991).

In sum, across the spectrum, communications and information are increasingly central; and our experiences are increasingly mediated by technology. Technology is crucial to understanding key contemporary questions about power, equality, justice and identity. Technology is ubiquitous, and central to our everyday lives, routines and culture. Debates about culture need to take account of this dimension of technology. Specifically, in developing a cultural analysis, I would suggest that we need to get beyond a number of dominant orthodoxies. First, there is the notion that new technology is merely the latest in the armoury of weapons with which the capitalist class exploits the working class (Webster & Robins 1986). While a class analysis seems to me useful in understanding some dimensions of technology, there are other aspects of technology – and I have raised some of these – which seem more amenable to a cultural than an economistic analysis. The meanings of technology cannot be "read off" from some broader structure, nor are they reducible to the intent of one class or group. Secondly, there is the traditional humanist faith in some natural, unalienated person, untainted by science and technology. In contrast, human capacity is inextricably linked to technologies, and technologies embody the human, thus the boundaries between human and machine are fluid (Haraway 1991). Thirdly, there is the notion that we can simply appropriate for counter-cultural use technologies designed as instruments of control. While there are progressive possibilities at the point of consumption, and technology is a contested terrain, these possibilities will always be constrained by the encoding of the particular technology in question.

Accordingly, in understanding technology as culture, prevailing sociological approaches are largely inadequate because of their focus on the *initial* stage in the life of a technology; and because they restrict their focus to the *utility* of a technology, ignoring the *symbolic* dimension. In my view, we need to look at more than the *origins* of technological artefacts: technology both shapes, and is shaped by, lived, everyday, interpretative practices.

References

Barry, J. A. 1991. *Technobabble*. Cambridge, Mass.: MIT Press.

Bijker, W. E. 1992. The social construction of fluorescent lighting, or how an artifact was invented in its diffusion. In *Shaping technology / building society: studies in sociotechnical change*, W. E. Bijker & J. Law (eds). Cambridge, Mass.: MIT Press.

Bijker, W. E., T. P. Hughes, T. J. Pinch (eds) 1987. *The social construction of technological systems: new directions in the sociology and history of technology*. Cambridge, Mass.: MIT Press.

Bloomfield, B. P. 1989. On speaking about computing. *Sociology* **23**, 409–26.

Braverman, H. 1974. *Labor and monopoly capital*. New York: Monthly Review Press.

Callon, M. 1986. The sociology of an actor-network: the case of the electric vehicle. In *Mapping the dynamics of science and technology*, M. Callon, J. Law, A. Rip (eds). London: Macmillan.

Cockburn, C. & S. Ormrod 1993. *Gender and technology in the making*. London: Sage.

Cowan, R. S. 1987. The consumption junction: a proposal for research strategies in the sociology of technology. In *Shaping technology / building society: studies in sociotechnical change*, W. E. Bijker & J. Law (eds). Cambridge, Mass.: MIT Press.

Forty, A. 1986. *Objects of desire: design and society 1750–1980*. London: Thames and Hudson.

Foucault, M. 1980. *Power/knowledge: selected interviews and other writings 1972–1977*. Hemel Hempstead, England: Harvester Wheatsheaf.

Giddens, A. 1990. *The constitution of modernity*. Cambridge: Polity.

Haraway, D. 1991. *Simians, cyborgs and women*. London: Free Association.

Hill, S. 1988. *The tragedy of technology*. London: Pluto.

Hughes, T. 1986. The seamless web: technology, science, etcetera, etcetera. *Social Studies of Science* **16**, 281–92.

Johnson, J. 1988. Mixing humans and non-humans together: The sociology of the door-closer. *Social Problems* **35**, 298–310.

Knights, D. & H. Wilmott 1990. *Labour process theory*. London: Macmillan.

Kopytoff, I. 1986. The cultural biography of things: commoditisation as process. In *The social life of things: commodities in cultural perspective*, A. Appadurai (ed.). Cambridge: Cambridge University Press.

Law, J. 1987. Technology and heterogeneous engineering: the case of Portuguese maritime expansion. In *Shaping technology / building society: studies in sociotechnical change*, W. E. Bijker & J. Law (eds). Cambridge, Mass.: MIT Press.

Mackay, H. & G. Gillespie 1992. Extending the social shaping of technology approach: ideology and appropriation. *Social Studies of Science* **22**, 685–716.

MacKenzie, D. & J. Wajcman (eds) 1985. *The social shaping of technology*. Milton Keynes, England: Open University Press.

Meyrowitz, J. 1985. *No sense of place: the impact of electronic media on social behaviour*. Oxford: Oxford University Press.

Miller, D. 1987. *Material culture and mass consumption*. Oxford: Basil Blackwell.

Moores, S. 1993. *Interpreting audiences. The ethnography of media consumption*. London: Sage.

Noble, D. 1984. *Forces of production*. New York: Knopf.

Pacey, A. 1983. *The culture of technology*. Oxford: Basil Blackwell.

Papanek, V. 1971. *Design for the real world*. London: Thames and Hudson.

Pinch, T. J. & W. E. Bijker 1984. The social construction of facts and artefacts: or how the sociology of science and the sociology of technology might benefit each other. *Social Studies of Science* **14**, 399–441.

Poster, M. 1990. *The mode of information: poststructuralism and social context*. Cambridge: Polity.

Rheingold, H. 1991. *Virtual reality*. New York: Summit.

Rheingold, H. 1994. *The virtual community: finding connection in a computerised world*. London: Secker & Warburg.

Roszak, T. 1988. *The cult of information*. London: Paladin.

Silverstone, R. & E. Hirsch (eds) 1992. *Consuming technologies: media and information in domestic spaces*. London: Routledge.

Volosinov, V. 1973. *Marxism and the philosophy of language*. New York: Seminar Press.

Webster, F. & K. Robins 1986. *Information technology: a Luddite analysis.* New Jersey: Ablex.

Woolgar, S. 1985. Why not a sociology of machines? The case of sociology and artificial intelligence. *Sociology* **19**, 557–72.

CHAPTER 17

The temporal landscape of global/izing culture and the paradox of postmodern futures

Barbara Adam

Introduction

This chapter focuses on the temporality of global/izing[1] culture and the concept of "postmodernism" as a means to delineate and explain some of the characteristic features of this culture. Where Norris (this volume) attacks postmodern analyses for their relativism and, consequently, their inadequate basis for a progressive politic, I want to demonstrate how the concept of postmodernism is inappropriate for grasping the dynamics of contemporary life. Postmodern analyses are useful, important even, for the deconstruction of some of the key assumptions that have facilitated the development of global/izing culture, but tend to thwart critical and active engagement with the consequences of these cultural processes. That is, they crucially stop where the implications of their insights would need to be translated into action. Through this focus on time and the temporal features of global/izing culture, I demonstrate our inescapable involvement in the constitution of this culture. It is my intention to provide not only insights into the paradoxes surrounding the concept of postmodernism, but also pointers towards a path of critique and active intervention.

I begin by outlining the temporal features of global/izing culture which, in turn, demonstrates the inescapability of personal involvement. Next, I use the focus on time to identify some of the shortcomings of the concept of postmodernism for theorizing this contemporary culture. Finally, I identify points of departure and argue for the need for engagement with the future, for political action after postmodernism.

Global/izing culture

Mass migration, people dying from starvation and the ravages of civil war, the destruction of public buildings and private dwellings by guns, missiles and mortar shells, the devastation wrought by earthquakes, floods, hurricanes and volcanoes – all are events from across the world that we can witness on television in the comfort and safety of our living rooms. Such events may move us to political activity or charitable action: pressing a few buttons, for example, we can make the difference between life and death to a person, family or village on the other side of the globe. Alternatively, they may make us turn away and actively shut out the suffering and distress; or they may leave us untouched, impatiently waiting for the next instalment of a favourite soap or sporting event.

We know so much – too much – and so little. We know more than we can encompass in our daily actions and less than we need in order to feel confident that our actions make a difference. In global/izing culture, the vastness of available knowledge and choice seem to stand in an inverse relation to the availability of options. We are informed about global warming, acid rain, the depletion of the ozone layer and the dangers of nuclear power. We know of the link between our personal actions and the dying forests in Sweden, the skin cancers in Australia, and the fates of many animal species. *In the context of global/izing knowledge, our choices for action are limitless but our options are restricted and ambiguous.* And yet, irrespective of whether or not we feel personally touched by the misery, suffering and annihilation of fellow human beings, animals and plants, our actions and inactions, concerns and ignorances inescapably tie us to their fate. Thus, environmental hazards, for example, confront us with the realization that we are connected to brother worm, sister meson and daughter of a thousand years hence. That is to say, we are networked into a global community of being – past, present and future – whether or not we are members of CND, Amnesty International or the World Wildlife Fund, whether we subscribe to publications such as the *New Internationalist* or support Greenpeace. Through the industrial way of life, we share environmental threats with other beings. Moreover, global/ized finance ties our personal existence to the mis/fortunes of peoples across the world; and we are part of the global network of communication irrespective of whether or not we make transatlantic phone calls, communicate through electronic mail, or "save air miles".

I want to propose that *we can speak of a global/izing culture when people as private citizens are tied into global processes and, consequently, have the potential to be concerned about global issues and the capacity to get personally involved in social, cultural and ecological matters from across our earth.* I want to distinguish this global/izing culture from the much longer-term institutional processes of globalization that have extensively occupied social scientists for the last 20 years and have led to lively debates (but little consensus) about the specific form of globalization, its motive force and its proper analysis.[2]

At an institutional level, globalization clearly reaches back to the early Middle Ages and beyond; as such it is not a new development. Thus, for example, Giddens's (1990: 64) definition of globalization as "the intensification of world-wide social relations which link distant localities in such a way that local happenings are shaped by events occurring many miles away and vice versa" is not confined to the twentieth century. We can recognize it in the missioneering activities of the early Christians, in the trading cultures of the ancient and the modern world, and in the colonizing zest of a few European nations. Thus, Christianity imposed a global rhythm of work, prayer and feast days. It therefore was, and in a diminished capacity still is, a truly global influence on everyday practices and traditions in which "the basic routines of life revolved around the four great pivots of Christmas, Easter, Lammas and Michaelmas" (Thrift 1988: 56). Later on, Protestantism globalized not only a particular work ethic but also a relation to time as money (Weber 1904–5/1989). There can be no doubt that these religious influences were felt in cities and rural areas the world over, that they were truly global influences. Equally longstanding is the globalization of trade; that is to say, it too may be traced back to the early Middle Ages and goes hand in hand with the expansion of Christianity. A similar case for globalization as an extended historical process can be made about colonial processes that brought the world under the rule of a small number of European nations. This particular globalization is, in turn, closely tied to the expansion of world markets, a process dominated by a few nation states, with Britain as a key protagonist. For some theorists like Hall, therefore, globalization is integral to the rise (and decline) of contemporary Western nations like Britain. He argues that we cannot think about the formation of British society "and all the things that give it a kind of privileged place in the historical narratives of the world, outside of the processes that we identify with globalization" (Hall 1991: 19). In contrast to these *institutional* processes of globalization, the concept of global/izing culture involves the networking of *private citizens* into our earth as a physical, social and cultural environment, providing them with the potential for direct access to its processes.

Beyond this distinction between the very long historical development of institutional globalization and the contemporary personal experience of global/izing culture it is important to appreciate that global/izing culture is not merely a spatial concept. That is to say, while the images of the globe, the earth, the world are spatial ones, the processes of globalization are fundamentally dependent on time, unthinkable without specific temporal developments. In this chapter, I want to bring to our attention some of the temporal characteristics that underpin global/izing culture since these are particularly pertinent for taking our analyses beyond postmodern theories that emphasize contextual subjectivity at the expense of metanarratives and totalizing tendencies. The focus on time forces us to engage simultaneously with embodied, embedded particularity and global/izing processes, that is, with temporally based difference and universalized, artefactual time. I am referring here, in particular, to the developments, at the turn of this century, of the wireless telegraph and to the standardization of time. These two innovations are associated respectively with the global/ized present and the rationalization of local times into standard time and world time.

Mapping the temporality of global/izing culture

The global/izing present

The sinking of the *Titanic* in the early hours of 14 April 1912 can be taken as an event that shows how technological developments created the base for experiencing a *global present*, a central aspect of global/izing culture. Where a disaster like the sinking of a ship at high seas would have been destined to become a secret of the sea only a few decades earlier, by 1912 it had become a collectively knowable, global event that created "a new sense of world unity" and allowed the peoples of many lands "to share a common grief" (quoted in Kern 1983: 67). The creation of a global present through the wireless telegraph, therefore, promoted a sense of global connectedness among people who formerly had been isolated by distance. With the development of the wireless telegraph, the sending and receiving of information became almost simultaneous. By the early part of this century, this technological innovation had become an essential part of a global network of communication that linked the cities of the world as well as land stations and ships at sea.

Equally important was the development of the telephone. It too allowed for virtually instantaneous communication across vast distances. Years, months and days of waiting for a reply had been reduced to fractions of seconds, to a gap that was almost imperceptible. *Together, these innovations in communication changed the relationship between time and movement across space: succession and duration were supplemented by seeming simultaneity and instantaneity. The present was extended spatially to encircle the globe: it became a global present.* This opened up an unbridgeable gap between the speeds at which information and physical bodies could travel across space, a discrepancy ranging from the speed of light to the pace of walking. Today, this gap is routinely incorporated into the anticipations, plans and actions of members of industrial and industrializing societies whether these involve travel, satellite television, the movement of troops and equipment to the scene of modern warfare or the interaction of people with their computers. It forms an integral part of the taken-for-granted reality of global/izing culture.[3]

Fraser (1987: 196) proposes that "the width of the social present is determined by the time necessary to make people take concerted action. In its turn, that period depends on the distances involved and the speed with which messages may be carried." It is thus the capacity for global simultaneity that transformed the social present into a global one. The existence of such a global present meant not merely that business meetings could take place between people in Beijing, London, New York and Tokyo without any of the participants having to leave their desks. It meant also that events in one part of the world could have almost instantaneous effects on the other side of the globe and send ripples through the entire network. Furthermore, these processes are largely beyond the control of those involved since the combination of instantaneity of communication with simultaneity of networked relations no longer functions to the principles of mechanical interaction. Stockmarkets are a case in point: excitement or problems in one financial centre have inescapable and often unpredictable effects on the rest. "The new level of interconnectivity", Poster (1990: 3) points out, "heightens the fragility of social networks." The enormous speed coupled with multiple, simultaneous, reflexive connections creates a world of increased contingency and uncertainty. Not only that, the massively expanded knowledge bases also simultaneously lead to a proportional reduction in personal knowledge and predictive power: *the global present is simultaneous, instantaneous and all-encompassing; it is for us a virtual reality, knowable only with the aid of science and technology.* Its status of virtual reality (see also Winston, this volume) applies irrespective of content. It applies equally to distant human tragedies, threatened species, environmental disasters, political developments and World Cup football: the universal and the particular, the im/material and the virtual, the personal and the objective interpenetrate and mutually implicate each other.

Standard time and world time

Closely associated with the technological creation of a global present are the very important developments of *standard time* and *world time*,[4] the rationalization of clock and calendar time across the globe. Standard time brought to an end the myriad of local times and dates used by the peoples of the world. During the later part of the nineteenth century travellers moving from the East to the West Coast of the United States, for example, encountered different local times in every town they went through until, in 1883, the US railroads inaugurated a uniform time. By 1884, Greenwich was installed as the zero meridian and the earth divided into 24 equal zones, each one hour apart. Though it took many years for this standard time to get adopted worldwide,[5] its establishment constituted the beginning of the *global day*, a day made up of the same disembedded twelve hours, irrespective of context and number of daylight hours, where the hour between 9 and 10 o'clock is the "same" hour irrespective of whether it is summer or winter, the dry or rainy season, on the Equator or in the northern hemisphere. This development goes hand in hand with the adoption of a globally synchronized, unified time, with Britain the centre of rationalized time zones and France the source of world time. At 10.00 am 1 July 1913 the Eiffel Tower transmitted the first time signal across the globe. Wireless signals travelling at the speed of light displaced local times and established one time for all people on this earth: 1913 is thus the beginning of *world time*.[6]

Both standard time and world time are crucial material conditions for the global network of communication in both information and transport. They are fundamental to a twentieth-century concept of globalization and to the development of global/izing culture: world time, the universal day, and the global present provide the framework for the development of a *global perspective*. Such a global perspective became a potential reality once the whole world came into reach, in principle at least, at the everyday personal level: when people can hear on the radio or watch on their TV screen events and tragedies occurring on the other side of the globe, when it takes no more than two days to reach any destination, when, at the press of a button, a personal donation can affect the livelihood or survival of people in another part of the world. The famines, civil wars and political struggles in the African subcontinent, the massacre at Tiananmen Square, the burning oilfields in Kuwait, the plight of the civilians in the bitter civil war raging in the former Yugoslavia, Norway's decision to lift the ban on hunting certain species of whales are inescapably, global events, subject for all to see, pass judgement on and exert pressure.

The capacity for a global perspective is clearly a totalizing tendency in the material condition of contemporary culture that runs counter to the postmodern argument against universalism. But, it is a global/izing feature that demands a conceptualization beyond the "either-or mode" that still persists, even in postmodern theory. That is to say, the unique, the particular and the contextual do not displace but are inescapably implicated in the universal. Moreover, for members of global/izing culture there is no "outside" from whence they could be "innocent bystanders" or "objective observers". This means we can no longer retain an attitude of non-involvement.

> In the electric age, when our central nervous system is technologically extended to involve us in the whole of mankind and to incorporate the whole of mankind in us, we necessarily participate, in depth, in the consequences of our every action. It is no longer possible to adopt the aloof and dissociated role of the literate Westerner. (McLuhan 1964/ 1973: 12)

In global/izing culture, responsibility therefore extends beyond representatives in local and national governments to the private citizen: it inescapably connects the global with the local and personal.

Global/izing pasts and futures

With reference to time, the shift in emphasis from sequence and duration to instantaneity and simultaneity extends not just to the global present and world time but also to global/izing pasts and global futures. Where peoples of ancient cultures used (and still use) rituals and myths to keep alive and recreate the past in the present, members of global/izing culture primarily use science and technology for this task. With electronic information storage and retrieval infinite pasts can effortlessly be kept in the present and summoned up at will. Through carbon dating, spectrometry and X-rays, for example, layers of multiple pasts are made transparent in the present; no place is too remote, no past too distant. Moreover, with the aid of science and technology, we rediscover what was (and still is) taken for granted in ancient cultures: the global interconnectedness of all life forms past, present and future; our common dependence on water, soil and air. We get to recognize our shared conditions for wellbeing as well as our vulnerability to harm (Sheldrake 1990, Beck 1992a,b, Benton 1993). Finally, we can speak of a global future – a further totalizing feature of global/izing culture – when all or at least a significant number of people across the globe share, in the short and long term, important dimensions of their lives. I have in mind such examples as the future of debt and destitution for countries on the receiving end of the Western commitment to "development", the ecological effects of the industrial way of life, and the lack of control for globally networked processes.

When, in 1949, US President Truman defined a substantial part of the world as "underdeveloped", he set in progress the global agenda of "development", the goal to bring the "Third World" "up to" the "First" or at least the "Second World's" standards. He had thus begun a secular missioneering project of proportions equal if not superior to that of the Christian and Muslim religions: the world was to be Westernized and embrace industrialism, capitalism, technology and democracy. "The guiding light of international development policy", Sachs (1992: 17) points out, "was to create societies of paid workers and consumers everywhere", importing technology and experts from the West, producing industrial goods with money borrowed from Western banks. Since, however, the interest rates to be paid to Western banks over the years far outstrip the original loans, those countries pay for and finance the increasing material wealth of the West while descending on the well-documented spiral of debt and dependency (e.g. George 1988). Far from narrowing the gap between rich and poor, the global project of "development" has dramatically sharpened the inequalities of power and wealth. It is a global/izing future that does not bode well for the majority of peoples on this earth.

The industrial societies' twin imperative of growth and technological innovation with its effects on the global environment indicates global/izing futures of environmental crises where GNP – Gross National Product – simultaneously constitutes a measure of Gross National *Pollution*. Dependence on continuing growth and consumption, in other words, cannot be separated from the inevitable need for obsolescence and the growth in waste. Moreover, since technology is regarded as the central tool for progress and as generator of successful development, it seems inevitable that the depletion of non-renewable resources, coupled with the attendant steep rise in pollution, become an integral part of global/izing Western/izing futures. Those unintended consequences of the industrial way of life permeate the land, sea, earth, air and surrounding atmosphere of our planet. They affect perpetrator and innocent alike. (Well, not quite, since the producers of hazards have a tendency to ensure that the poor and powerless are affected first and foremost.) Even societies not yet touched by industrialization and those resisting the Western path are nevertheless subject to the unplanned futures of technological development since its effects cannot be contained within their countries of origin.[7]

Most pertinent to this creation of global/ized present futures and future presents is, of course, the development of nuclear power and its associated threat of radiation.[8] Nuclear weapons are tested in the more remote regions of our world from where their radiation permeates ecosystems and affects all of us to varying degrees and intensity. Nuclear material is located across the world on land, in the sea and in the air. It is stored deep in the earth and on the bottom of the oceans. It is harnessed for both benign and hostile power and it encircles our earth in satellites. It engulfs the globe affecting all life on earth with its potential threat: the aftermath of radiation may be immediate or take decades, even millennia, to reveal. It is a *global future for all* irrespective of location, nationality and political persuasion. It forms an in/visible, virtual reality that constitutes presents for hundreds, even thousands, of potential generations hence. With the nuclear threat, moreover, the industrial system is no longer capable of dealing with its own unknowable future: we have no institutions, now or in the foreseeable future, which could deal with the worst imaginable case of a nuclear war or even a major nuclear fall-out (May 1989). As a global threat that permeates our present as well as our long-term future, the nuclear hazard creates not just the present future and future present but the *potential end in the present*. With nuclear power, global/izing culture loses its basis for belief and trust in continuity and future presents.

The future of global/izing culture, moreover, is constituted by unintended and uncontrollable effects of planned and intended actions. Yesterday's hailed inventions are today's sources of cancers, global warming, ozone depletion and dying forests, their impact rarely tied to time and space. Globally networked and temporally disbursed over millennia, those unintended consequences tend to elude traditional economic and scientific control. They consequently force us to take account of potential consequences of actions that can only be known with the benefit of hindsight. *In such situations, the past is no longer a reliable guide to the future.* Equally, once the potential outcome of cultural activity is character-ized by globalization and temporal uncertainty, and once the time lags of cause and effect span from nanoseconds to millennia, both risk calculation and socio-political engineering become highly problematic social practices. Such spatially and temporally dispersed uncertainty poses barriers to effective action because our capacity to predict and control is dependent on processes gov-erned by sequential, linear causality. In other words, the simultaneity and instantaneity of global information and environmental effects in conjunction with non-linear, networked processes render our efforts ineffective, elude our conventional modes of controlling the future.

If, however, global/izing culture is marked by historically unprecedented characteristics, if its multitude of features co-exist simultaneously in a mutually permeating way, and if we are personally implicated in and thus responsible for those globalized processes and their contingent effects without being able to rely on conventional modes of control, then these features must be allowed to permeate not just our everyday, our economic and our political understand-ing but also our assumptions in cultural studies and our theories. They need to become an integral part of cultural theory in the same way as the key features of the Enlightenment had penetrated the work of the "founding fathers" of social science and their successors. Postmodernist theorists have so far taken on this challenge. We need to ask, therefore, to what extent the concept of postmodernism can actually cope with this task.

Here and now, then and there: concern with the postmodern concept

I want to question whether the concept of postmodernism, particularly in terms of its temporality and the implicit dualistic schema of "once there was and now there is", could possibly provide us with the wherewithal to grasp the complexity of global/izing culture. I want to query, further, whether its explicit focus on the past can help us to understand and engage with the future. This means I am neither concerned to discuss the different theoretical approaches to postmodernism, nor to arbitrate between the various critical responses to it. Instead, I want to focus on the concept itself in order to explore post-modernism/postmodernity in terms of implicit principles and strategies for knowing.

Attention on postmodernism as a conceptual tool becomes important as soon as we acknowledge the constitutive nature of knowledge. That is to say, the concept and its underlying premises require attention once we accept as fact that cultural theorists change and construct the worlds they study through the very process of description and explanation, that the knowledge they produce is constitutive of the social world they study (see Atkinson & Coffey, this volume). It is necessary since, as Giddens (1990: 15–16) puts it, "[sociological] knowledge spirals in and out of the universe of social life, reconstructing both itself and that universe as an integral part of that process". This means that concepts need to be *appropriate* to their role as constructors of immediate and long-term futures. Looked at in this way, the concept of postmodernism needs to be scrutinized for its capacity to embrace temporal complexity and to facilitate an active involvement with contingent global/ized and global/izing futures.

We have established that global/izing culture is a process – contemporary and ongoing – that it is characterized by networked complexity and multiple temporalities ranging from duration and succession to simultaneity and instantaneity. It exhibits the past and constructs the future in the present: past, present and future interpenetrate and mutually implicate each other to a point where their neat separation becomes meaningless. Most importantly, the future plays a dominant role; projected, contingent and uncertain, it is a key driving force for action at the personal and institutional level.

Irrespective of the theories we associate with the terms postmodernism and postmodernity, the concepts are constituted on a dualistic basis: here and now, then and there, once there was and now there is. Postmodernity and postmodernism are defined in relation to what they are *not* – modernity and modernism. They thus define complexity through the simplicity of a binary code, contingency and temporal implication through comparison with an a-temporal past. They set up static before-and-after conditions instead of temporally extended, open, future-oriented processes. That is to say, the prefix of post- not only delimits the substantive scope of the subject matter but also transforms ongoing and embedded processes into disembedded, static states. There is a tendency, moreover, to create a historical "other" and generalize this "other" into an a-historical, a-contextual, hierarchically positioned caricature that bears no resemblance to the complexity of contextual, embedded societies: the "before" connotes a simpler, less developed phase from the postmodern state that succeeds it. Thus, postmodernity and postmodernism are not only defined by their past other, they also create that other. This means both concepts are totalizing in their sweep and by implication total in their exclusions – an unintended consequence of the concepts, which runs counter to some of the features of global/izing culture outlined in this chapter.

Understanding rooted in such a conceptualization is thus not viable: it is problematic at the substantive level of depiction and at the political level of action. Global/izing culture implicates each one of us in its processes. It is a world of difference without others, a world of networked complexity and multiple ambiguity, contingency and un/certainty. This means that we live in a world that is no longer centrally constructed around dualistic principles but we continue to think with the concepts and categories of either–or, once-there-was–now-there-is, them–us, there and then–here and now, East–West, left–right. It means, further, that we participate in the creation of contingent futures but look to the past for guidance to effect their control. To attempt to understand global/izing culture through the concepts of postmodernity and postmodernism is to be presented with a case where the concepts are out of step with the reality they seek to explicate. Instead of the implicit binary code inherent in the prefix "post", we need code combinations, code syntheses and neither-nor approaches; we need to embrace the future – contingent, ambiguous, uncertain, multiple – and use temporally open concepts that do not re-embed us in the conceptual mode of "either-or" choices. Most importantly, we need to accept our implication in those global/izing processes and take responsibility for our past-, present- and future-creating actions.

> The twentieth century has been a unique period in world cultural history. Humankind has finally bid farewell to that world which could with some credibility be seen as a cultural mosaic of separate pieces with hard, well-defined edges. Because of the great increase in the traffic in culture, the large-scale transfer of meaning systems and symbolic forms, the world is increasingly becoming one not only in political and economic terms, as in the climactic period of colonialism, but in terms of its cultural construction as well, a global ecumene of persistent cultural interaction and exchange. (Hannerz 1991: 107)

This global ecumene irrevocably ties our personal concerns to collective responsibilities for the long-term future. These connections are not simulacra and not mere texts but, as McLuhan (1964/1973: 12) insisted, they are "the consequences of our every action".

Ironically, the concepts of postmodernity and postmodernism come to their limits precisely where analyses of global/izing cultures become pertinent and interesting: when they encounter personal global/ized relations – the sociocultural equivalent to contextual/izing total/izing tendencies, and meta-narratives – when they are confronted with the need to actively *engage* with the materiality of globalized existence. They are silent with respect to contingent, uncertain but largely predetermined futures and the in/visibility, im/materiality and levelling tendency of environmental hazards. They fail to encompass the loss of "other" in the face of increased difference, and lack the capacity to embrace questions of value, morality, responsibility and engagement. These pressing features of global/izing culture challenge cultural studies to produce theories that acknowledge the relativity of knowledge while enabling us to be effective, responsible, embedded and embodied participants in the construction of contemporary pasts/presents/futures. This, of course, necessitates that the constitutive power of knowledge is not only something that is theorized but something to be centrally taken account of in the praxis of cultural studies. As constructors of social reality, in other words, we are obliged to take a moral and political stand; we have to come to terms with our inevitable involvement in global/izing processes and the need for active engagement with the future. Taking account of the future and responsibility for posterity becomes an inescapable, moral imperative for cultural theory.

Notes

1. I use the concept of "global/izing" in order to emphasize the processual, open-ended nature of globalization and globalized culture.
2. Thus, theories of the "world system" and ceaseless capital accumulation (Wallerstein 1974, 1990, 1991) compete with analyses of transnational processes (Keohane & Nye 1971, Hannerz 1990, 1991, Robertson 1990, 1991, Sklair 1991) and colonialism (Hall 1991), Beck's (1992a,b) analysis of the "global risk society" with Giddens's (1990, 1991) theory of "time-distantiation" and "disembedding processes of high modernity". Some writers identify new local-global connections (Giddens 1990, Hannerz 1990, 1991), others stress inequalities between centre and periphery (Hannerz 1990, 1991, Wallerstein 1990, 1991). The same terms, however, are not necessarily used from compatible perspectives and thus result in very different analyses. I am thinking here, for example, of the writings of Hannerz (1990, 1991) and Wallerstein (1990, 1991) on centre-periphery, or of Beck (1992a,b) and Giddens (1990) on risk.
3. Kern (1983) provides a seminal analysis of the changes that took place in material culture at the turn of this century and their effects on the experiences of and approaches to time and space.
4. For excellent accounts of these developments see Kern (1983) and Fraser (1987); also Nguyen (1992).
5. In the more remote regions of our earth life is, of course, still organized on the basis of variable time and uneven hours.
6. Like all processes of rationalization this one too has its weak points where rationality collapses into irrationality: in the Aleutian Islands in the South Pacific, where eastern and western time zones meet, we can celebrate a birthday twice or miss it altogether by simply crossing the time line which passes between the Islands.
7. For social science analyses of ecological futures see, for example, Yearly (1991); Beck (1992a, b, 1993); Adam (1994a: Ch. 6; 1994b).
8. For analyses of nuclear futures see, for example, May (1989), Adam (1990), Adam & Allan (1994), Allan (1995).

References

Adam, B. 1990. *Time and social theory.* Cambridge: Polity and Philadelphia: Temple University Press.

Adam, B. 1994a. *Timewatch. The social analysis of time.* Cambridge: Polity.

Adam, B. 1994b. Running out of time: global crisis and human engagement. In *Social theory and the global environment*, M. Redclift & T. Benton (eds), 92–112. London: Routledge.

Adam. B. & S. Allan 1994. Minutes to midnight: time, truth and the nuclear apocalypse. Paper presented at *Against Time: Anachronism and the Human Sciences* conference, University of Exeter, England, December 1994.

Allan, S. 1995. "No truth, no apocalypse": investigating the language of nuclear war. In *Studies in communication*, T. McCormack & R. Avery (eds), 171–214. Greenwich, Connecticut: JAI Press.

Beck, U. 1992a. From industrial society to risk society: questions of survival, social structure and ecological enlightenment. *Theory, Culture and Society* **9**, 97–123.

Beck, U. 1992b. *Risk society. Towards a new modernity.* London: Sage.

Beck, U. 1993. *Die Erfindung des Politischen.* Frankfurt: Suhrkamp.

Benton, T. 1993. *Natural relations. Ecology, animal rights and social justice.* London: Verso.

Fraser, J. T. 1987. *Time, the familiar stranger.* Amherst: University of Massachusetts Press.

George, S. 1988. *A fate worse than debt.* London: Penguin.

Giddens, A. 1990. *The consequences of modernity.* Cambridge: Polity.

Giddens, A. 1991. *Modernity and self-identity: self and society in the late modern age.* Cambridge: Polity.

Hall, S. 1991. The local and global: globalization and ethnicity. In *Culture, globalization and the world-system*, A. King (ed.), 19–40. London: Macmillan.

Hannerz, U. 1990. Cosmopolitans and locals in the world culture. In *Global culture, nationalism, globalization and modernity*, M. Featherstone (ed.), 237–52. London: Sage.

Hannerz, U. 1991. Scenarios for peripheral cultures. In *Culture, globalization and the world-system*, A. King (ed.), 107–28. London: Macmillan.

Keohane, R. O. & J. S. Nye Jr (eds) 1971. *Transnational relations and world politics.* Cambridge, Mass.: Harvard University Press.

Kern, S. 1983. *The culture of time and space 1880–1919.* London: Weidenfeld & Nicolson.

May, J. 1989. *The Greenpeace book of the nuclear age. The hidden history of the human cost.* London: Gollancz.

McLuhan, M. 1964/1973. *Understanding media.* London: Routledge & Kegan Paul.

Nguyen, D. T. 1992. The spatialisation of metric time: the conquest of land and labour in Europe and the United States. *Time and Society* **1**, 29–50.

Poster, M. 1990. *The mode of information.* Cambridge: Polity.

Robertson, R. 1990. Mapping the global condition: globalization as the central concept. In *Global culture, nationalism, globalization and modernity*, M. Featherstone (ed.), 15–30. London: Sage.

Robertson, R. 1991. Social theory, cultural relativity and the problem of globality. In *Culture, globalization and the world-system*, A. King (ed.), 69–90. London: Macmillan.

Sachs, W. 1992. Development. A guide to the ruins. *The New Internationalist* **223**, 4–27.

Sheldrake, R.1990. *The rebirth of nature. The greening of science and God.* London: Century.

Sklair, L. 1991. *The sociology of the global system.* Hemel Hempstead, England: Harvester Wheatsheaf.

Thrift, N. 1988. Vicos Voco. Ringing the changes in the historical geography of time consciousness. In *The rhythms of society*, M. Young & T. Schuller (eds), 53–94. London: Routledge.

Wallerstein, I. 1974. *The modern world-system.* New York: Academic Press.

Wallerstein, I. 1990. Culture as the ideological battleground of the modern world-system. In *Global culture, nationalism, globalization and modernity*, M. Featherstone (ed.), 31–56. London: Sage.

Wallerstein, I. 1991. The national and the universal: can there be such a thing as world culture? In *Culture, globalization and the world-system*, A. King (ed.), 91–106. London: Macmillan.

Weber, M. 1904–5/1989. *The Protestant ethic and the spirit of capitalism.* London: Unwin Hyman.

Yearly, S. 1991. *The green case. A sociology of environmental issues, arguments and politics.* London: HarperCollins.

Index